APRÈS SKI

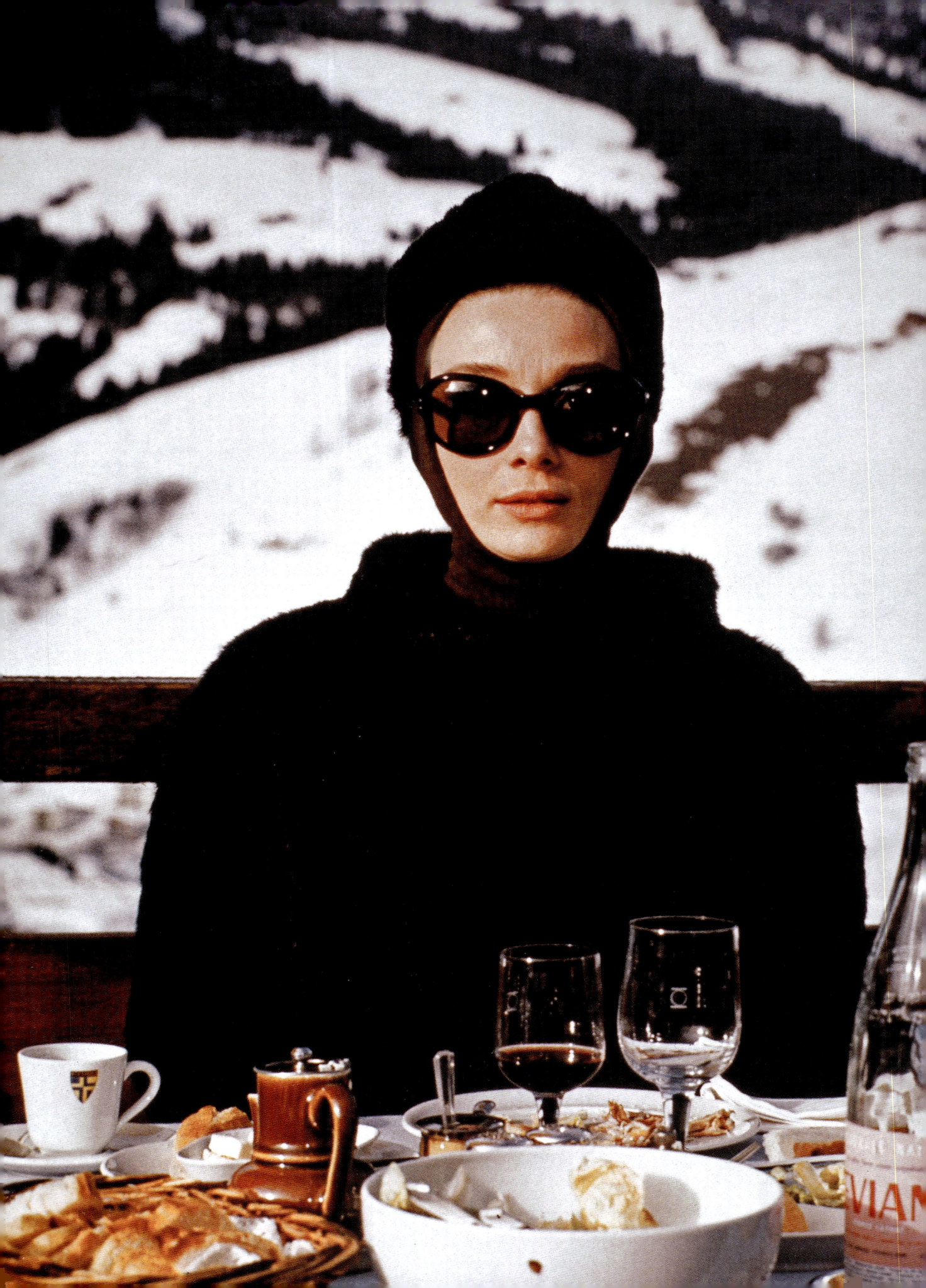

APRÈS SKI

THE SCENE, THE STYLE, THE MENU

Erin Isakov

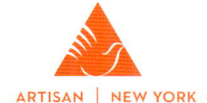

ARTISAN | NEW YORK

Library of Congress Cataloging-in-Publication Data is on file.

ISBN 978-1-64829-394-8 (hardcover), 978-1-64829-398-6 (ebook)

Design by Nina Simoneaux

Artisan books may be purchased in bulk for business, educational, or promotional use. For information, please contact your local bookseller or the Hachette Book Group Special Markets Department at special.markets@hbgusa.com.

The publisher is not responsible for websites (or their content) that are not owned by the publisher.

The Hachette Speakers Bureau provides a wide range of authors for speaking events. To find out more, go to hachettespeakersbureau.com or email HachetteSpeakers@hbgusa.com.

Published by Artisan,
an imprint of Workman Publishing,
a division of Hachette Book Group, Inc.
1290 Avenue of the Americas
New York, NY 10104
artisanbooks.com

The Artisan name and logo are registered trademarks of Hachette Book Group, Inc.

Printed in China (APO) on responsibly sourced paper

Cover © 2025 Hachette Book Group, Inc.

10 9 8 7 6 5 4 3 2

To all the mountain adventurers who pioneered the skiing lifestyle

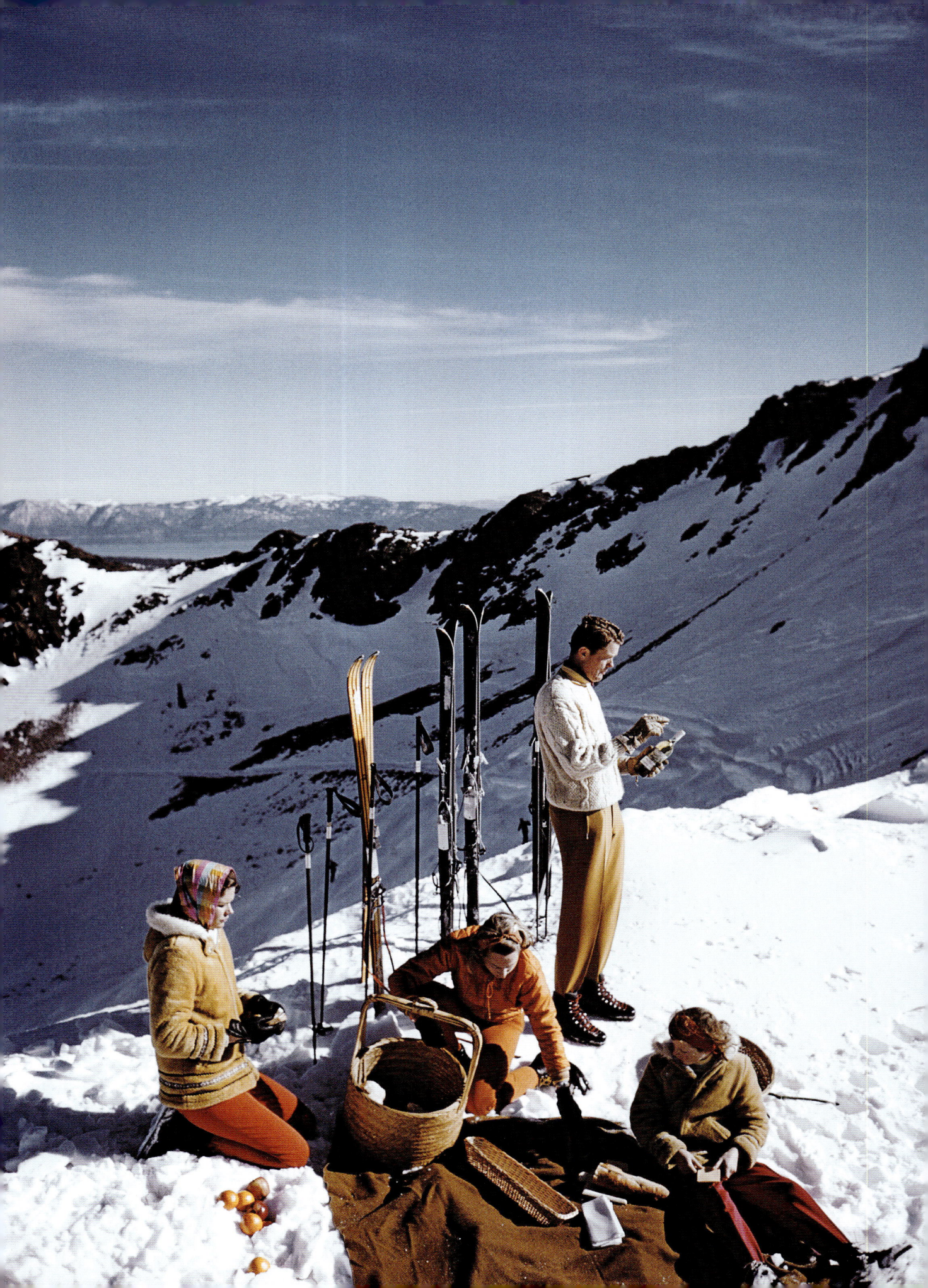

CONTENTS

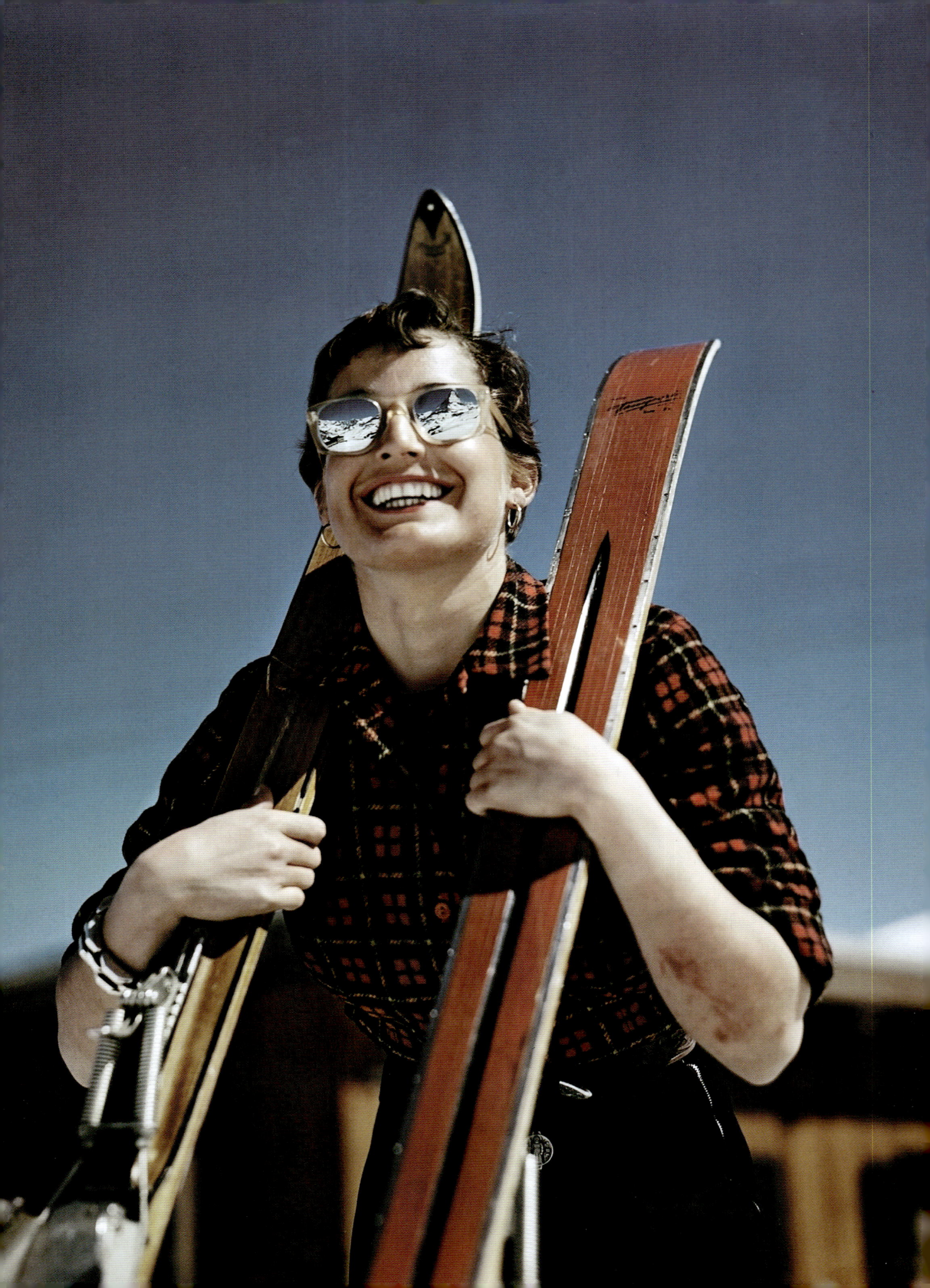

Introduction

SKIING ISN'T JUST A SPORT; it's a way of life. For generations, skiers have traveled across the globe not only to enjoy the powder but also to indulge in the glamour, refreshments, vistas, and revelry following a great day on the mountain. This time is referred to as après-ski (literally, "after ski"), and it's when skiers catch their breath, swap stories, toast to the day's adventure, and refuel their bodies. It can also be a time to simply let loose and party.

Après-ski may traditionally begin right after skiing, but it can extend into the early morning hours. It can be rowdy or relaxed, family friendly or far from it. Traditions vary by region and even by resort. No matter where or how you prefer to unwind after a day on the slopes, what happens after skiing has helped shape the experience of the sport for generations.

Aiming to serve as both visual inspiration and a guidebook, the following pages will take you on a nostalgia-fueled journey through the most stylish eras and best après-ski spots around the globe as well as offer recipes for quintessential après-ski food and beverages.

As much as this book is intended as a celebration of the many facets of après-ski, it is also a love letter to the wider world of skiing. The story of my life began in a ski town: My parents met while my dad worked as a ski patroller and my mom sold lift tickets at California's Mammoth Mountain Ski Area in the 1970s. I was put on skis as soon as I could walk, and have since traveled across countries and continents to ski and snowboard mountain ranges around the world. As an adult, I took my passion for the sport and the style icons of the golden era of skiing (including my own parents) and turned it into my livelihood, cofounding the women's skiwear brand Erin Snow with my husband in 2003.

I hope you share my love for this world, and that these pages and the images that fill them inspire you to create your own après-ski look or gathering, whether at home or away at your next mountain destination.

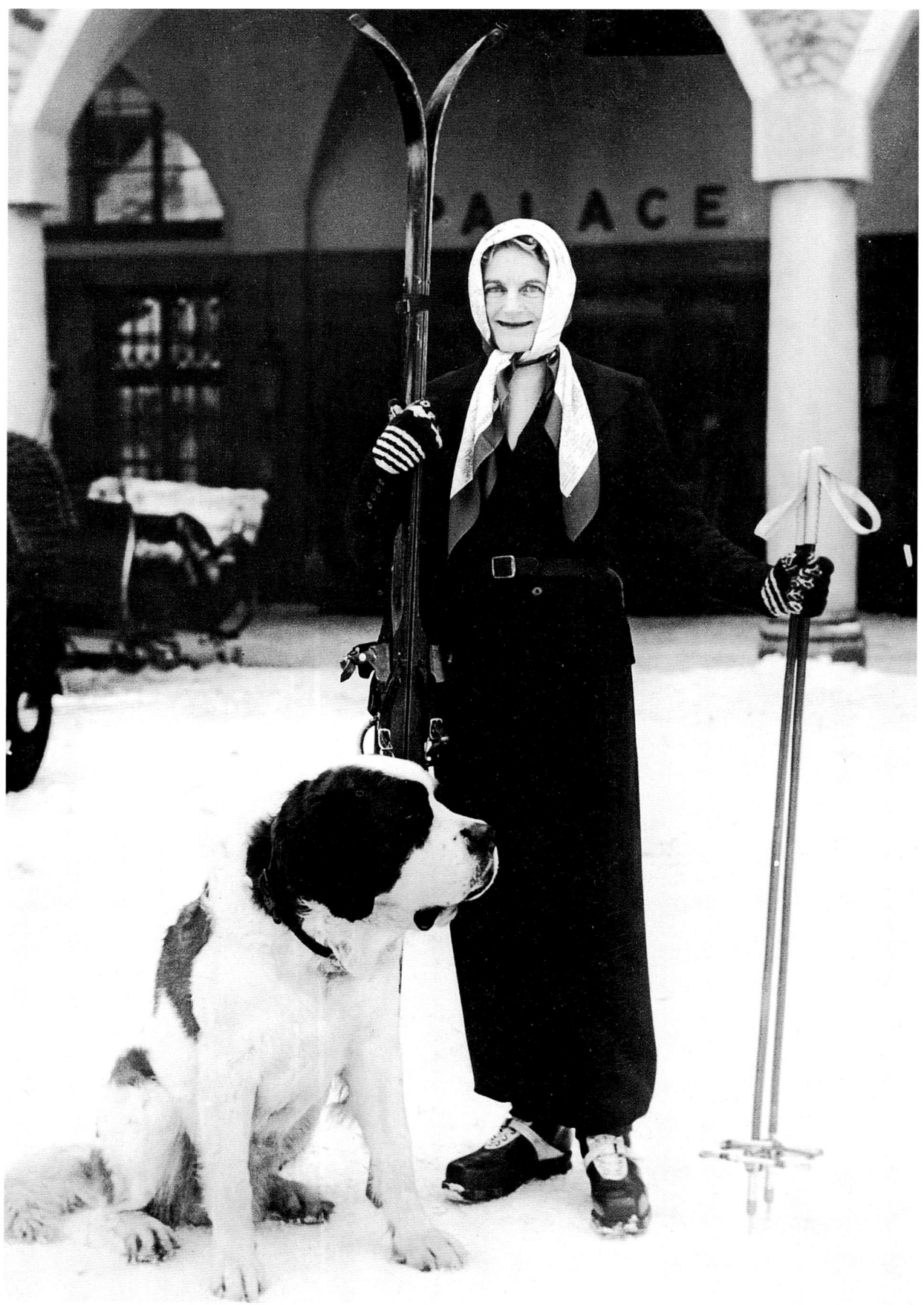

The Birth of
Après-Ski

THE MODERN SKI HOLIDAY was effectively conceived in St. Moritz, Switzerland, in 1864, when, according to legend, local hotelier Johannes Badrutt convinced a group of Englishmen to visit his Engadiner Kulm Hotel during the winter. (Until then, tourists mainly visited the region in the summer.) Dressed for harsh conditions upon their December arrival in St. Moritz, the Englishmen were stunned to find bright sunshine, soft snow, and fresh air. They enjoyed themselves so much that they stayed on as guests at the Kulm Hotel until springtime and thereafter returned year after year, bringing family and friends. Building on his father's success, Johannes's son Caspar opened the five-star Badrutt's Palace Hotel in 1896. This glamorous ski hotel and the glitzy town of St. Moritz soon became a ski destination for the world's rich and famous. After World War I, both the sport and the concept of the ski holiday gained momentum, with the Engadin valley at the center of it all. Even today, extravagance and decadence run wild in St. Moritz.

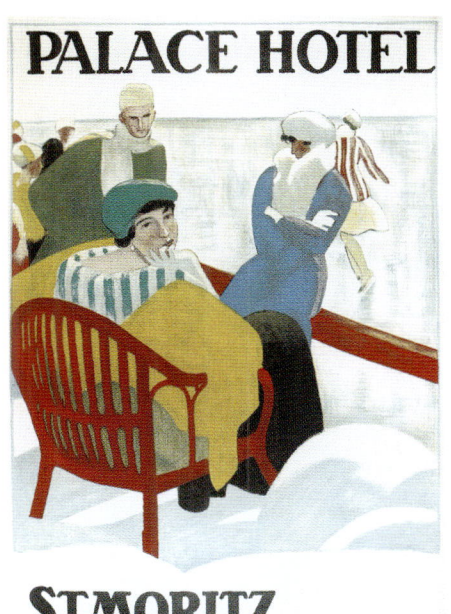

◀ Clementine Churchill, the wife of Sir Winston Churchill, with her Saint Bernard in front of Badrutt's Palace Hotel during her 1937 winter holiday in St. Moritz

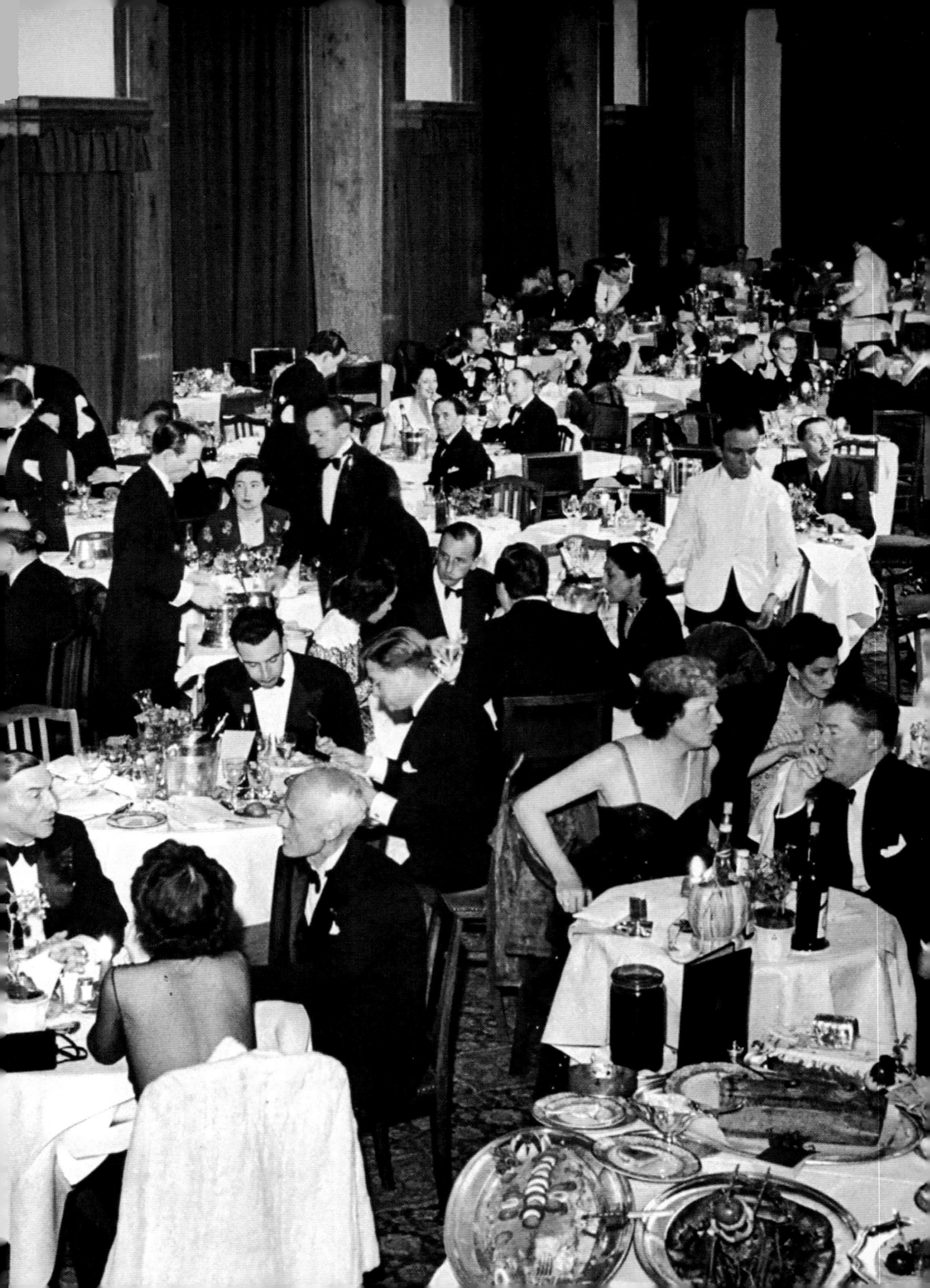

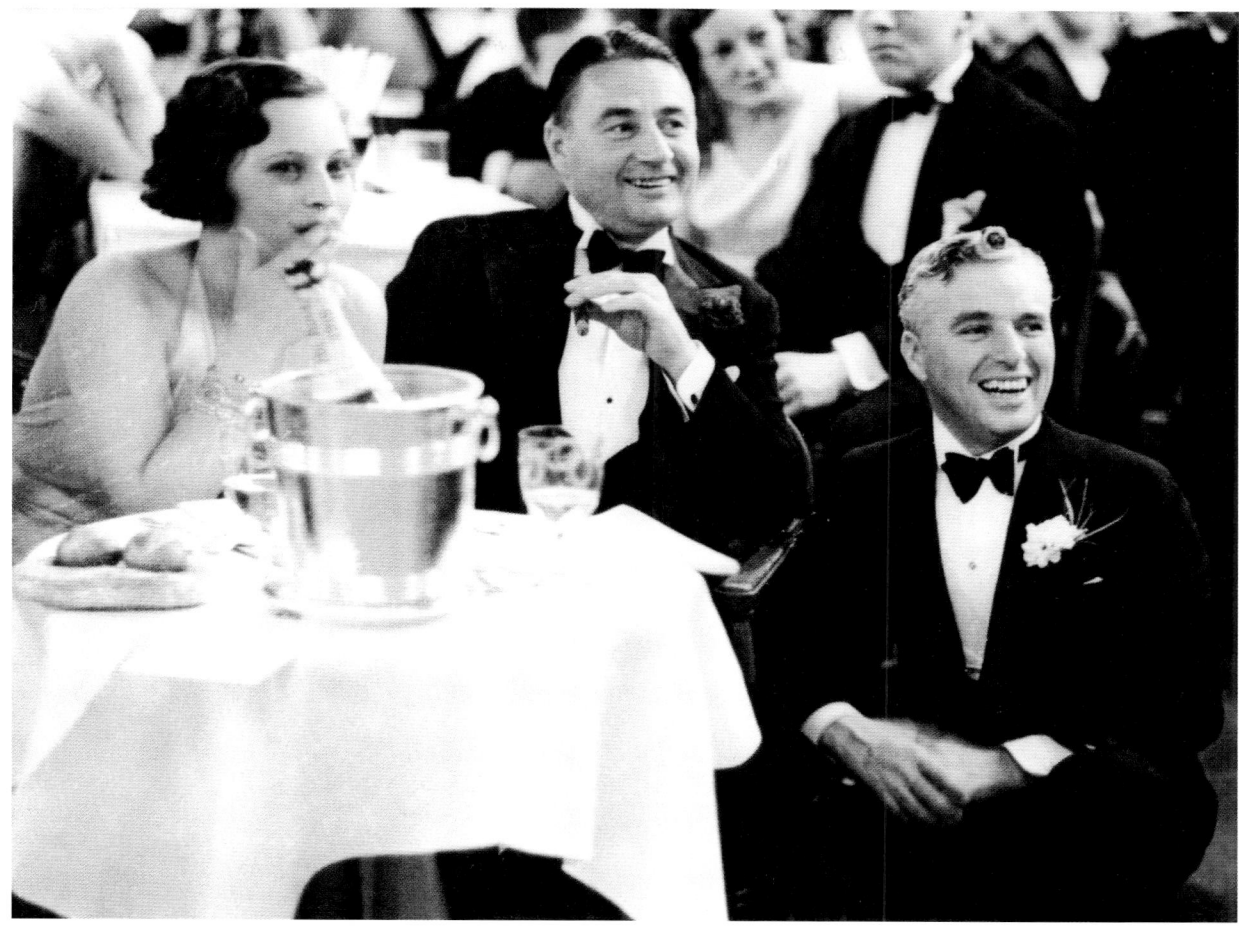

▲ In the 1930s, St. Moritz saw its popularity as a ski destination soar while Badrutt's Palace Hotel played host to illustrious events featuring Hollywood stars, socialites, and prominent figures, such as Charlie Chaplin (right) and his brother Sydney, seen here at a formal wintertime gala at the hotel around 1932.

◄ These extravagant galas and dinners continued into the following decades in St. Moritz, establishing the resort town as a beacon for those seeking a lavish après-ski environment. A formal dinner at the Palace Hotel in 1947 is pictured here.

Skiing arrived relatively late to the United States, with the help of Scandinavian immigrants who, with millennia of skiing history, brought their equipment and traditions, sparking intrigue among their new neighbors. In the early part of the twentieth century, Americans with means took ski holidays to Europe, returning home to form ski clubs, cut trails, and establish their own hills. The US even hosted the 1932 Winter Olympics in Lake Placid, New York. Soon after, America began developing its own resorts to rival those of Europe.

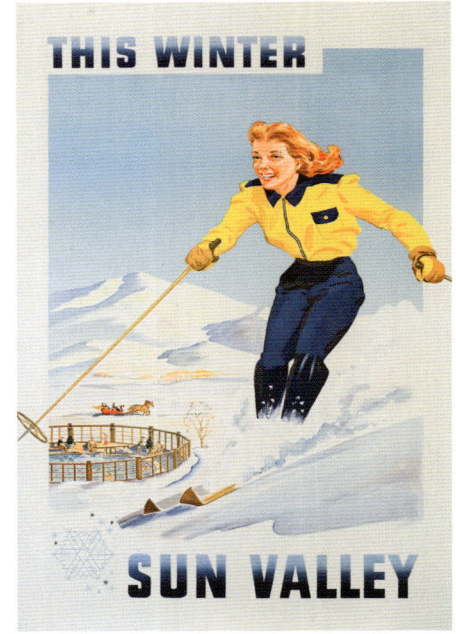

Opened in 1936, the Sun Valley Lodge in Sun Valley, Idaho, became the marquee lodging choice at America's first destination ski resort. Sun Valley was the birthplace of the chairlift, hosted the world's first ski school, and was home to several celebrities, including Ernest Hemingway, who completed *For Whom the Bell Tolls* in suite 206 (now room 228) of the lodge. Hemingway was initially lured to the fledgling resort town in 1939 with a free stay at the lodge alongside other celebrities as part of a campaign to attract tourists. He later made a home in nearby Ketchum, Idaho, and is buried there.

Sun Valley was also home to the first generation of America's self-proclaimed "ski bums," young people who flocked to the fun, often making ends meet by working odd jobs to support their ski-town lifestyle.

Perhaps the most famous of those young ski enthusiasts was Warren Miller, who launched his long and storied ski filmmaking career in Sun Valley with his first feature film, *Deep and Light*, in 1950. Miller went on to direct and narrate a ski movie each year for the remainder of his film career, featuring some of the best skiers of their times tackling incredible terrain in beautiful scenery around the world. These films helped entice and inspire

▸ A visitor relaxing après-ski at the then-new Sun Valley Lodge, 1937

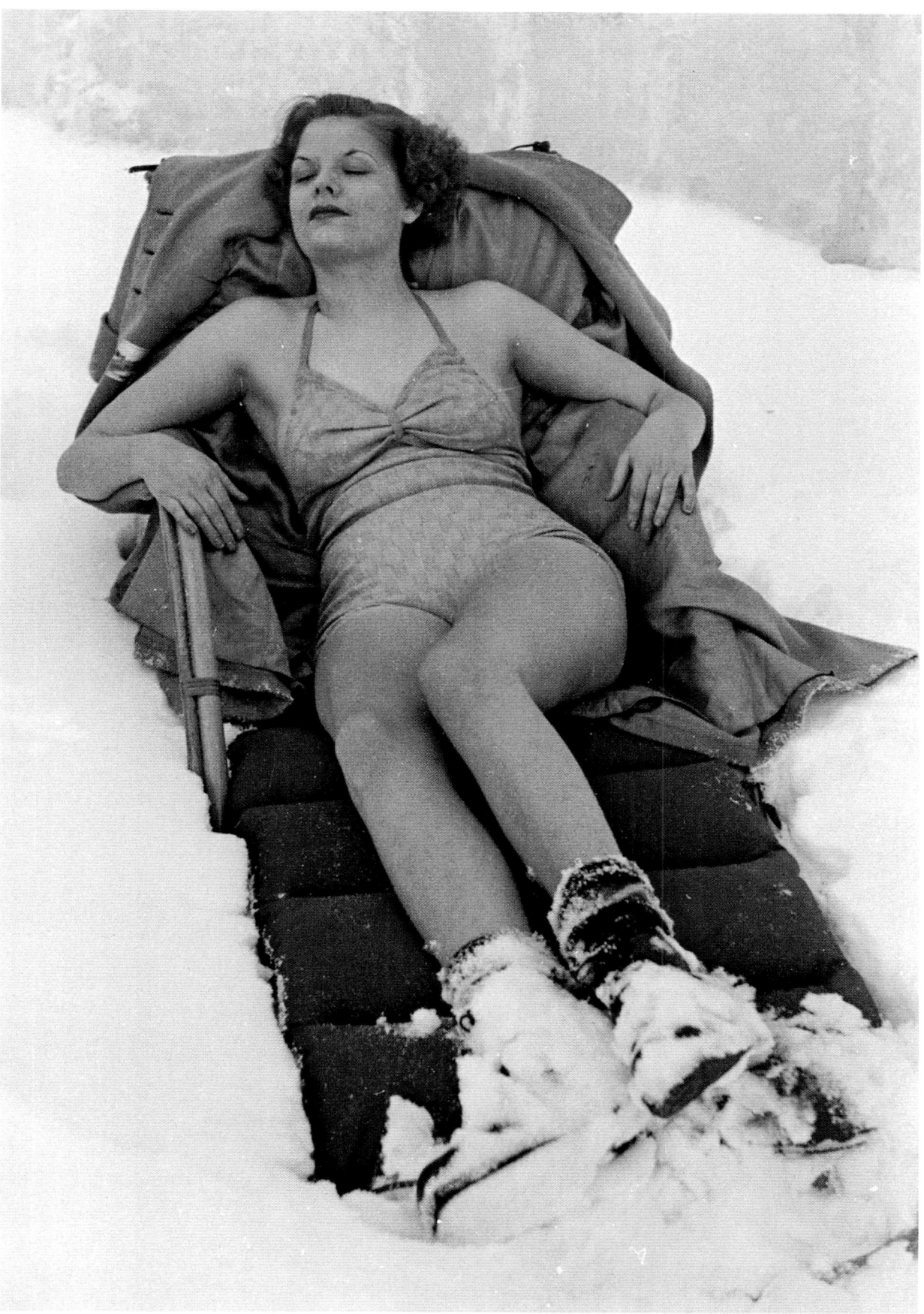

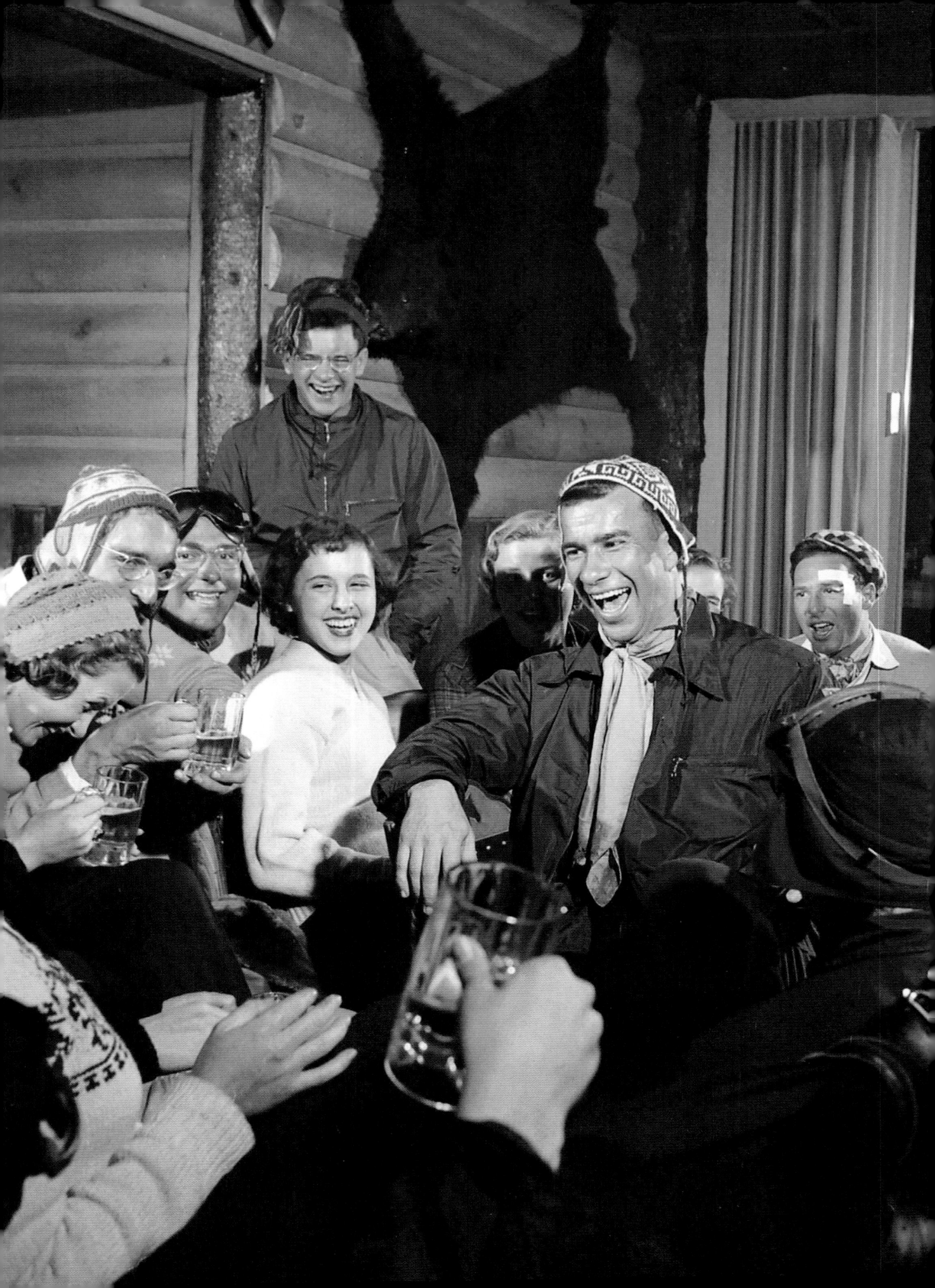

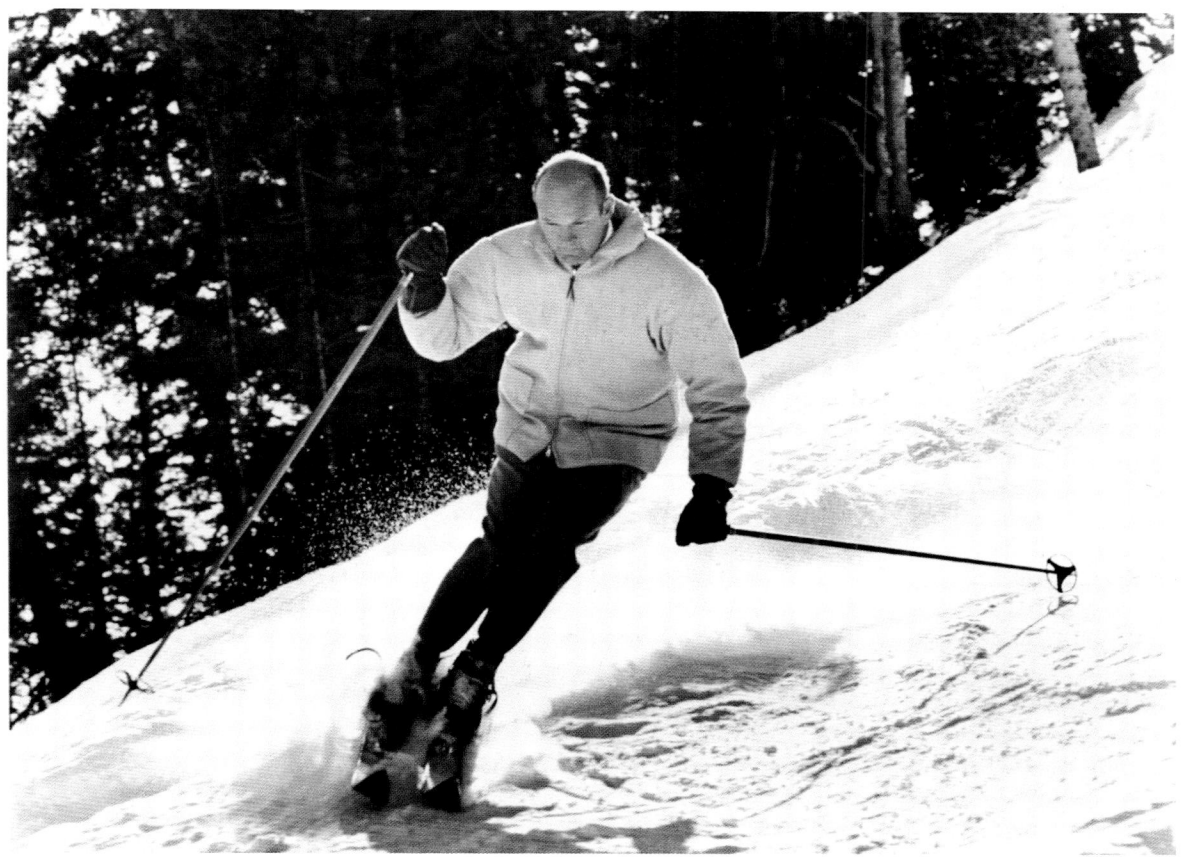

generations of skiers and continue to do so today. Showings of the annual Warren Miller film came to mark the unofficial start of each ski season and helped glamorize the sport and the ski lifestyle for decades.

While the modern ski holiday was born toward the end of the nineteenth century, the practice boomed following World War II as a way to escape and celebrate life. Europeans returned in droves to resorts in Switzerland, France, Austria, and Italy. In America, skiing gained popularity with help from skilled skiing soldiers returning from Europe (including the legendary 10th Mountain Division, whose members later founded or were affiliated with more than sixty resorts across the US, including Vail, Stratton, Whiteface, and Aspen). Sun Valley was soon joined by newly developed ski resorts across North America and much of the world, where college students, families, veterans, executives, and stars mingled side by side on the slopes, fostering a festive après-ski scene.

▲ Director Warren Miller skiing for his 1967 film *Ski on the Wild Side*

◄ Ski bums enjoying a rowdy and carefree evening after a day of skiing in Sun Valley, 1950

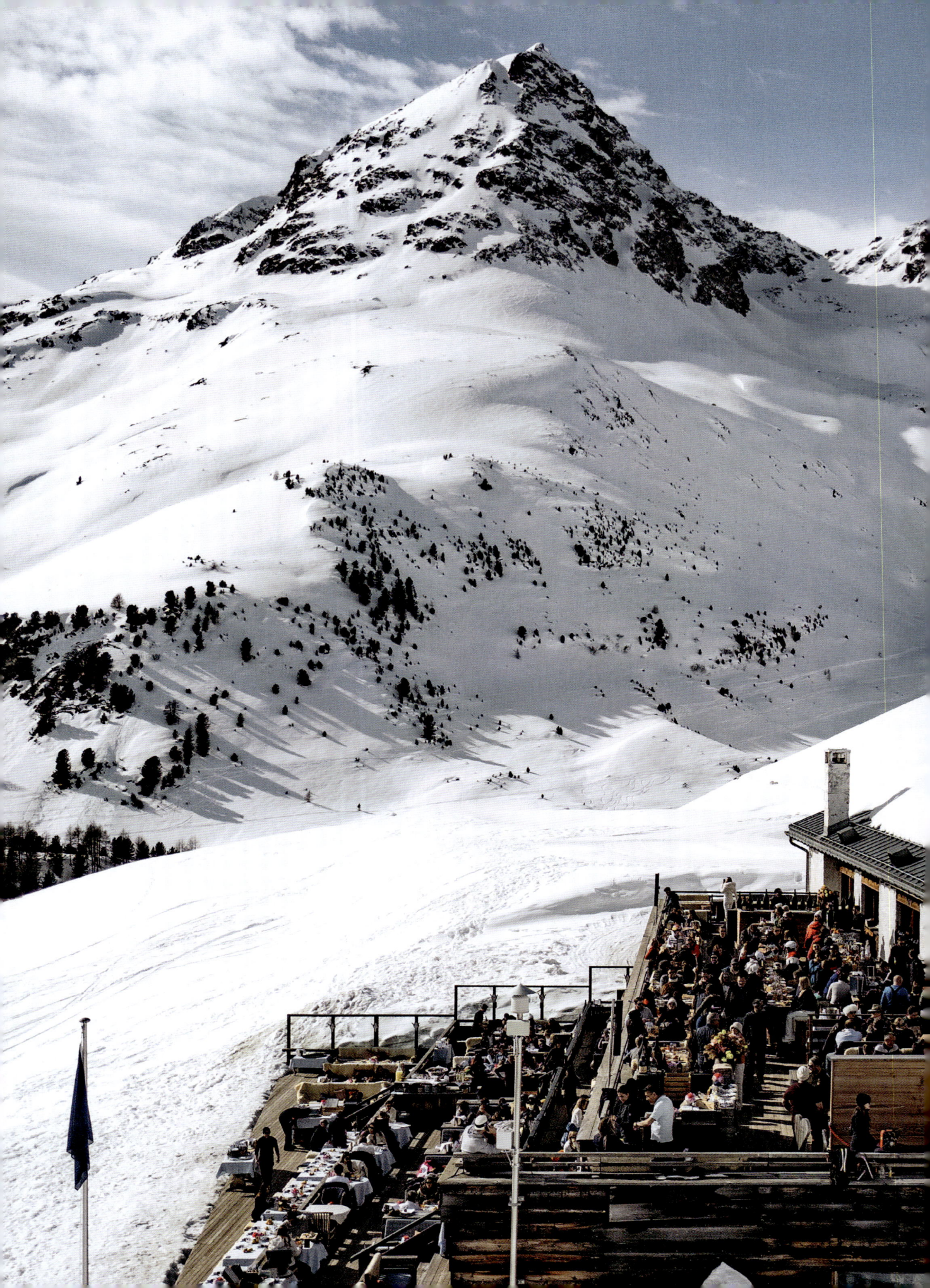

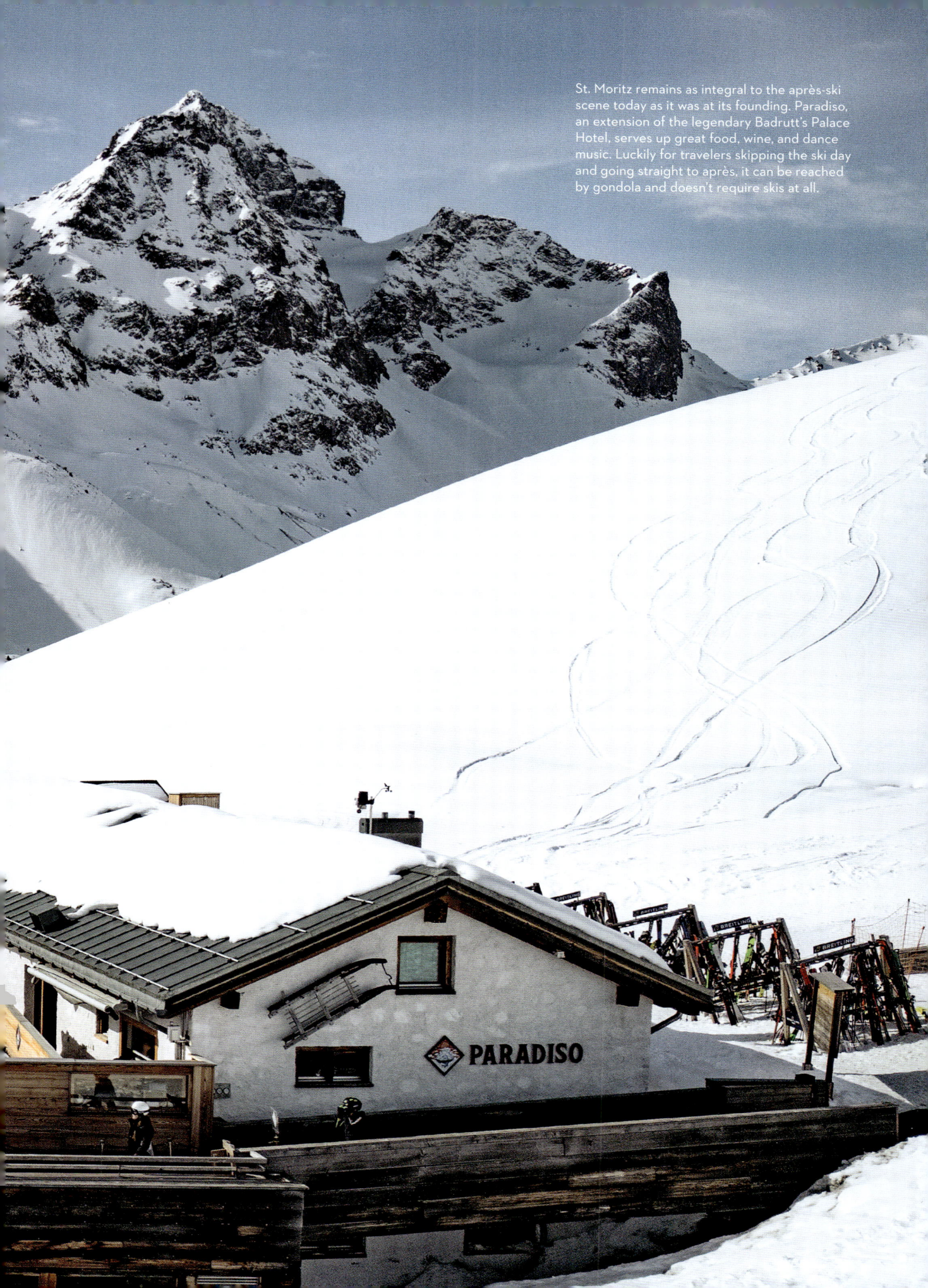

St. Moritz remains as integral to the après-ski scene today as it was at its founding. Paradiso, an extension of the legendary Badrutt's Palace Hotel, serves up great food, wine, and dance music. Luckily for travelers skipping the ski day and going straight to après, it can be reached by gondola and doesn't require skis at all.

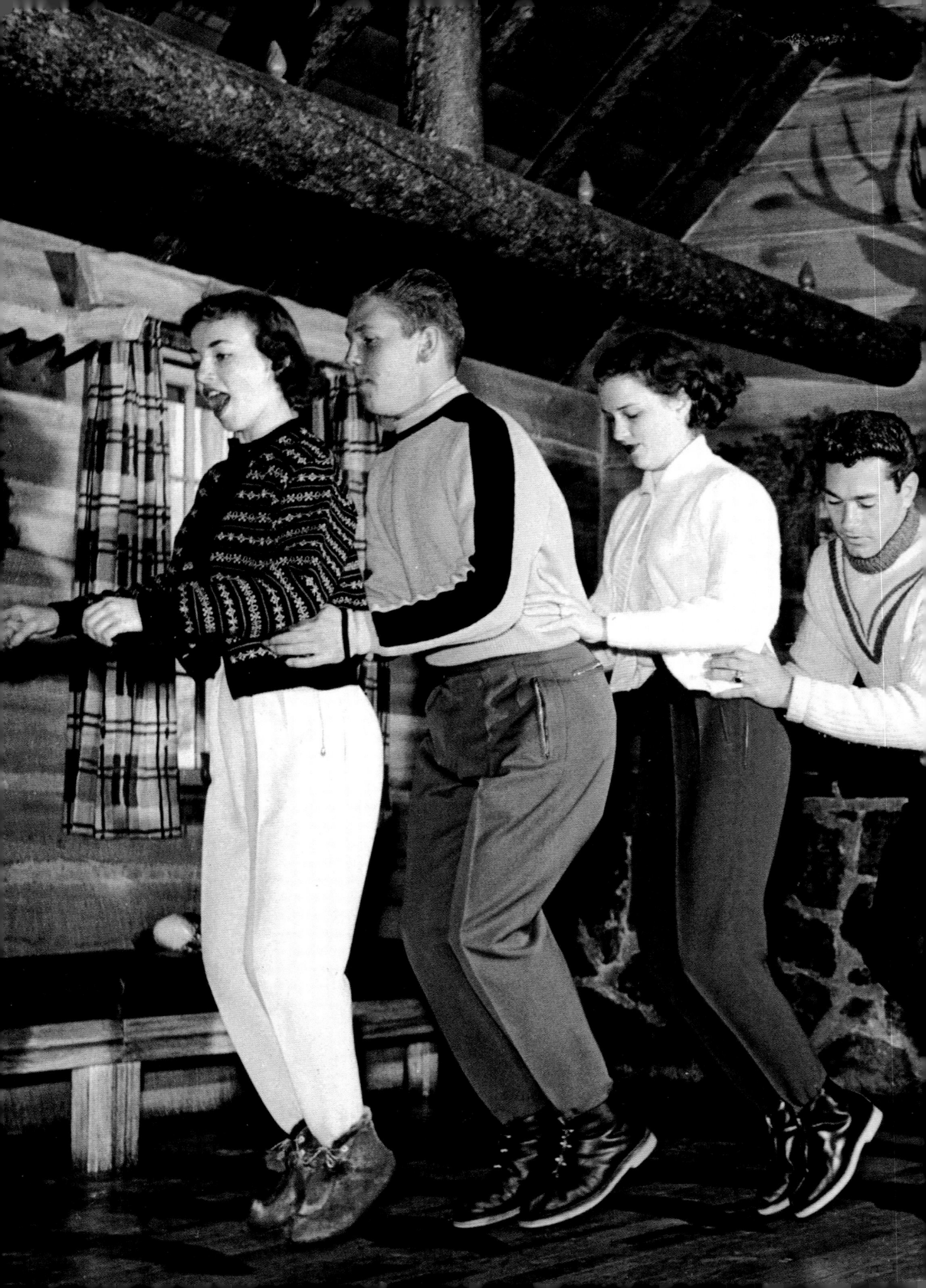

The Scene

Glide into a slope-side bar or make your way back to the base area to strip off some layers; it's time for après-ski. Perhaps your afternoon will be filled with snow beach sunbathing, sipping cocktails in a ski lodge, or dancing on tables in a world-famous nightclub—or all three. For others, a more family-friendly experience might be in order, with sledding and soaking in an outdoor pool. Either way, there is an après setting to fit every taste and mood.

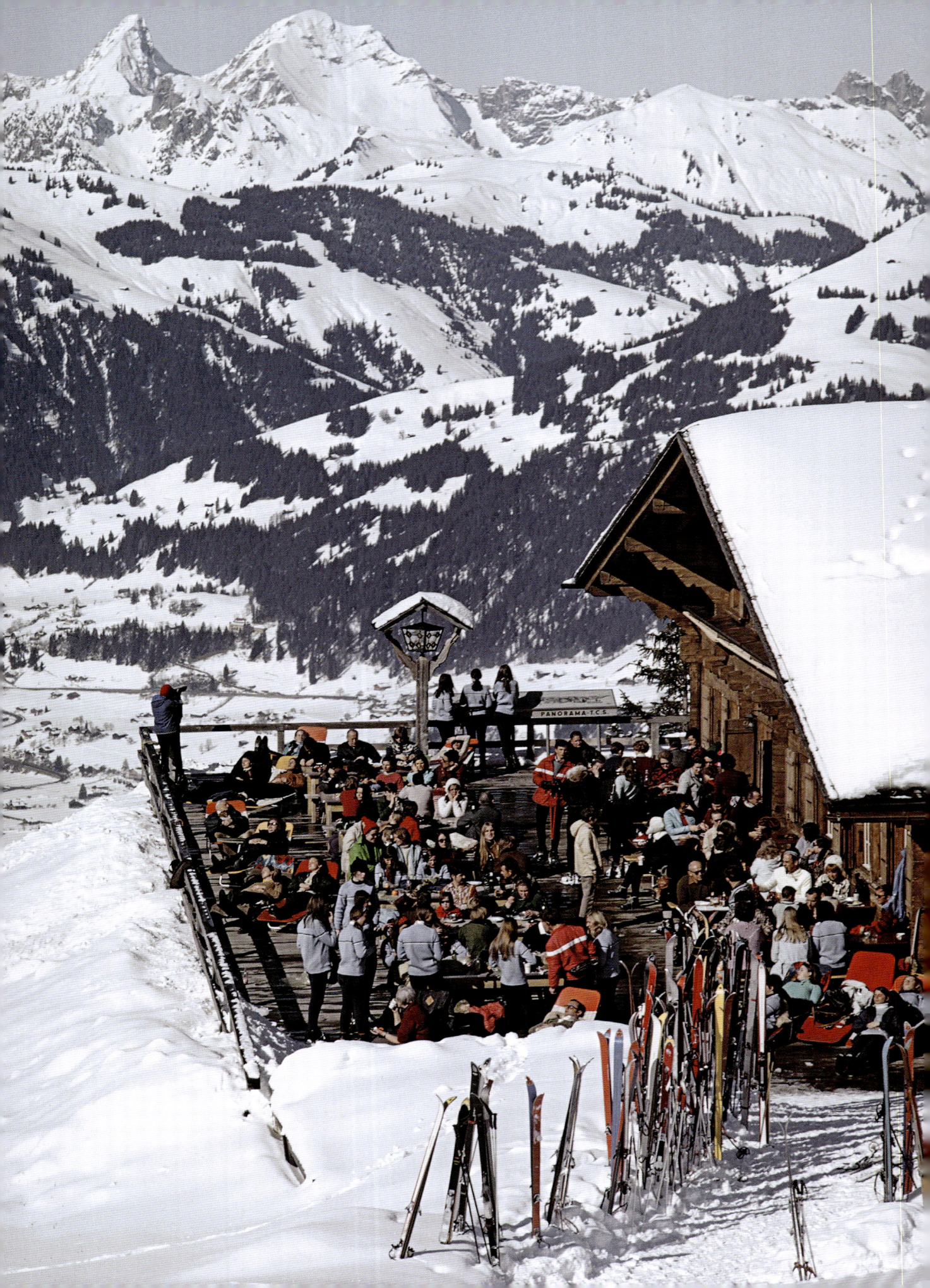

Mountainside Dining

—

One of the great pleasures at the end of a ski day is schussing to a mountain eatery for good music, great food, and preferably a nearby gondola for a safe ride down after an Aperol Spritz or two. A handful of elite private clubs sit atop the slopes of tony ski towns, such as the historic Eagle Club in Gstaad, Switzerland, and the younger Aspen Mountain Club in Aspen, Colorado (recently renamed as AspenX). These clubs have notoriously counted royals, film stars, and financiers among their members and regulars. For a lucky few in Montana, membership at the Yellowstone Club includes skiing an entire private mountain resort. However, many resorts worldwide are home to picture-perfect mountainside spots that are available for everyone to enjoy.

◀ Founded in Gstaad, Switzerland, in 1957 by Charles Greville, the seventh Earl of Warwick, the Eagle Club has long served as a social lunch club for royals, celebrities such as Sir Roger Moore, and designers such as Valentino.

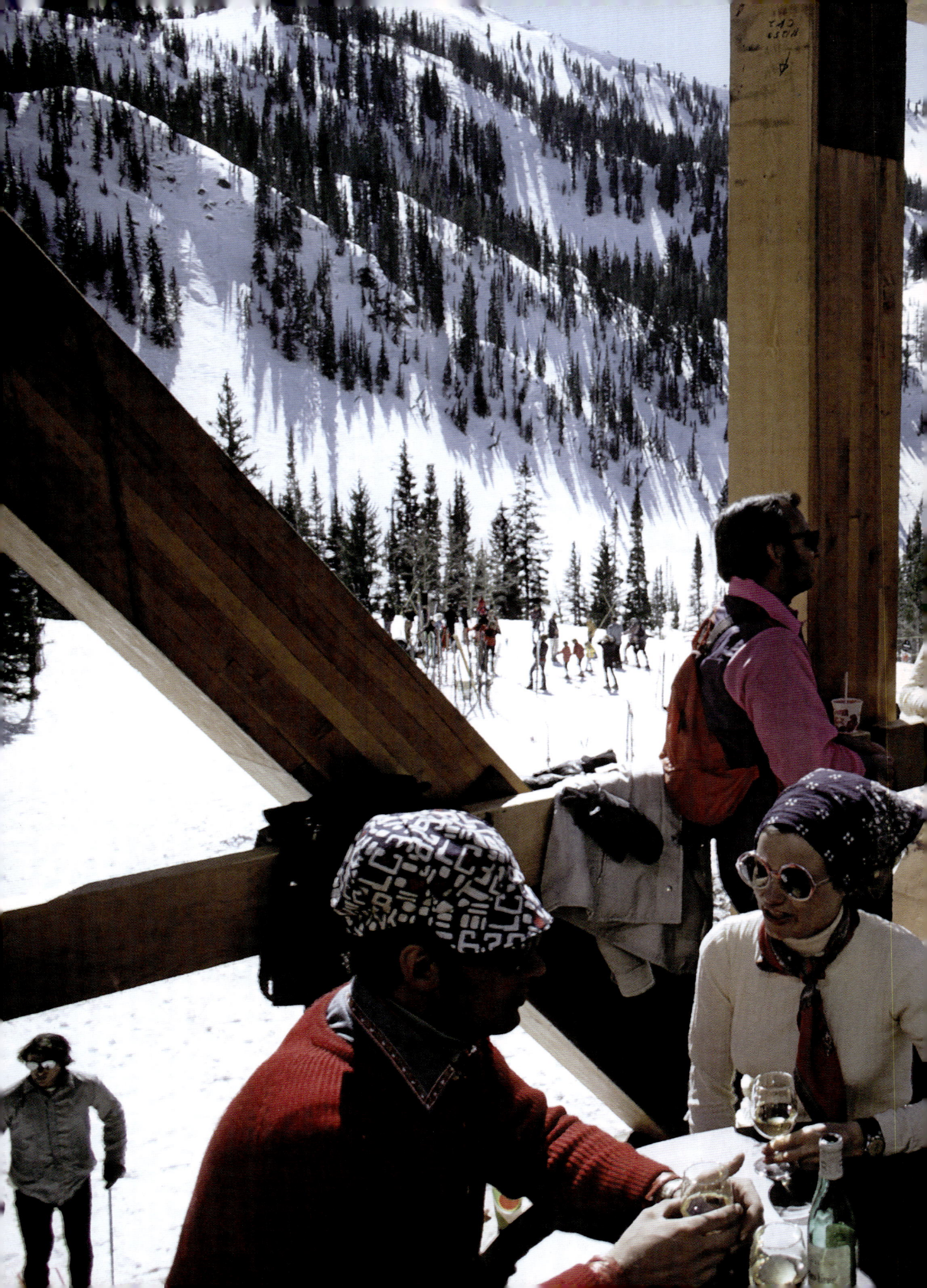

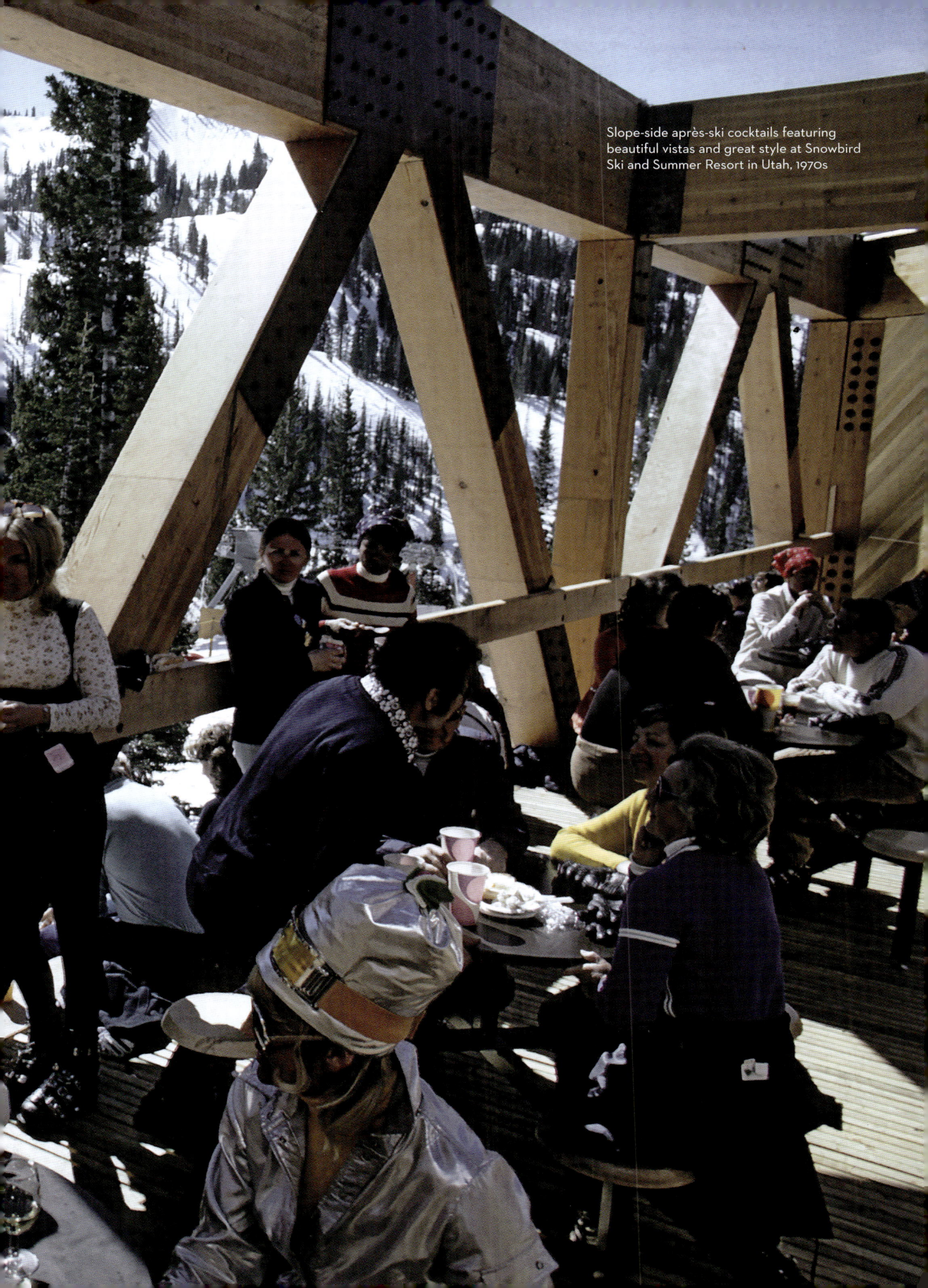

Slope-side après-ski cocktails featuring beautiful vistas and great style at Snowbird Ski and Summer Resort in Utah, 1970s

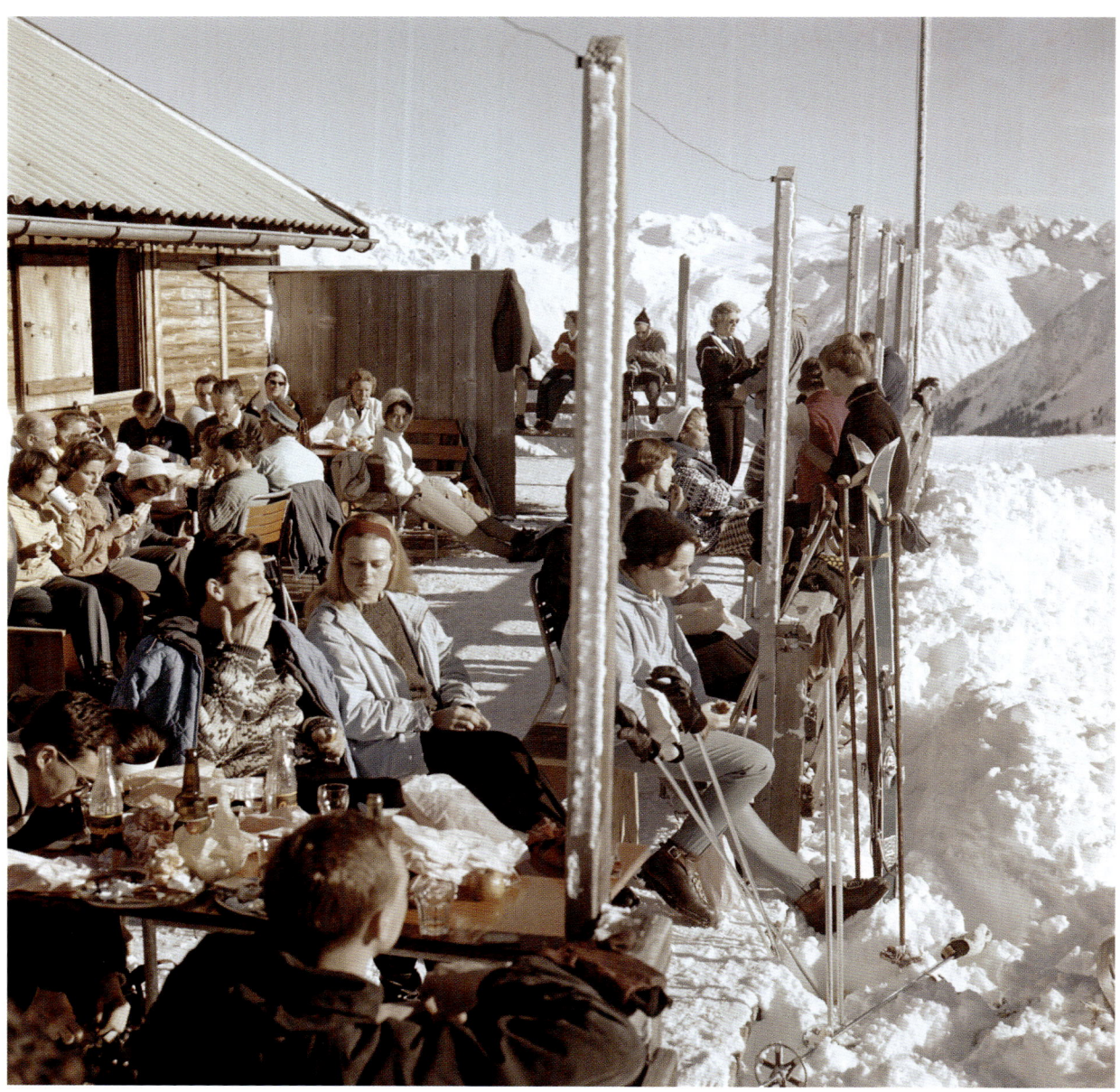

▲ Skiers enjoying après-ski drinks and food with a breathtaking view from above the tree line in Klosters, Switzerland, 1960

▶ Aspen Highlands Ski Patrol showing off outside the Cloud Nine restaurant in 1975. High on the slopes of the Aspen Highlands mountain and accessible only by skis or snowboard, Cloud Nine remains a perennial hot spot, serving up midday food with a side of dancing, sometimes on furniture.

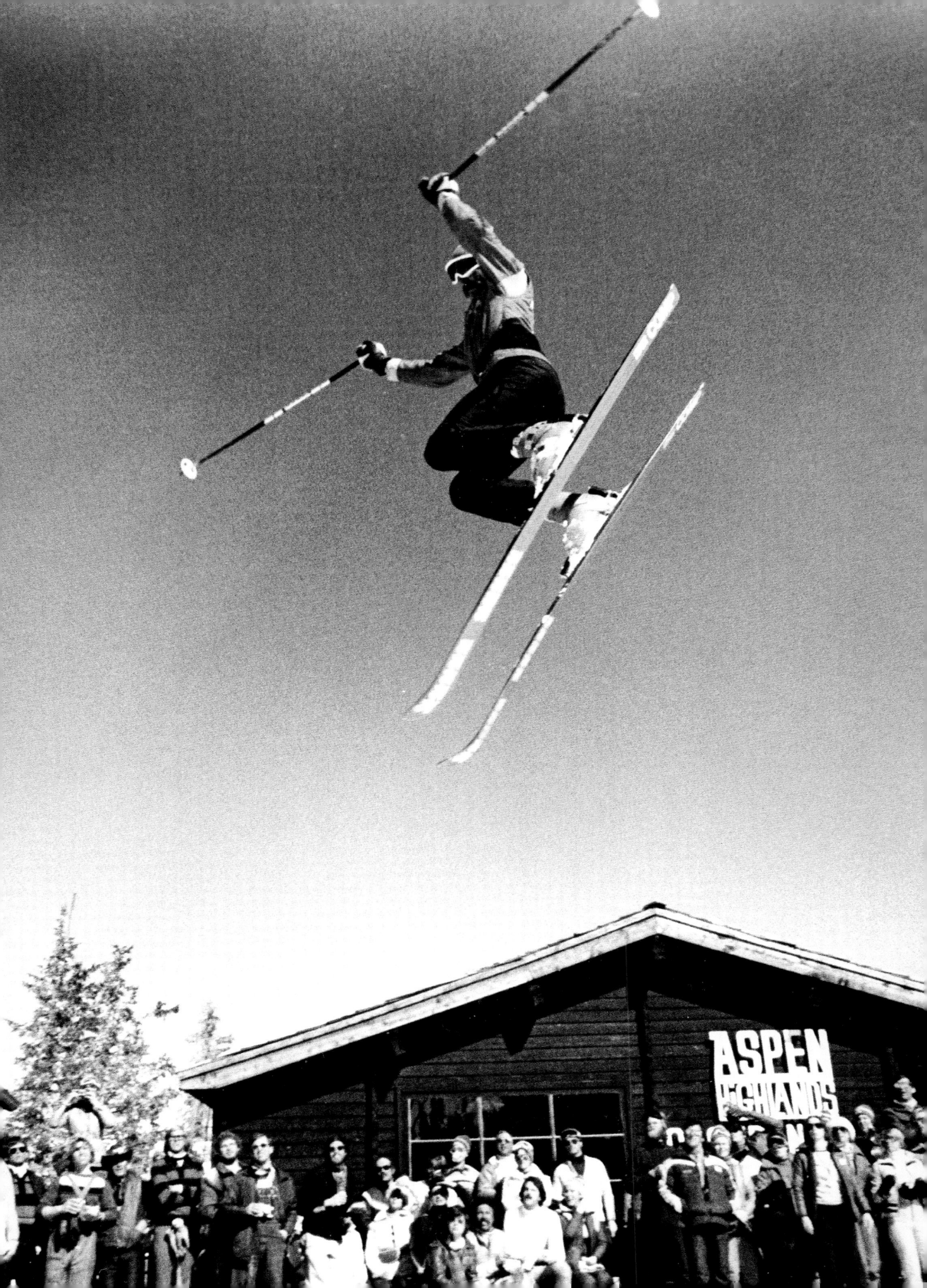

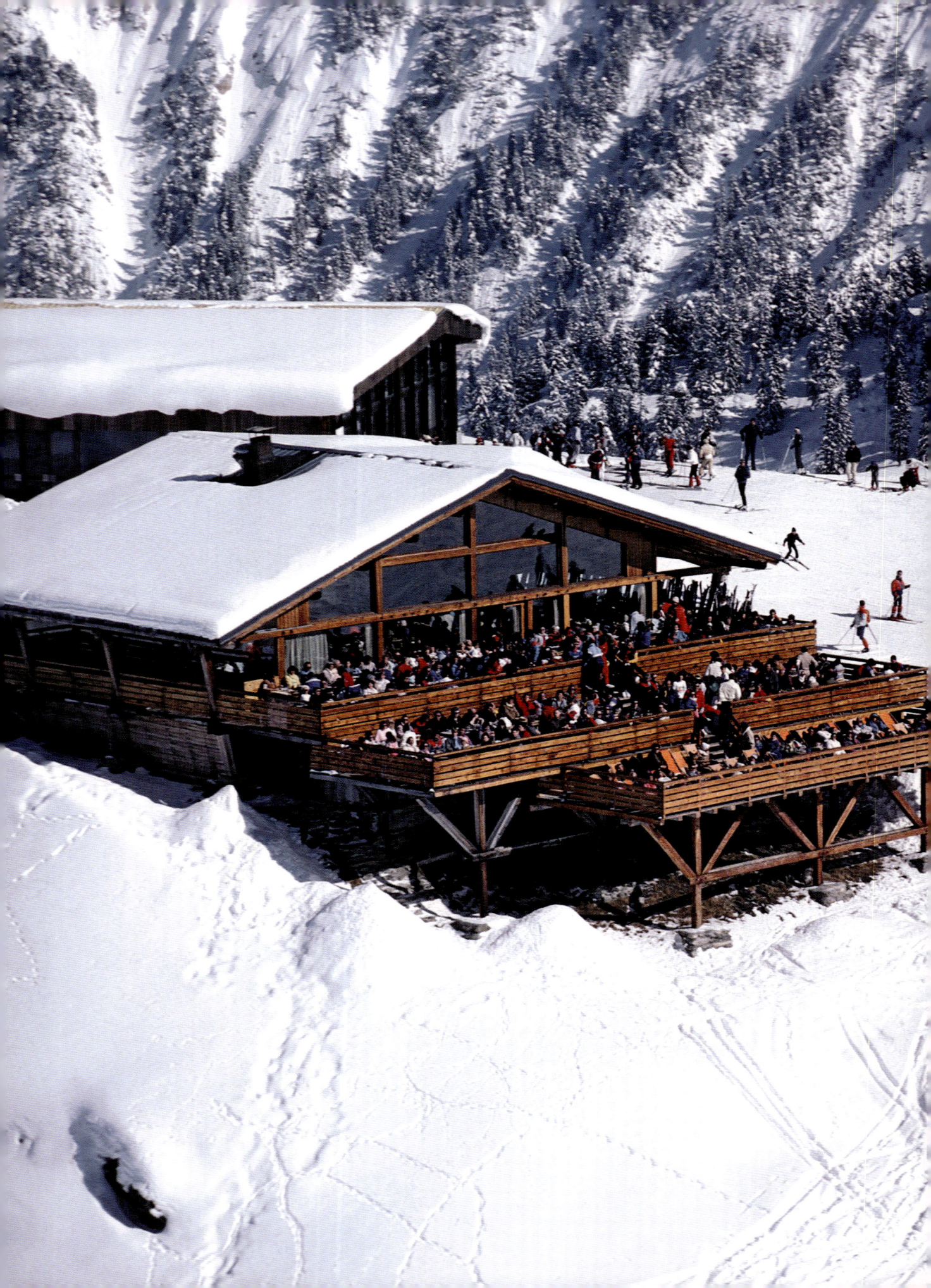

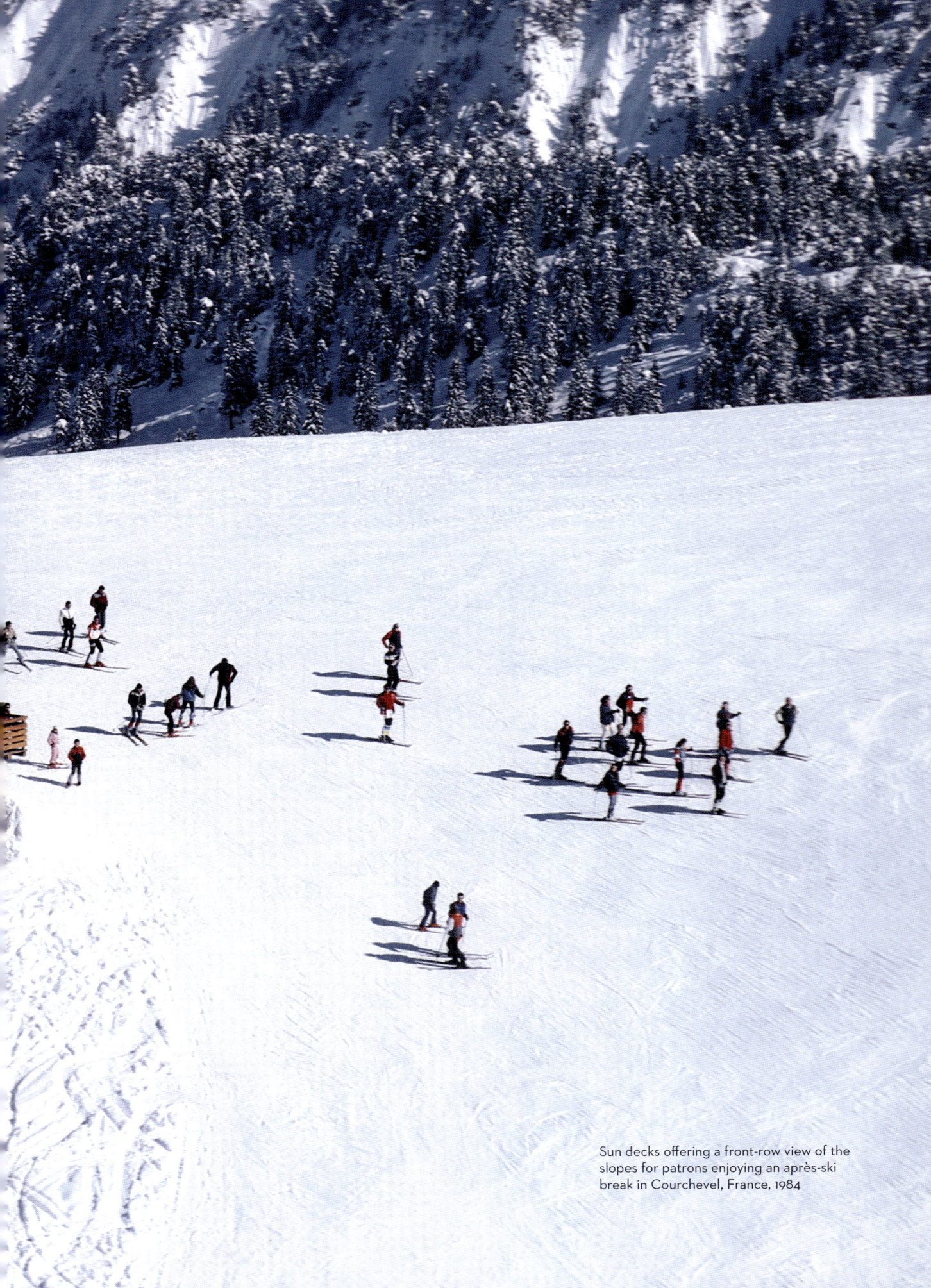

Sun decks offering a front-row view of the slopes for patrons enjoying an après-ski break in Courchevel, France, 1984

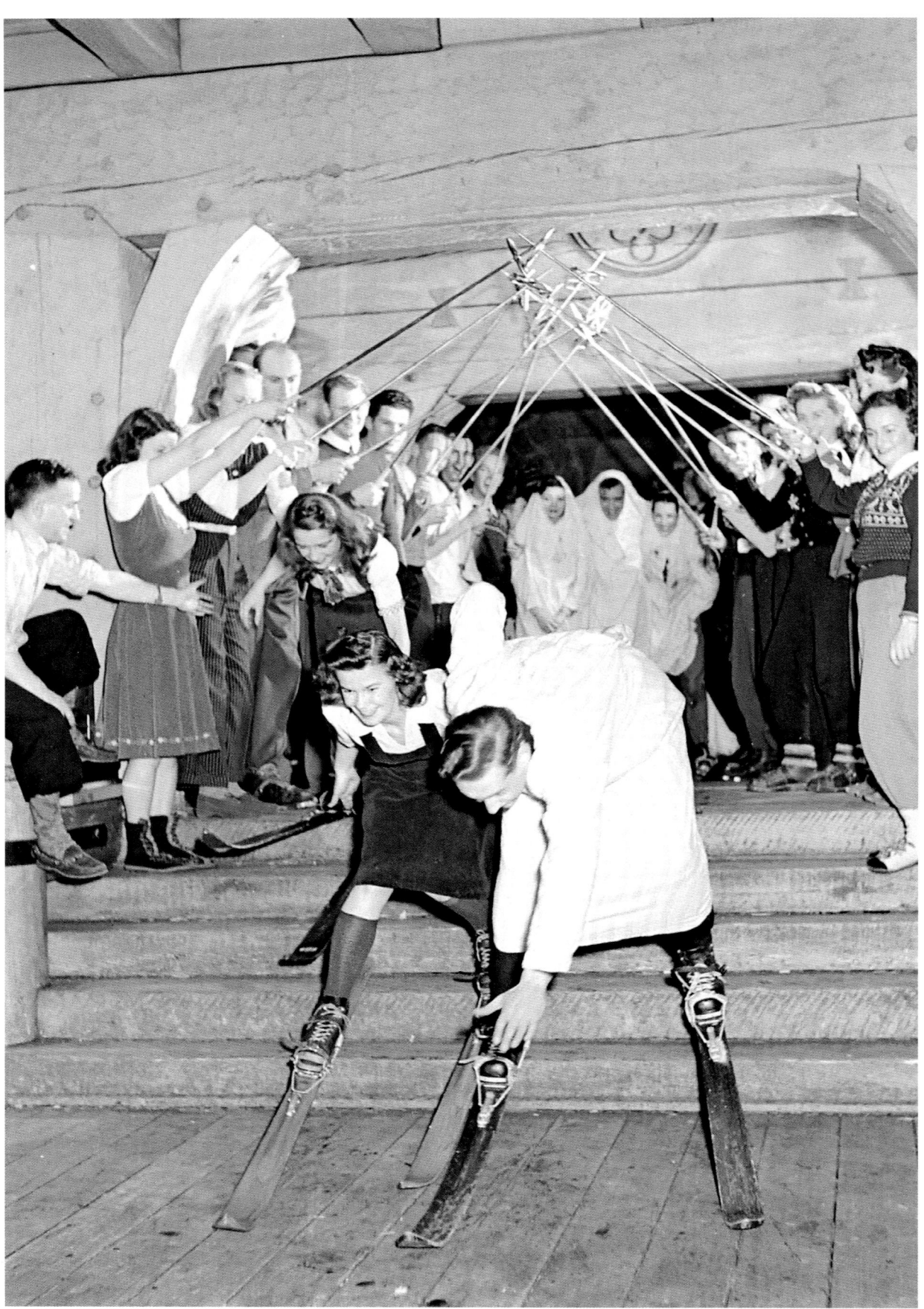

Chalets & Mountain Lodges

—

Whether it's a five-star hotel, family-friendly lodge, or private chalet, every ski enthusiast needs a home base. For well over a hundred years, après-ski traditions in these settings have included a varied combination of high- and lowbrow entertainment, including board games, aperitifs, and the occasional night of naughty fun.

◄ Timberline Lodge in Mount Hood, Oregon, hosted an annual ski club party known for its rowdy festivities, including creative indoor "skiing," as captured here by *Life* magazine in 1942.

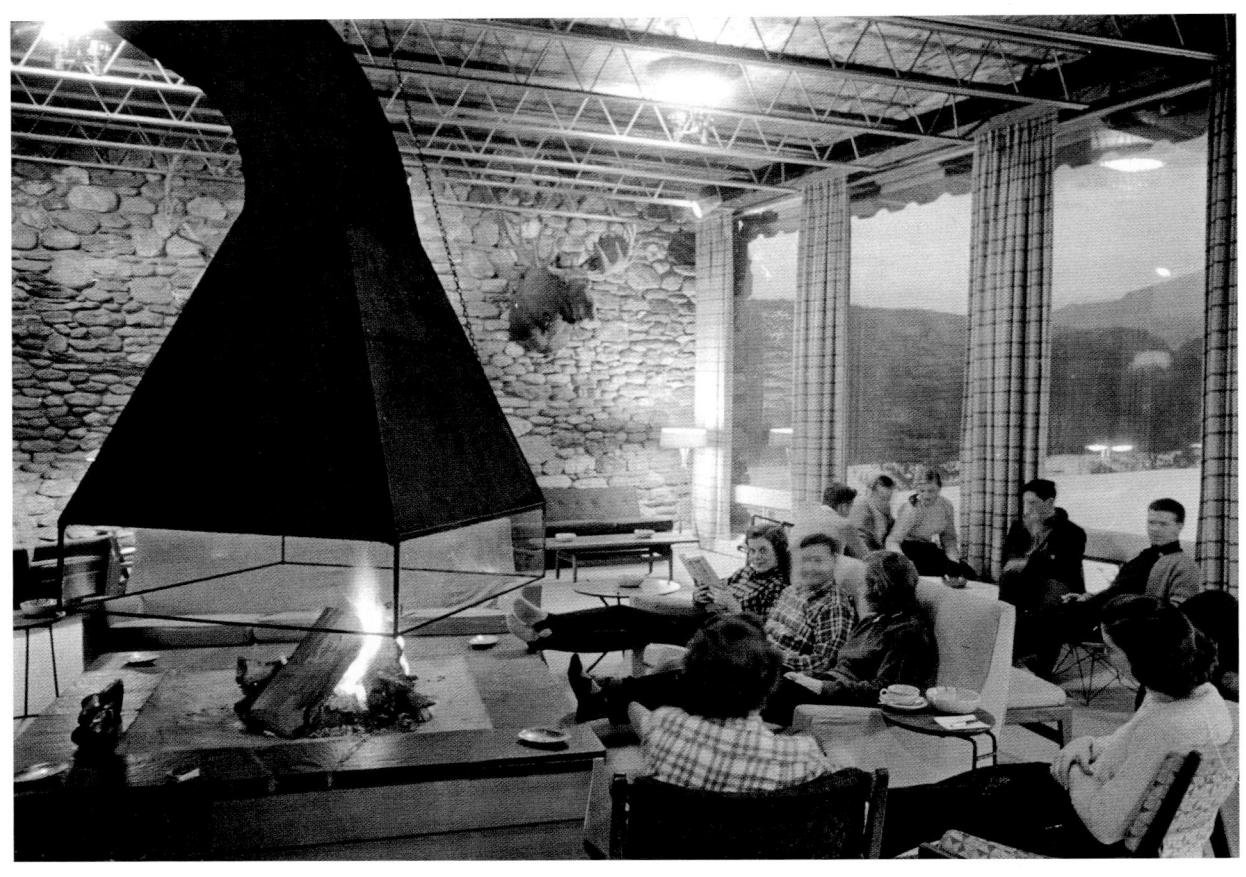

▲ The first stop for many people après-ski is a seat at a lodge in front of a fire. After you've unloaded outer layers and pulled off ski boots, this is an ideal place to warm up your extremities, enjoy a snack, and recharge after a long, cold day of skiing, as demonstrated here in Stowe, Vermont, 1957.

▶ Hunter S. Thompson at his home in Aspen, 1990

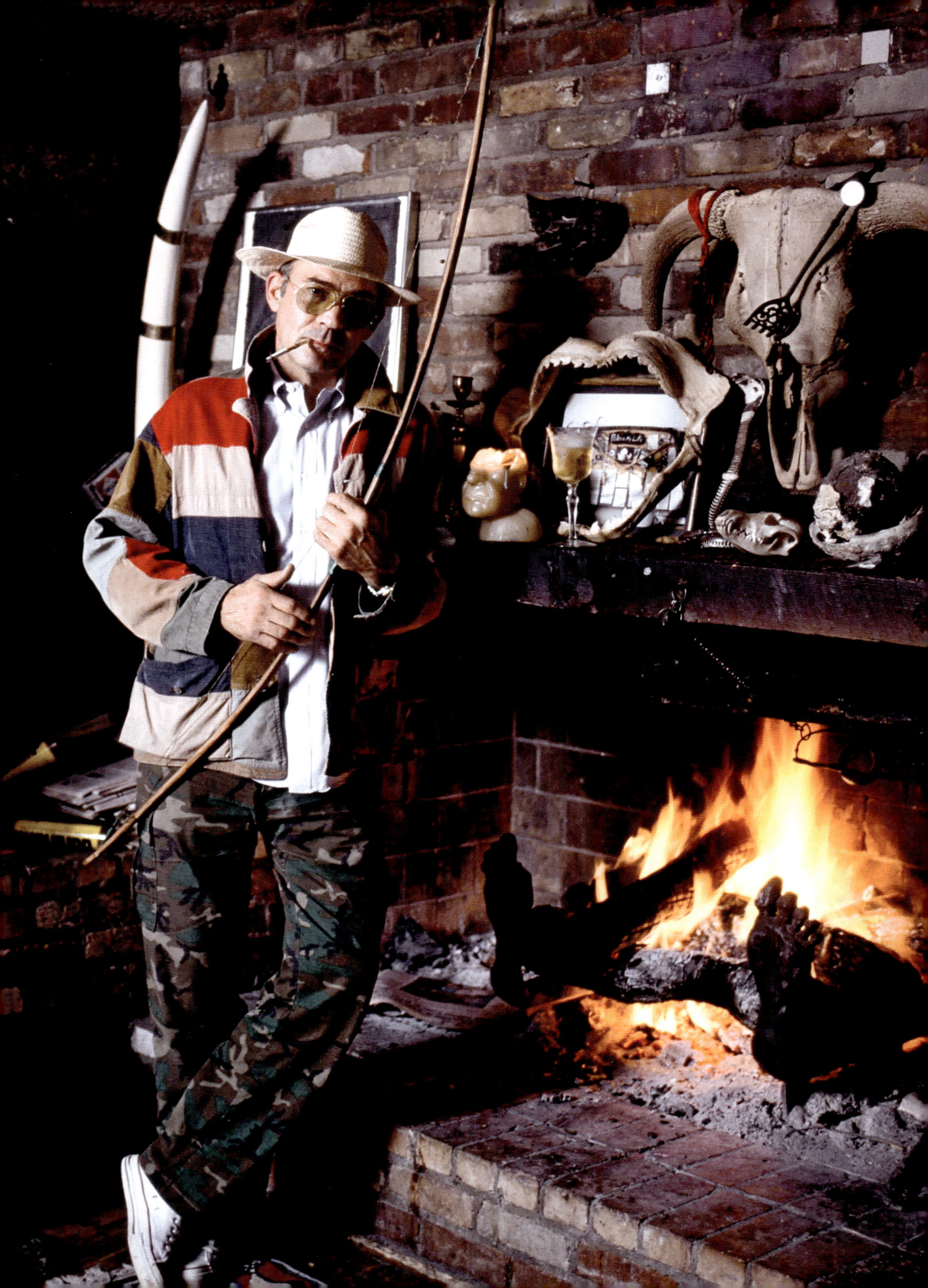

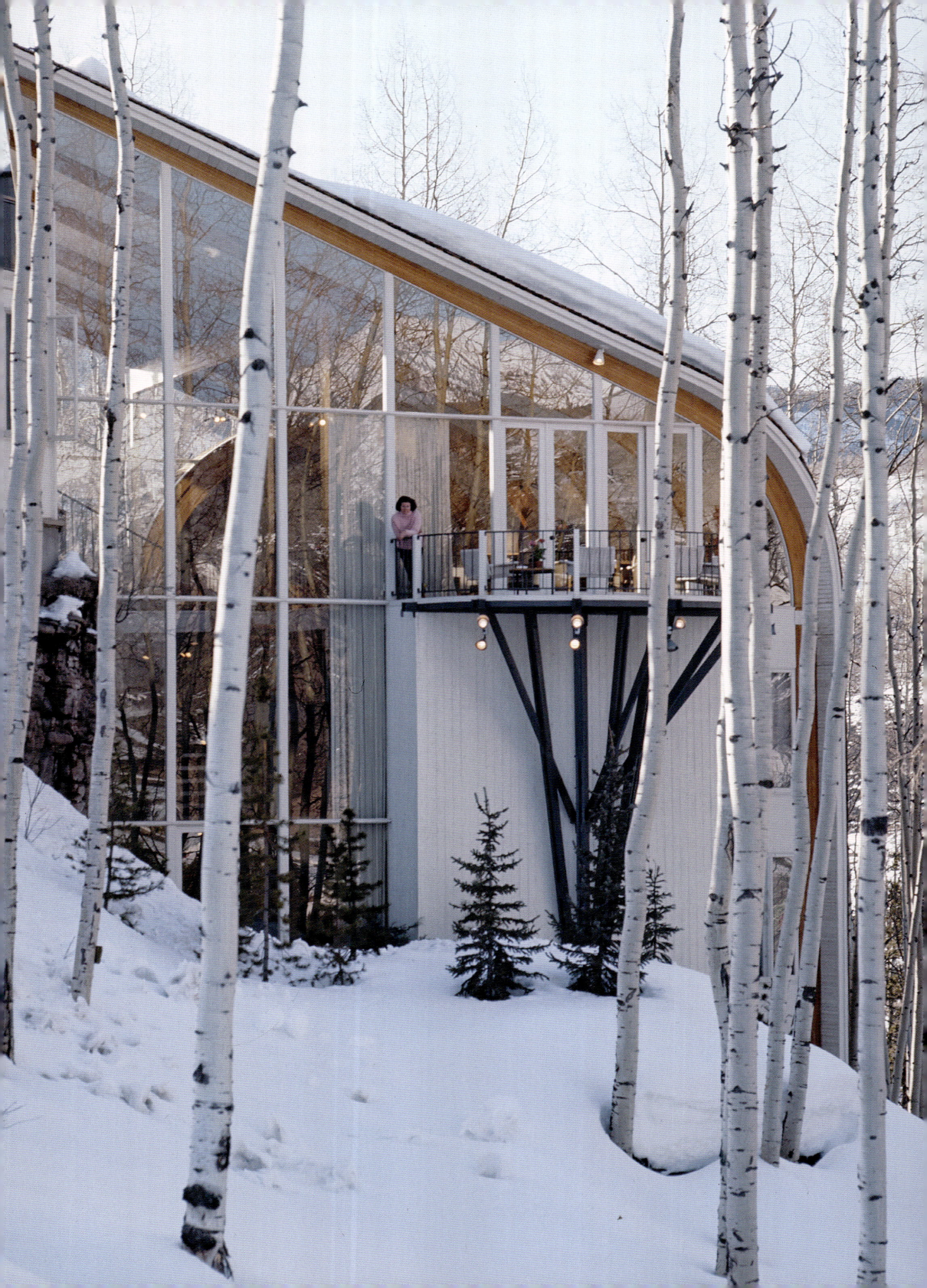

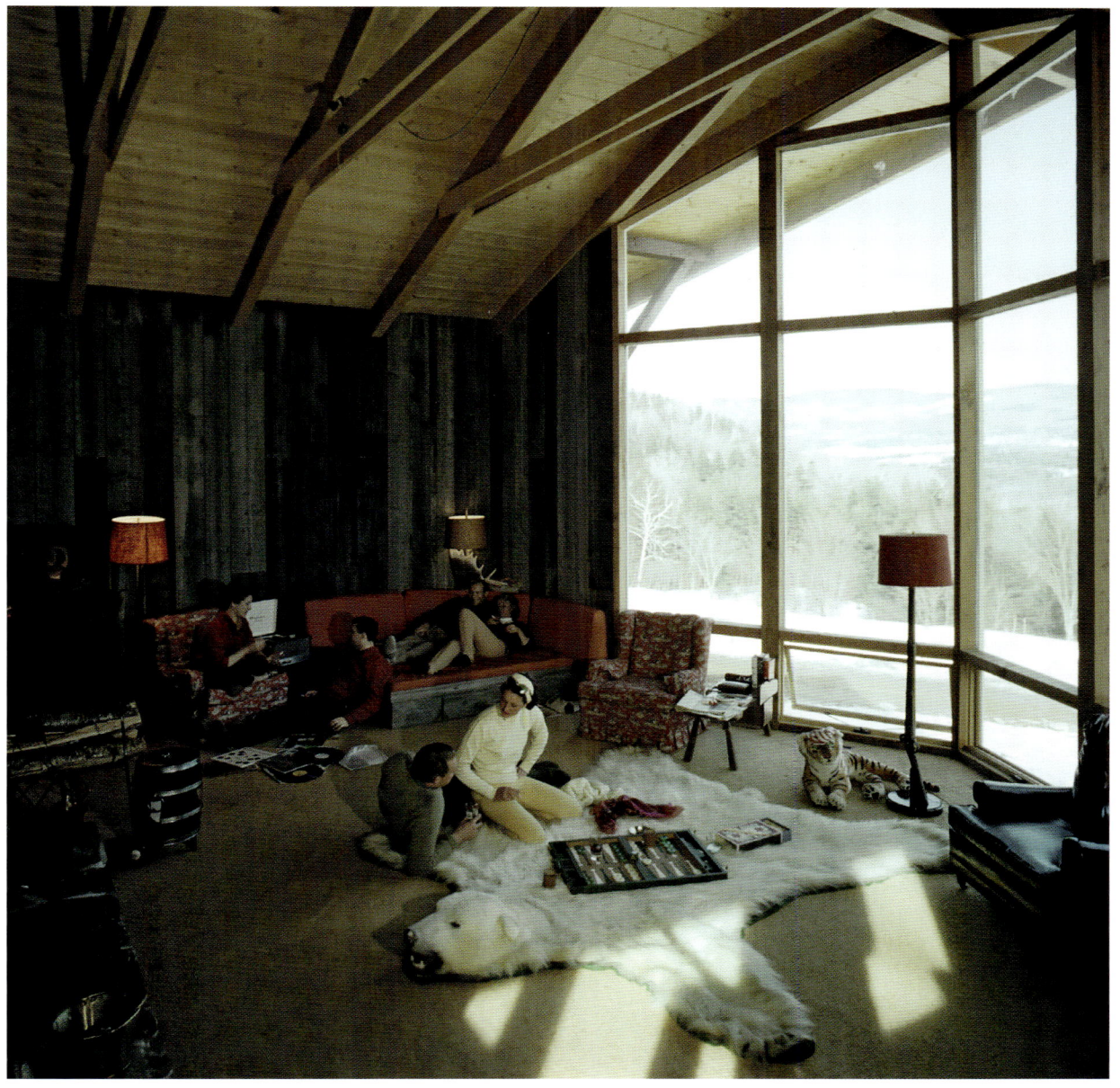

▲ A game of backgammon après-ski in a chalet at the Sugarbush Resort in Vermont, 1960

◀ This house built in the 1960s in Vail, Colorado, was designed to take in the incredible views and surrounding nature—a perfect après-ski venue.

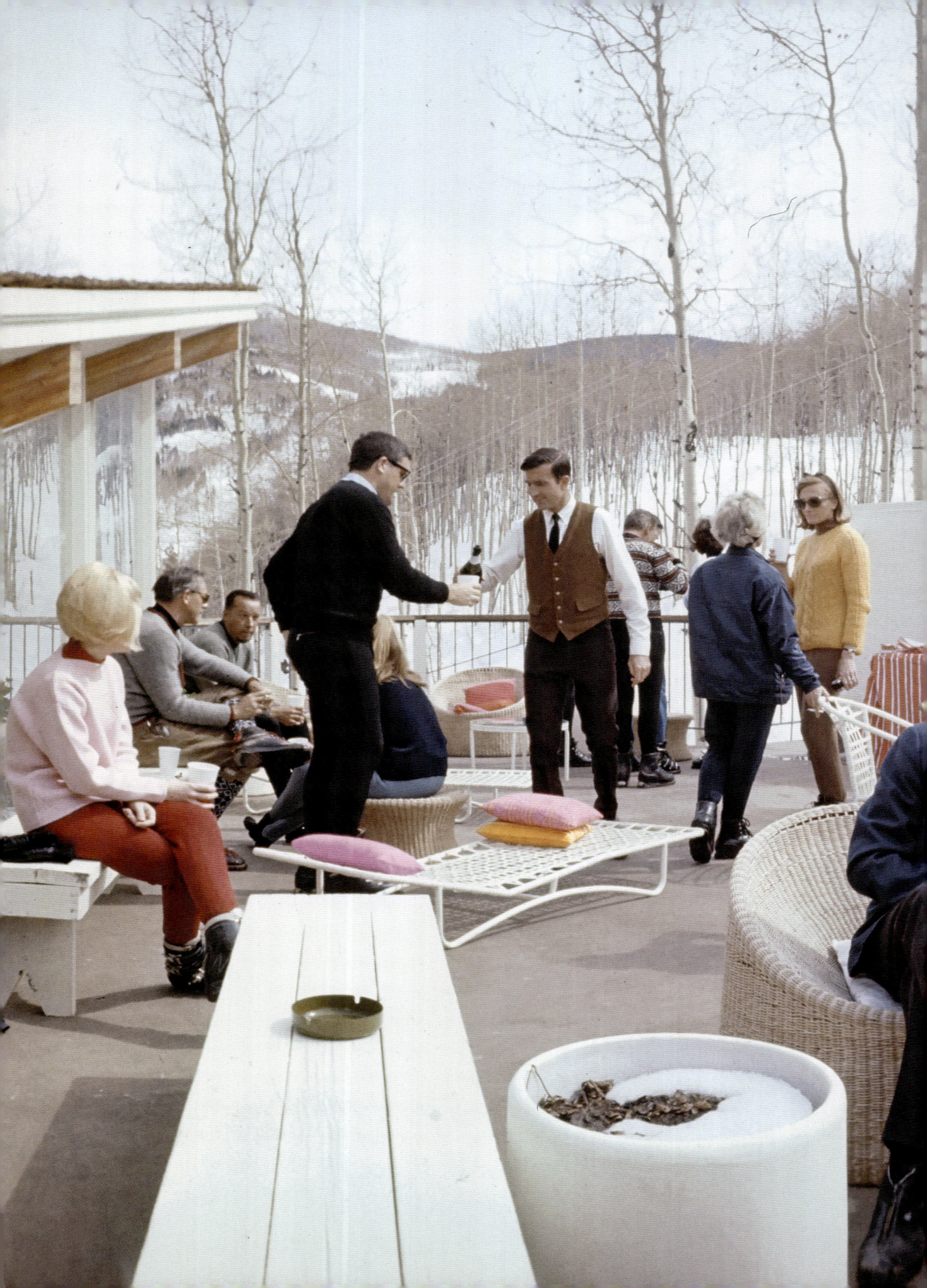

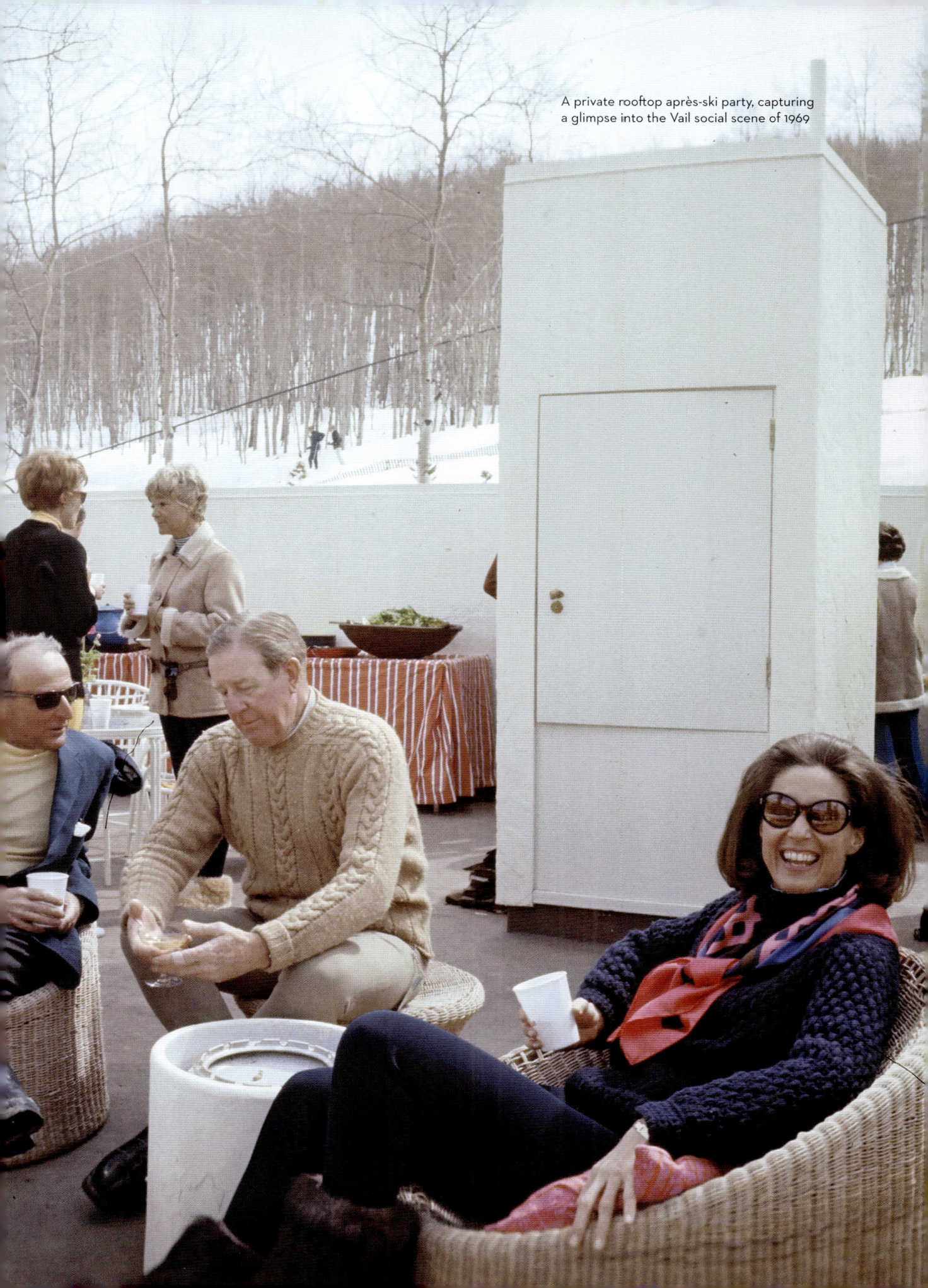

A private rooftop après-ski party, capturing a glimpse into the Vail social scene of 1969

THE
ICE BAR

It would be difficult to imagine a more perfect setting than an ice bar for an après-ski cocktail on a bluebird day. Built from blocks of ice and compacted snow, ice bars have been decorating après-ski scenes for nearly a century.

▼ Après-ski cocktails at the famed Badrutt's Palace Hotel ice rink bar in St. Moritz, 1947

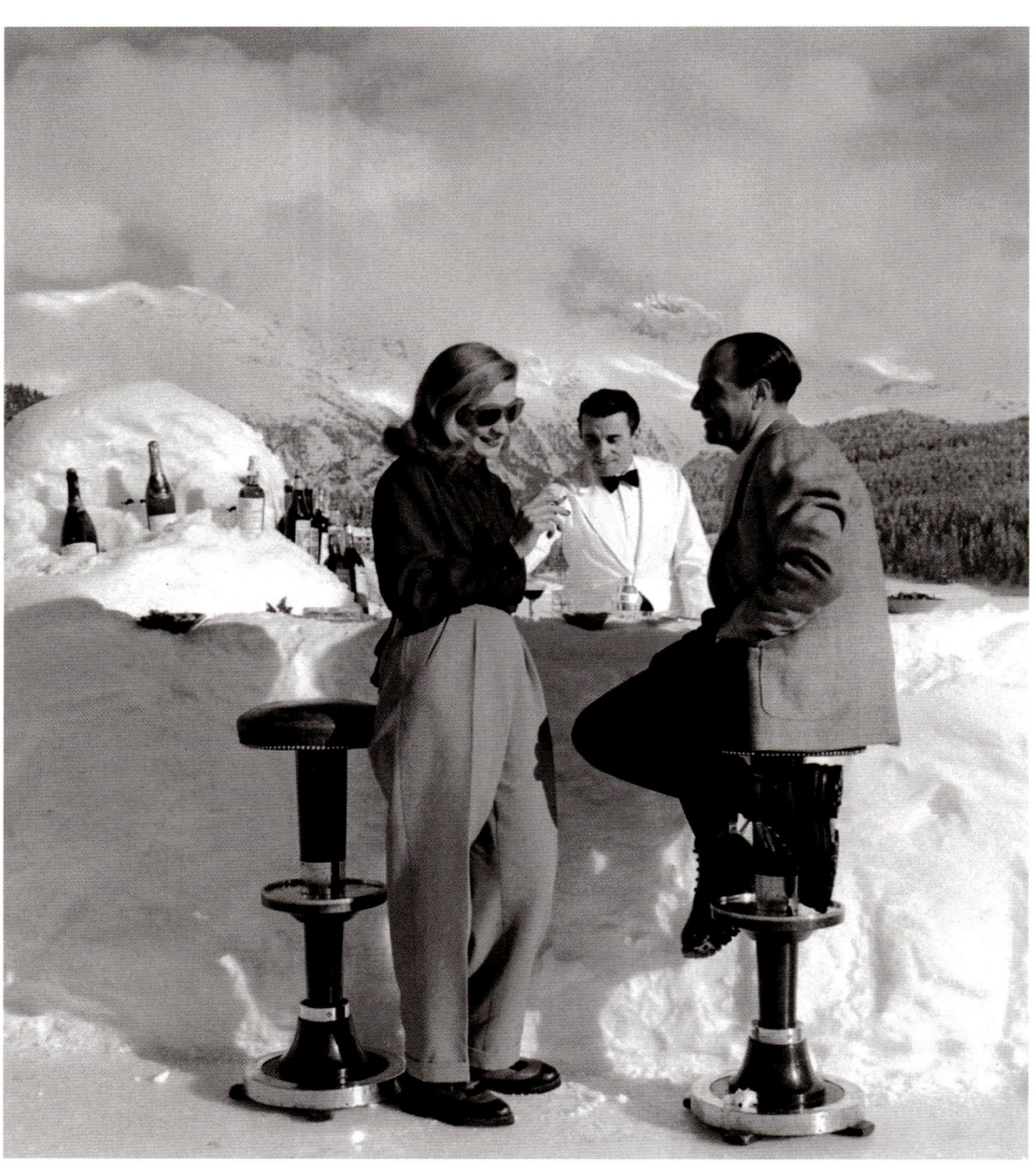

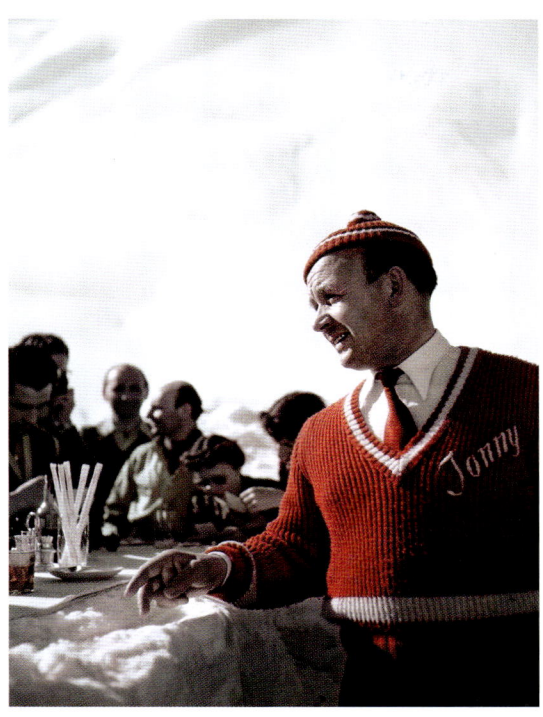

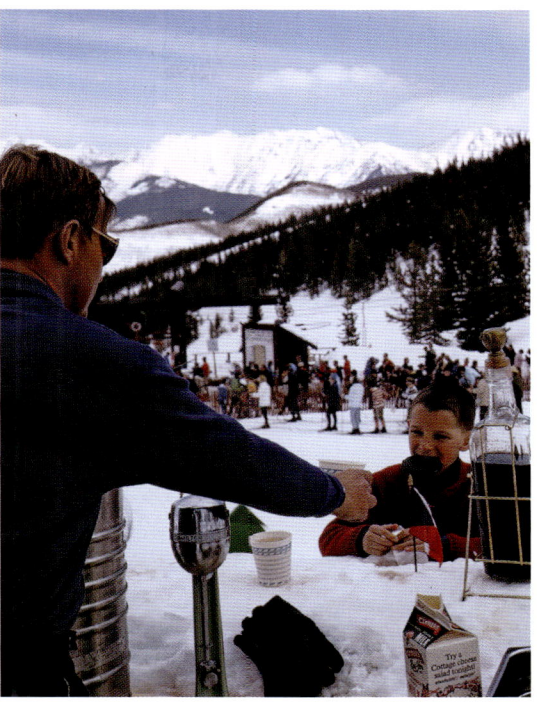

▲ The ice bar outside Hotel Edelweiss in Zürs, Austria, 1950

▲ A young customer at the Vail Ice Bar, 1964

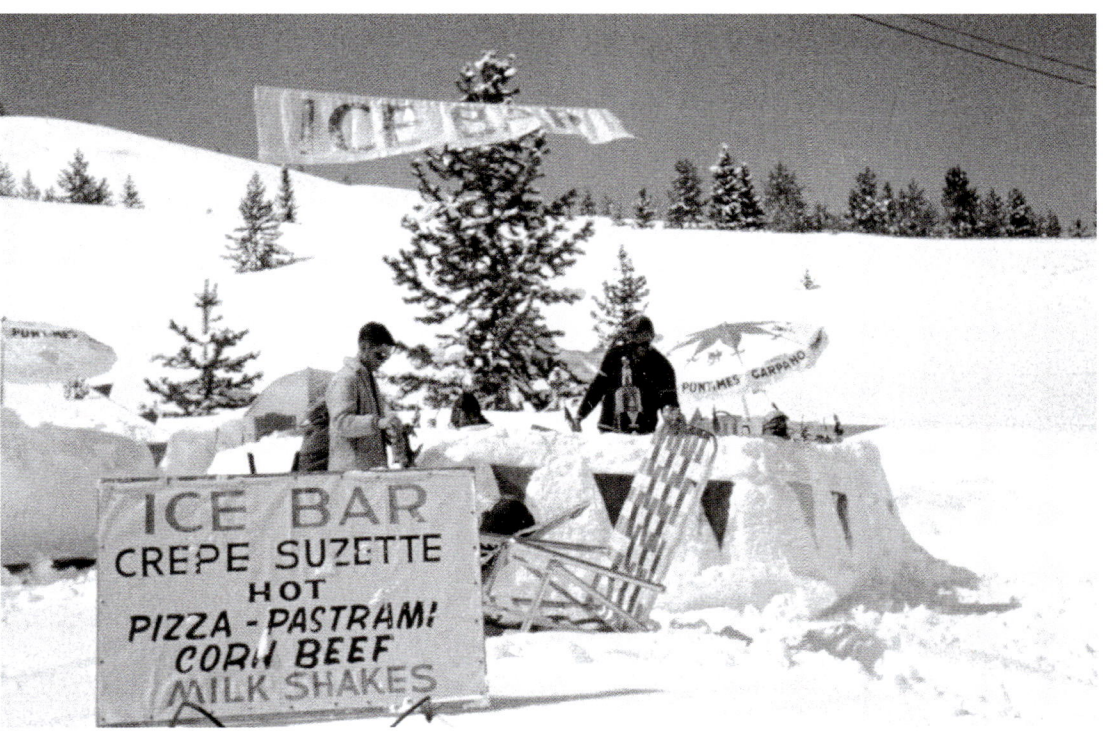

▲ Bill Whiteford, an early investor in the Vail Ski Resort, built a short-lived ice bar in the Mid-Vail area of the resort during the 1963–64 ski season.

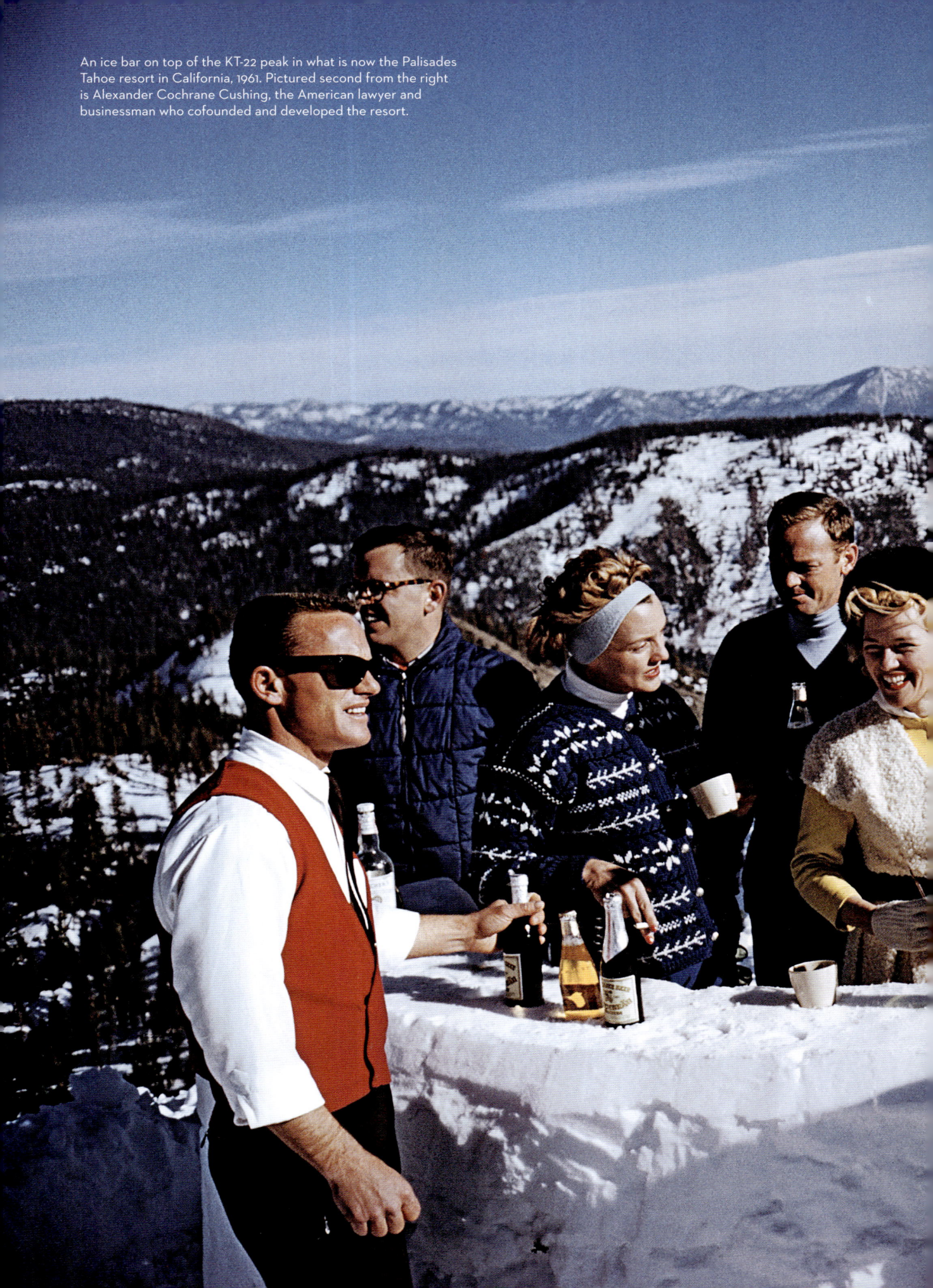

An ice bar on top of the KT-22 peak in what is now the Palisades Tahoe resort in California, 1961. Pictured second from the right is Alexander Cochrane Cushing, the American lawyer and businessman who cofounded and developed the resort.

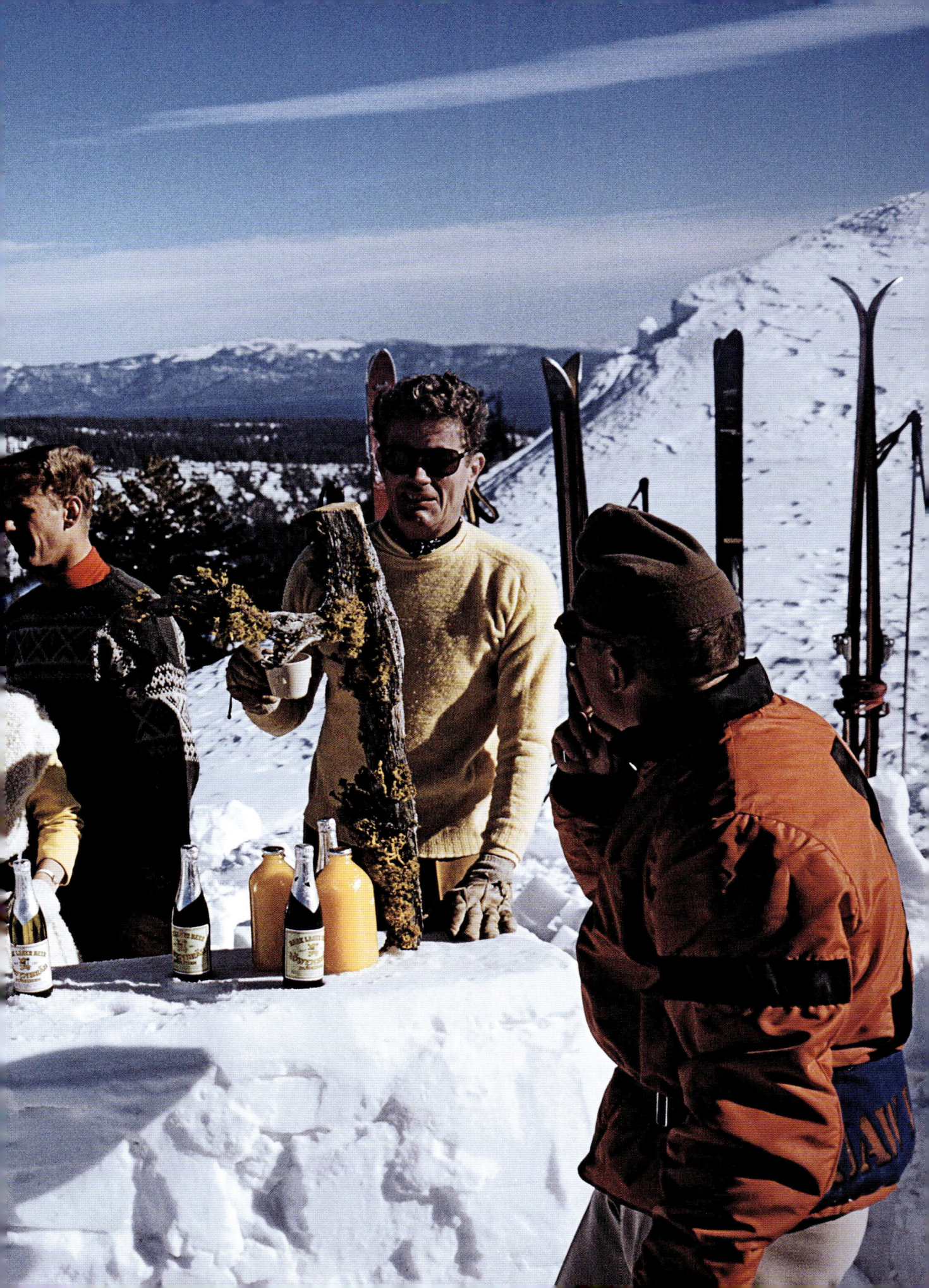

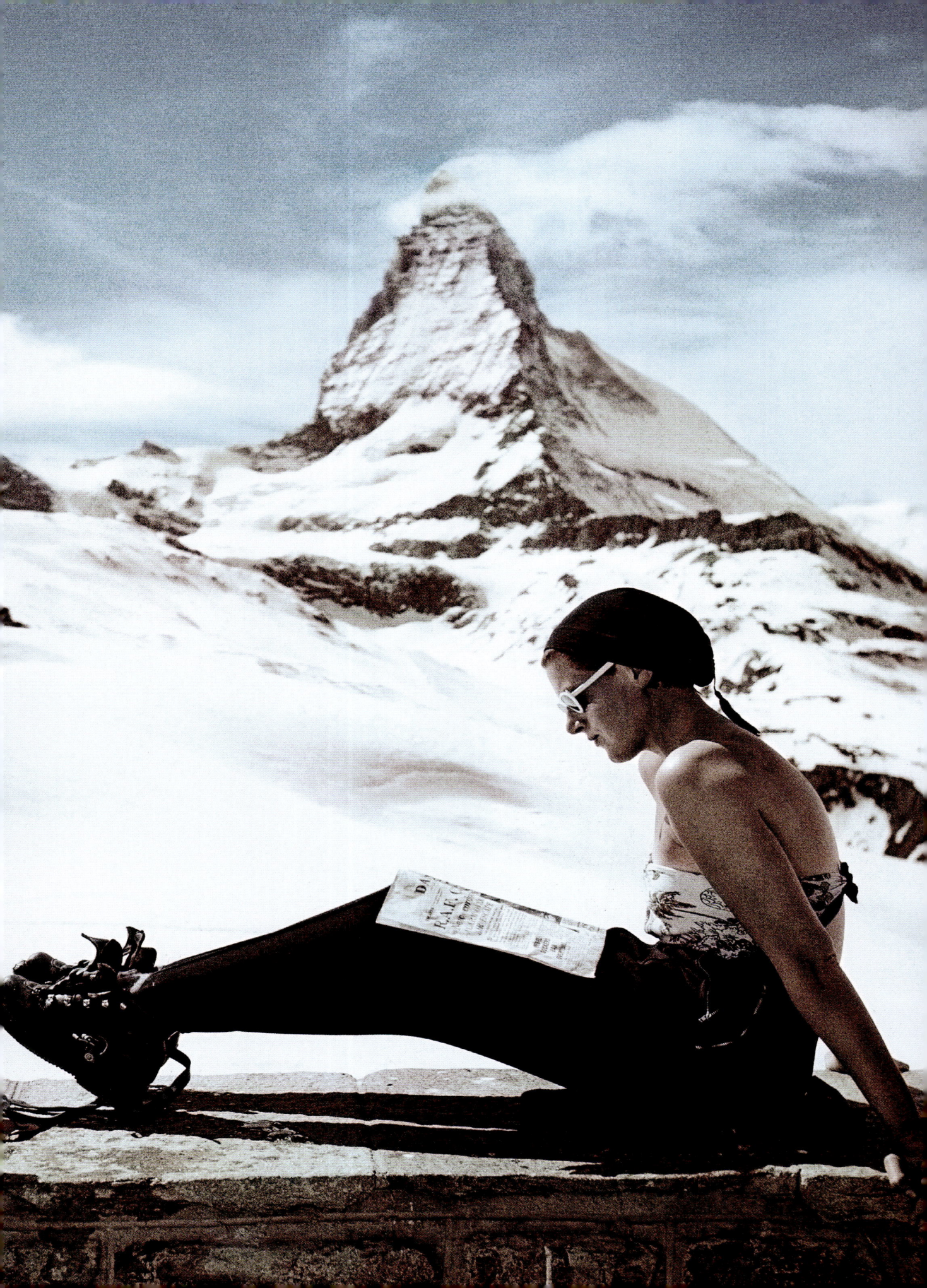

Snow Beach

—

Sunbathing isn't only for sandy beaches. After hours on skis, finding a comfortable spot to lounge and soak up the high mountain sun is an irresistible option. While this tradition has presumably existed for as long as there has been skiing, several high-profile "snow beaches" with food, drinks, and music have recently popped up at resorts worldwide. For those who do not ski, these spots are perfect for showing off mountain fashion or catching up with friends to kick off the après-ski festivities.

◄ Sunbathing après-ski within view of the Matterhorn in Zermatt, Switzerland, 1950

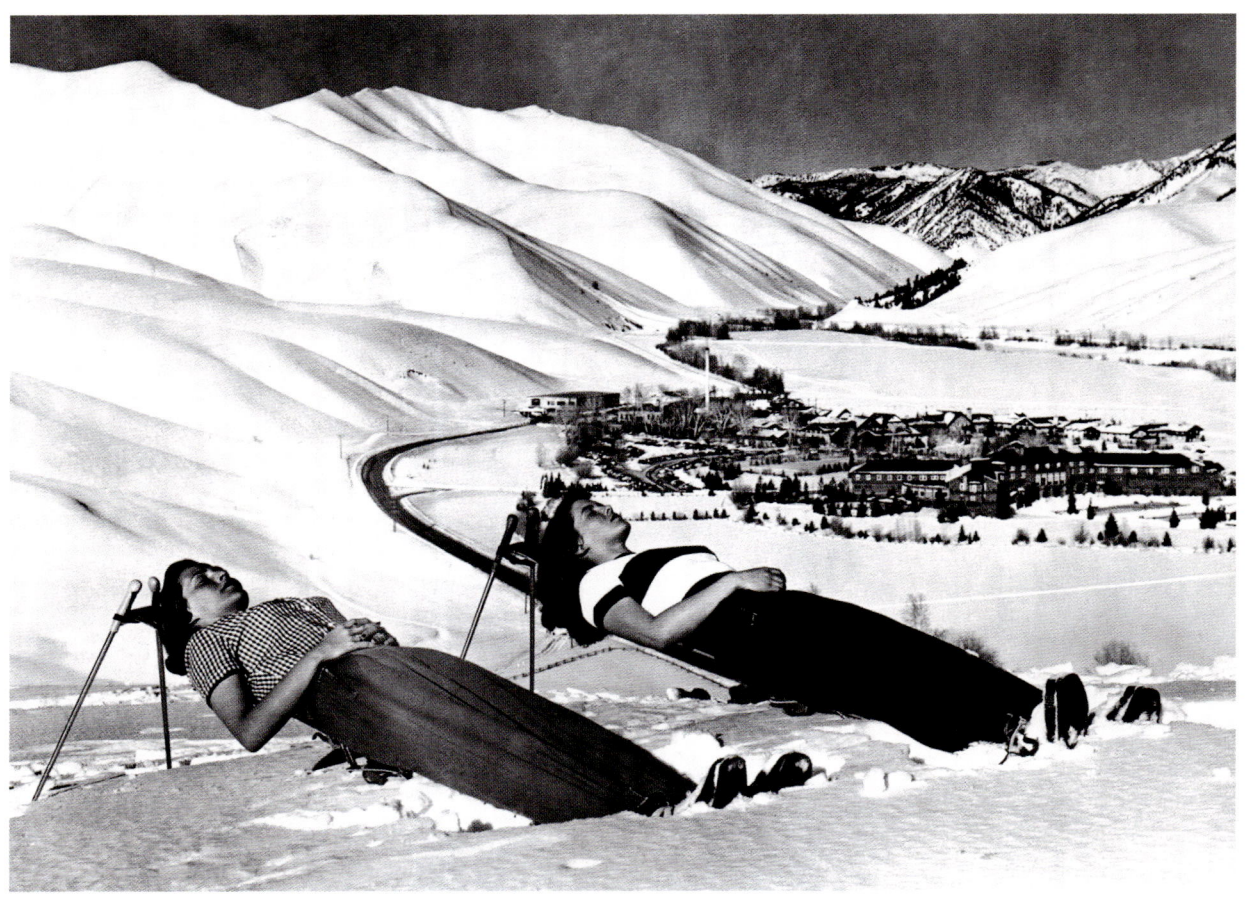

▲ No chair, no problem—skis can double as a seat back for lounging in the snow, as demonstrated in Sun Valley, 1950

▶ Après-ski enthusiasts young and old enjoying the scenery and the good weather in Verbier, Switzerland, 1964

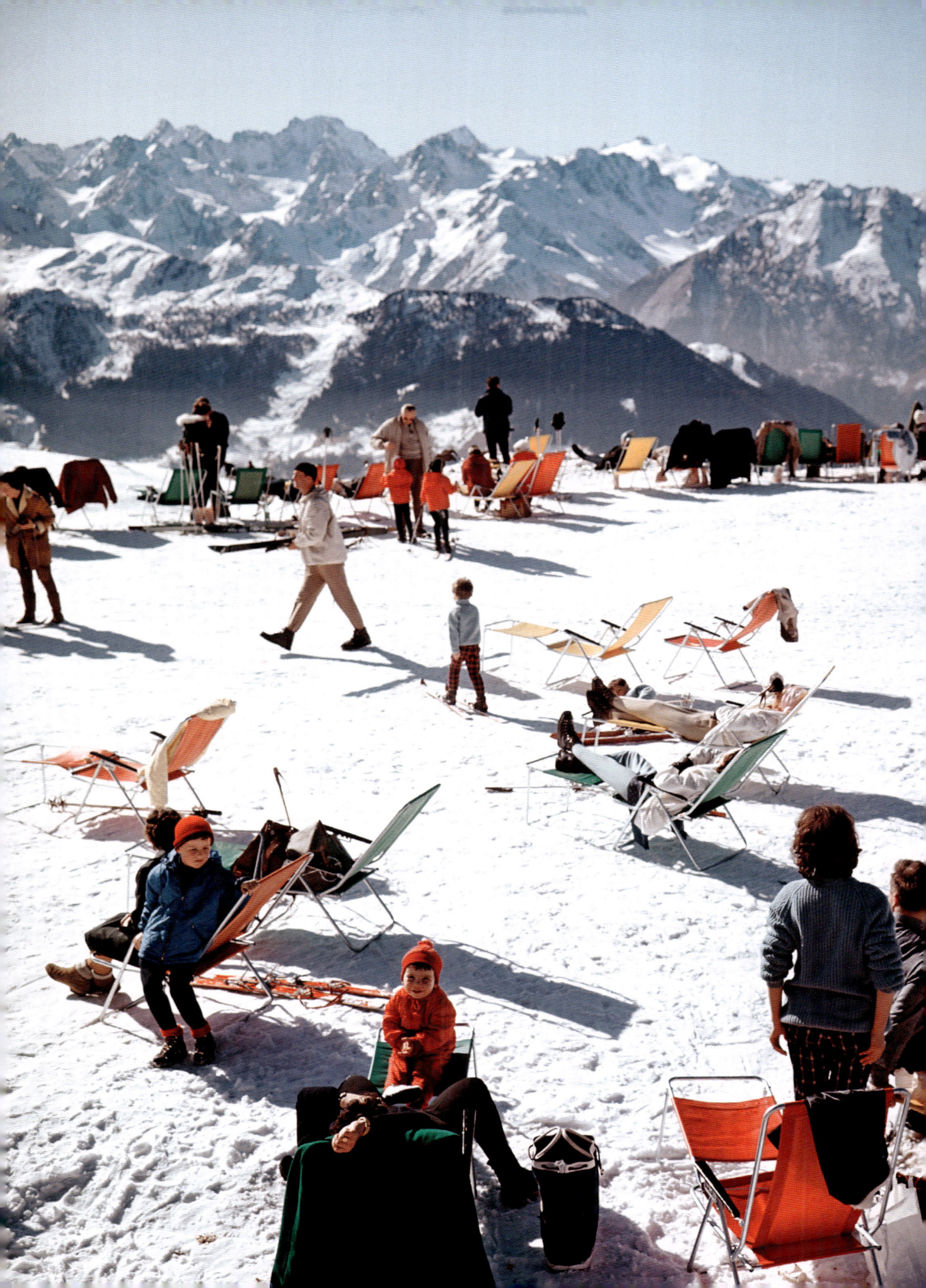

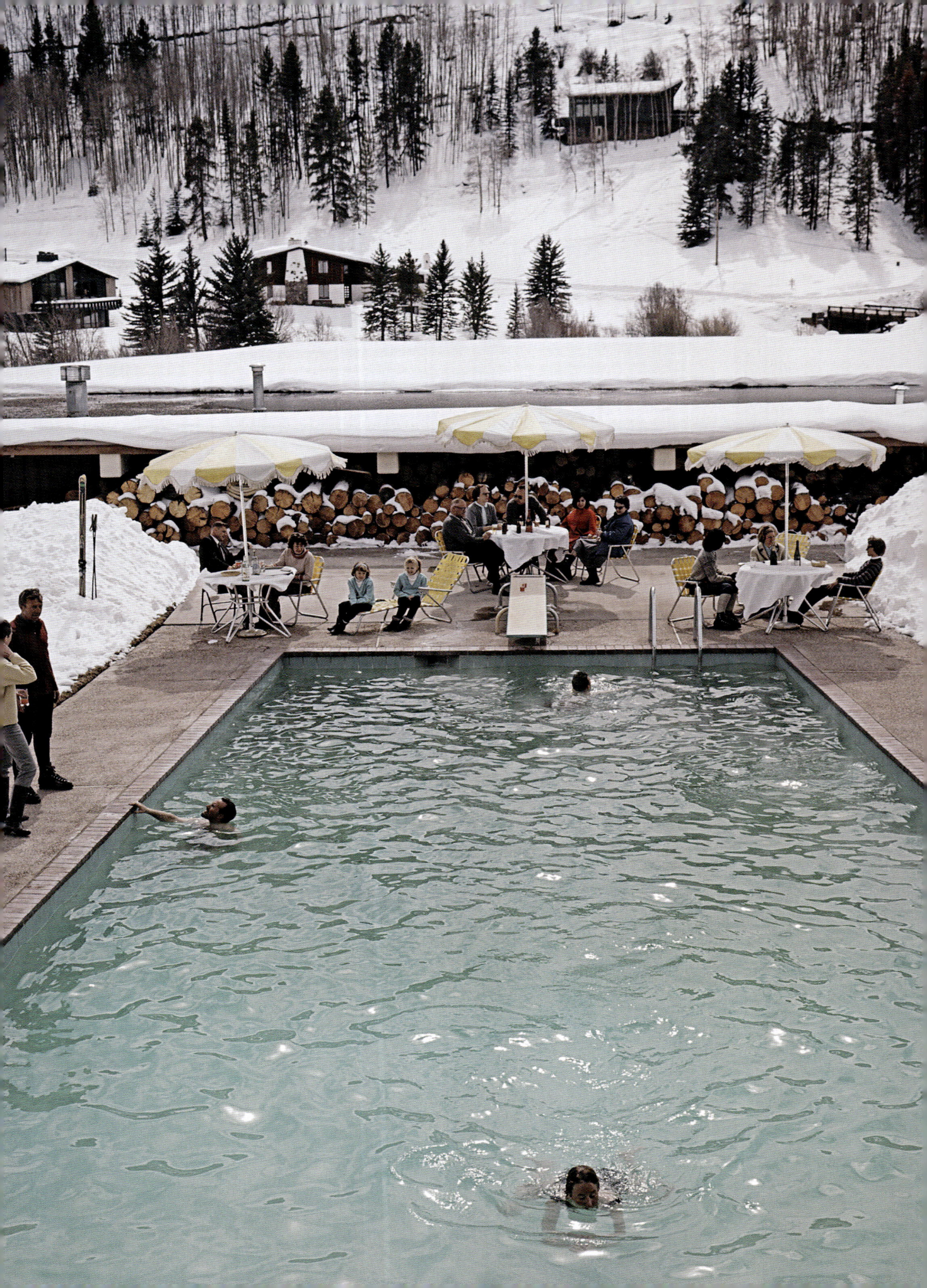

High-Altitude Pools

—

Sporting a bikini in the snow may seem dangerous, but immersing your body in a heated outdoor pool or hot tub is heaven after a long day on the slopes. It is also the ideal way to transition from a day of skiing to an evening of après-ski indulgence. Gorgeous mountain pools can be found far and wide, and truly unique—and therapeutic—experiences exist in the onsens of Japan as well as the thermal spas of Europe.

◀ A winter dip après-ski in Vail, 1964

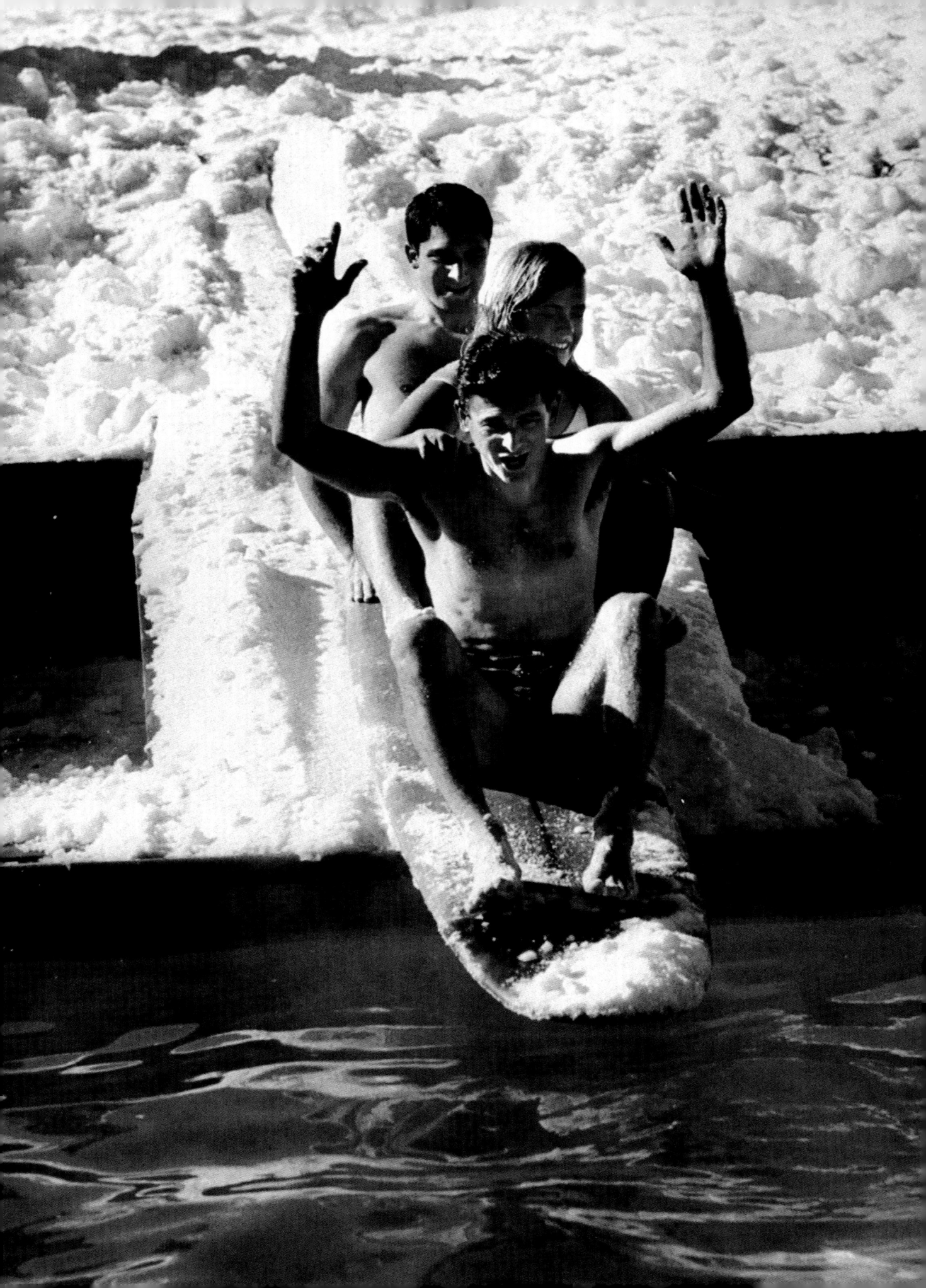

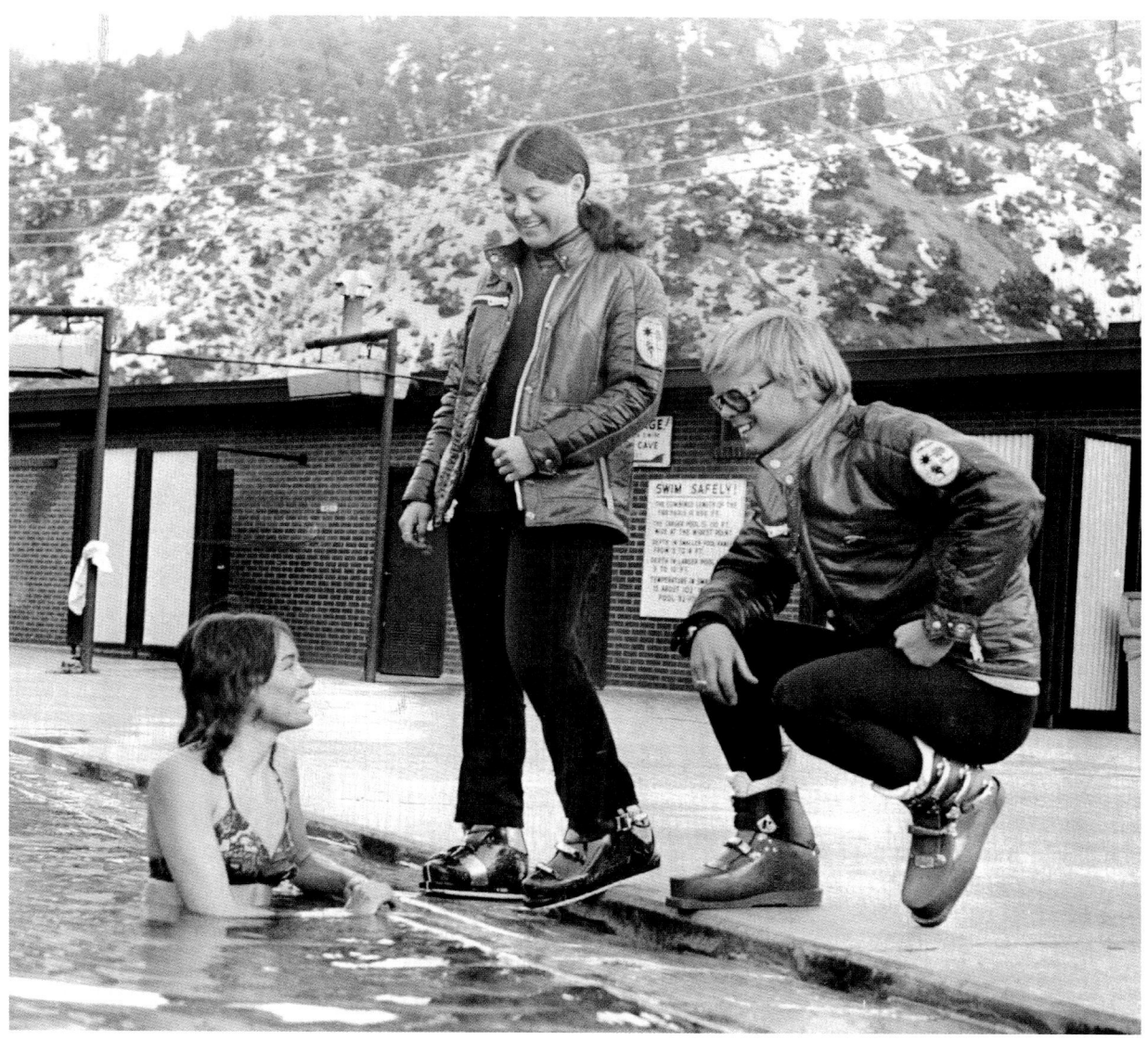

▲ Poolside après-ski at the Sunlight Mountain Resort, Colorado, in 1972

◀ A lot of people who love skiing also love surfing—just usually not at the same time. These college students invented a new way to enjoy après-ski poolside during a midwinter-break ski trip to Aspen in 1963.

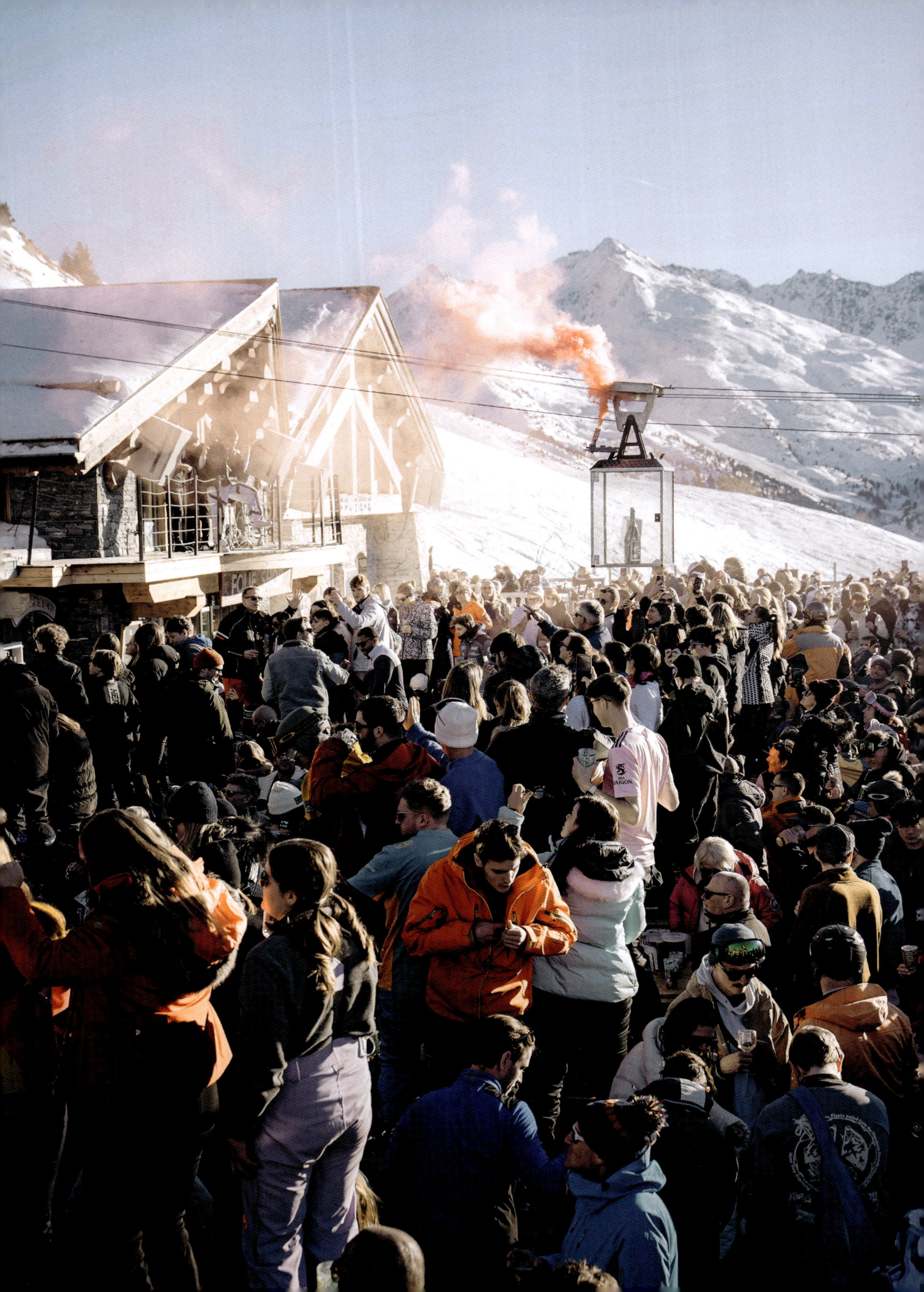

Ski Town Bars & Nightclubs

—

The wild side of après-ski can be found in local ski town nightclubs and bars. The Arlberg region of Austria is home to one of the most vibrant après-ski scenes in the world: the resort town of St. Anton, known for its massive beers, Jägermeister shots, and throngs of partygoers. In France, high-altitude party spot La Folie Douce has grown into an après-ski enterprise with multiple locations at top ski resorts across the Alps. Not to be outdone, North America boasts packed bars from Stowe, Vermont, all the way to Whistler, British Columbia (and everywhere in between).

◄ At La Folie Douce, founded in 1974 in Val d'Isère, dancing on tables in ski boots, watching fire dancers, and drinking an abundance of Veuve Clicquot are all highly encouraged.

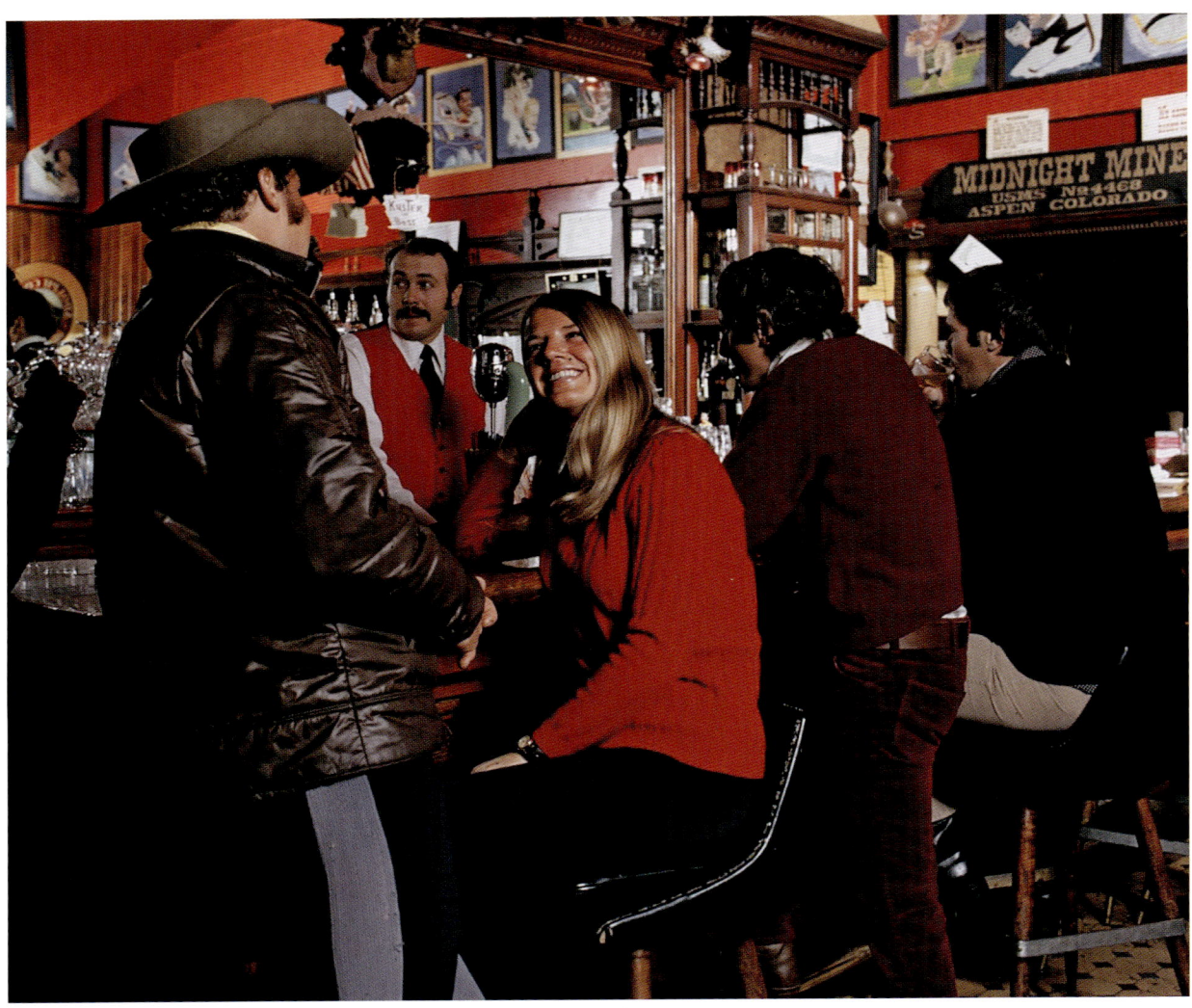

▲ The 1970s après-ski scene in Aspen, where stretch ski pants and cowboy hats paired perfectly

▶ Many of America's western ski resorts, including Jackson Hole Mountain Resort in Wyoming, were born out of mining and ranching towns. A visit to the town of Jackson offers skiing at one of the highest-rated mountains in the United States and a view of the majestic Teton Range as well as an opportunity to saddle up at the Million Dollar Cowboy Bar.

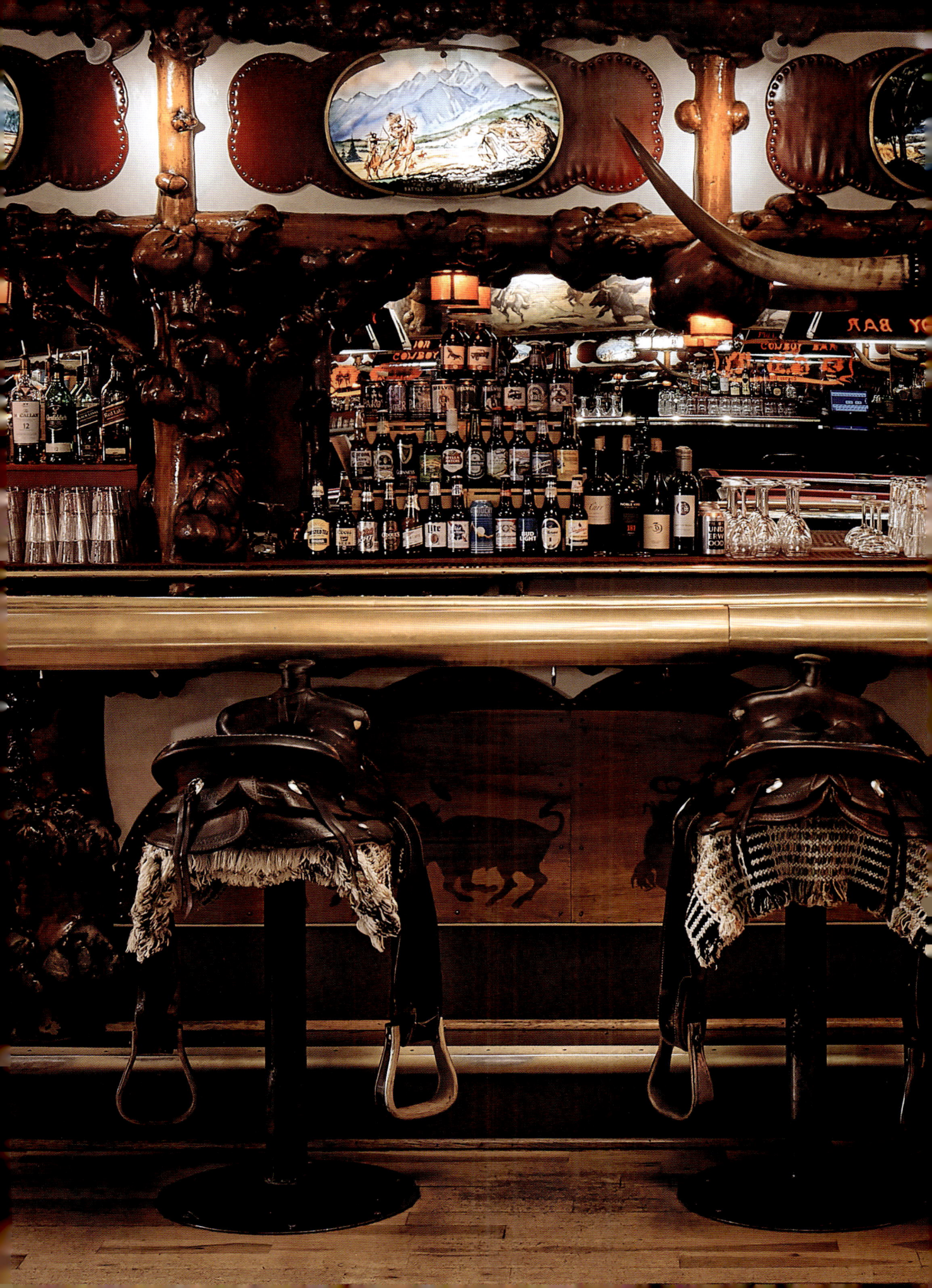

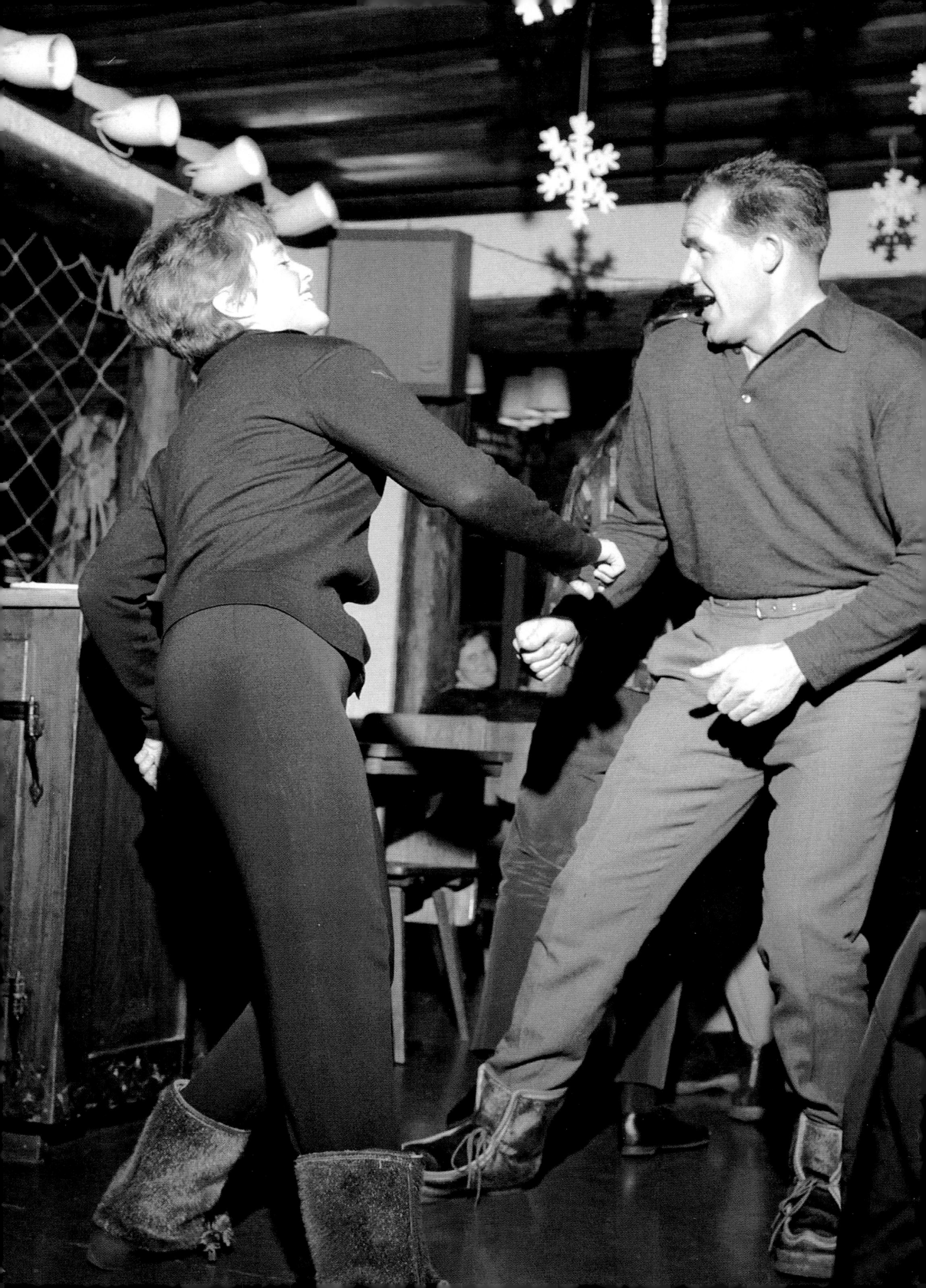

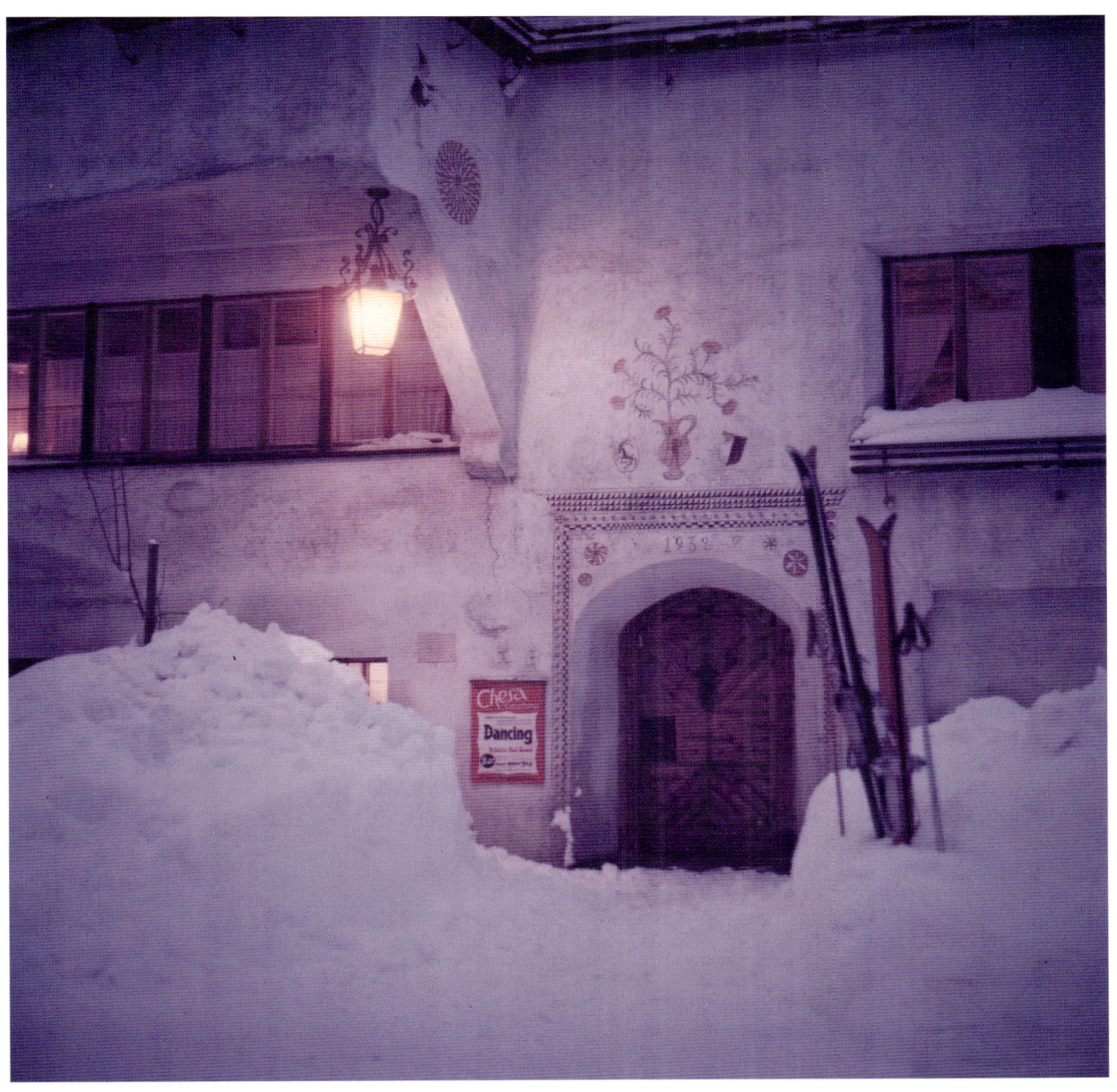

▲ Patrons could ski right up and dance all night at the legendary Chesa Bar at the Hotel Chesa Grischuna in Klosters, 1951.

◀ Dancing the Twist après-ski in Grindelwald, in the Jungfrau ski region of Switzerland, 1962

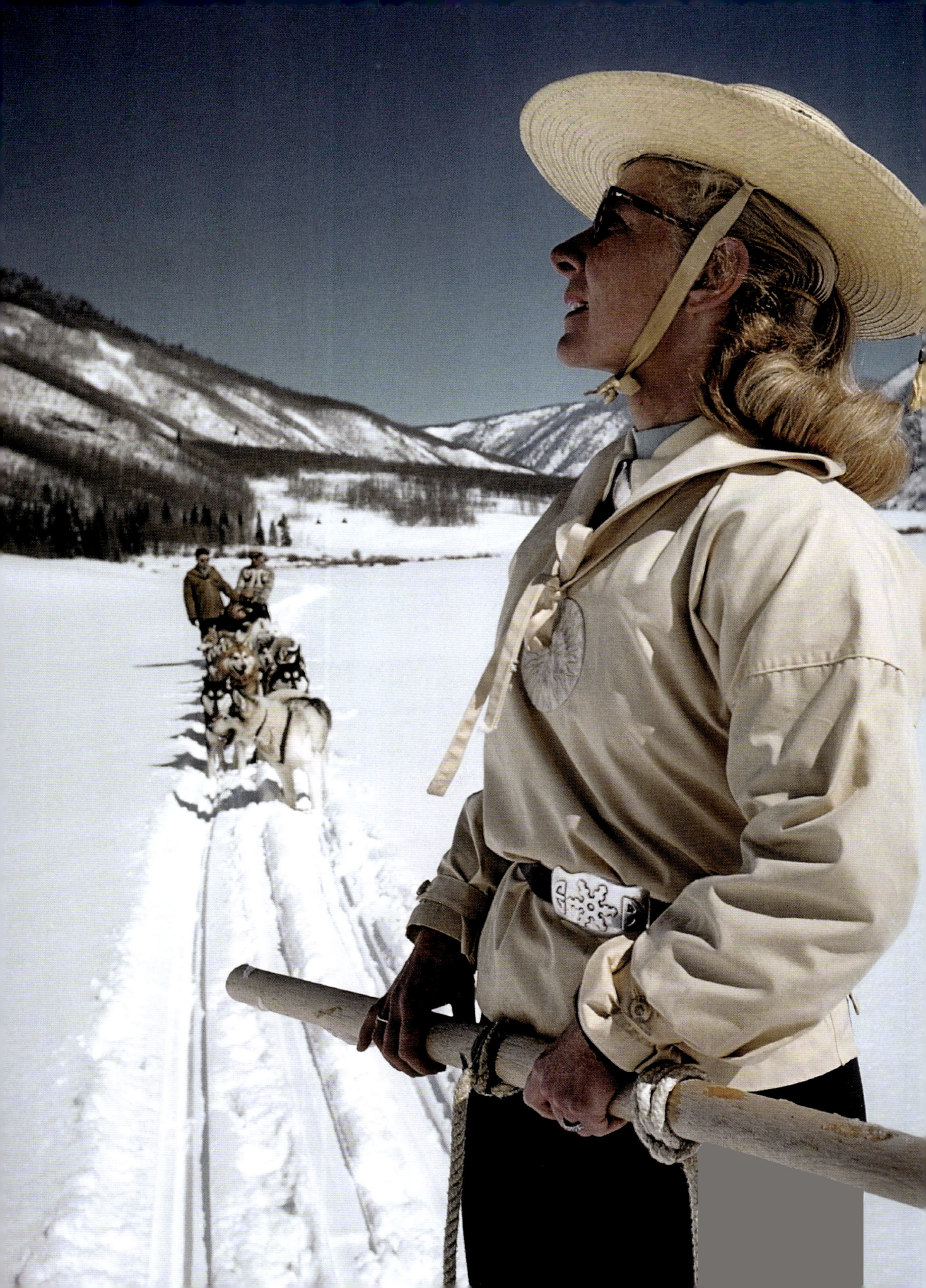

Fun & Games

—

When the skis come off, other toys come out. Ski towns are full of entertaining activities to enjoy après-ski, whether in the snow, on the ice, or even in the air. Sledding and ice-skating can be especially fun with the little ones or the young at heart, but given the high demand for thrills among ski enthusiasts, in places such as the Alps it is not uncommon to see brave participants run off the side of a cliff high atop the mountains with a parachute dragging behind.

◀ Taking in the view via a sled dog ride in Aspen, 1958

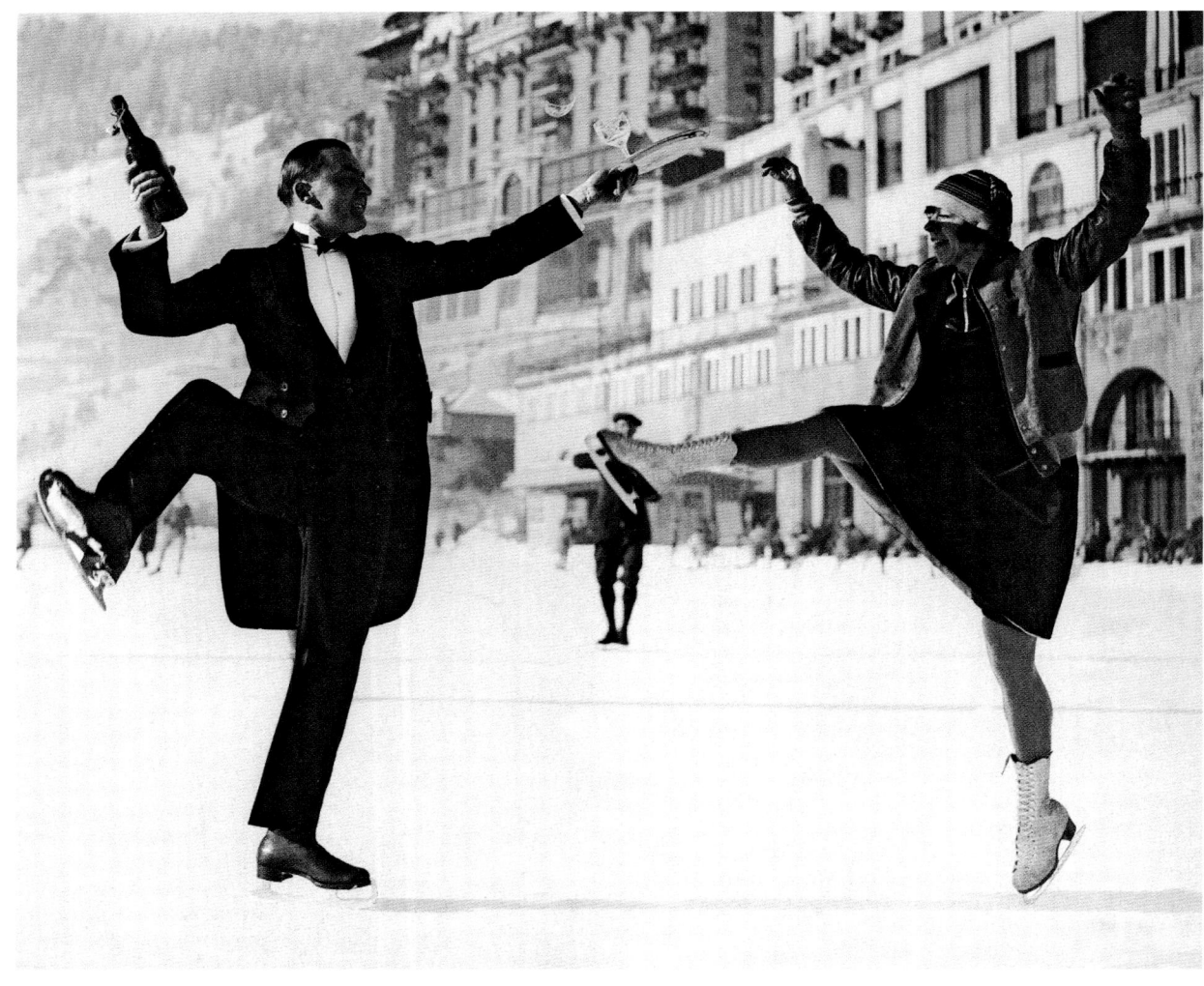

▲ A server from the Grand Hotel des Bains Kempinski and professional ice-skater Hilda Kaufman, known as "Hilda the Rocket," combine two favorite après-ski activities—ice-skating and cocktails—in St. Moritz in 1928.

▶ French pop singer Sheila riding a snow bike (essentially, a bicycle with skis instead of wheels) in Crans-Montana, Switzerland, 1969

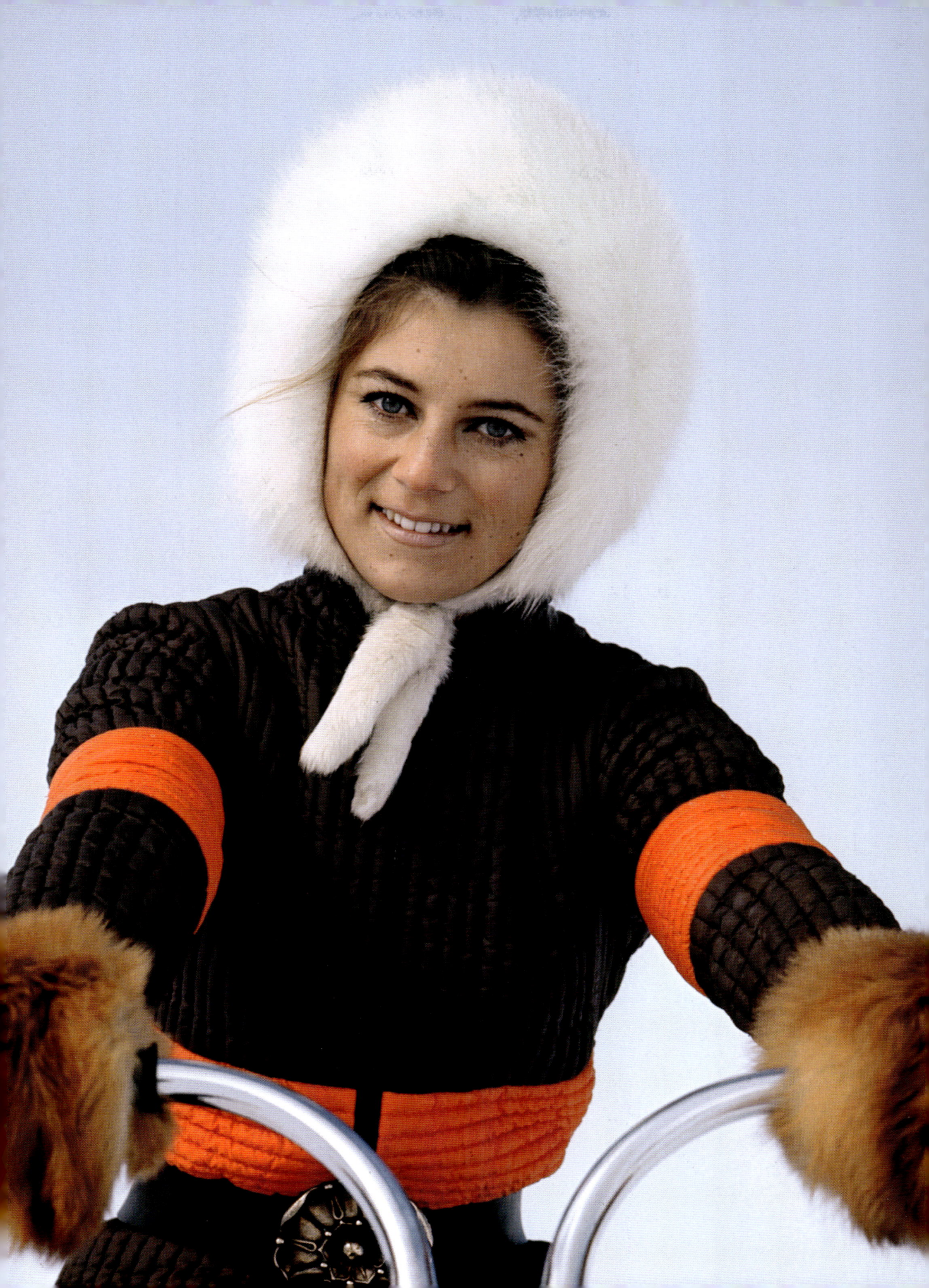

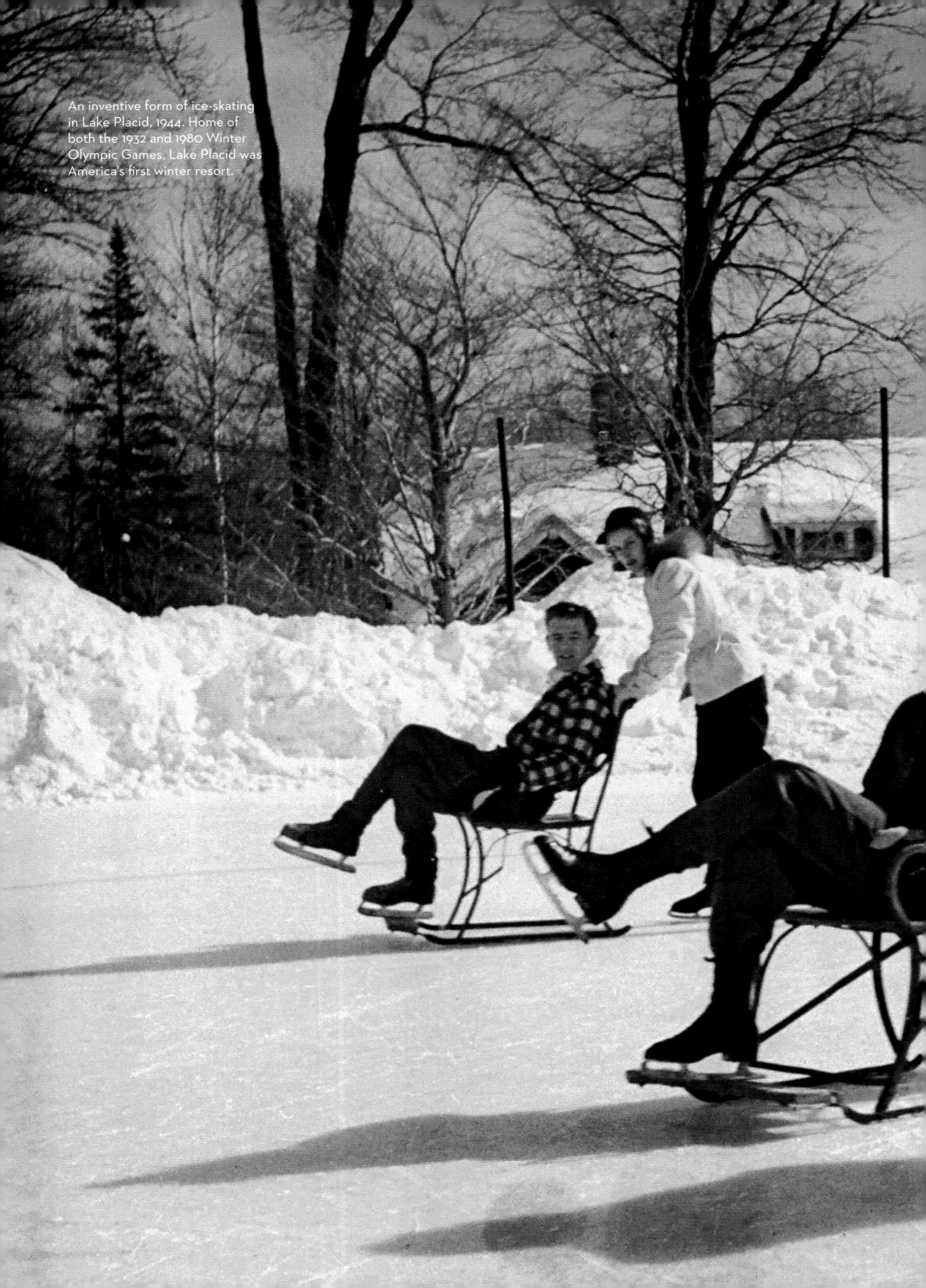

An inventive form of ice-skating in Lake Placid, 1944. Home of both the 1932 and 1980 Winter Olympic Games, Lake Placid was America's first winter resort.

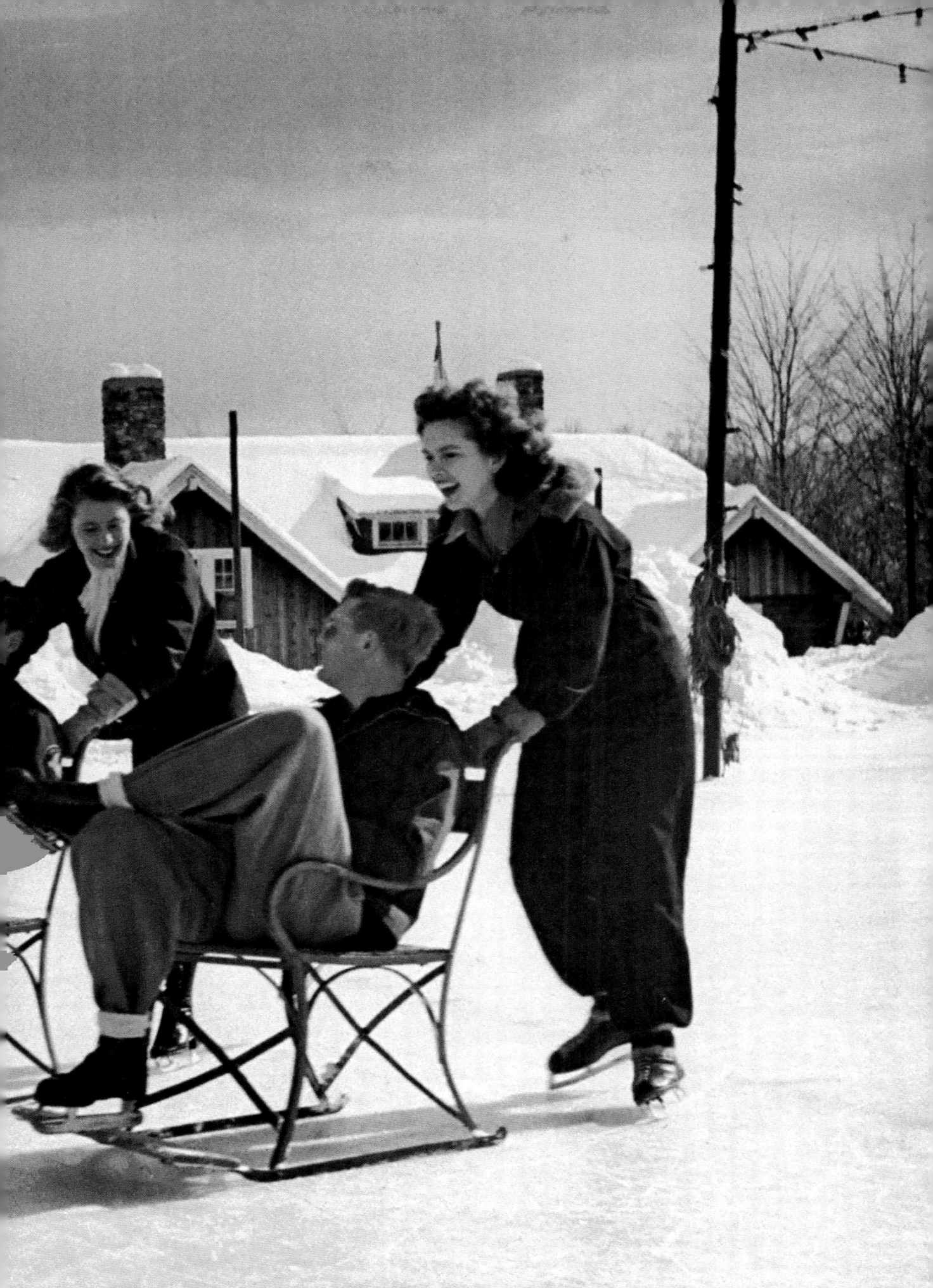

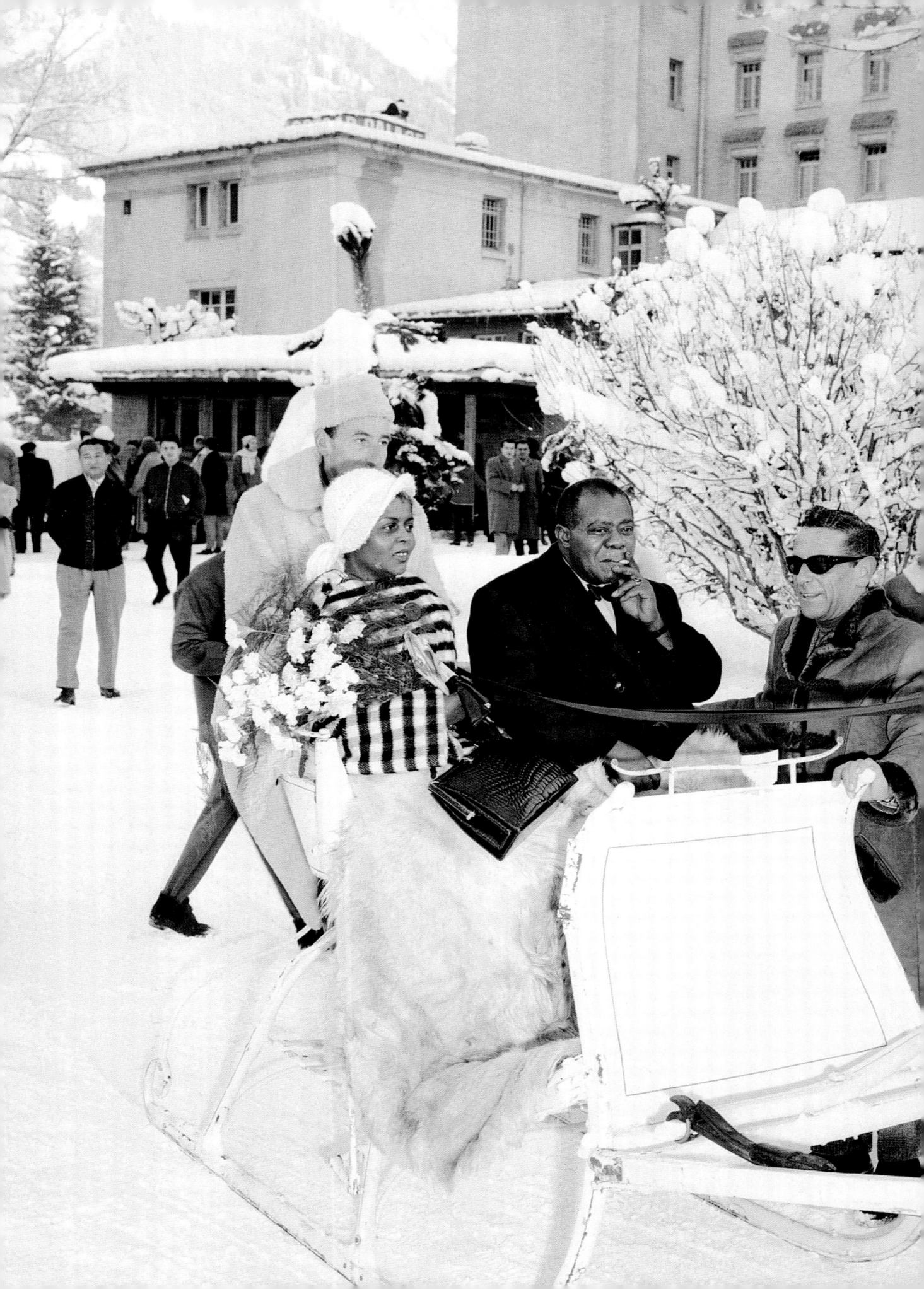

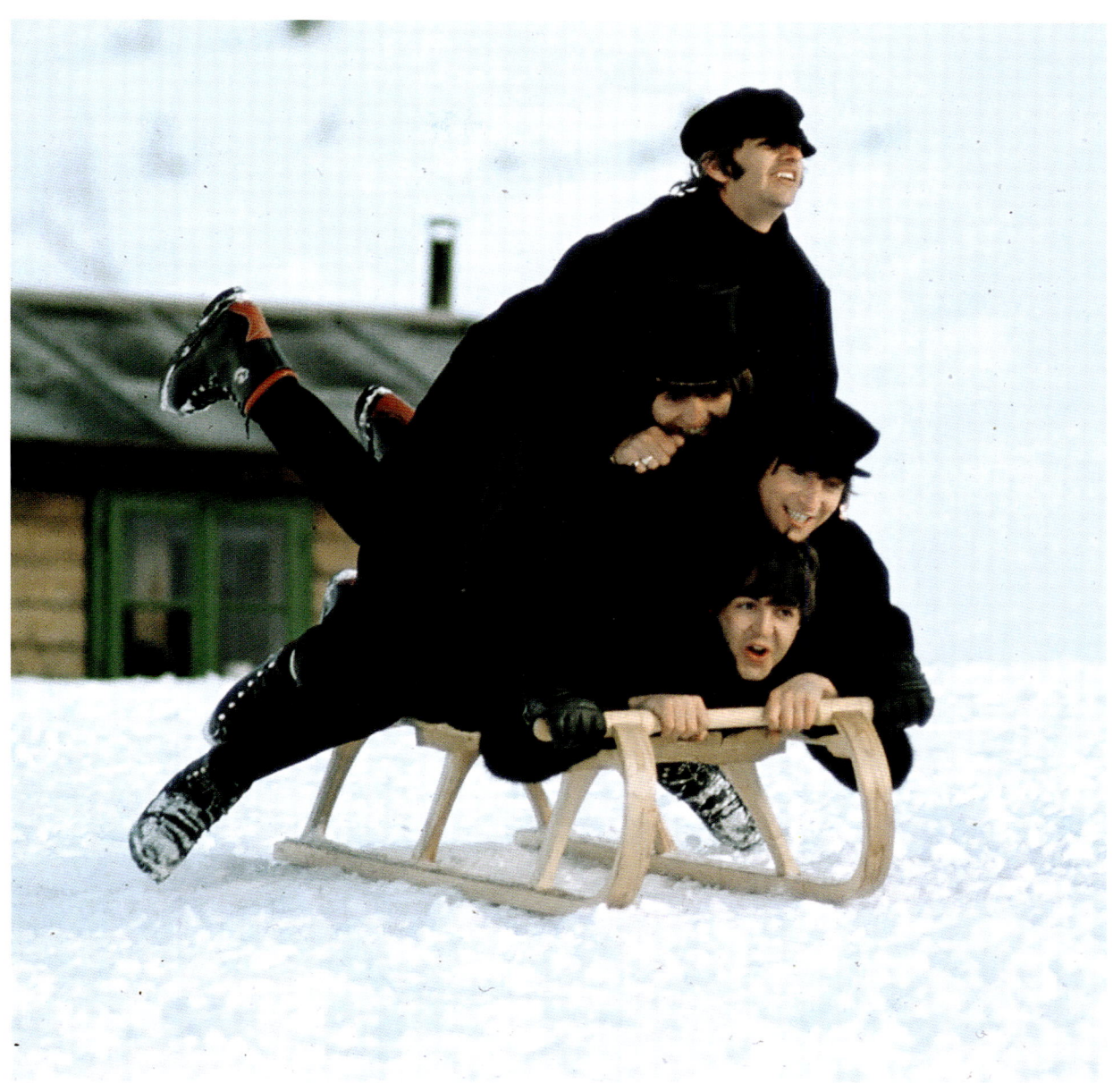

▲ A pileup of Beatles during the making of their film *Help!*, which was shot in 1965 in Obertauern, Austria

◀ Louis Armstrong with his wife, Lucille, riding in a horse-drawn sleigh in Gstaad, 1961

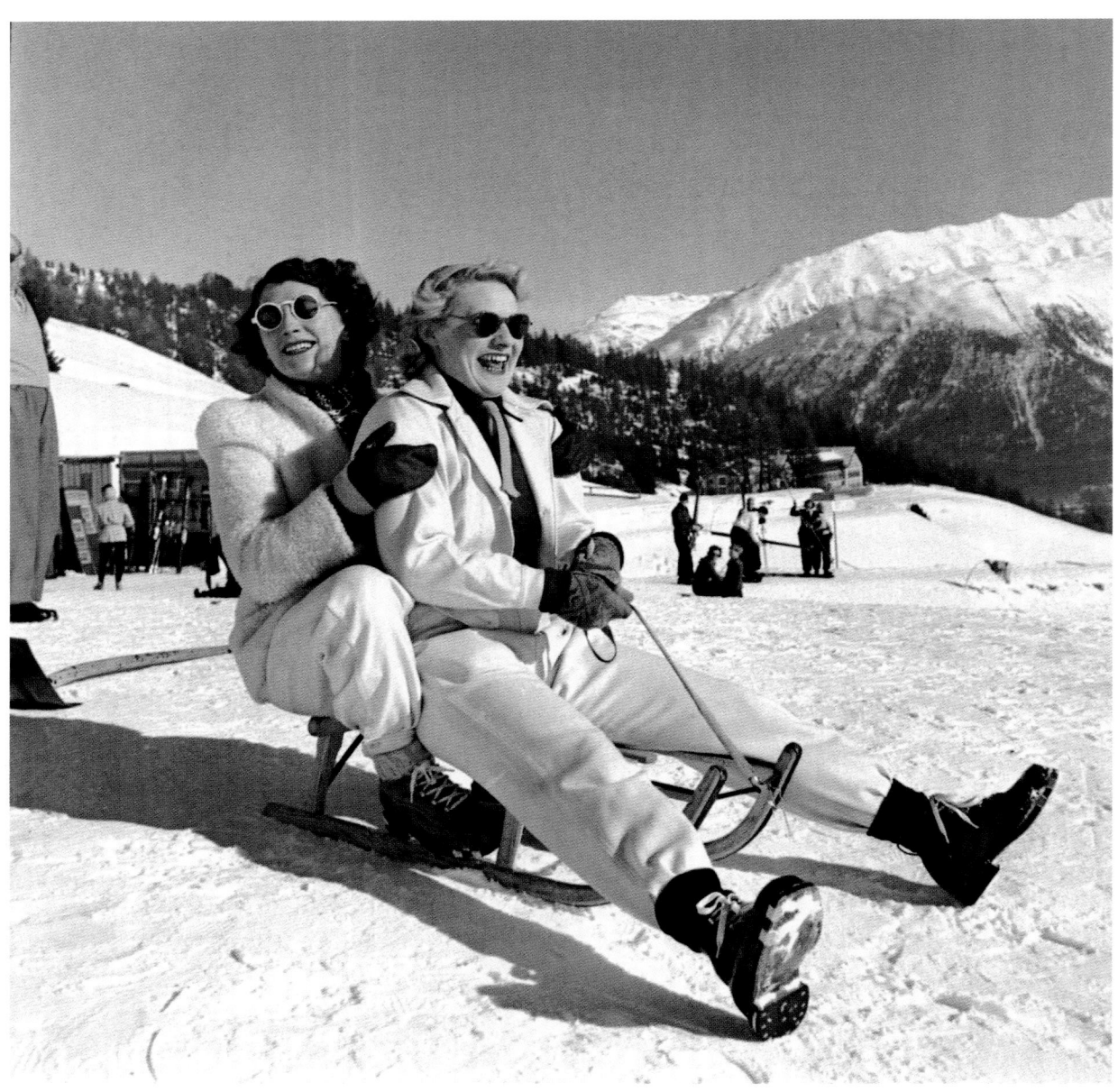

▲ Sledding in St. Moritz, 1947

▶ Brigitte Bardot curling at the Cortina d'Ampezzo
resort in Italy in the 1960s

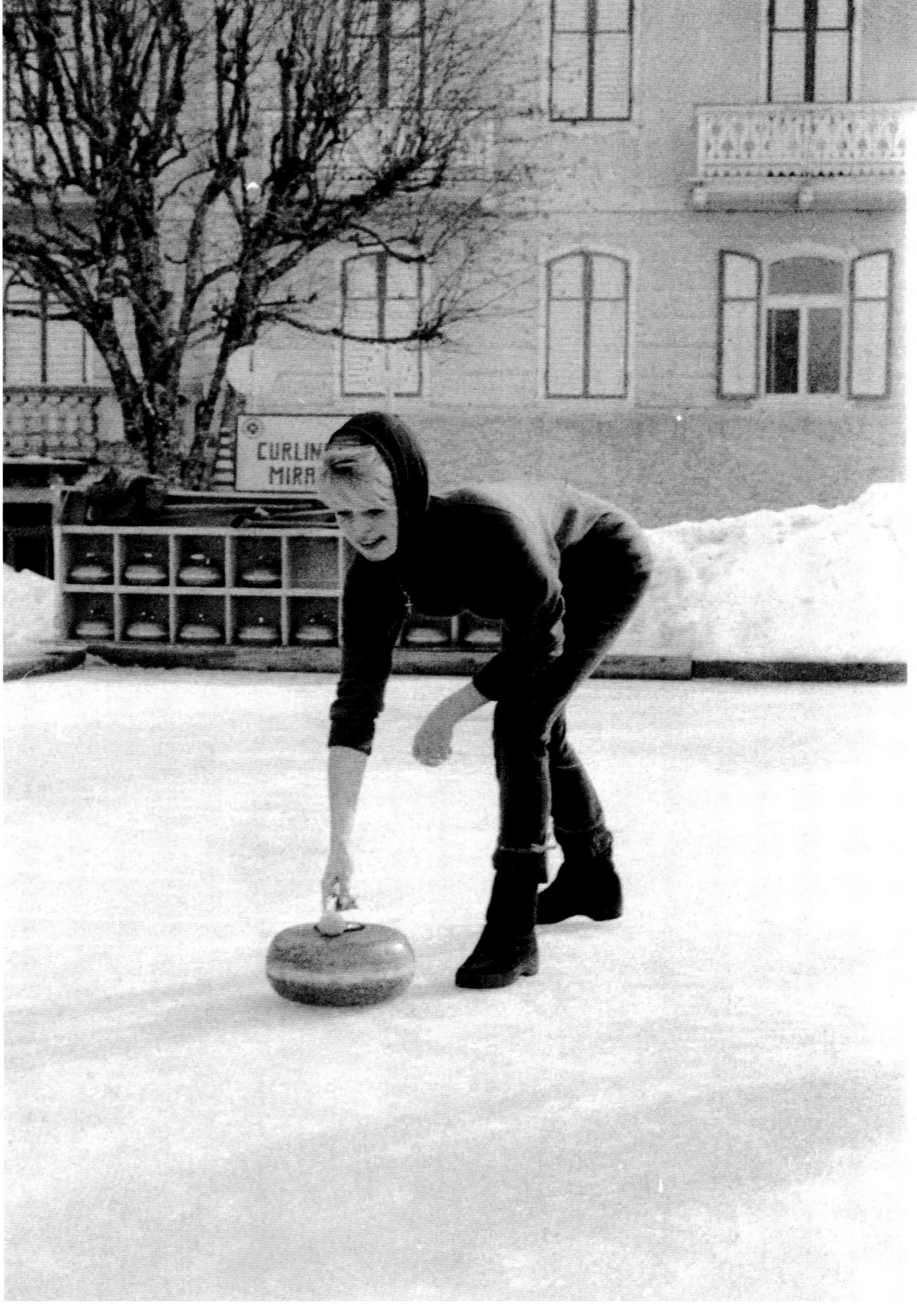

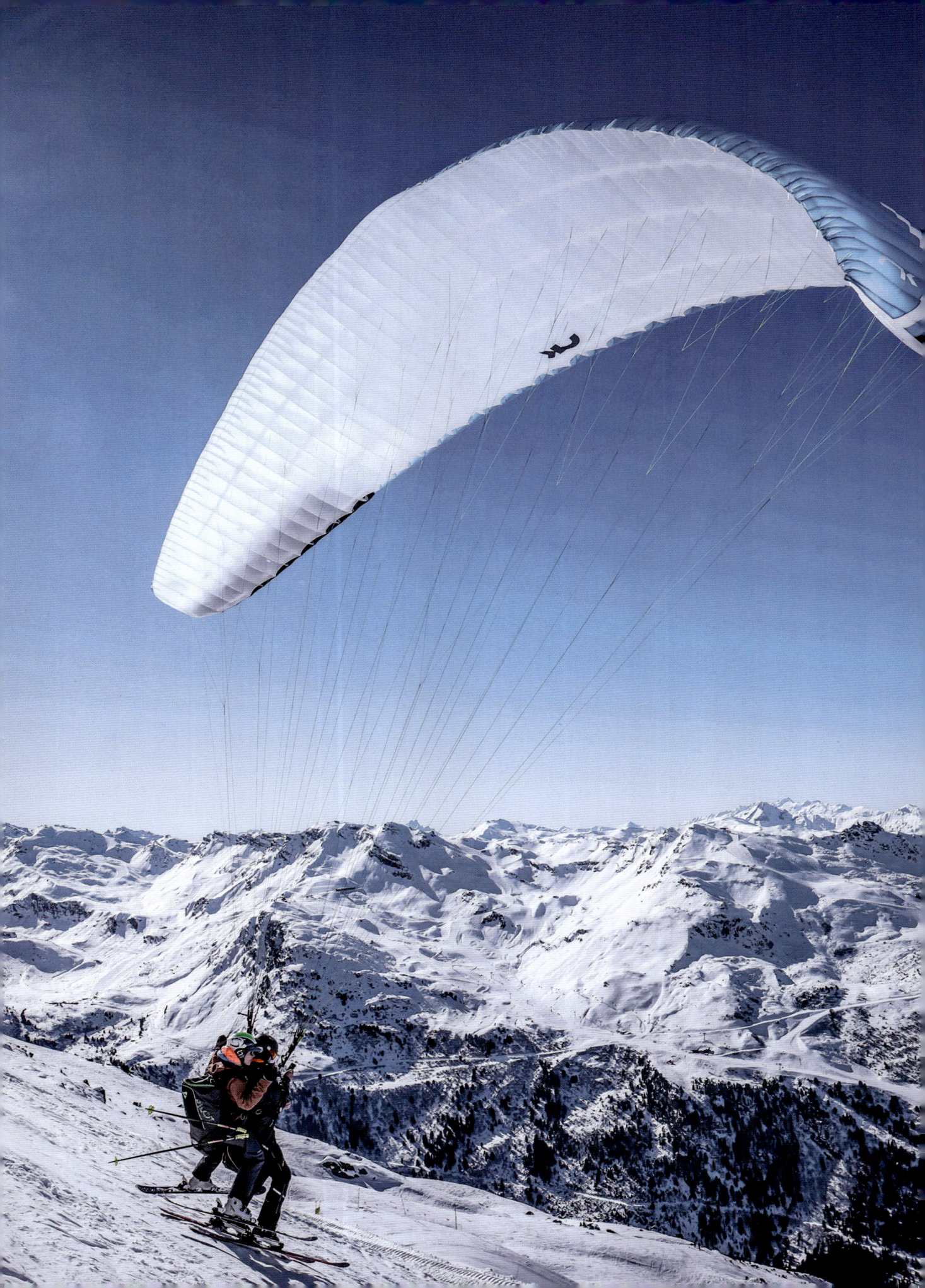

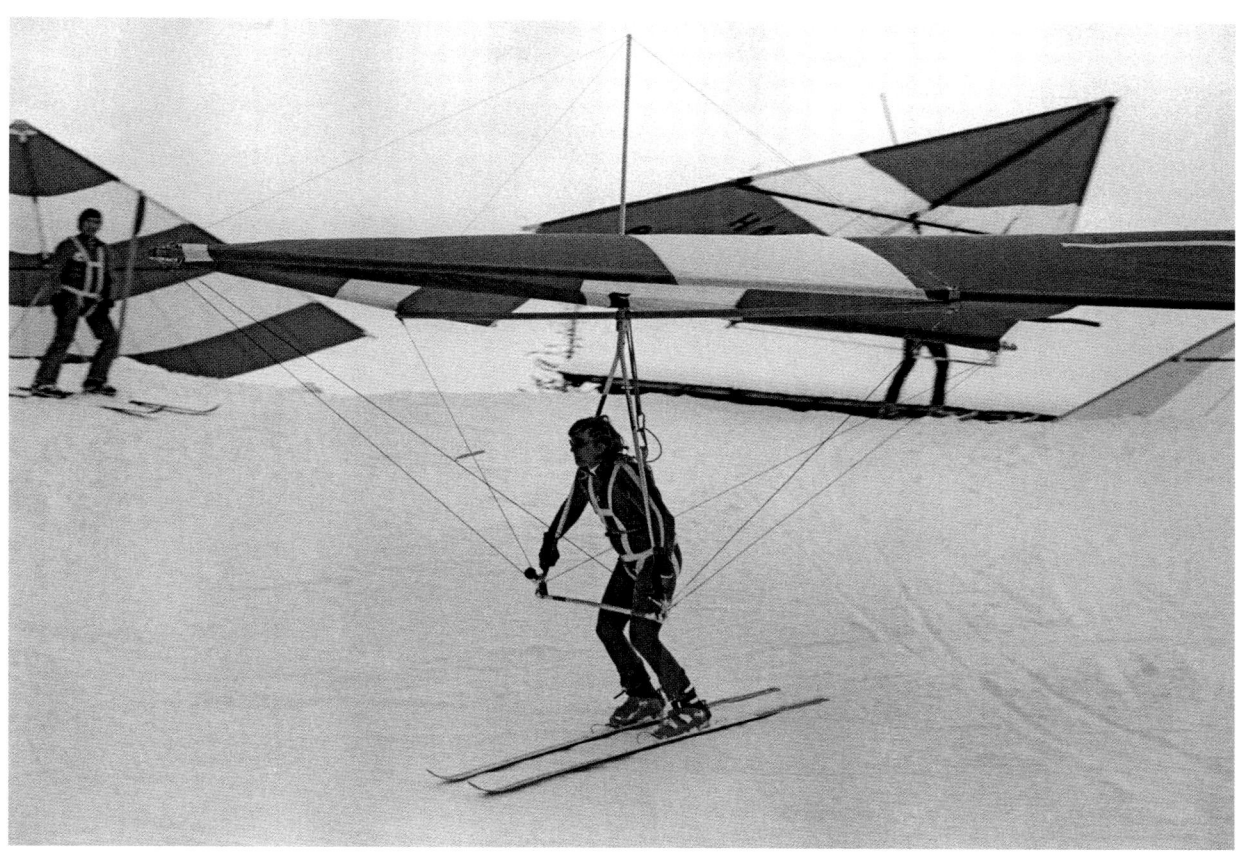

▲ A hang glider (or deltaplane) taking off on skis in Gstaad, 1975

◀ Tandem paragliding in Courchevel, 2023

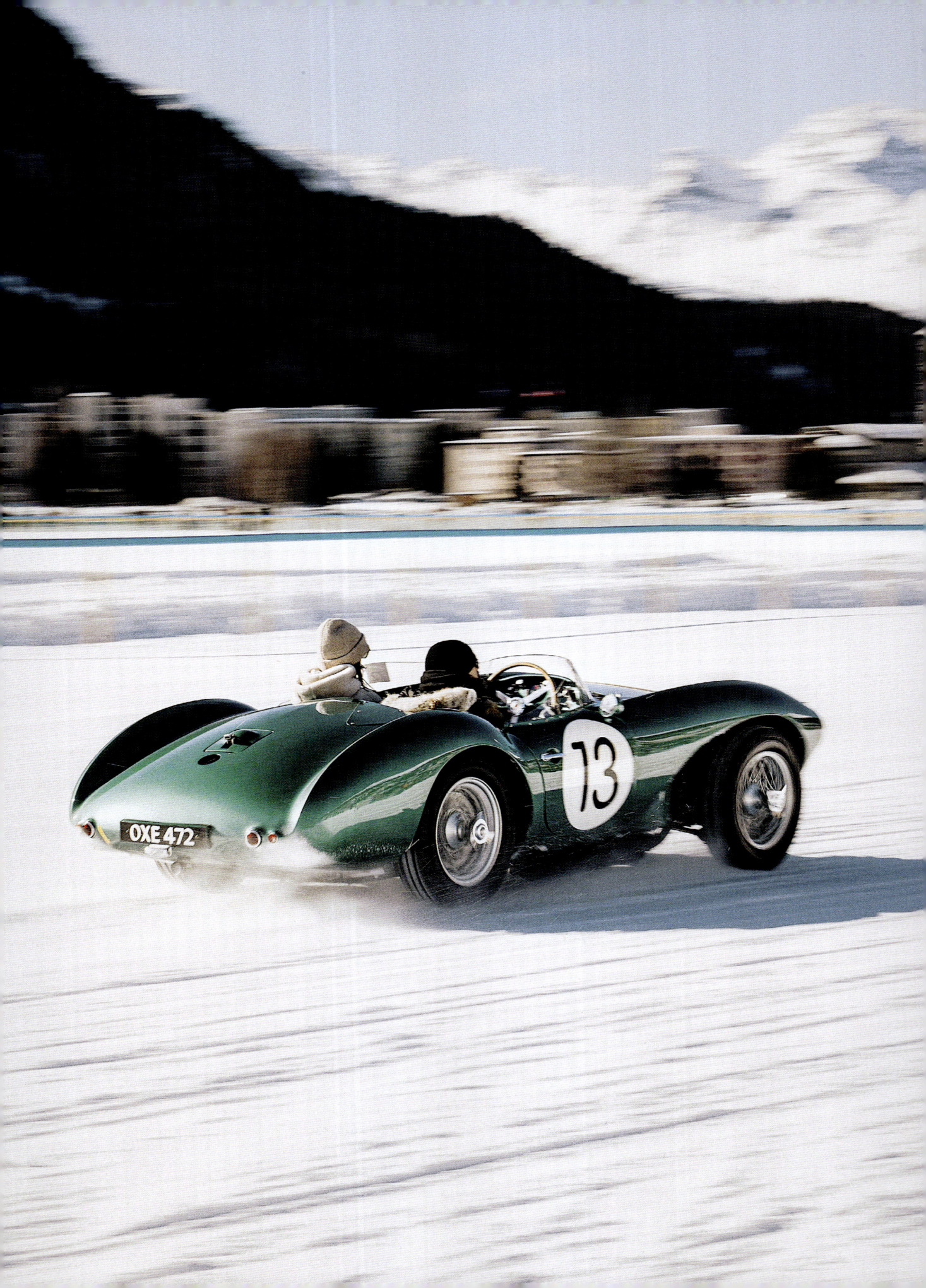

Ski Town Festivities

—

Drawing audiences from all over the world, gatherings such as the St. Regis World Snow Polo Championship in Aspen; the SnowDays Festival in Banff, Alberta; and the International Concours of Elegance in St. Moritz pack ski towns full of revelers. Visitors can ski in the morning, enjoy the events later in the day, and party late into the night.

◄ At the International Concours of Elegance, known as the ICE, car collectors and enthusiasts from all over the world come to the high Alpine resort town to witness a parade of cars on the frozen Lake St. Moritz.

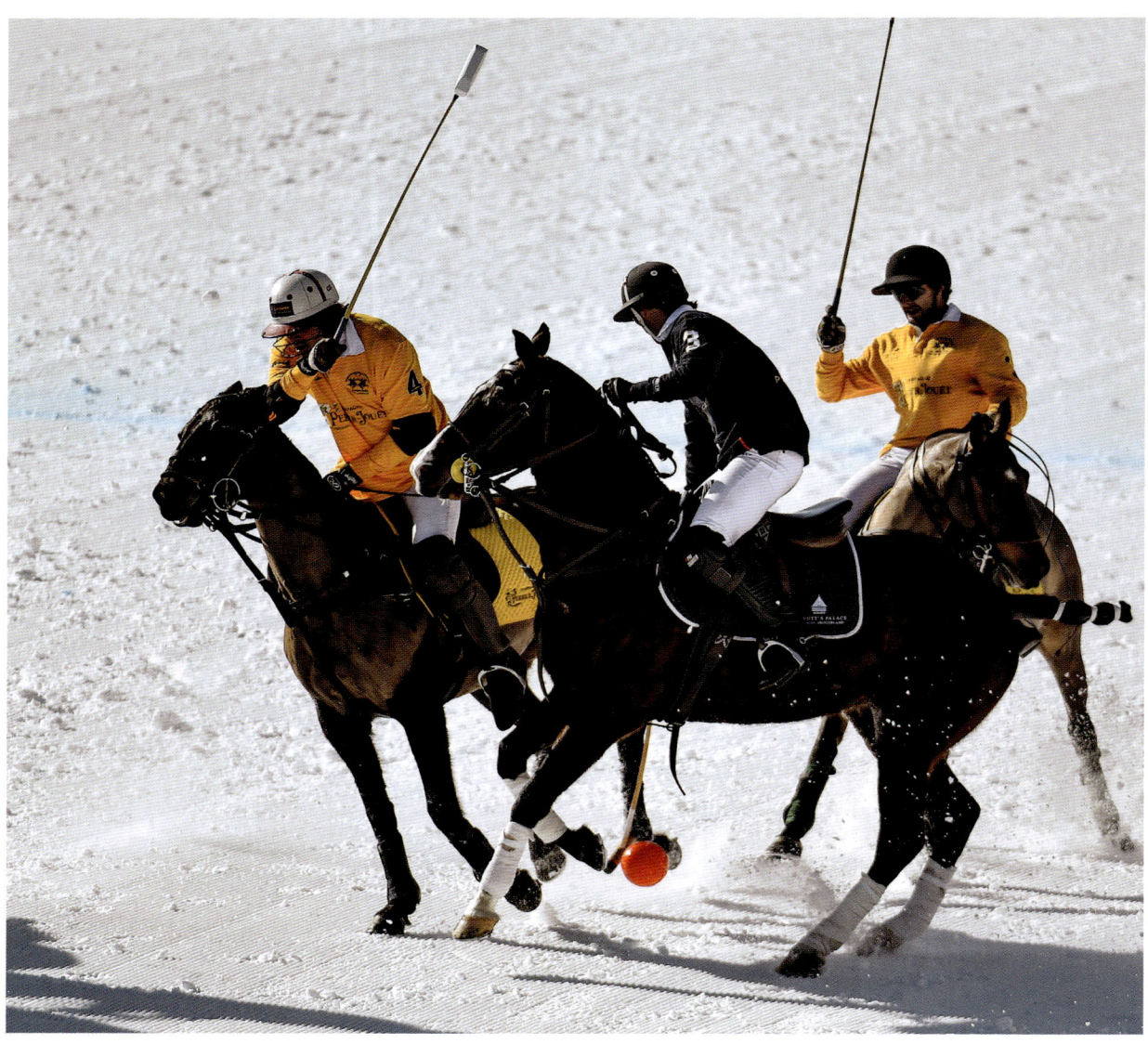

▲ Snow polo boasts events in Cortina d'Ampezzo, Kitzbühel in Austria, and Aspen, but the coveted Snow Polo World Cup is held each year in St. Moritz. Shown here is Team Badrutt's Palace Hotel playing against Team Perrier-Jouët in the 2016 Snow Polo World Cup.

▶ Not to be outdone by the prim and proper snow polo ponies, skijoring horses have become another high-octane après-ski passion. Skijoring involves standing on skis and being towed by various animals, including elk, reindeer, and dogs. The equine version got its start as a sport in the early 1900s and has evolved into something like a rodeo on skis.

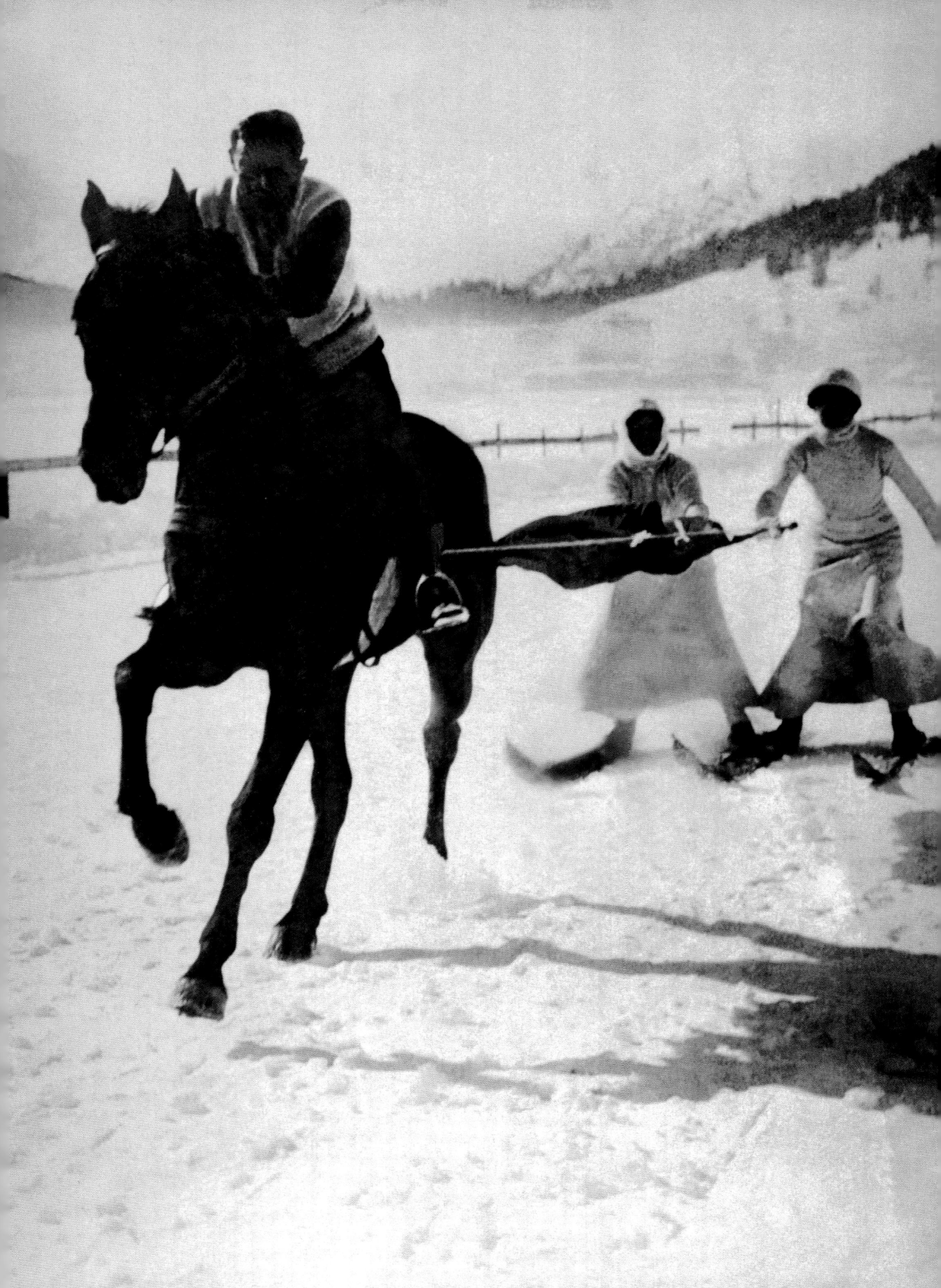

Ski Resorts for Every Après-Ski Scene

When the lifts stop running in the late afternoon, some resorts go to sleep, while others are just coming to life. Here's an at-a-glance guide to the resorts (and resort towns) for every type of enthusiast.

FOR BOOT-THUMPING DANCING ON TABLES

Ischgl (Austria)
St. Anton (Austria)
Val d'Isère (France)
Val Thorens (France)
Verbier (Switzerland)

FOR AN UNPRETENTIOUS GOOD TIME

Alta Badia (Italy)
Breckenridge (US)
Chamonix (France)
Jackson Hole (US)
Livigno (Italy)
Mammoth Mountain (US)
Portillo (Chile)
Queenstown (New Zealand)
Whistler Blackcomb (Canada)

TO SEE AND BE SEEN

Aspen Snowmass (US)
St. Moritz (Switzerland)

TO BE SEEN, BUT DISCREETLY

Courchevel (France)
Deer Valley (US)
Klosters (Switzerland)

TO BRING THE KIDS

Big Sky (US)
Lech (Austria)
Méribel (France)
Park City (US)
Stowe (US)
Sun Valley (US)
Vail (US)
Val Gardena (Italy)

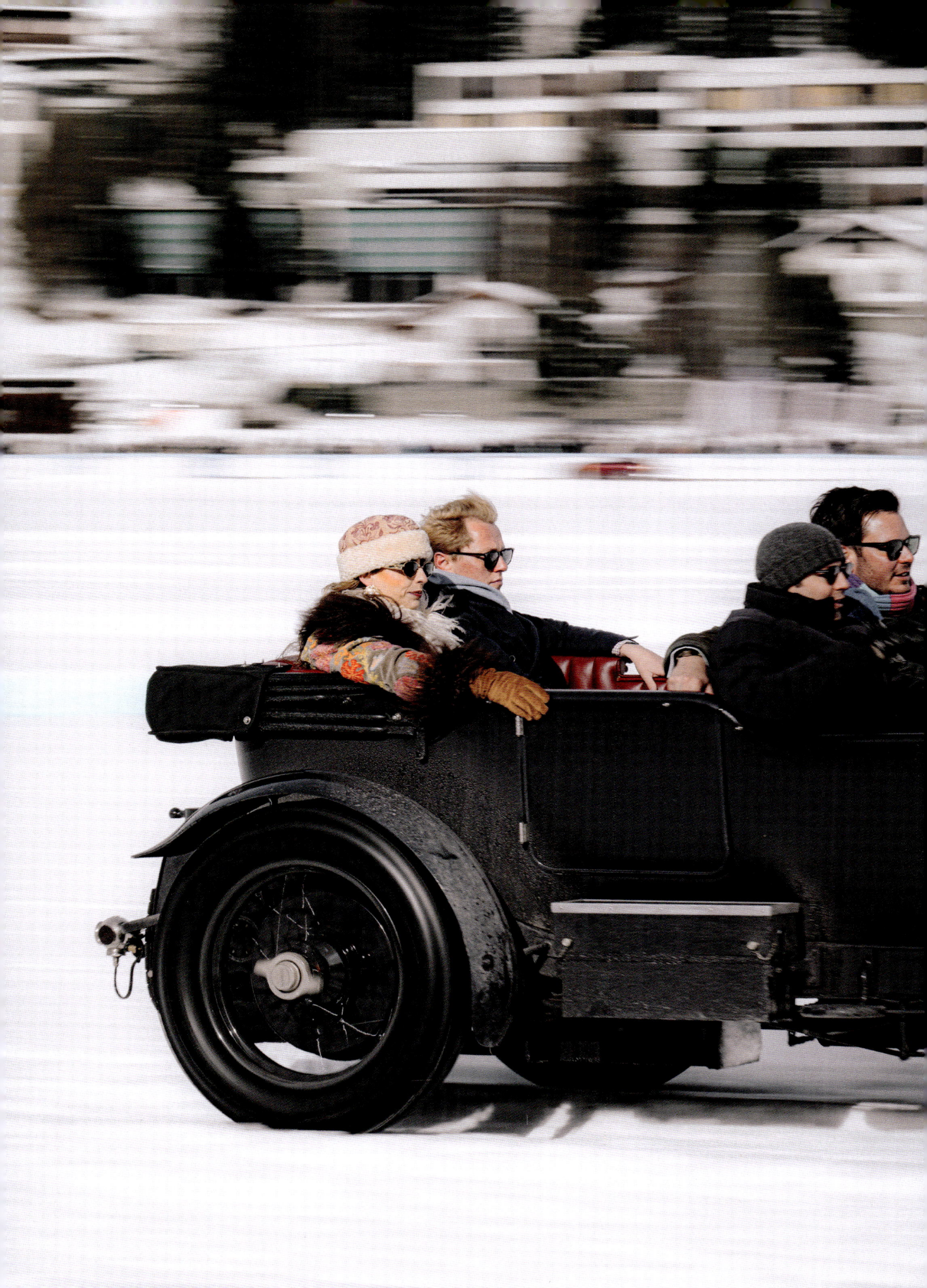

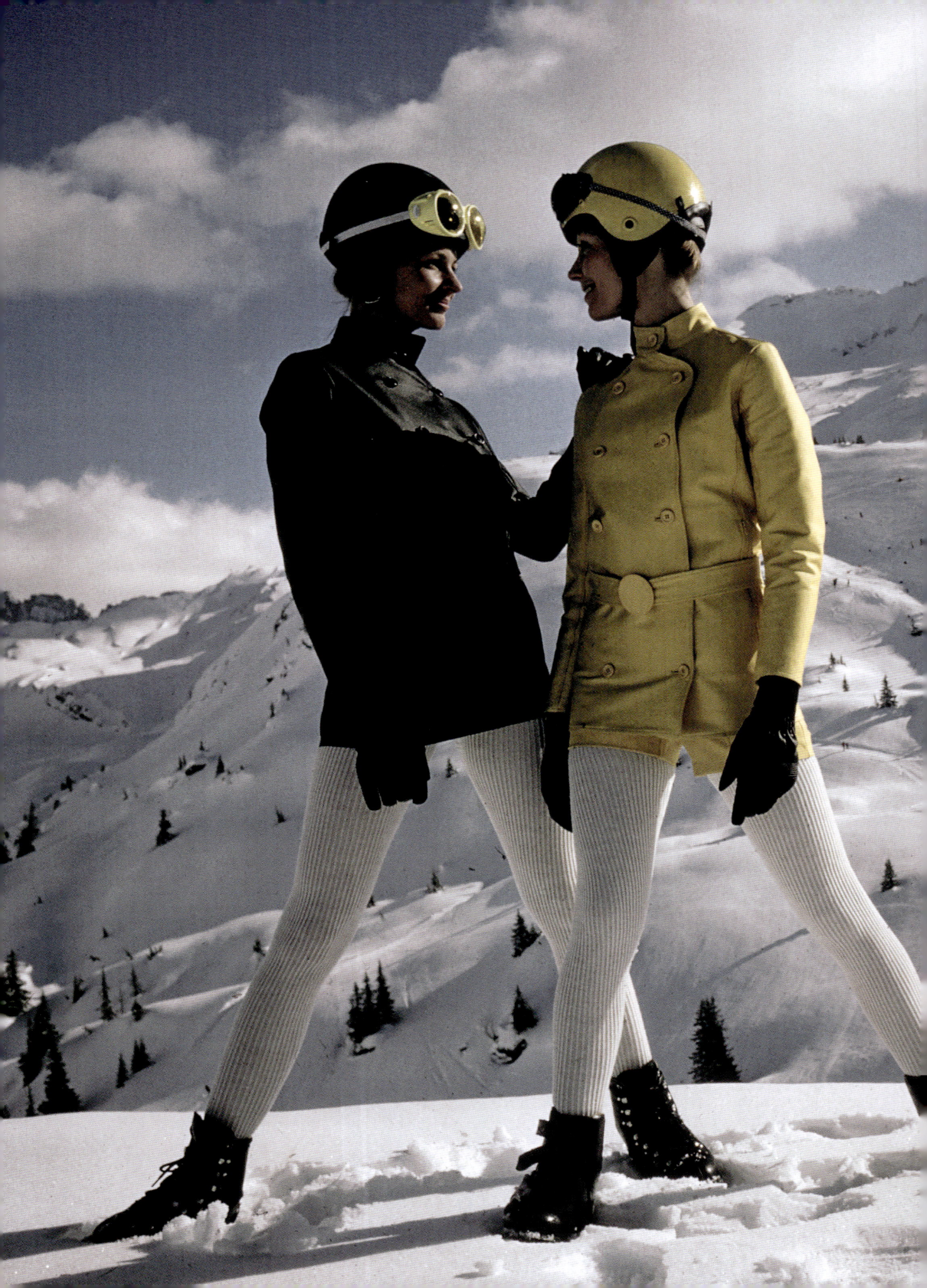

The Style

Skiing is a glamorous, sexy sport that takes place in gorgeous locations around the world, so it's no surprise that sty e defines après-ski. Eccentricities are welcome, and a unique point of view is admired. The fashion can be outrageously highbrow or unapologetically lowbrow—important styles and trends have been set throughout the eras of the sport by both camps. Since the turn of the twentieth century, the fashion of skiing has evolved from refined to wild, and more recently it has embraced its vintage roots and heritage, ushering in a new, chic era for the sport.

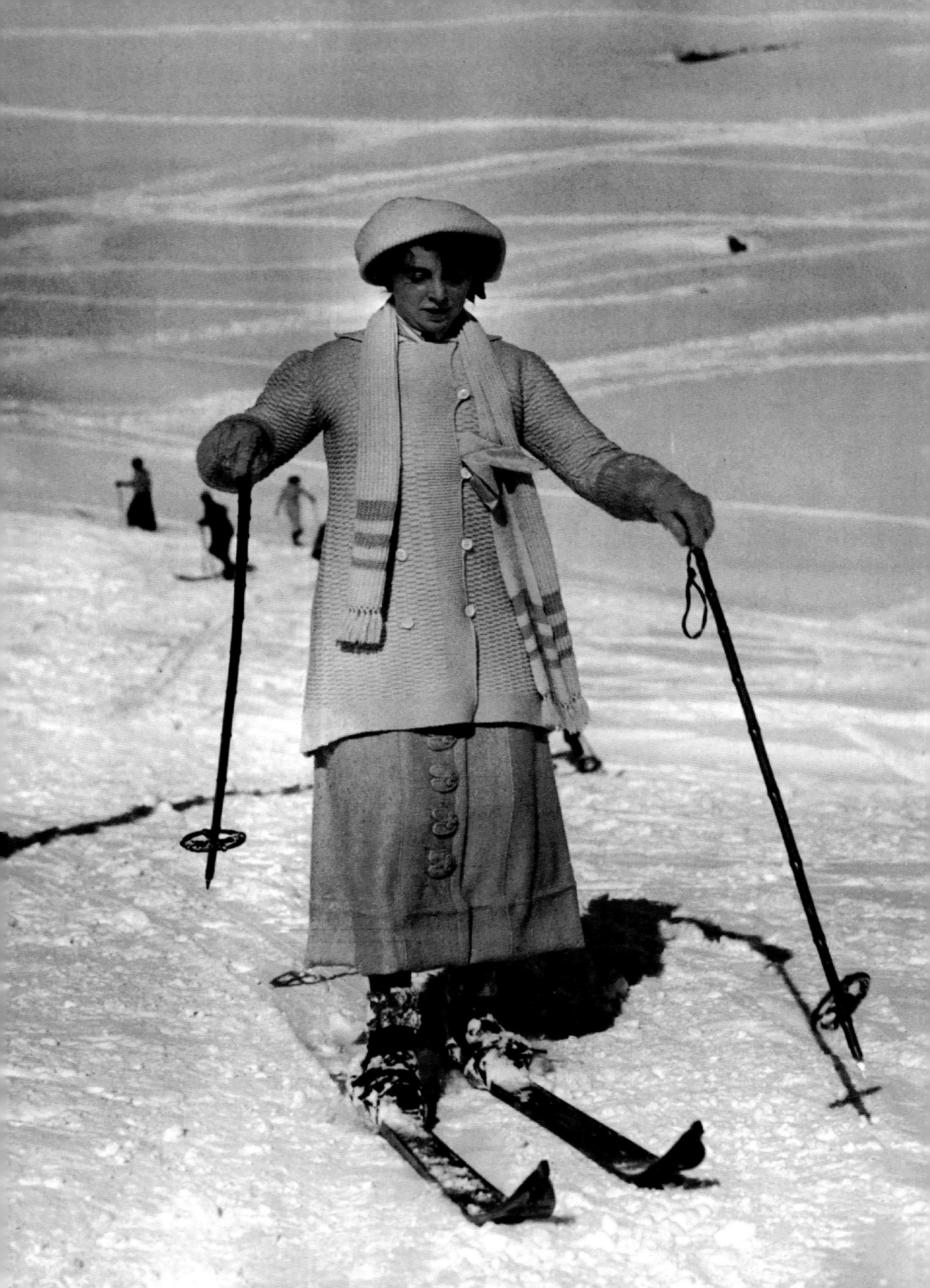

The Tailored Look

—

Like most fashion of its time, skiwear in the early twentieth century was tailored and formal. Skiers might dress much as they would for a day spent in town, with perhaps a few additional layers. Wool was the material of choice for apparel, and leather was the choice for boots. While these materials may not have been exactly comfortable or even practical, they did lay the foundation for the glamour and style historically associated with skiing.

◄ Constance Edwina, the Duchess of Westminster, skiing in a long skirt on New Year's Day, 1912, in Switzerland

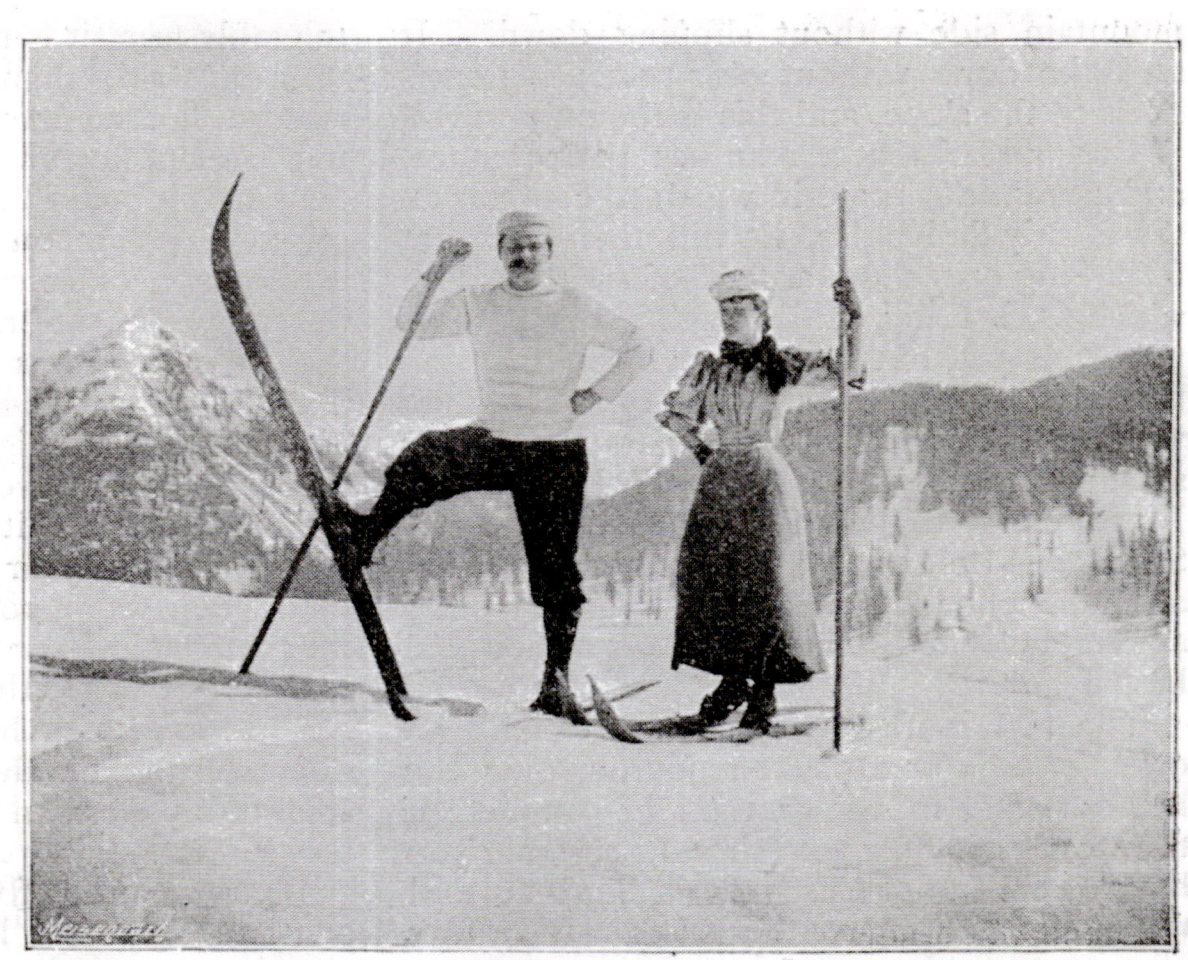

DR. CONAN DOYLE ON "SKI."

▲ Sir Arthur Conan Doyle, perhaps best known as the creator of the character Sherlock Holmes, wore wool tweed trousers while skiing with his sister Lottie in Davos, Switzerland, 1894.

▶ A skiwear advertisement from 1913 depicts the leather boots and long wool skirt worn by women in the era.

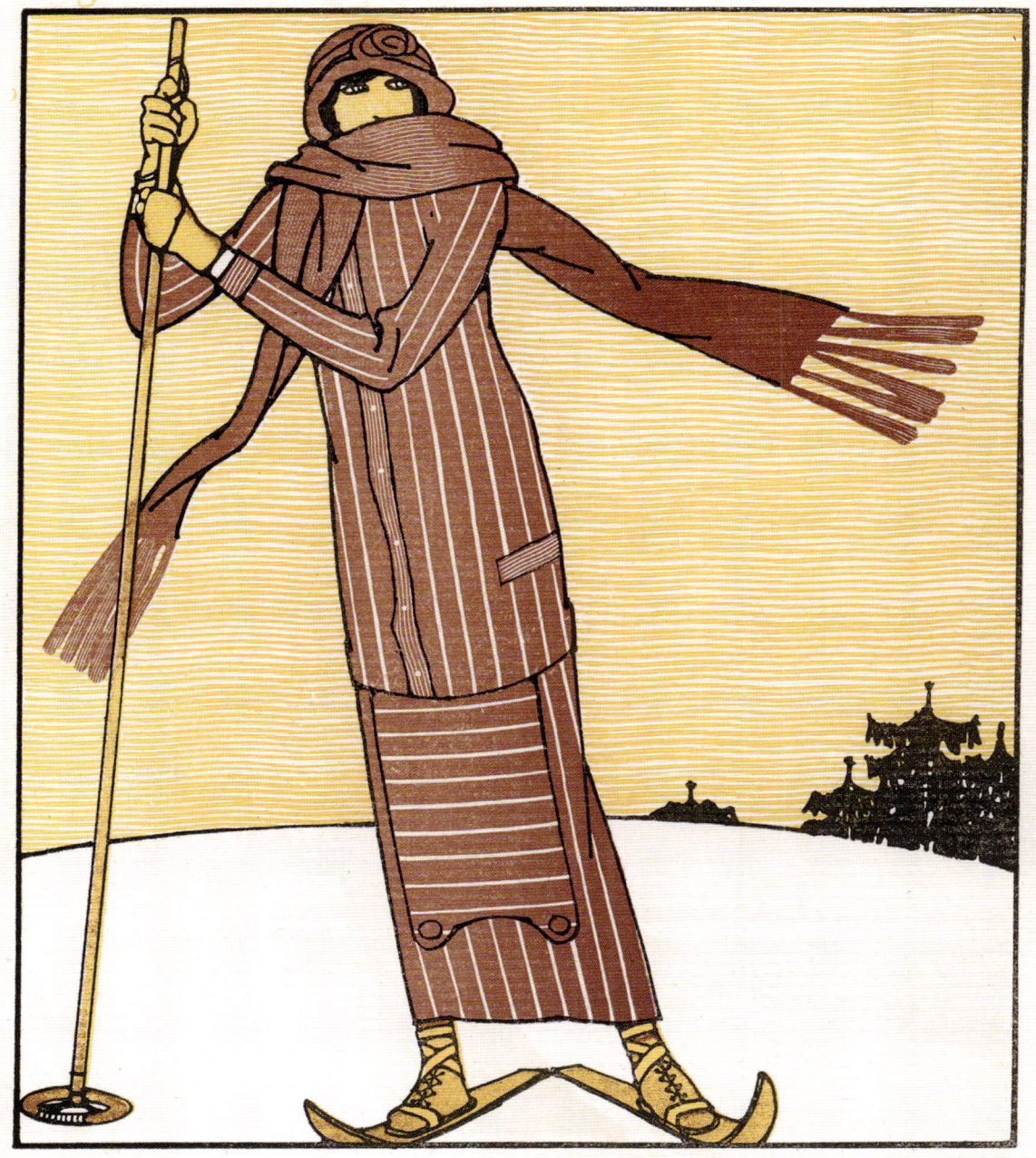

Costume en laine Shetland rayée de soie. La toque
et le cache-nez sont de feutre et de laine assortie.

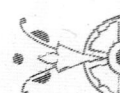

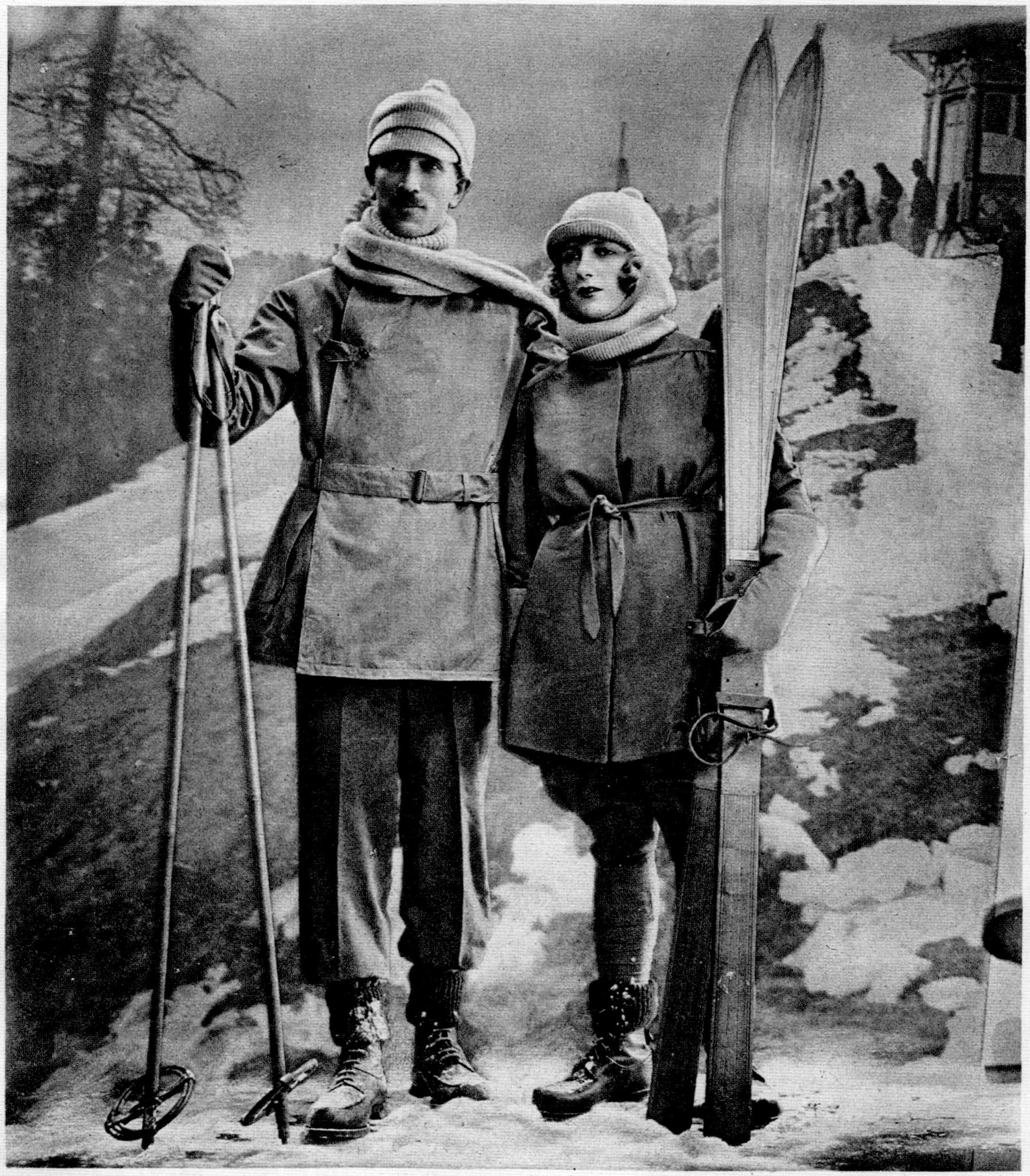

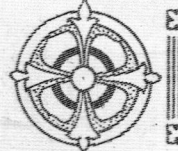
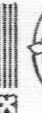
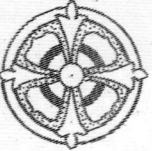

PRACTICAL SKI-ING OUTFITS

Designed and carried out in Proofed Gabardine by Burberry's, of the Haymarket.

PHOTOGRAPH BY ELWIN NEAME.

Skiwear
Gets Sporty

—

The first Winter Olympics, held in Chamonix, France, in 1924, included what we now call cross-country skiing, solidifying the transformation of skiing from a mode of transportation to an official sport, and a shift in ski fashion followed suit. Women finally broke free of skirts and opted for pants, just as men had been wearing, either in a knee-length knicker style or long, baggy, and cinched at the ankle to keep out snow. The inclusion of alpine (downhill) skiing in the 1936 Winter Olympics injected the burgeoning ski culture with a desire for a more streamlined, aerodynamic look, and soon pant designs evolved to an in-the-boot fit.

Whether on skis or in the lodge enjoying après-ski, the fashion was elegant—simply strip off the outer layers and head straight to teatime for hot drinks and conversation about perilous attempts at learning the then-new Arlberg method of skiing.

◀ A 1922 winter sports fashion advertisement by Burberry, showcasing a new pant option for women skiers

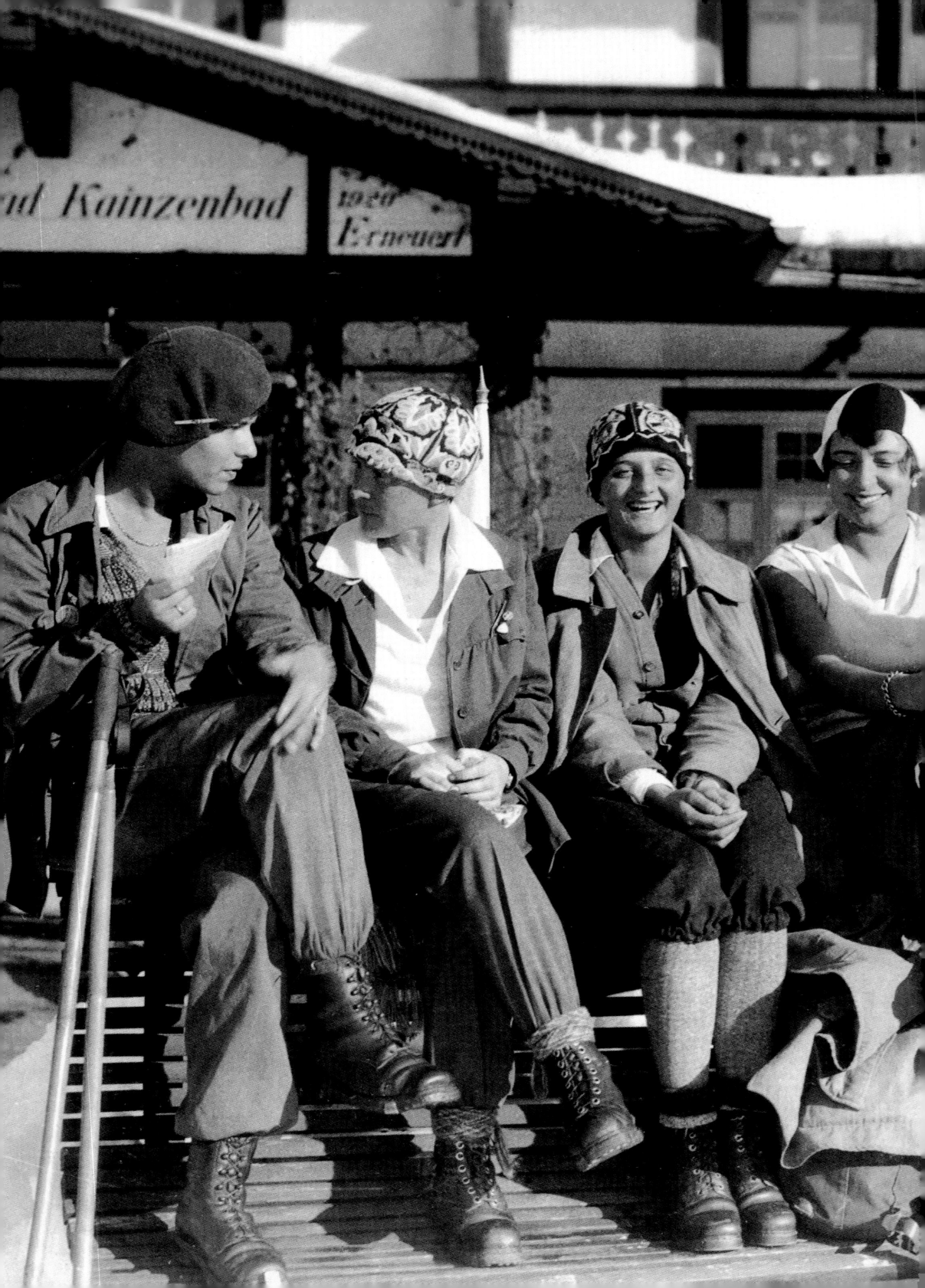

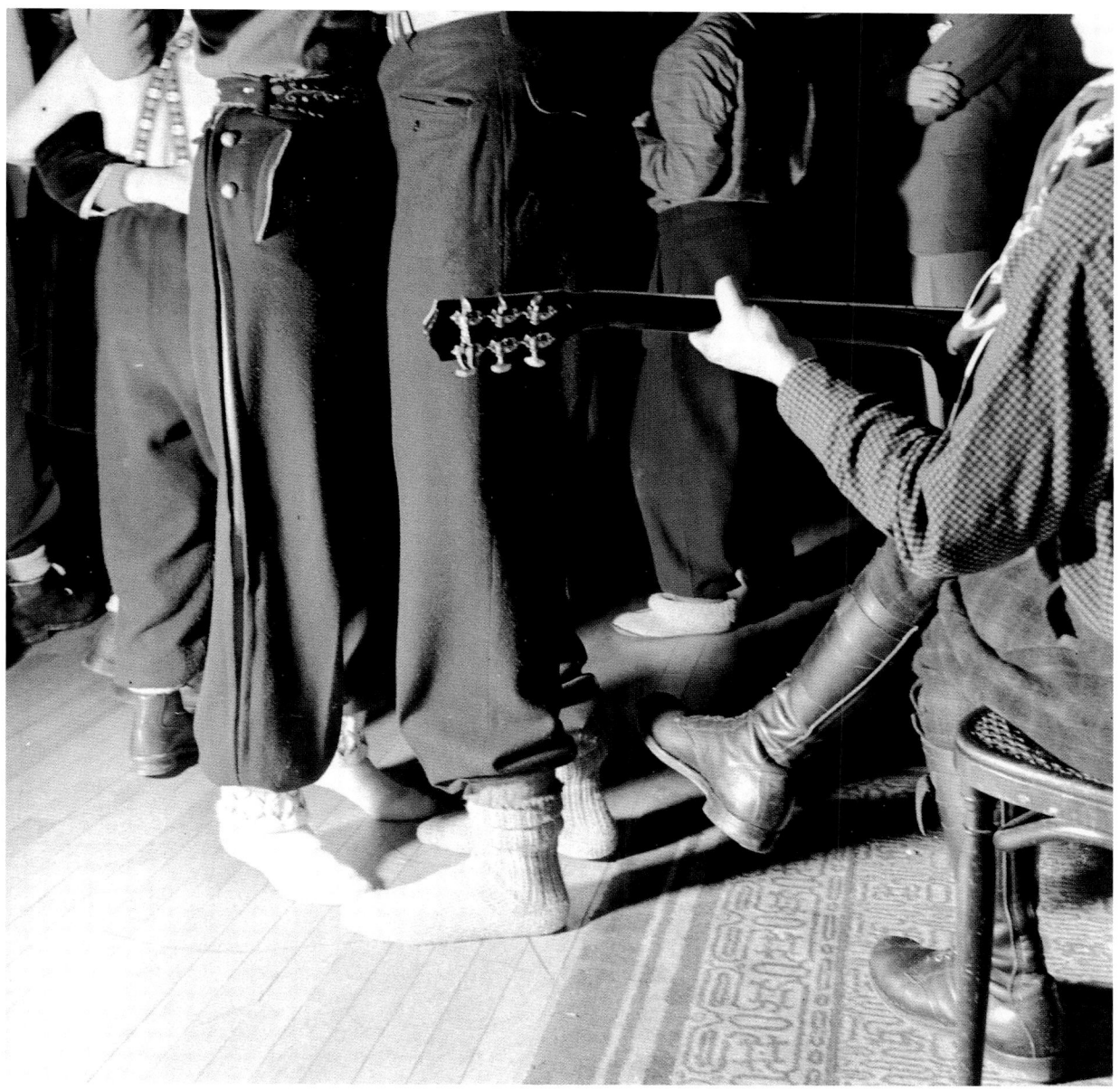

▲ Male and female college students wearing matching long wool pants at an après-ski party in 1938

◀ Skiers wearing knicker and long pant styles rest after a day on the slopes in what is now the Garmisch-Partenkirchen ski area, in the Bavarian Alps, circa 1927.

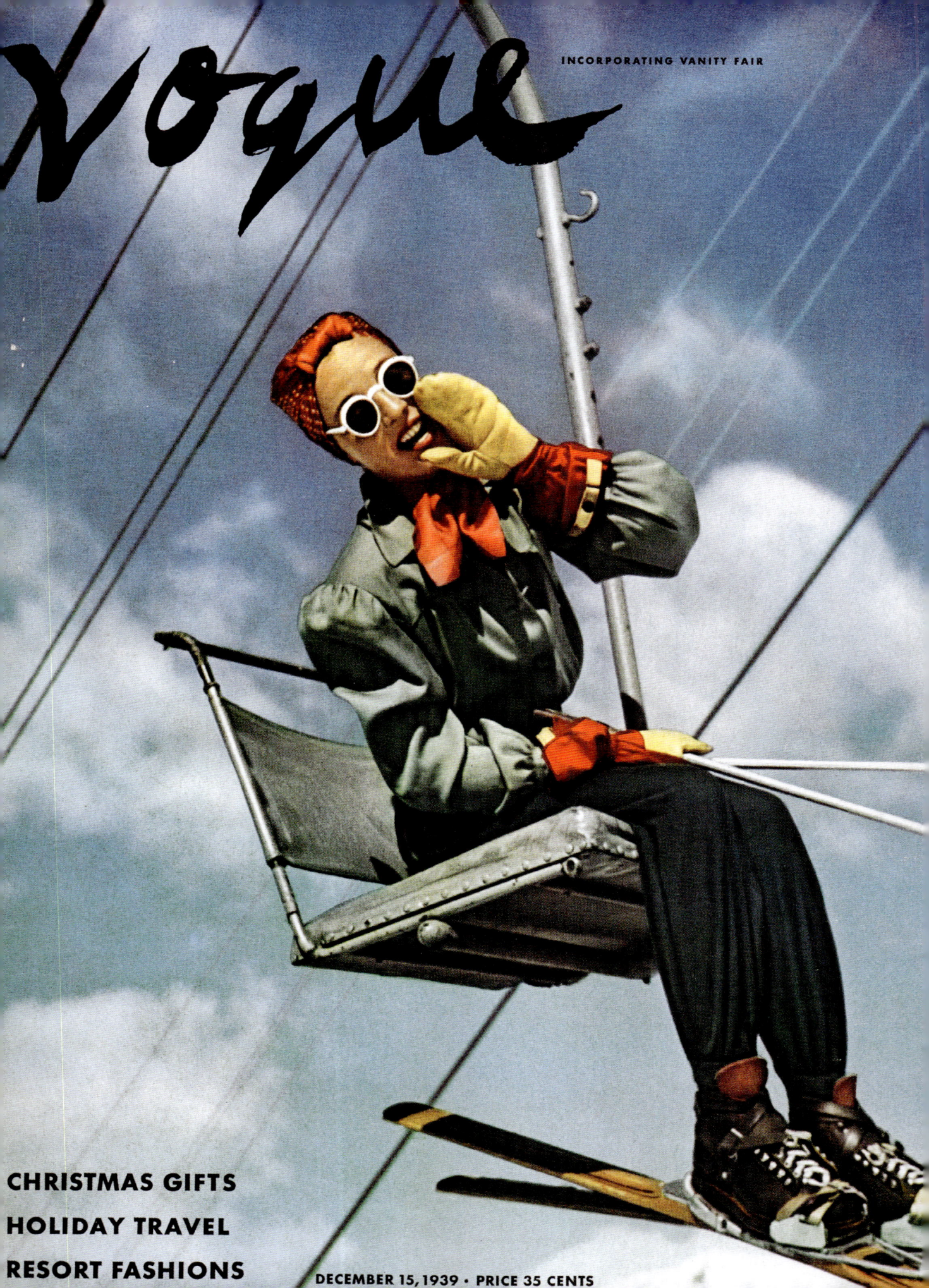

The New Look

—

The most impactful moment in the history of skiwear came with the invention of synthetic and, soon after, stretch fibers. The nylon fiber was developed in 1935 by Wallace Carothers at DuPont and became commercially available in 1940. Following World War II, skiing and skiwear began to explode in popularity around the world and especially in the United States. Nylon and highly elastic versions of it (such as Helanca, a stretchy nylon spun with wool) inspired a new crop of skiwear designers to innovate with color and fit. This forever changed the way people dress for skiing (and après-ski). There were, of course, the practical improvements for movement in the sport, but more important for fashion and the après-ski scene, things got a whole lot tighter and sexier.

◀ Hello, 1940s! Here comes a revolution in ski fashion, as captured for the December 15, 1939, cover of *Vogue*.

Fashion designer Emilio Pucci, widely known for his brightly colored prints, got his start in skiwear. A ski outfit he designed for a friend in Zermatt, Switzerland, caught the eye of photographer Toni Frissell, and her editor at *Harper's Bazaar*, the illustrious Diana Vreeland, asked Pucci to create a full ski collection for the December 1948 issue. He tapped the Oregon-based skiwear manufacturer White Stag to produce the collection and helped transform the way women dressed on and off the slopes.

In the same era, Montreal-based ski enthusiast and tailor Irving Margolese designed a slimmed-down ski pant that tucked inside the wearer's boot with a strap under the foot. He was able to ramp up to full production capacity in Canada soon after the end of World War II, while bombed European factories were still being rebuilt, and launched what became known as the Irving pant.

▶ A skier at Mont Tremblant, Canada, sporting newly-designed slimmer in-the-boot ski pants, 1945

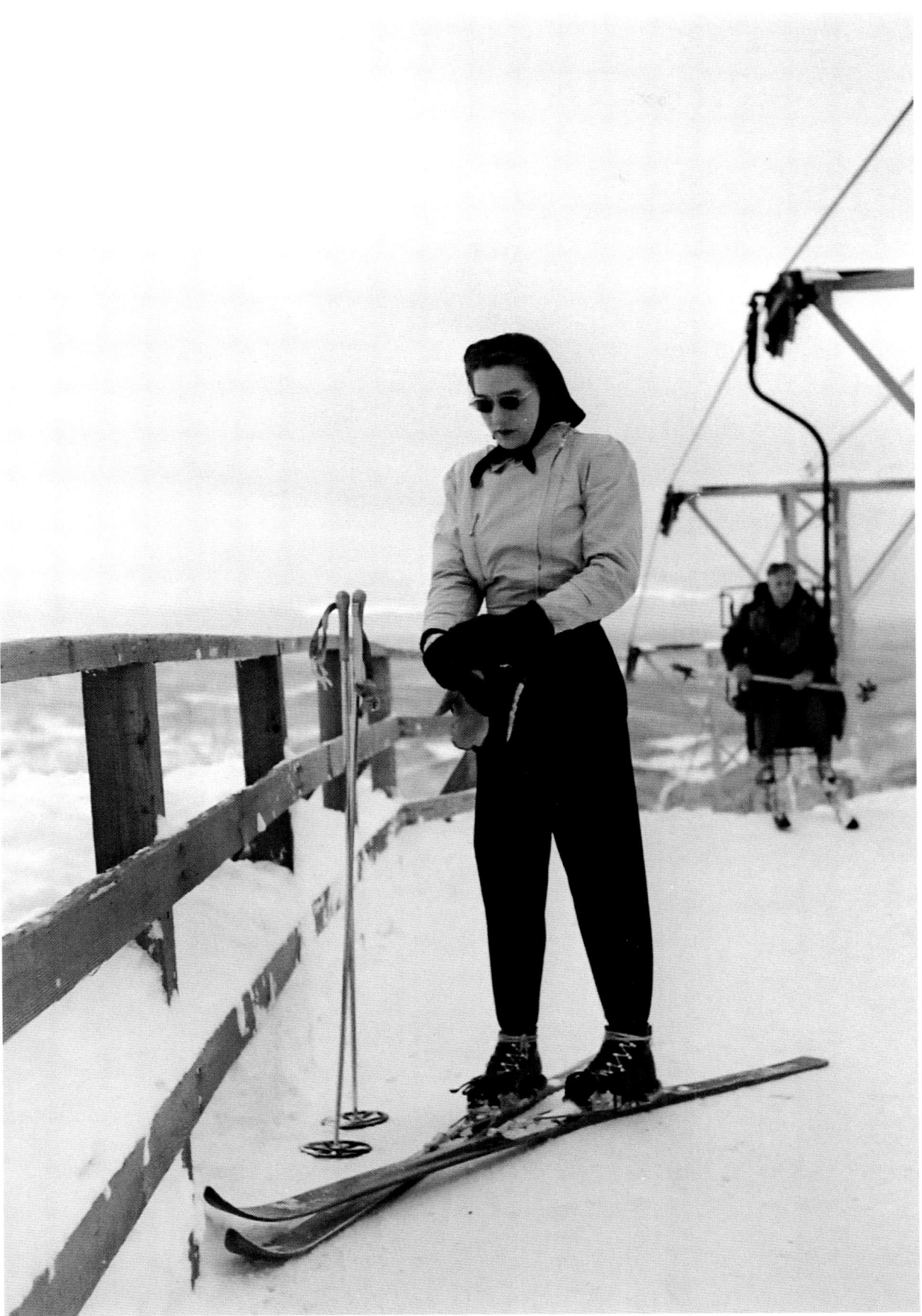

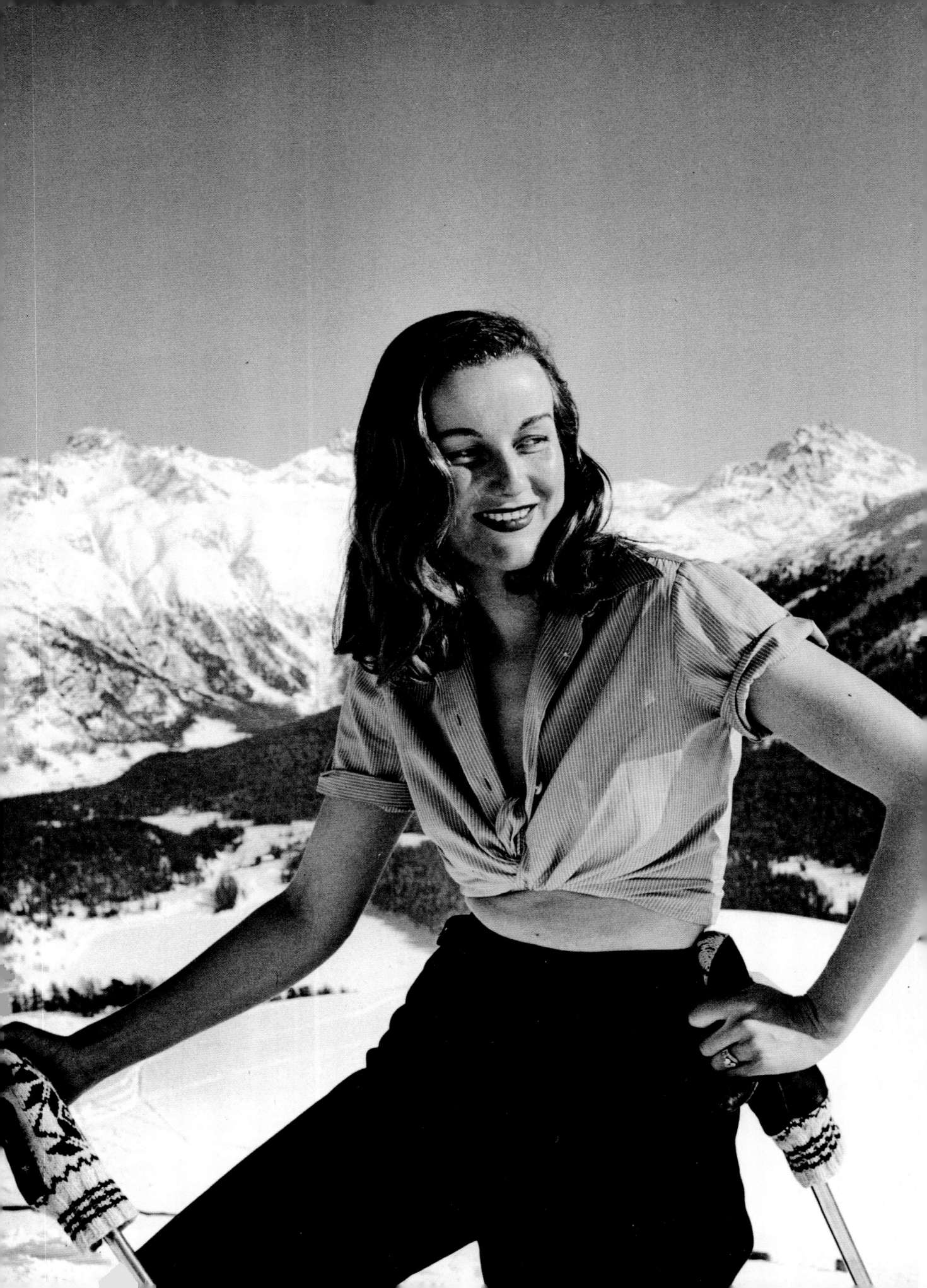

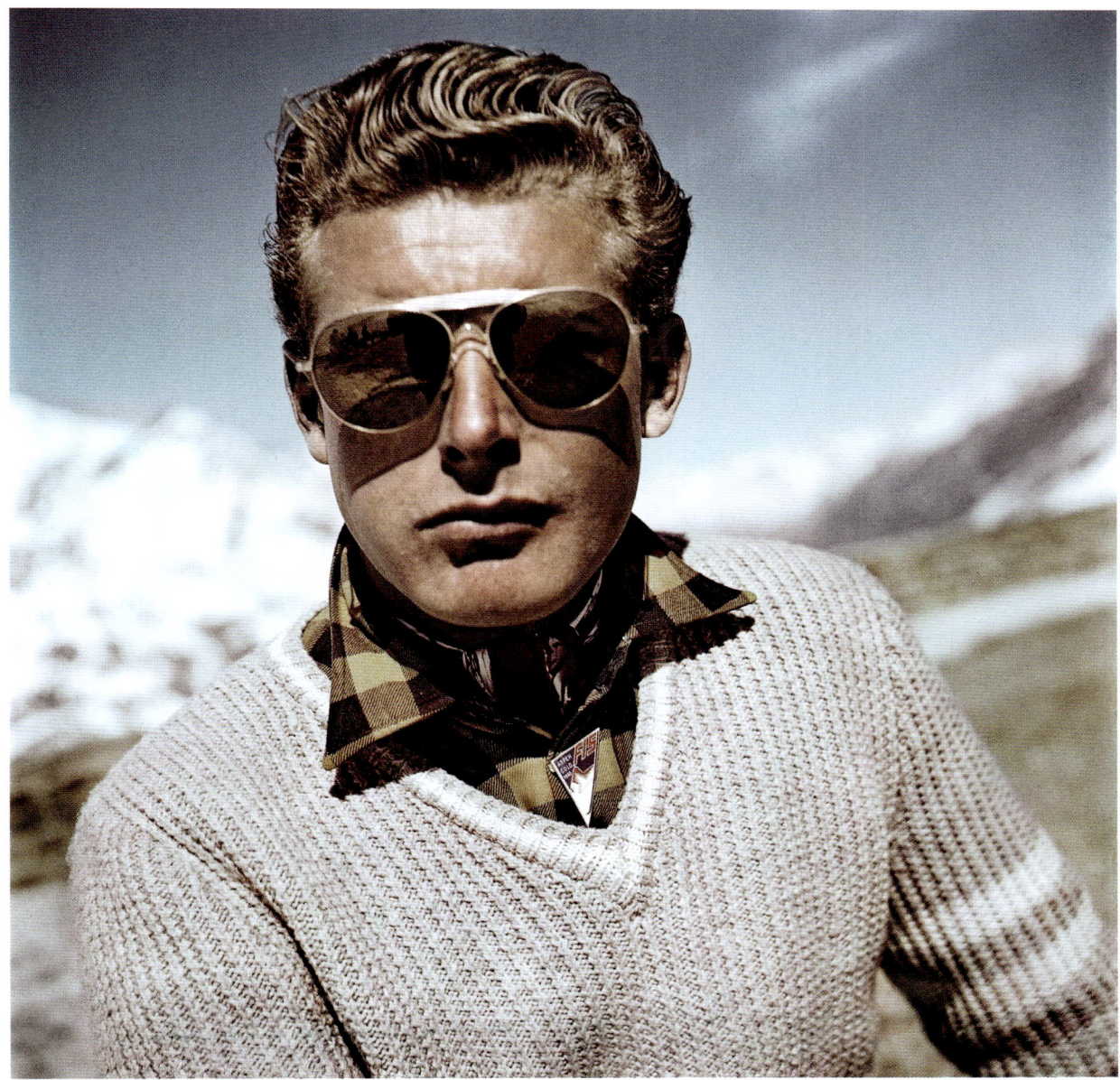

▲ Buttoned-up sport style in Zermatt

◀ The postwar 1940s ushered in a new era of celebrity and glamour for ski resorts, with business moguls and Hollywood stars flocking to destinations in Europe and North America. A new market for ski fashion emerged as well, with a distinctly stylish edge.

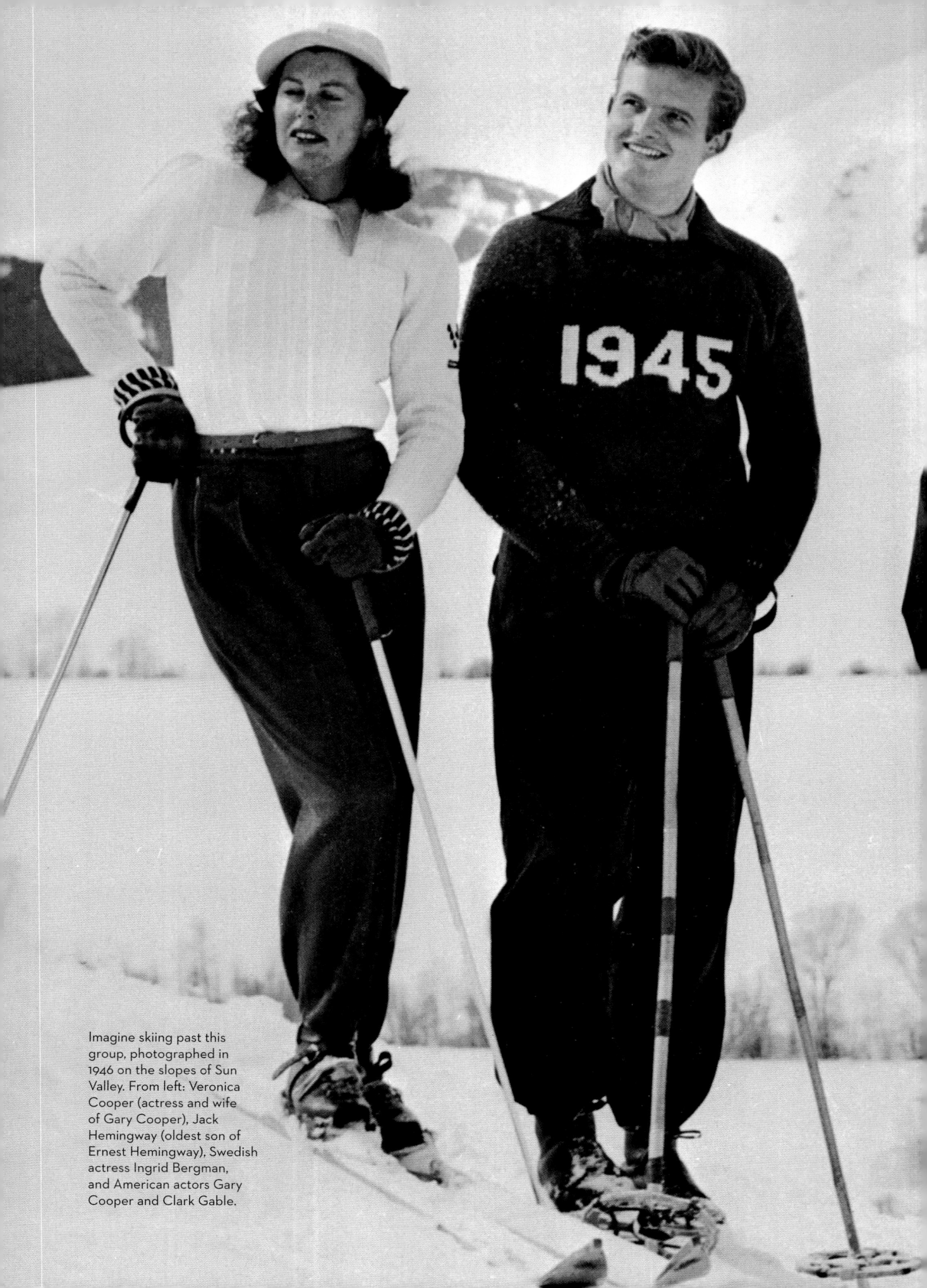

Imagine skiing past this group, photographed in 1946 on the slopes of Sun Valley. From left: Veronica Cooper (actress and wife of Gary Cooper), Jack Hemingway (oldest son of Ernest Hemingway), Swedish actress Ingrid Bergman, and American actors Gary Cooper and Clark Gable.

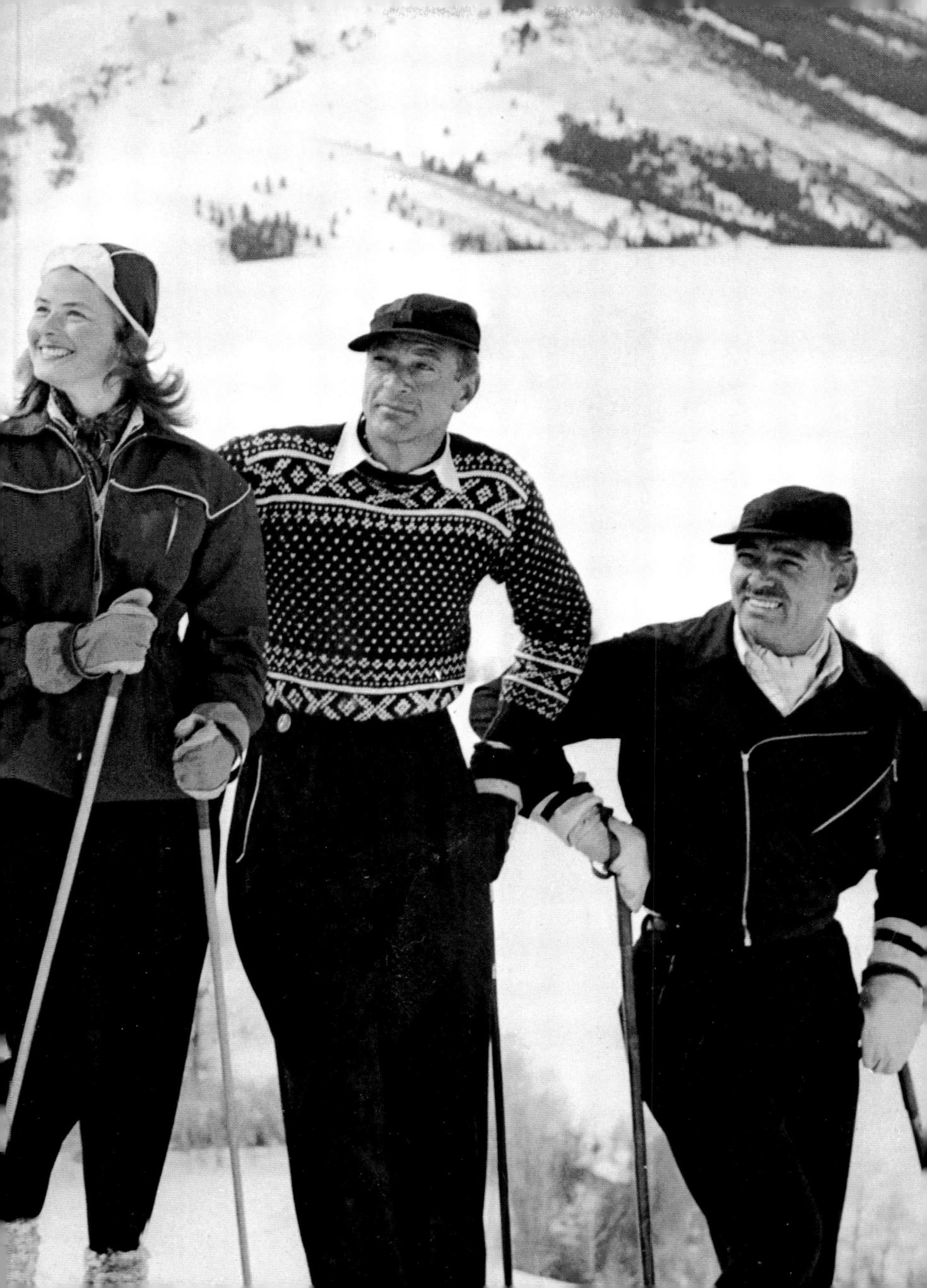

HEADWEAR

Accessories, including headwear, have always played a pivotal role in ski fashion. More so than on city streets, the slopes and lodges of ski resorts allowed for whimsical costume-like dressing opportunities. Knitwear, furry hats, Western styles, and more adventurous choices all have their place in après-ski.

▼ American model and avid skier Barbara Mullen wearing a knit pom-pom hat in Switzerland in 1960

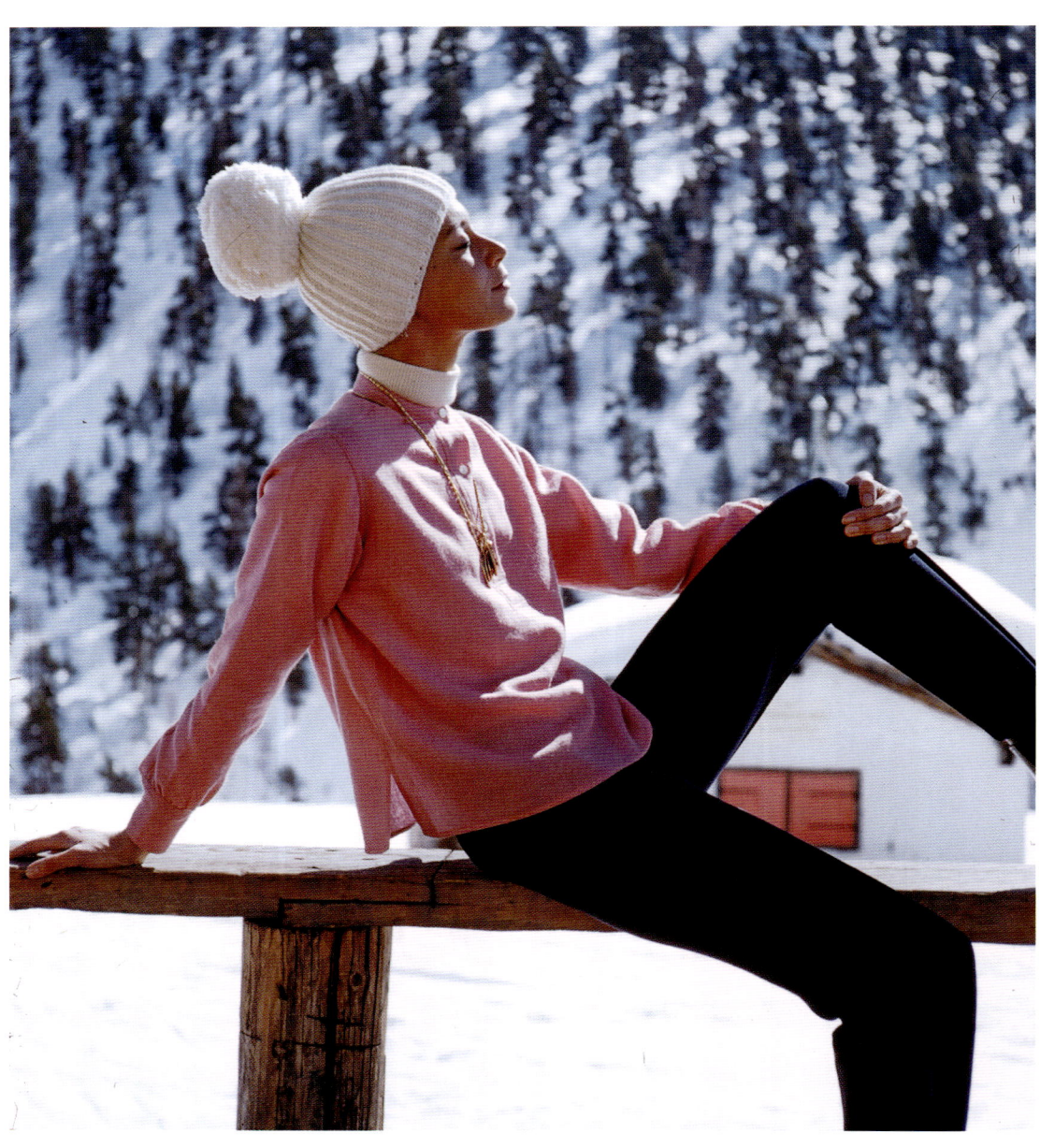

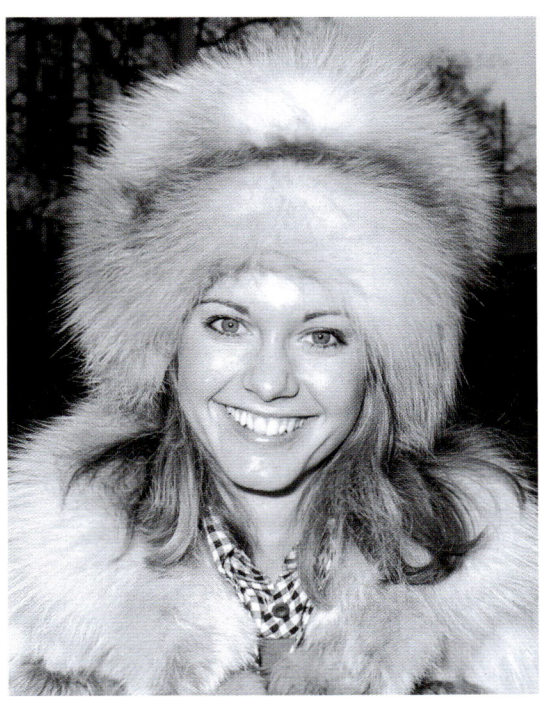

▲ Olivia Newton-John in an oversized furry hat in the 1960s

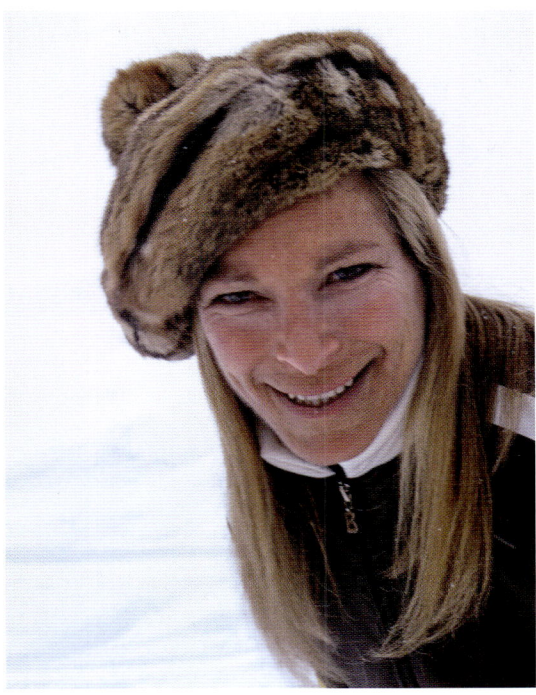

▲ Social fixture Nan Kempner wearing a fur beret in Vail, 1969

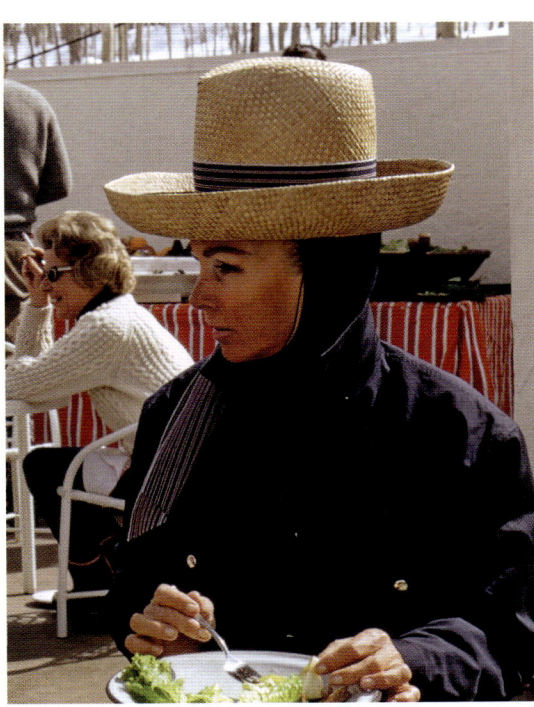

▲ A stylish 1960s take on après-ski headwear, with a knit balaclava worn under a tall, straw bowler-style hat

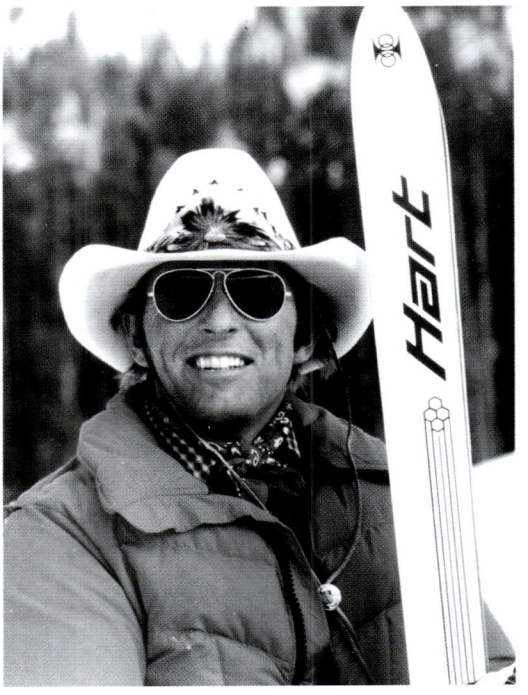

▲ Billy Kidd, the first American man to win an Olympic medal in alpine skiing, wearing his signature feather-trimmed Stetson

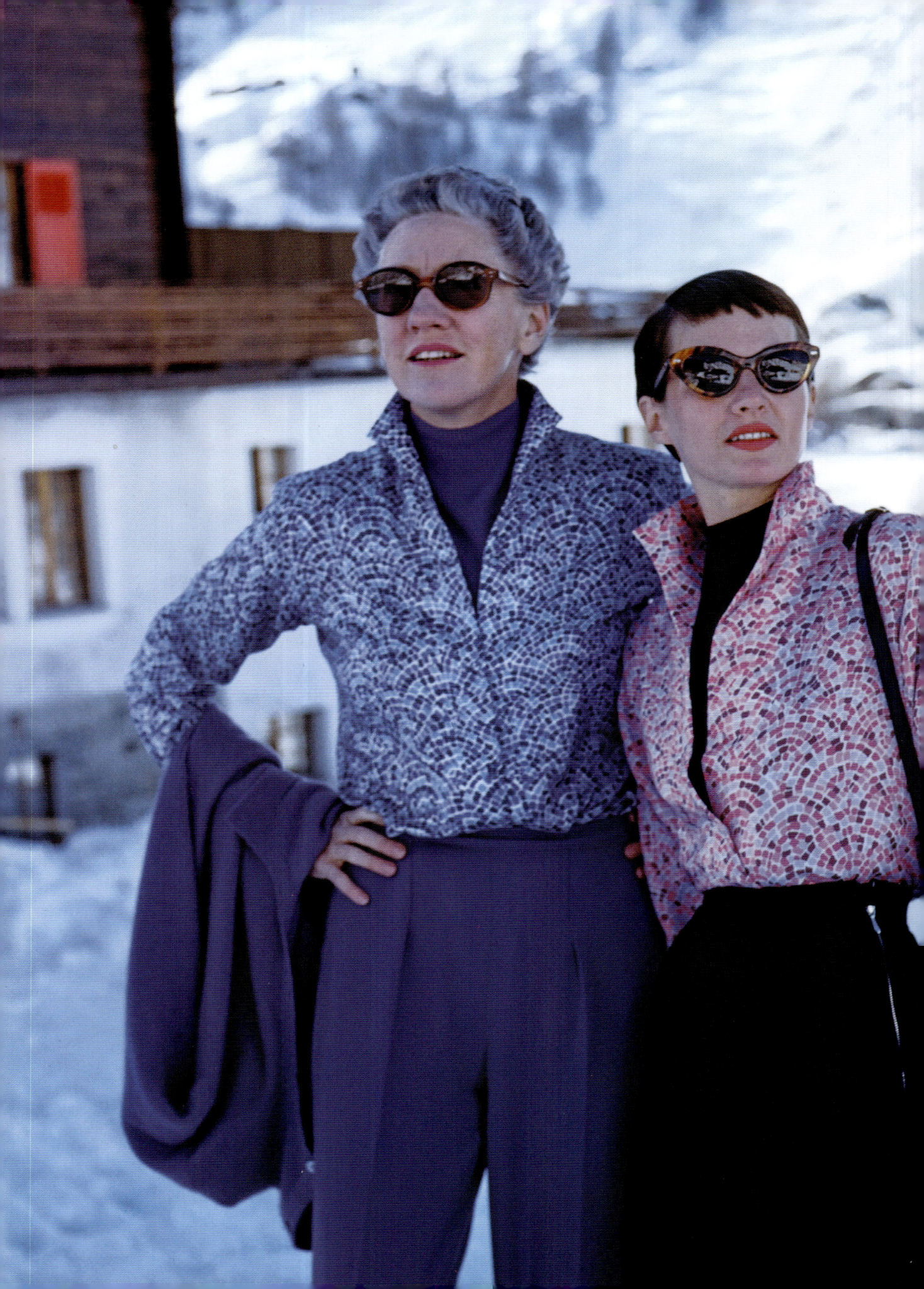

Tighter & Brighter

—

The final step in the evolution of ski fashion from thick, heavy, dark-colored wool to the bright, streamlined, slim silhouettes still popular today was the development of functional stretch fabrics, which improved mobility, helped a garment keep its shape even after being worn and then cleaned, and brought material even closer to the body for a better fit. These new fabrics changed the world of skiing, on and off the slopes, forever.

Combining the growing trend toward a slimmer-fitting pant with newly improved Helanca fabric, stretch ski pants in bright colors were born in the 1950s. Designer ski brands such as Bogner from Germany helped popularize this slimmer, brighter version of the ski pant.

The 1950s also saw fashion being designed and marketed specifically for après-ski. At resorts across North America and Europe, a new look could be seen: the slim, in-the-boot stretch ski pant paired with a cable-knit or Norwegian sweater and topped with a chic hat and eyewear. On the slopes, you'd throw on a jacket; for après-ski, you'd show off your sweater. In many cases, men and women sported a similar look.

◀ Toni Frissell (left) with friend Letha Gilbert in Zermatt wearing coordinating Pucci shirt-style silk parkas paired with slim in-the-boot pants, 1956

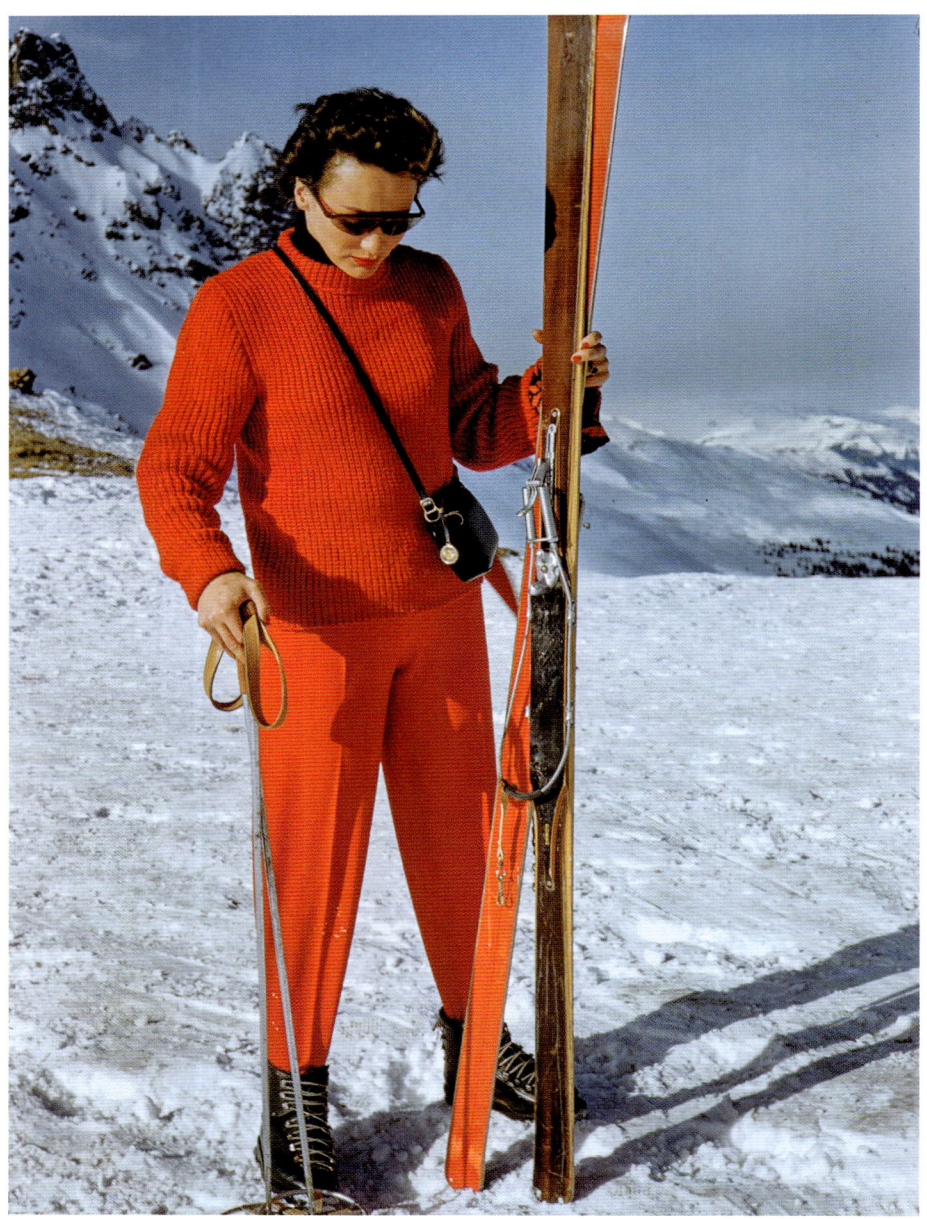

▲ Vibrant monochromatic ski looks, once again popular today, were pioneered by stylish skiers of this era, as shown here in Klosters, 1955.

▶ The street scene in 1950s Klosters showcased chic, timeless dressing.

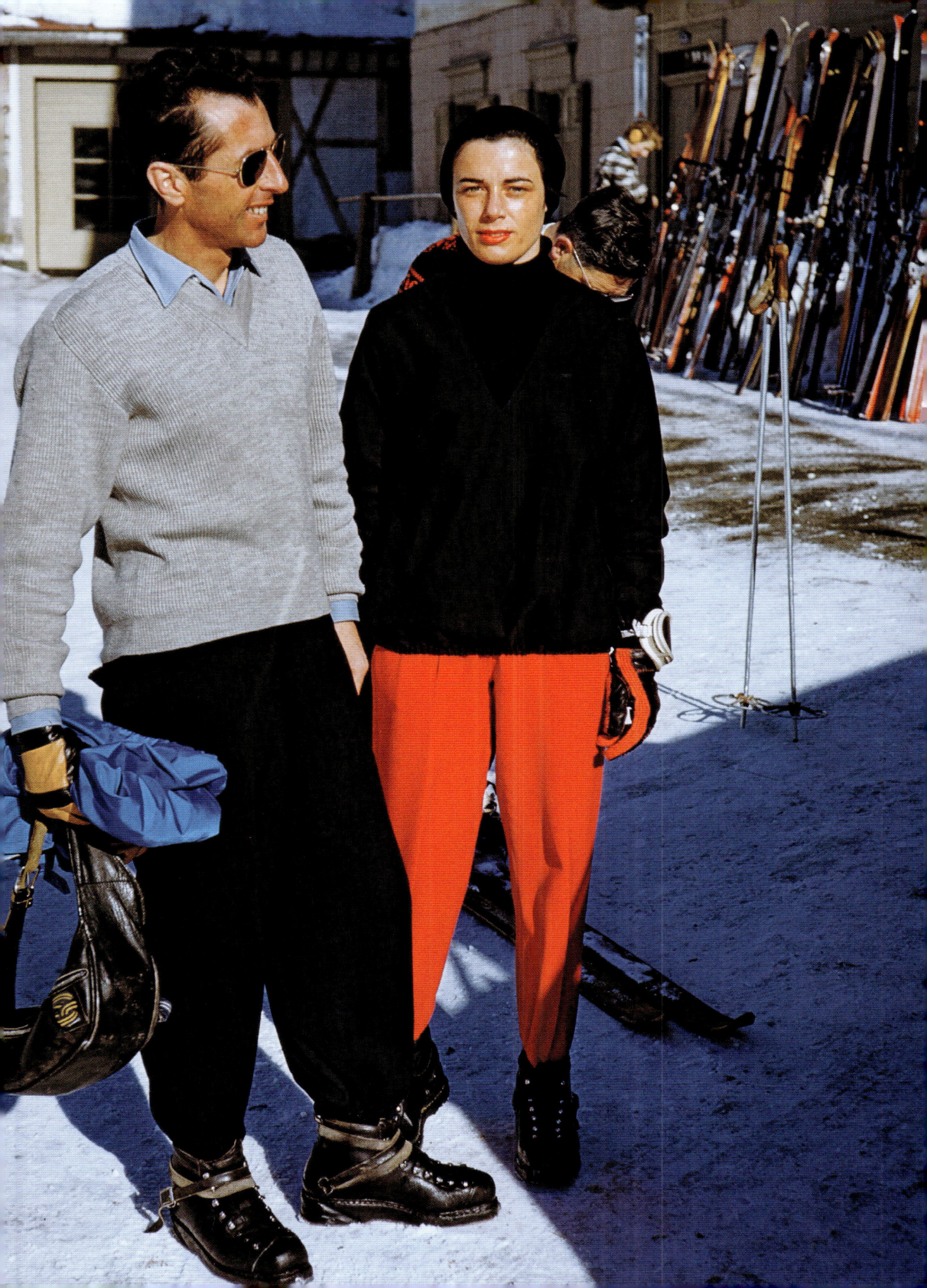

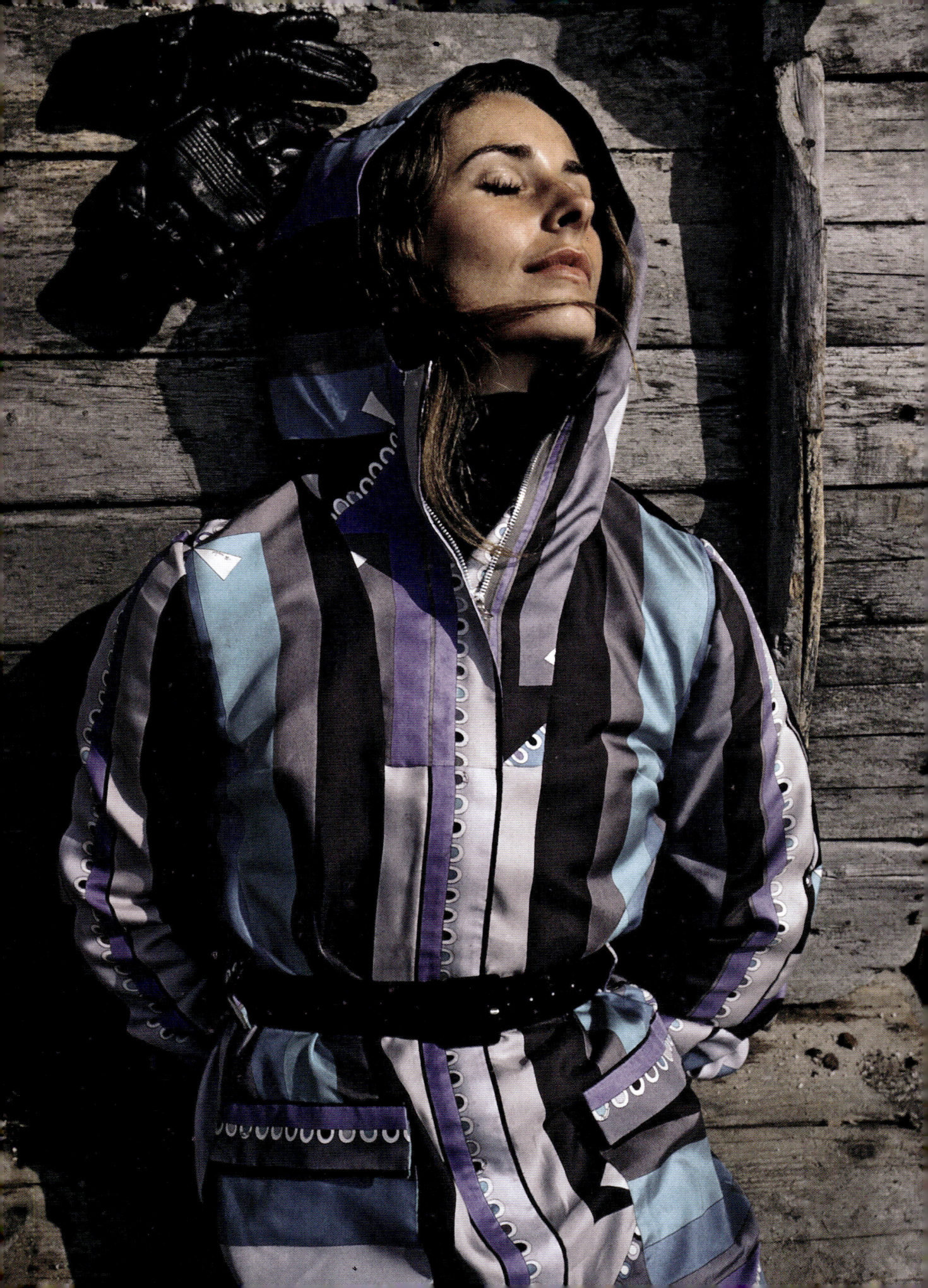

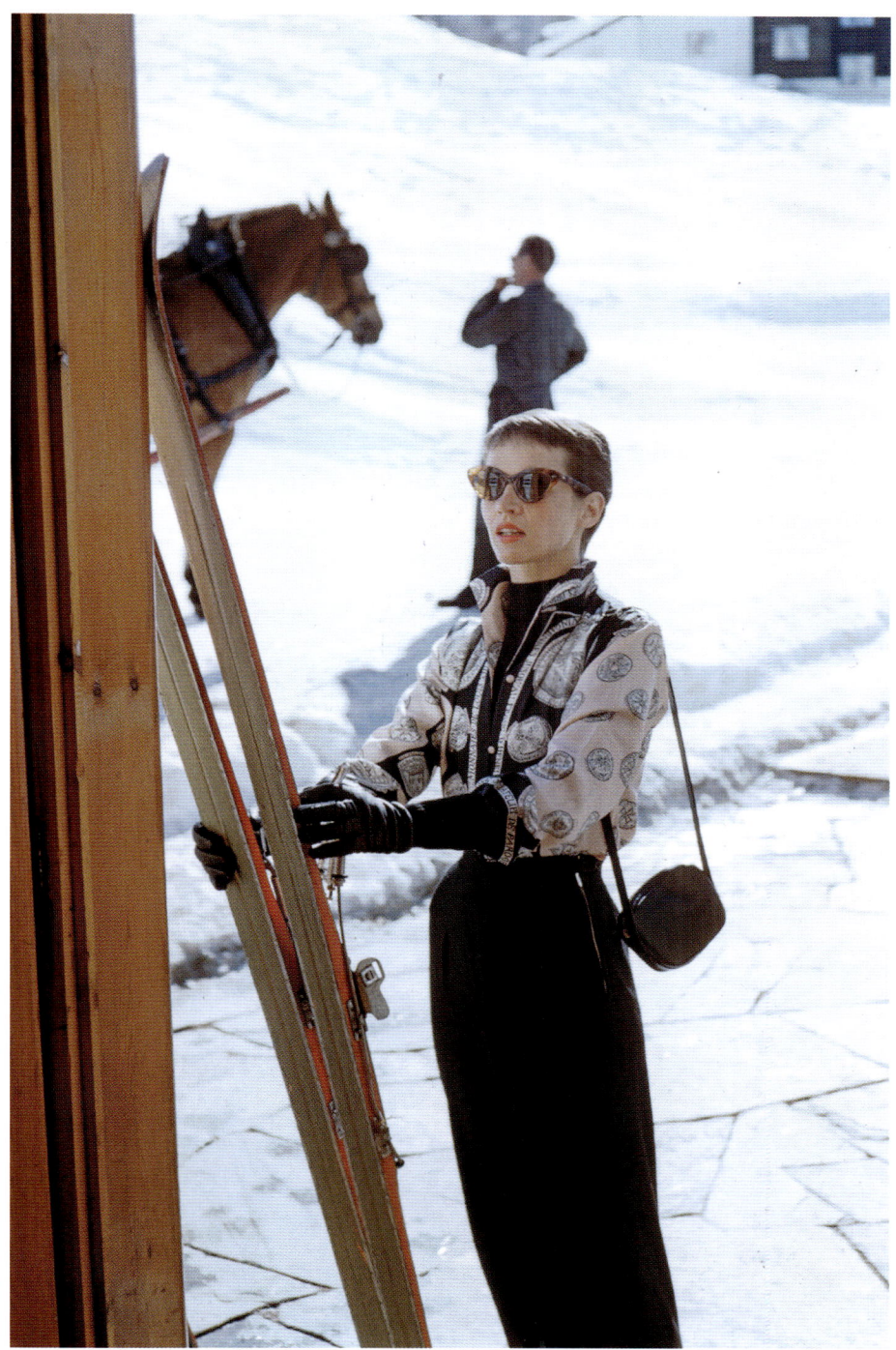

▲ Letha Gilbert wearing another printed shell top paired with slim pants in Zermatt, 1956

◀ Model Astrid Schiller, photographed for *Sports Illustrated* in an Emilio Pucci silk-printed ski parka in Val Gardena, Italy, 1969

EYEWEAR

Goggles are de rigueur on the slopes, mainly for practical purposes. They simply do the best job of protecting the eyes from ice and wind as skiers speed down runs. But while sitting slope-side après-ski, sunglasses are a significantly better choice. Many ski jackets are designed with interior pockets specifically for eyewear—make use of them and pack a pair of glasses to suit your style for après-ski.

▾ Princess Neslishah Sultan of Egypt (left) and Bourbon Princess Hedwige de la Rochefoucauld in fashion-forward outfits topped with chic eyewear strolling with social-fixture-turned-art-dealer Peter Zervudachi in St. Moritz in 1947.

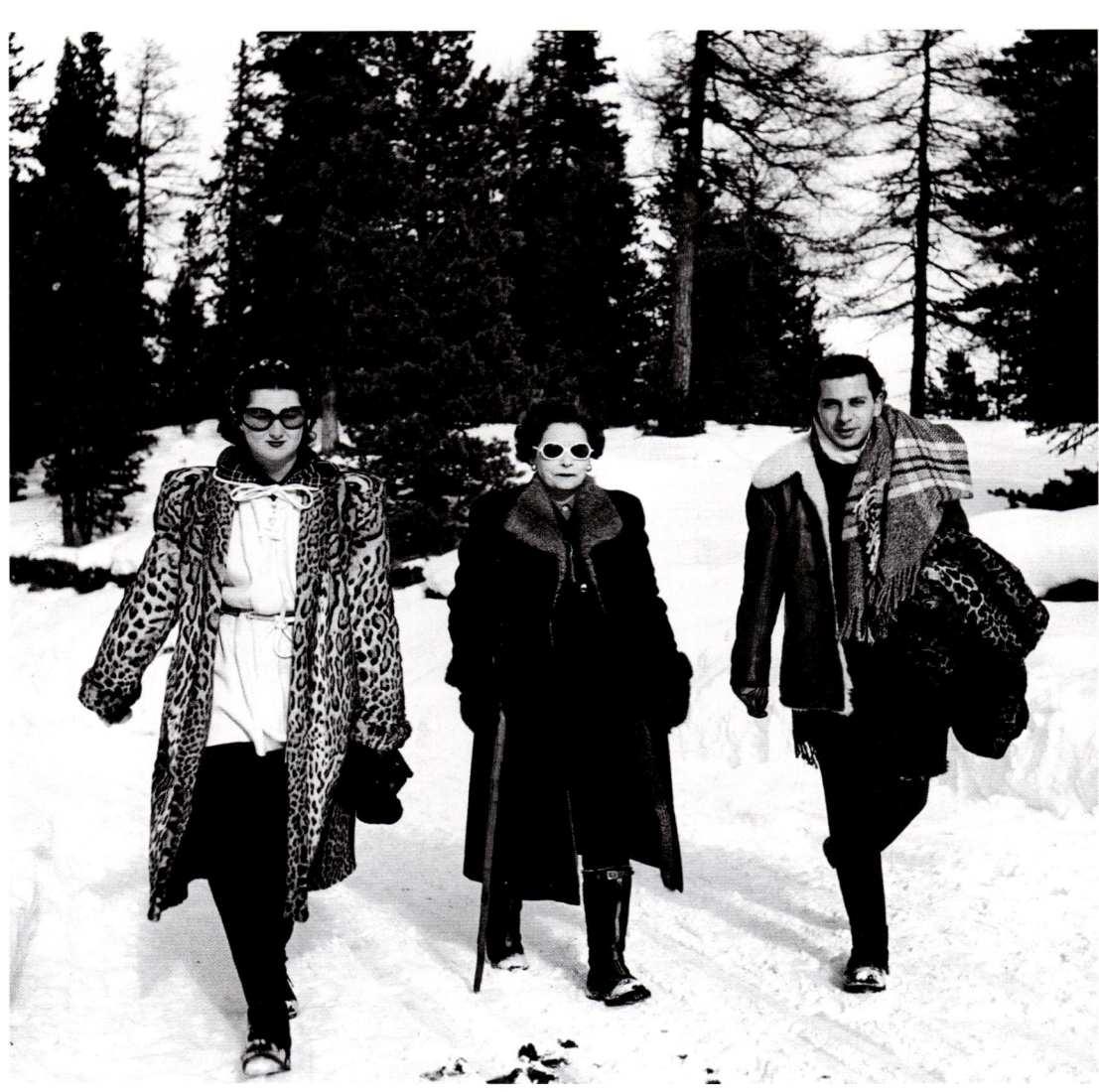

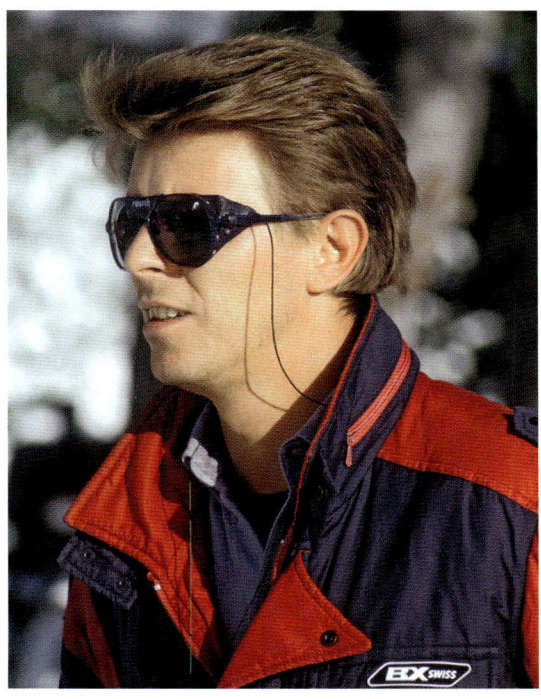

▲ Musician David Bowie wearing glacier-style sport glasses in Gstaad in 1986

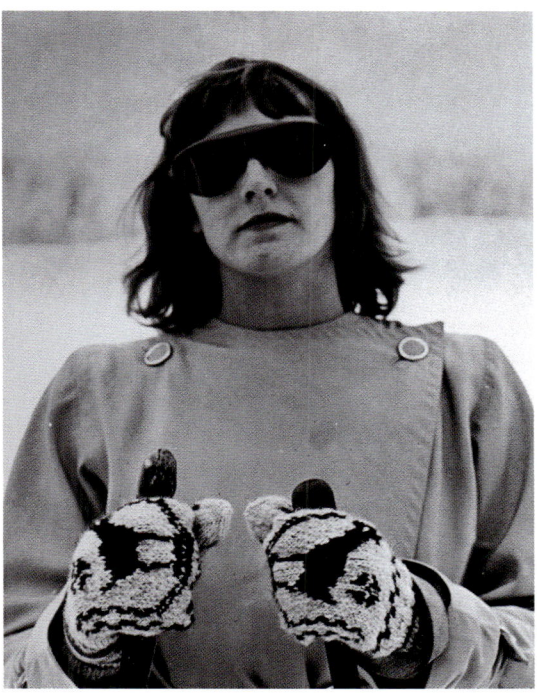

▲ Avant-garde eyewear worn at Pico Peak, Vermont, 1947

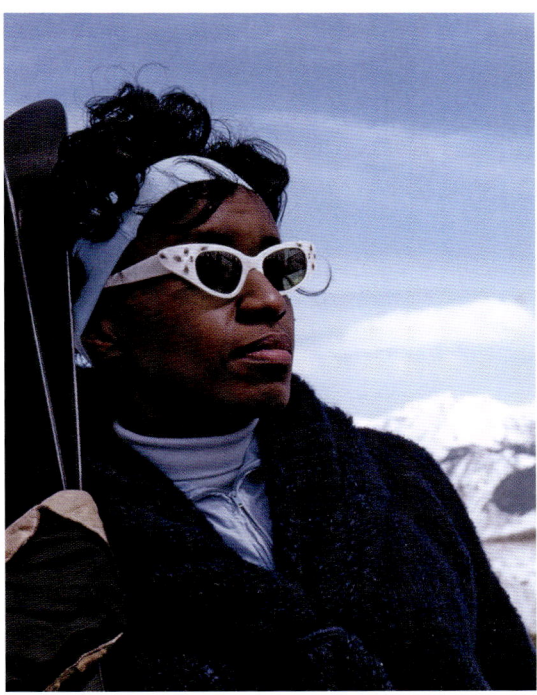

▲ Standout eyewear added a whimsical twist to classic skiwear for this skier in Vail in 1964.

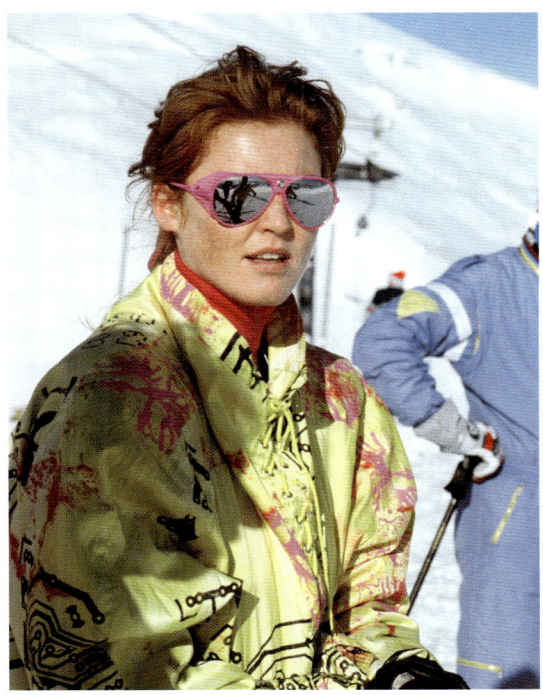

▲ Sarah Ferguson, Duchess of York, wearing bright pink glacier-style mirrored sunglasses in Klosters, 1987

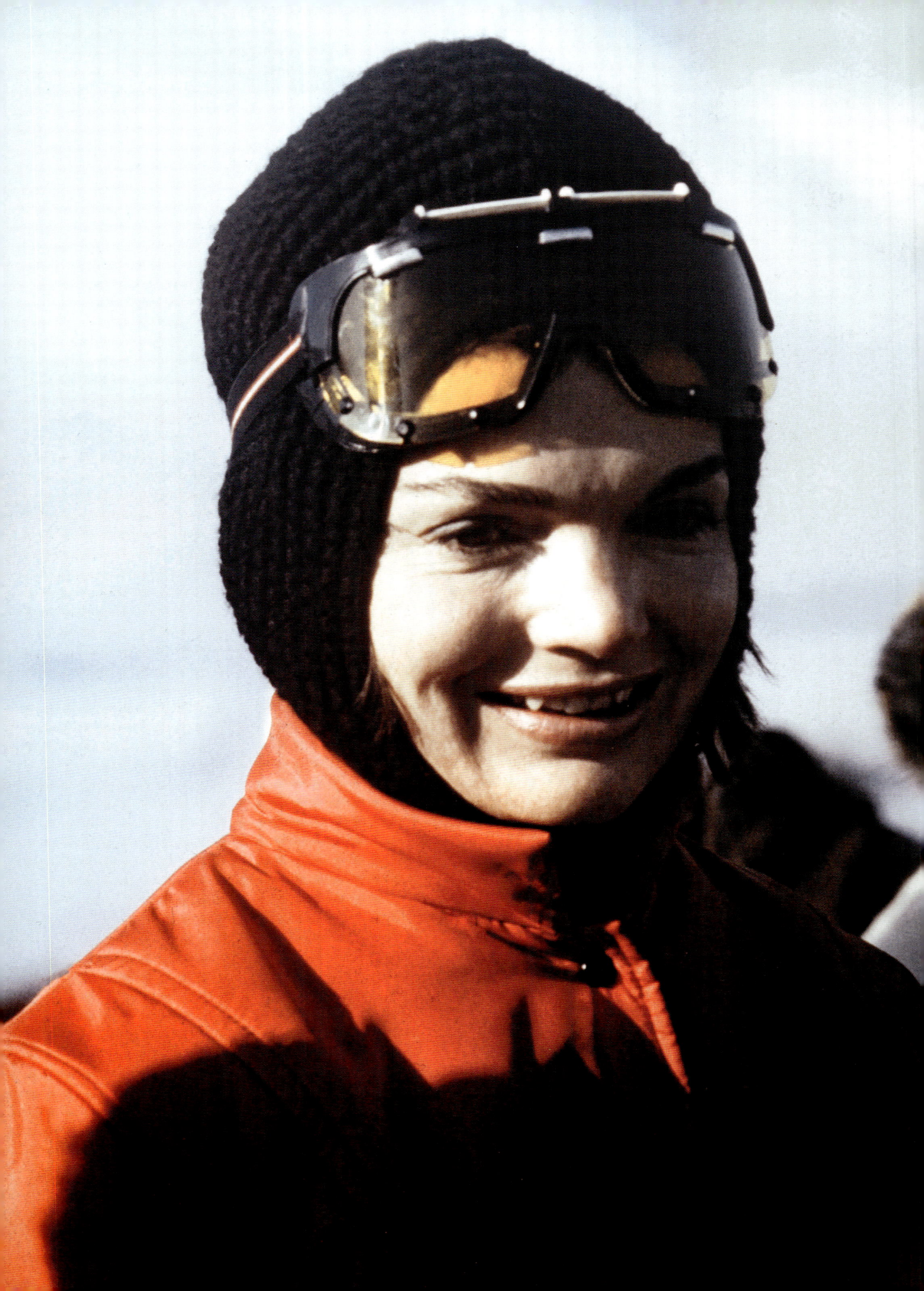

The Golden Era

—

With new ski resorts being developed around the globe and ski and après-ski fashion adding to the glamorous appeal of the skiing lifestyle, an iconic era filled with royals and celebrities blossomed in the 1960s and '70s. In the early 1960s, classic tailored looks were still the norm, including Norwegian sweaters and tapered stretch pants, but as the decade evolved, so too did the fashion. Mod looks made their way to ski resorts, in part thanks to Emilio Pucci and his innovative talent. Ski and après-ski fashion began to be less uniform and more forward-looking.

◄ Jacqueline Kennedy during a ski vacation in Gstaad, 1966

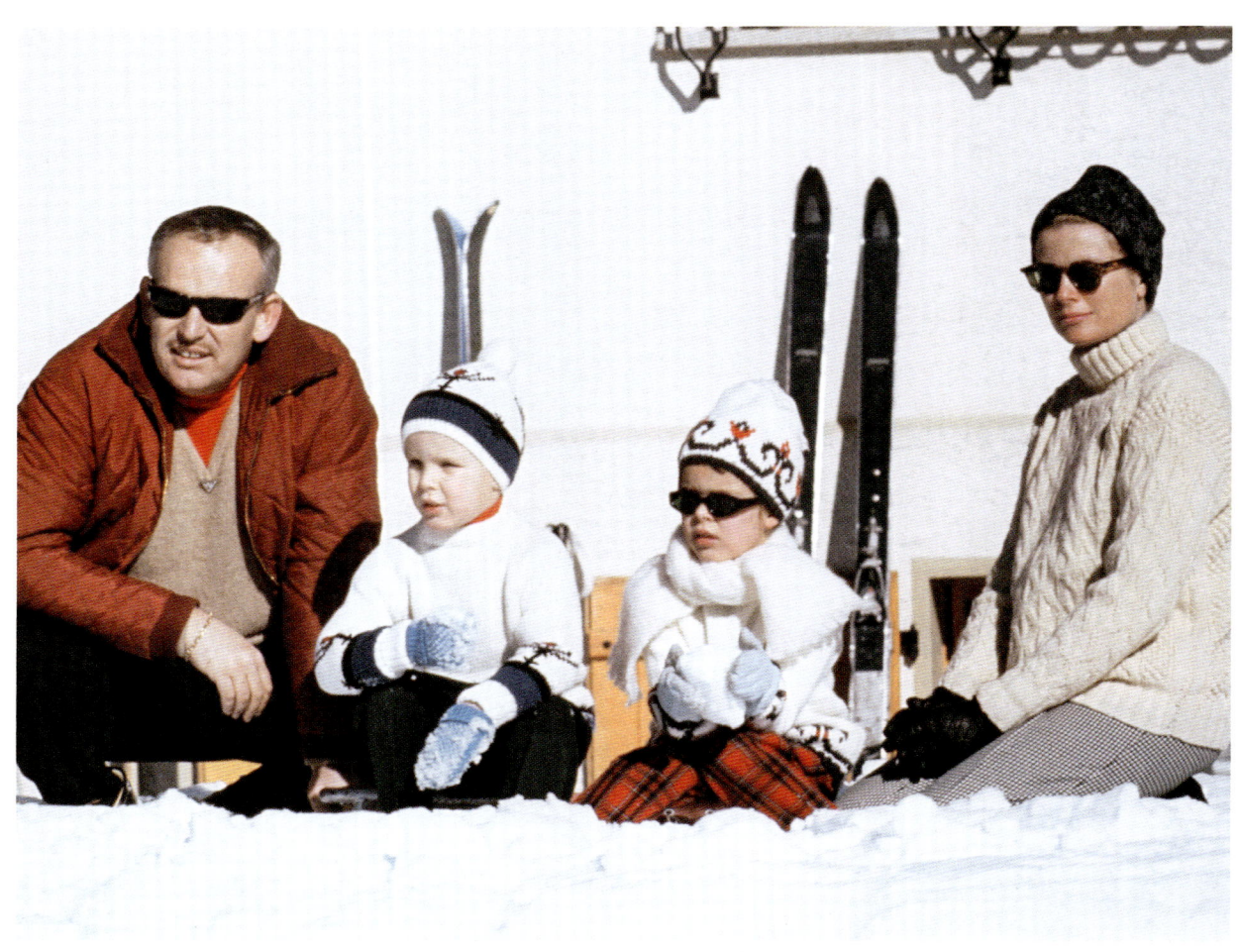

▲ The prince and princess of Monaco, Rainier III and Grace Kelly, with their children on a skiing holiday in Gstaad, 1964

▶ Queen Sirikit of Thailand wearing a tailored monochromatic look in Gstaad, 1961

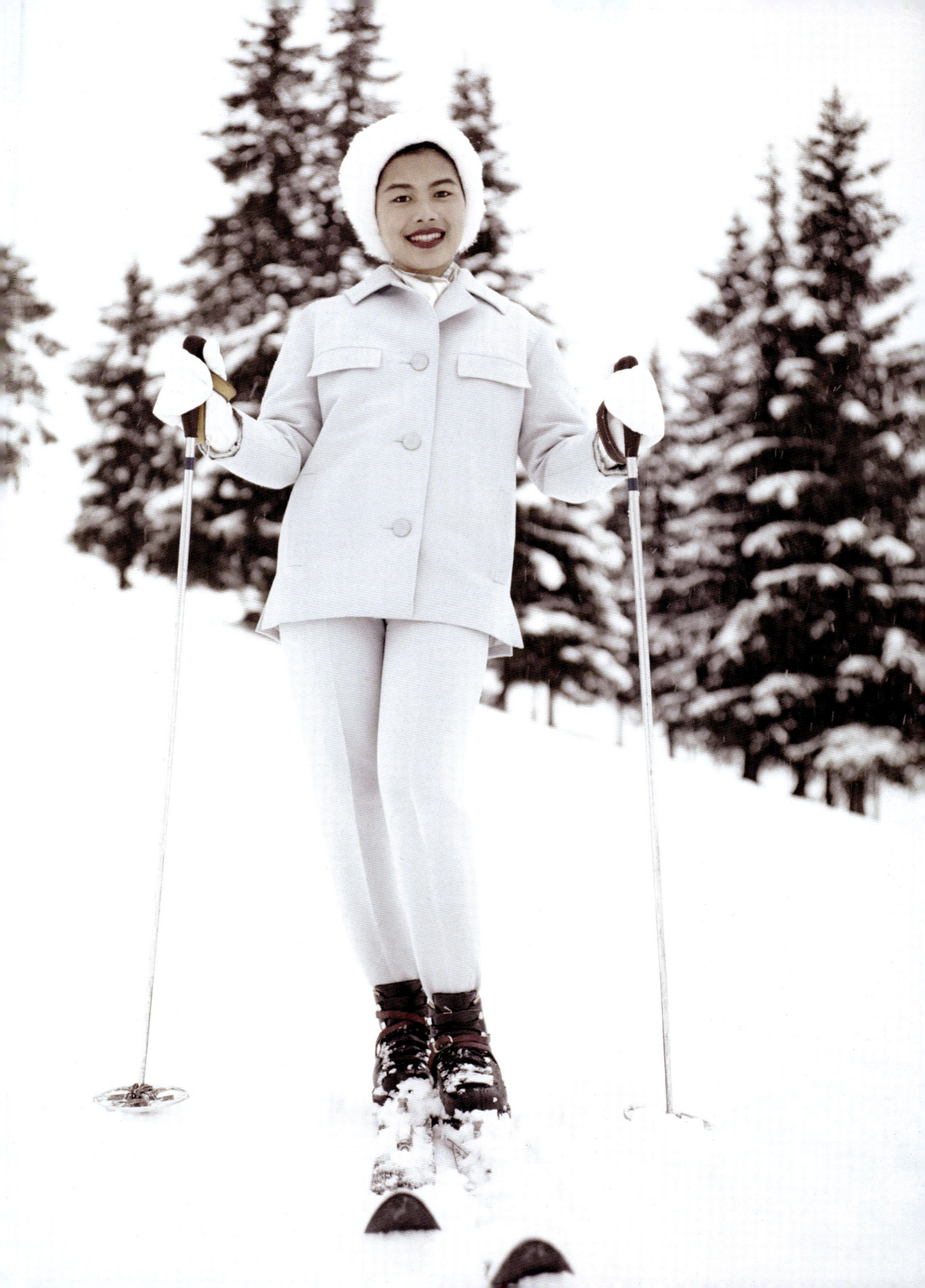

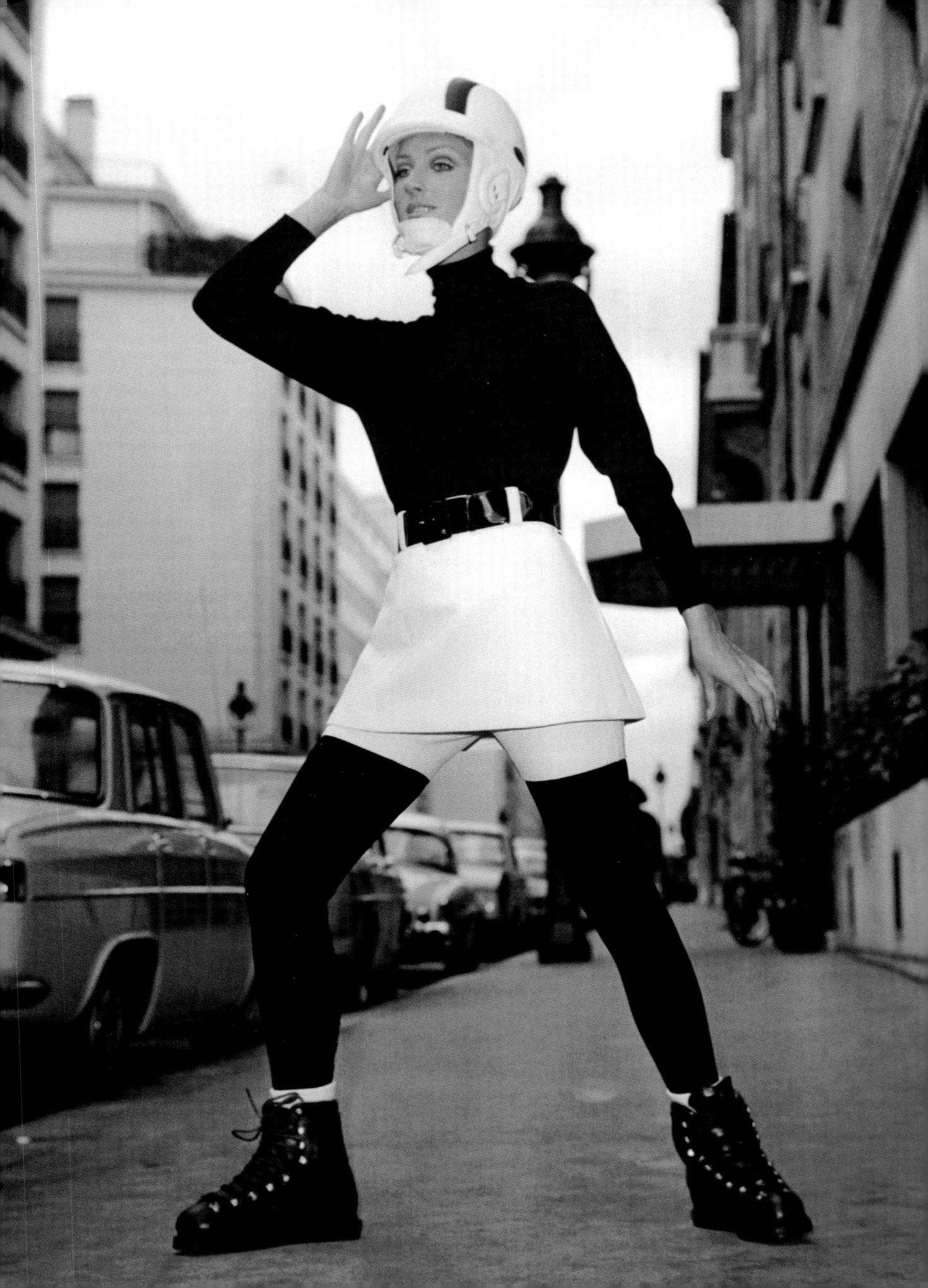

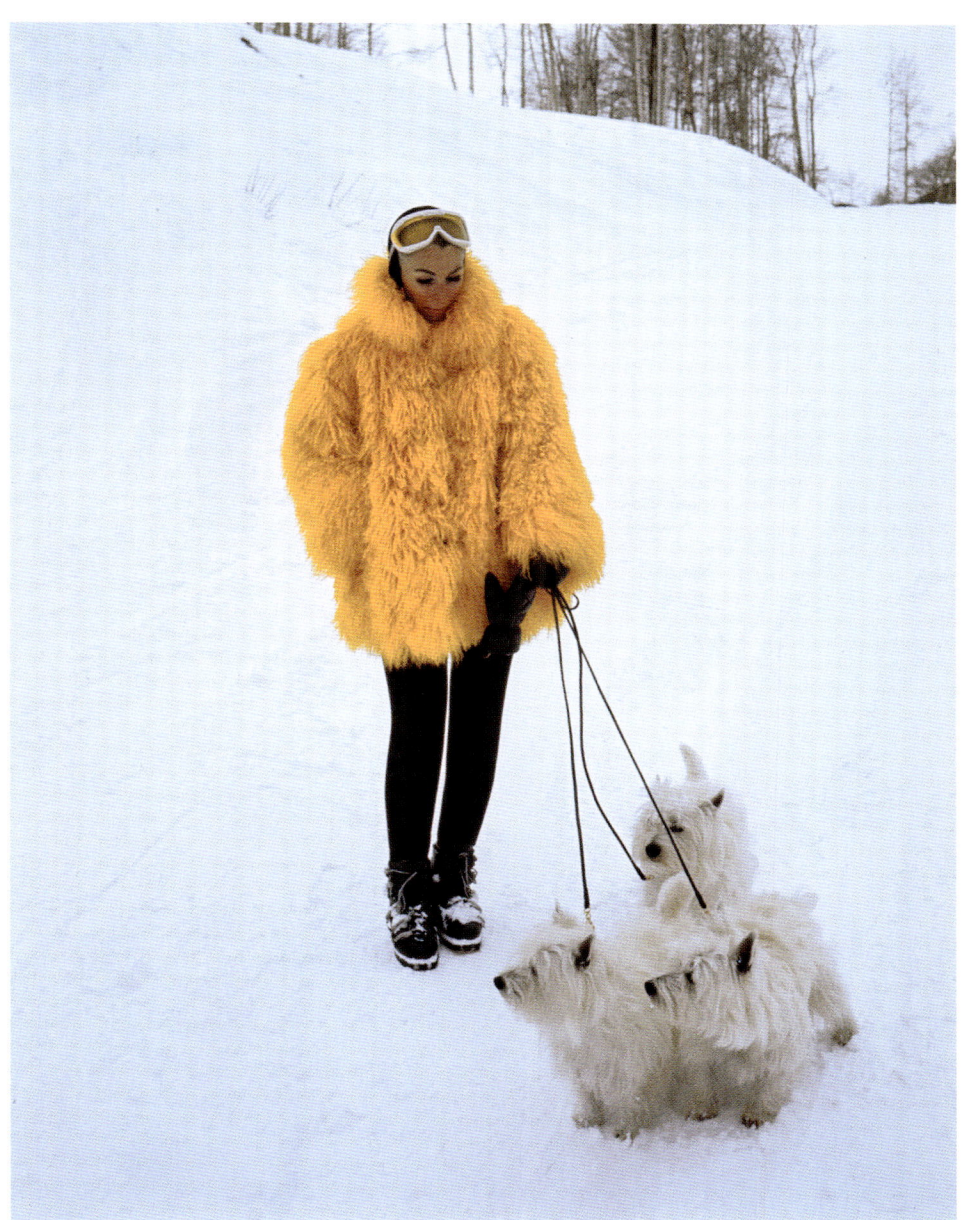

▲ Ann Bonfoey Taylor, the "grande dame" of Vail out for an après-ski stroll with her three Westies in 1967, wearing a shockingly bright Sherpa-style coat

◀ A model in Paris wearing the Emilio Pucci Winter 1967/1968 ski collection

107

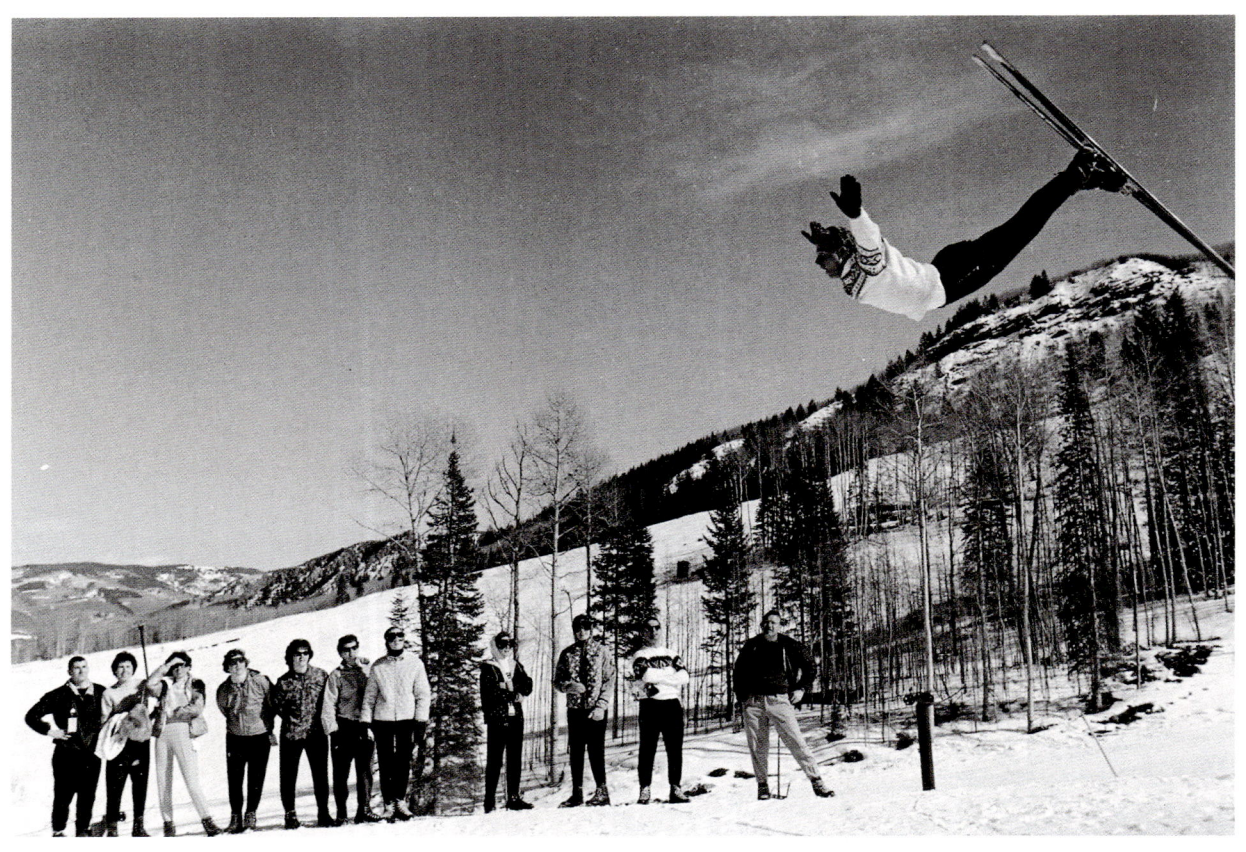

▲ A Norwegian sweater worn by one of the most famous Norwegian skiers of all time, Stein Eriksen. Eriksen not only helped change the style and form of how we ski but also became an ambassador of chic European ski fashion to resorts across America. Stein's legacy endures even today in Deer Valley, Utah, where one of the best carving runs in America and a stylish lodge bear his name.

▶ Coordinating Norwegian-style ski sweaters, 1964

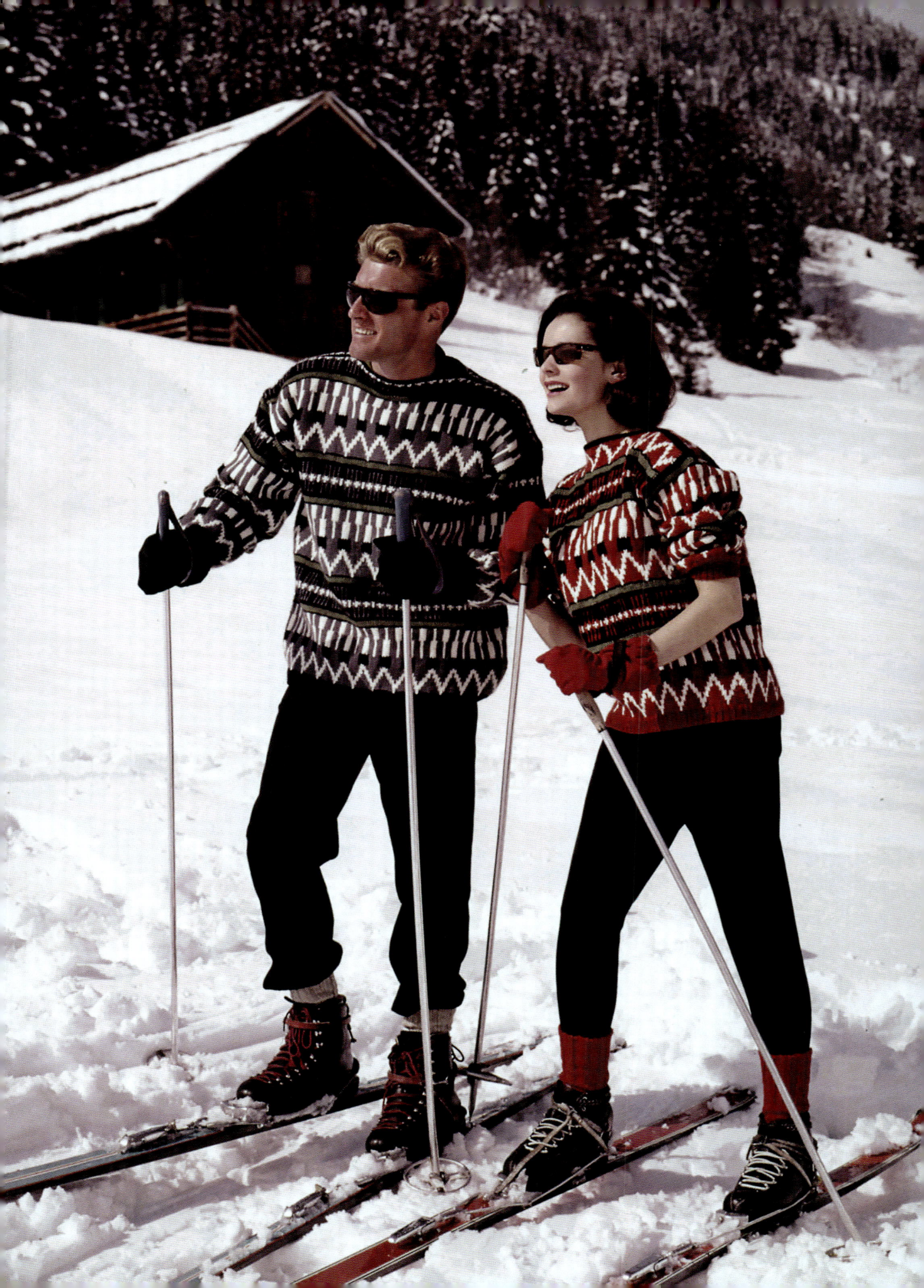

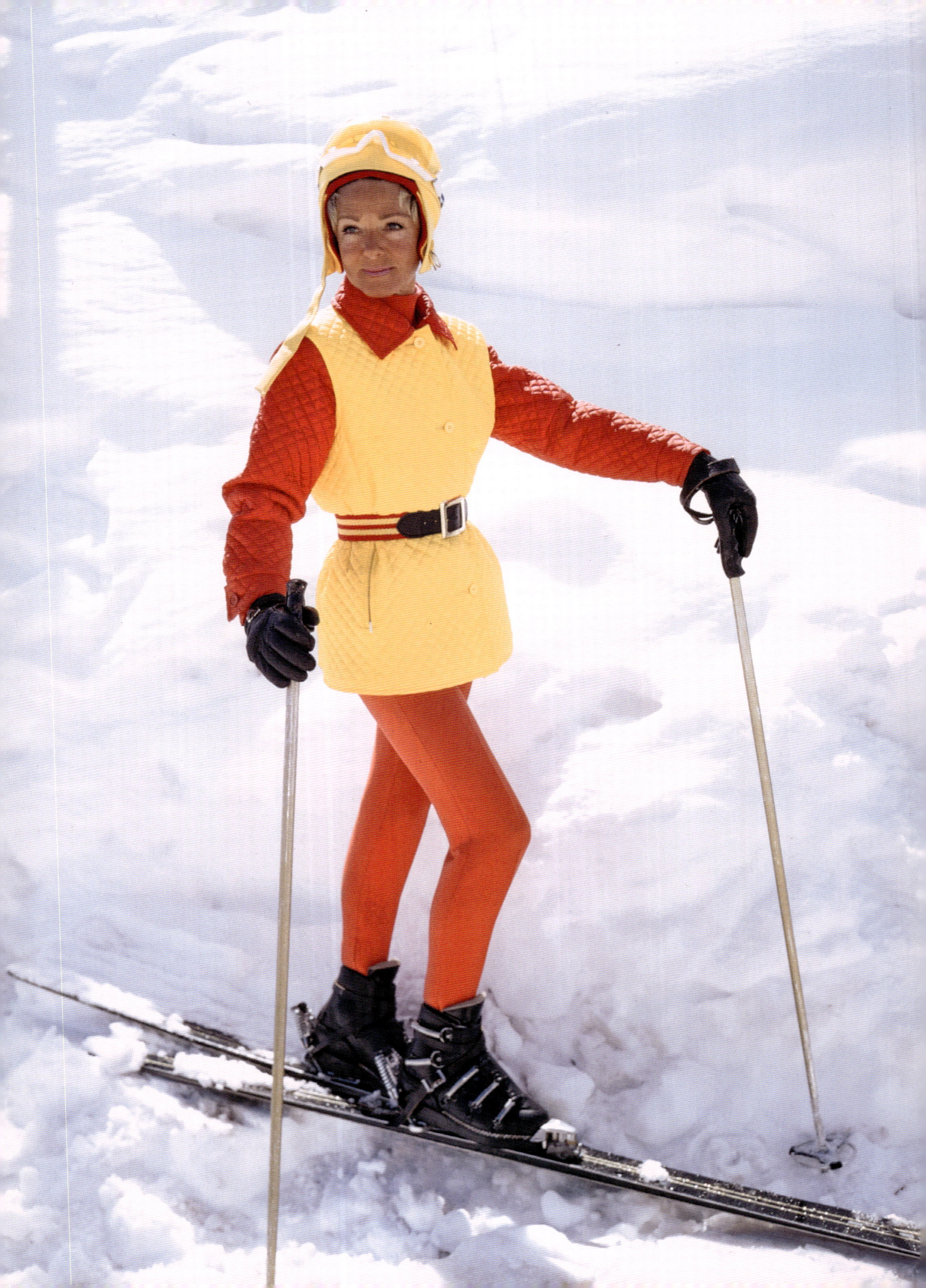

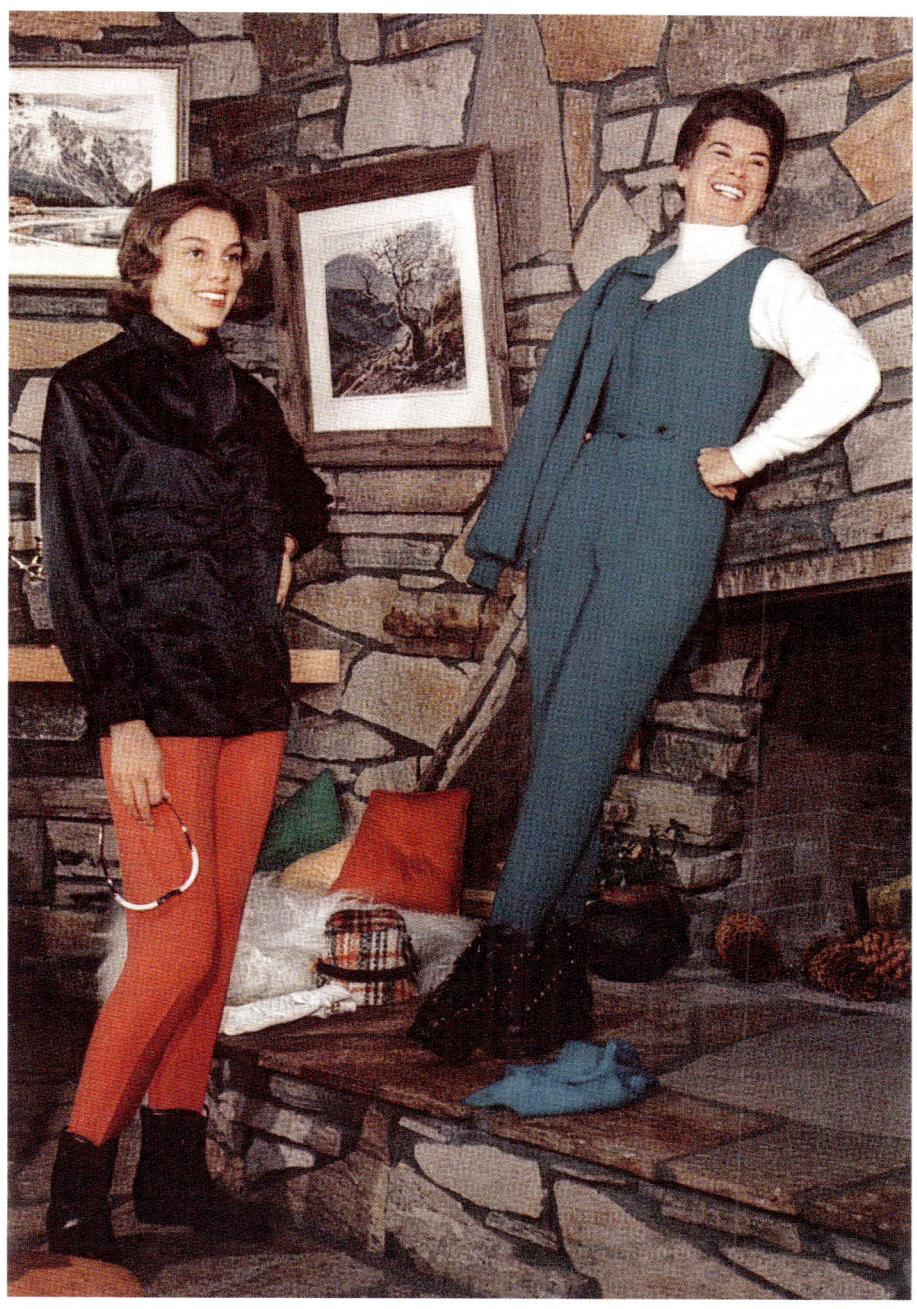

▲ Two models in vibrant stretch ski suits, circa 1960s

◀ Blanche Hauserman (who operated Vail's first skiwear boutique) wearing a brightly colored, fashion-forward ski look designed to transition from ski directly to après-ski in Vail, 1969

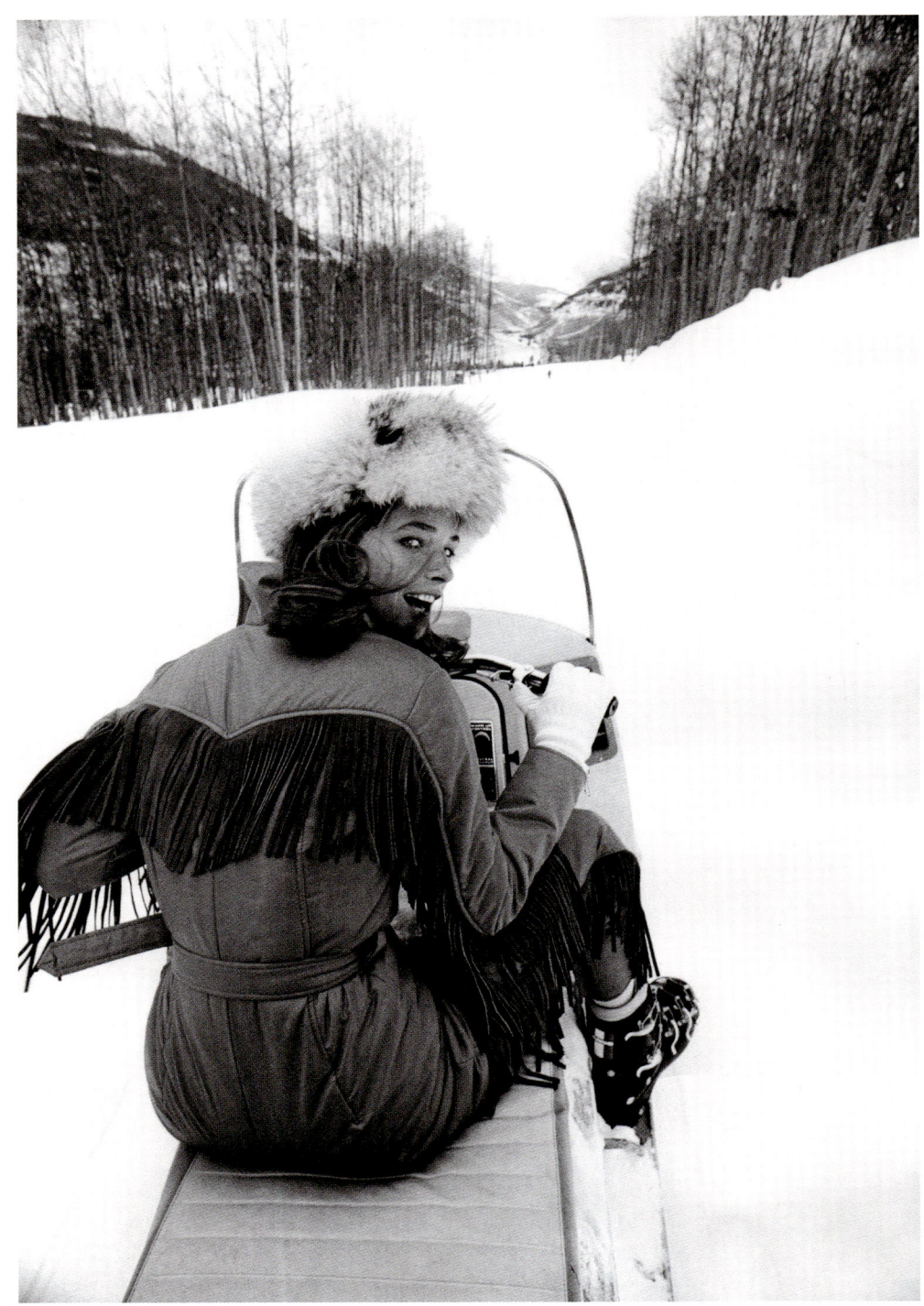

▲ Actress Charlotte Rampling wearing a western-wear inspired ski suit by White Stag on the back of a snowmobile in Colorado, 1970

▶ Colorful knitwear brought vibrant color and personal style mountainside in Gstaad, 1977.

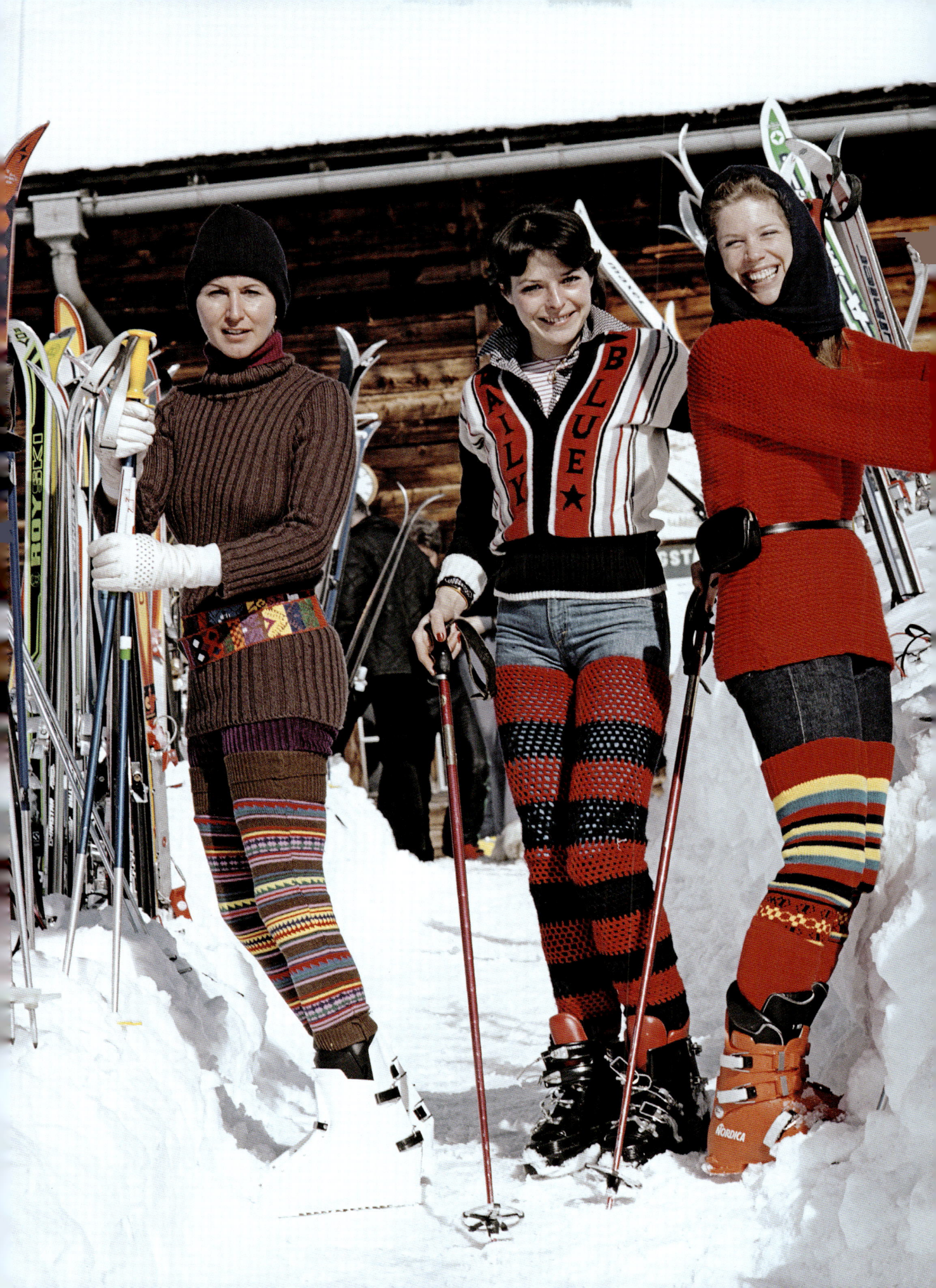

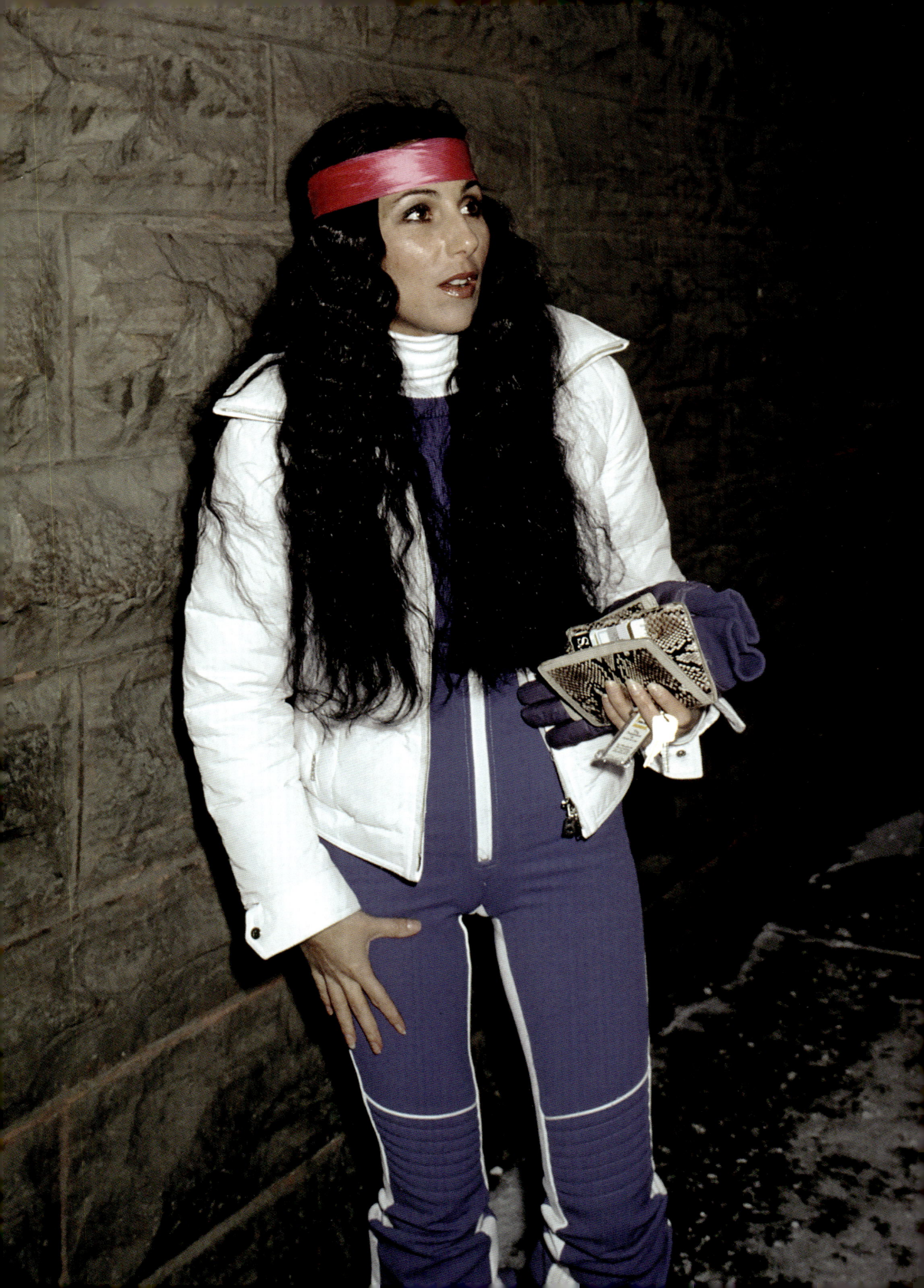

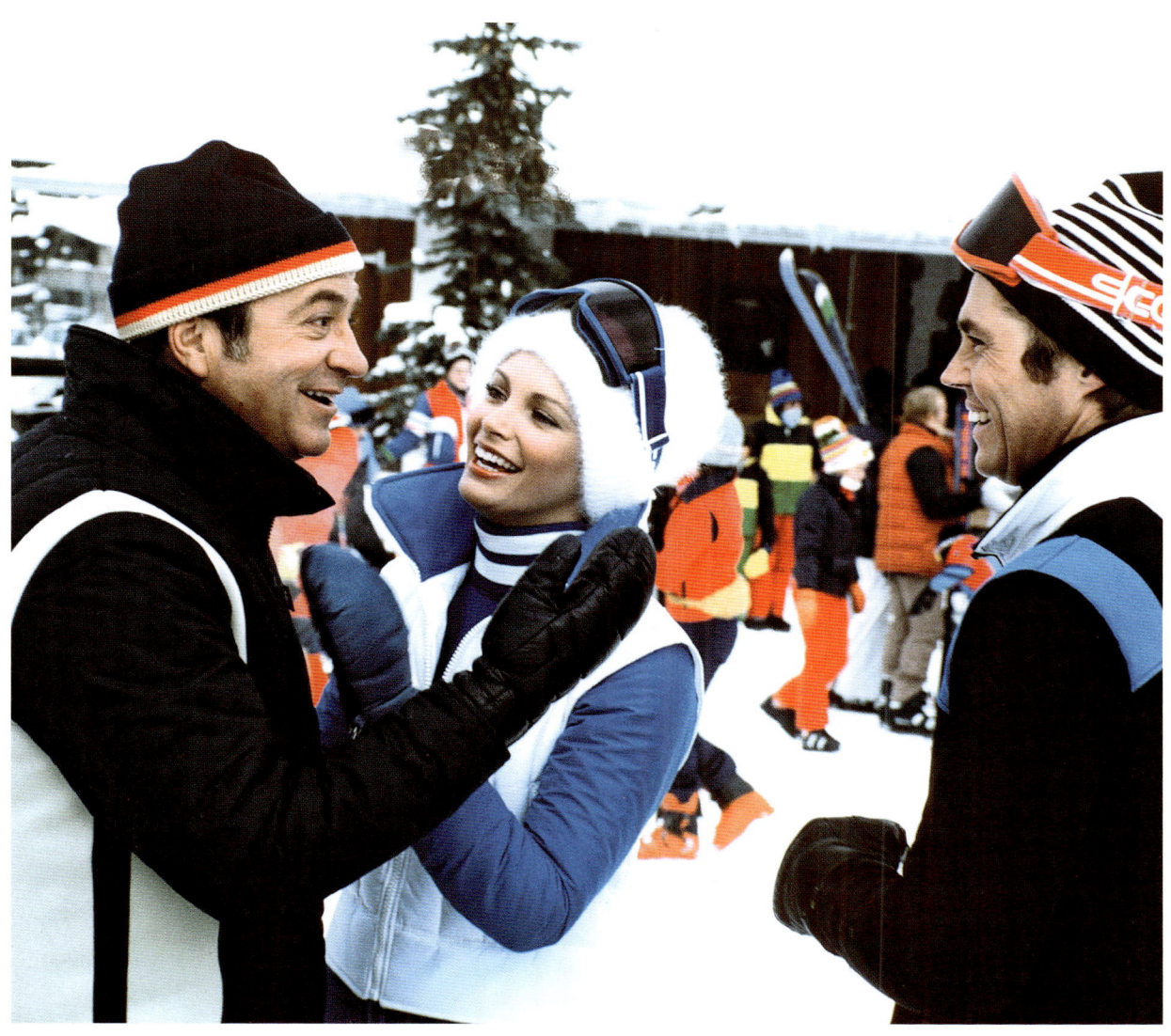

▲ Actors David Doyle (left), Jaclyn Smith, and Dennis Cole
wearing sleek sport-driven skiwear while on location in Vail
filming the 1979 "Terror on Skis" episode of *Charlie's Angels*

◀ Cher, photographed in 1977 in suspender pants
(aka salopettes) with racing stripes

SKIING AT THE MOVIES

In the golden era, skiers inspired Hollywood and Hollywood inspired the masses, with films such as the James Bond classic *For Your Eyes Only*, *Charade*, and *Downhill Racer* projecting the uniquely iconic style of skiing onto screens around the world.

▼ Roger Moore as James Bond in *For Your Eyes Only* (1981), with Lynn-Holly Johnson wearing a full-body stretch ski suit

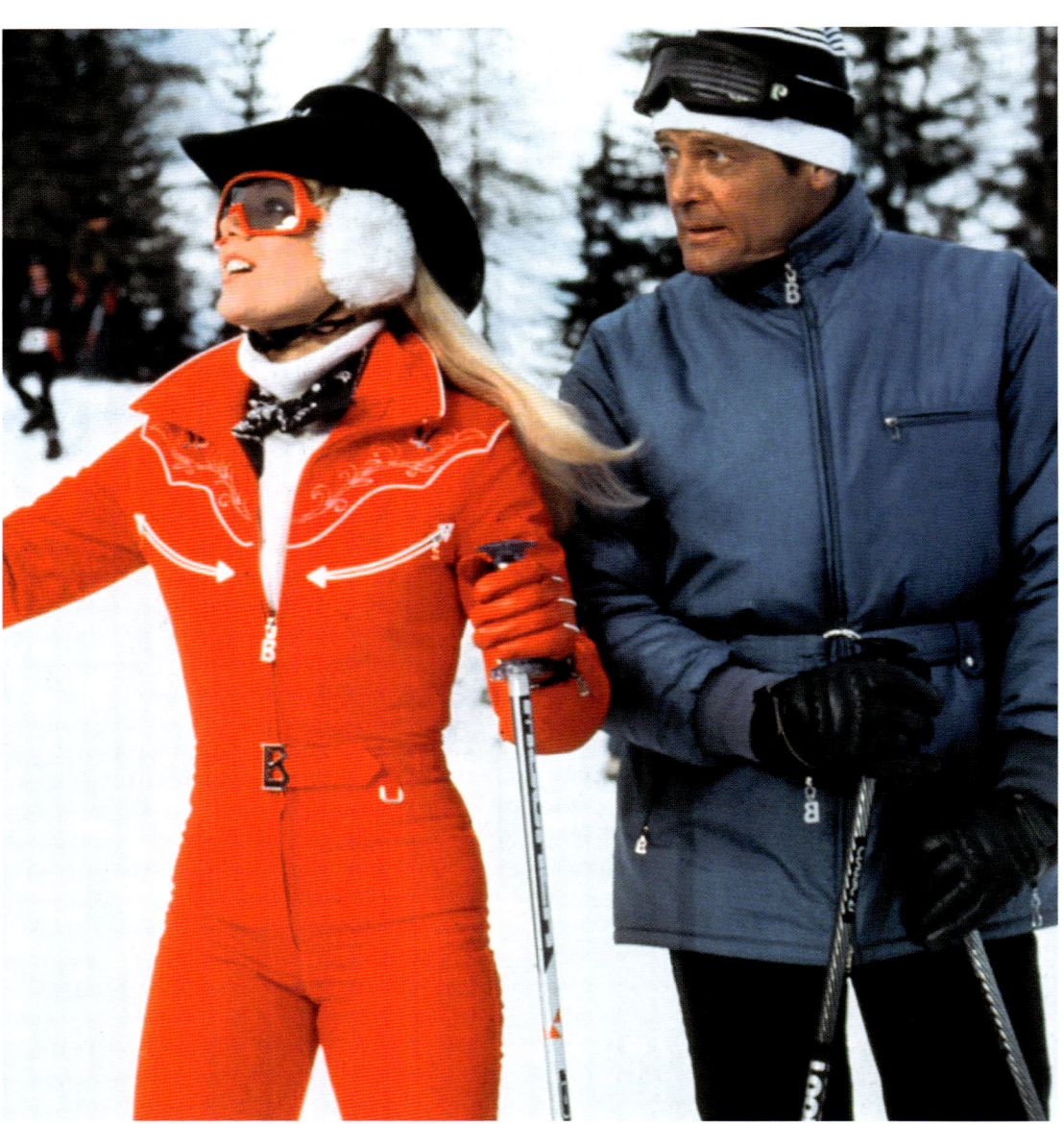

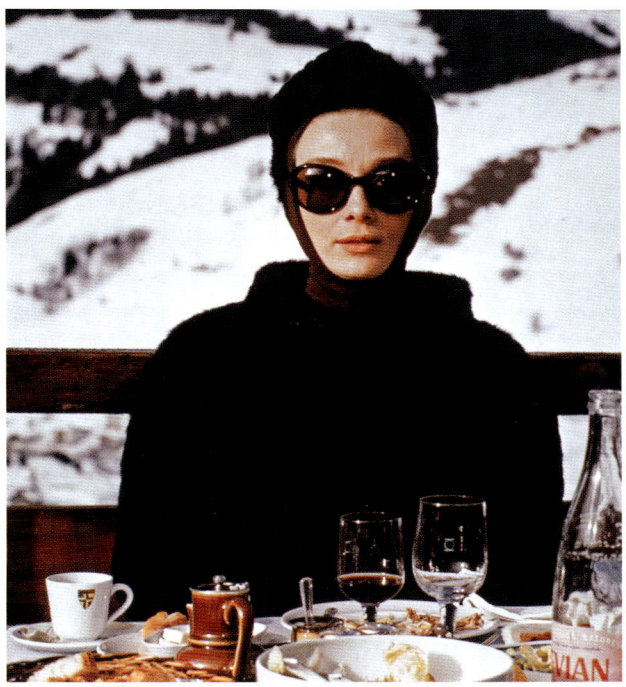

▲ In *Charade* (1963), Audrey Hepburn brought her iconic style to the French Alps, setting a new standard for après-ski fashion.

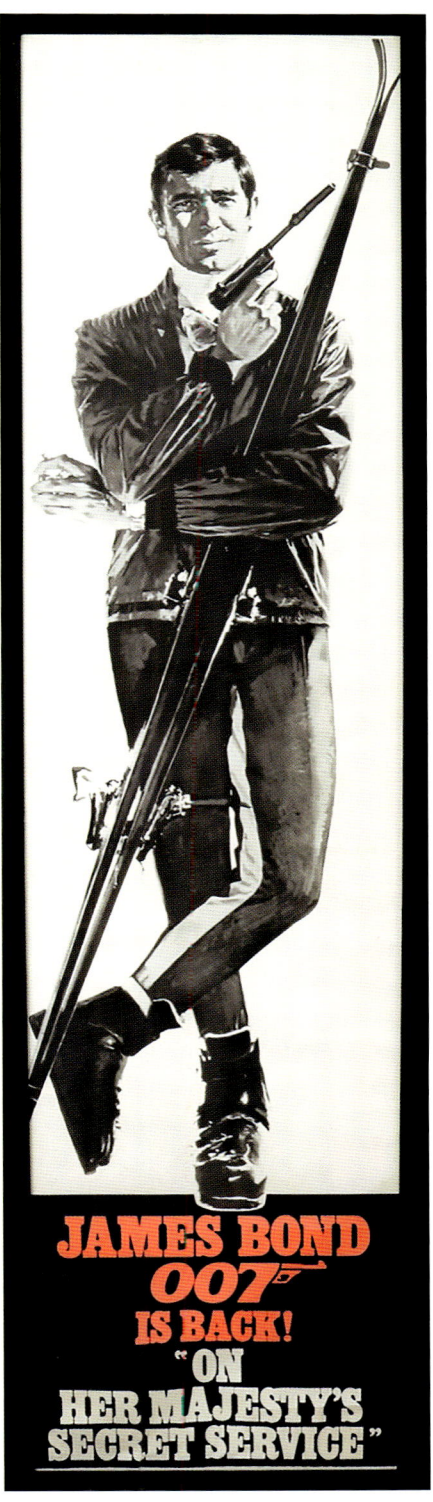

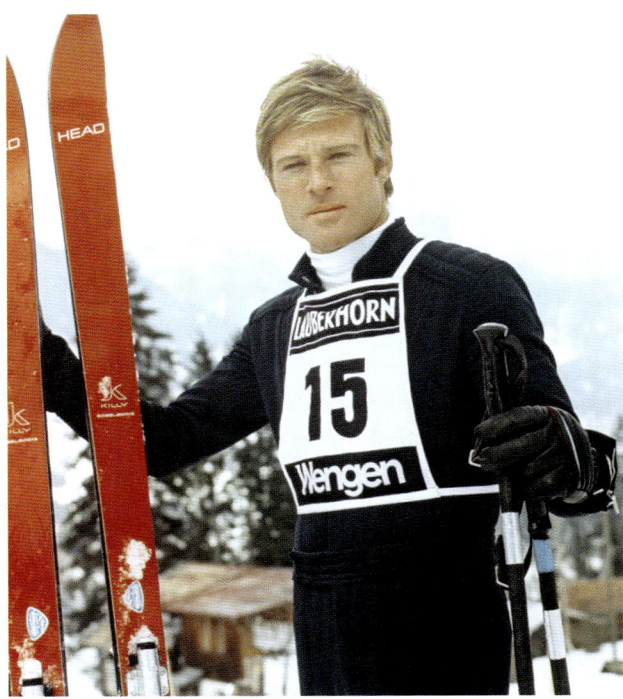

▲ The film *Downhill Racer* (1969) and its star, Robert Redford, meshed rugged American ski town fashion with speed-driven, sleek racing style and chic European glamour.

▲ *On Her Majesty's Secret Service* (1969), starring George Lazenby, was the first of many Bond films to include ski scenes.

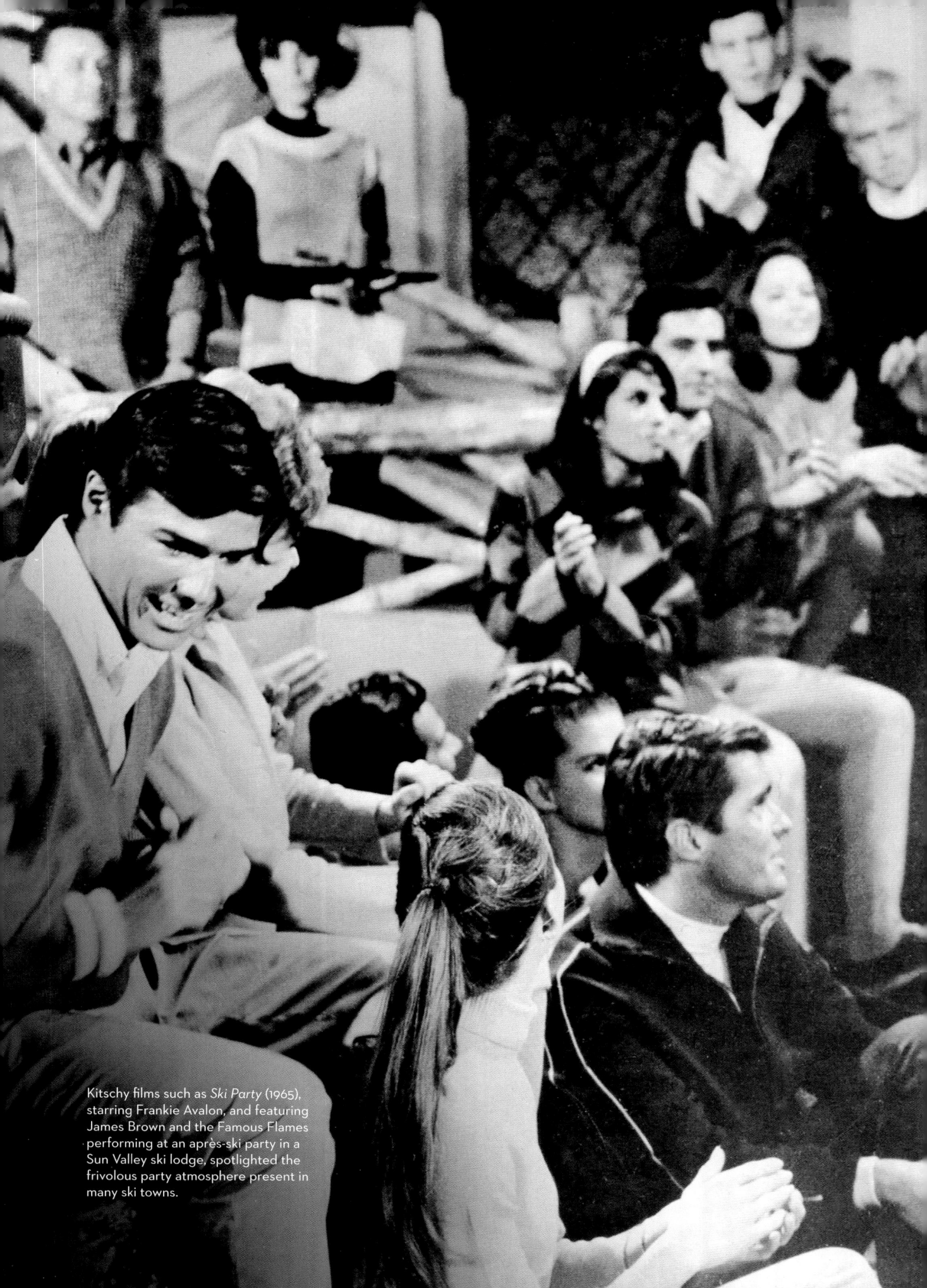

Kitschy films such as *Ski Party* (1965), starring Frankie Avalon, and featuring James Brown and the Famous Flames performing at an après-ski party in a Sun Valley ski lodge, spotlighted the frivolous party atmosphere present in many ski towns.

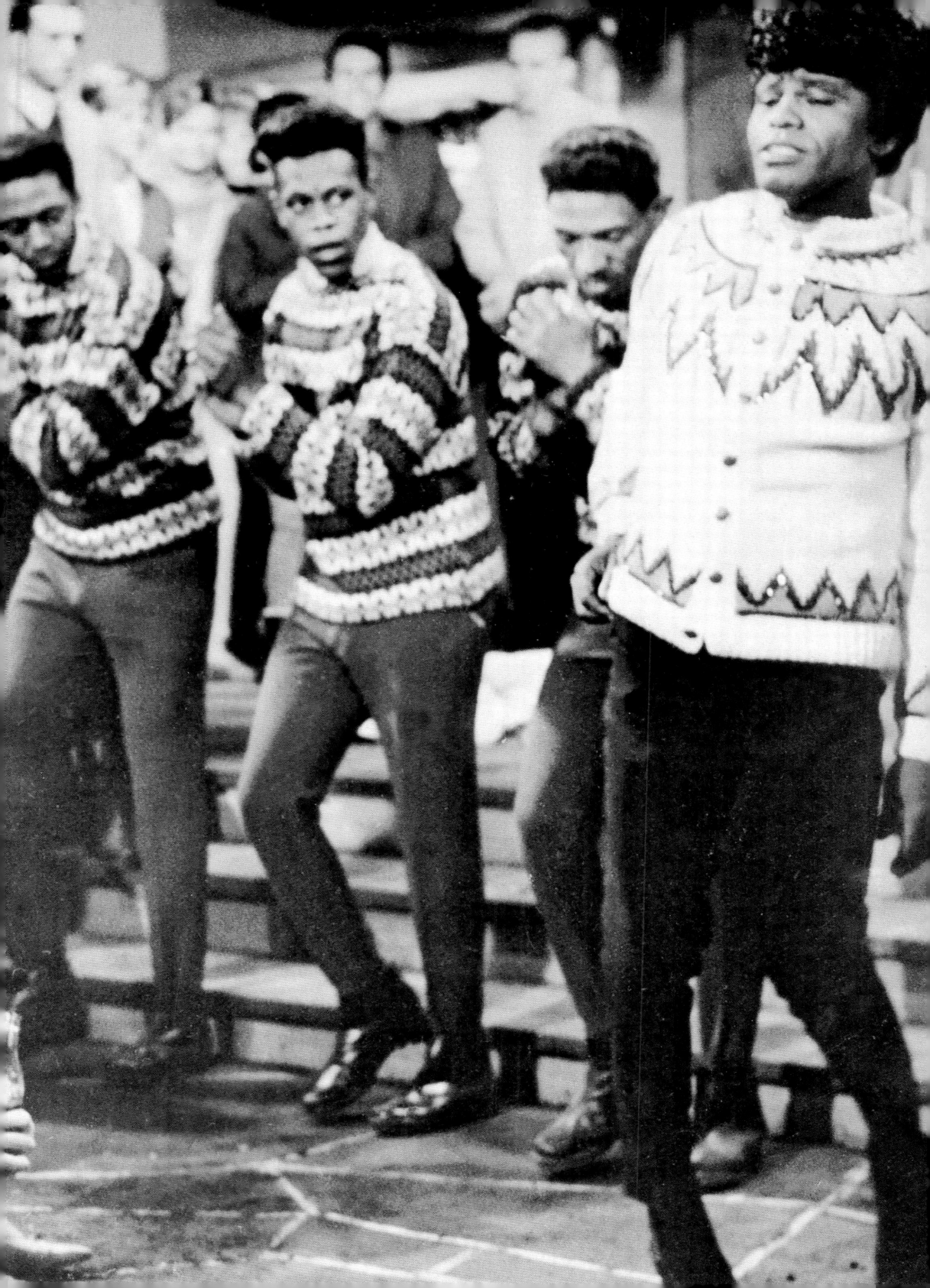

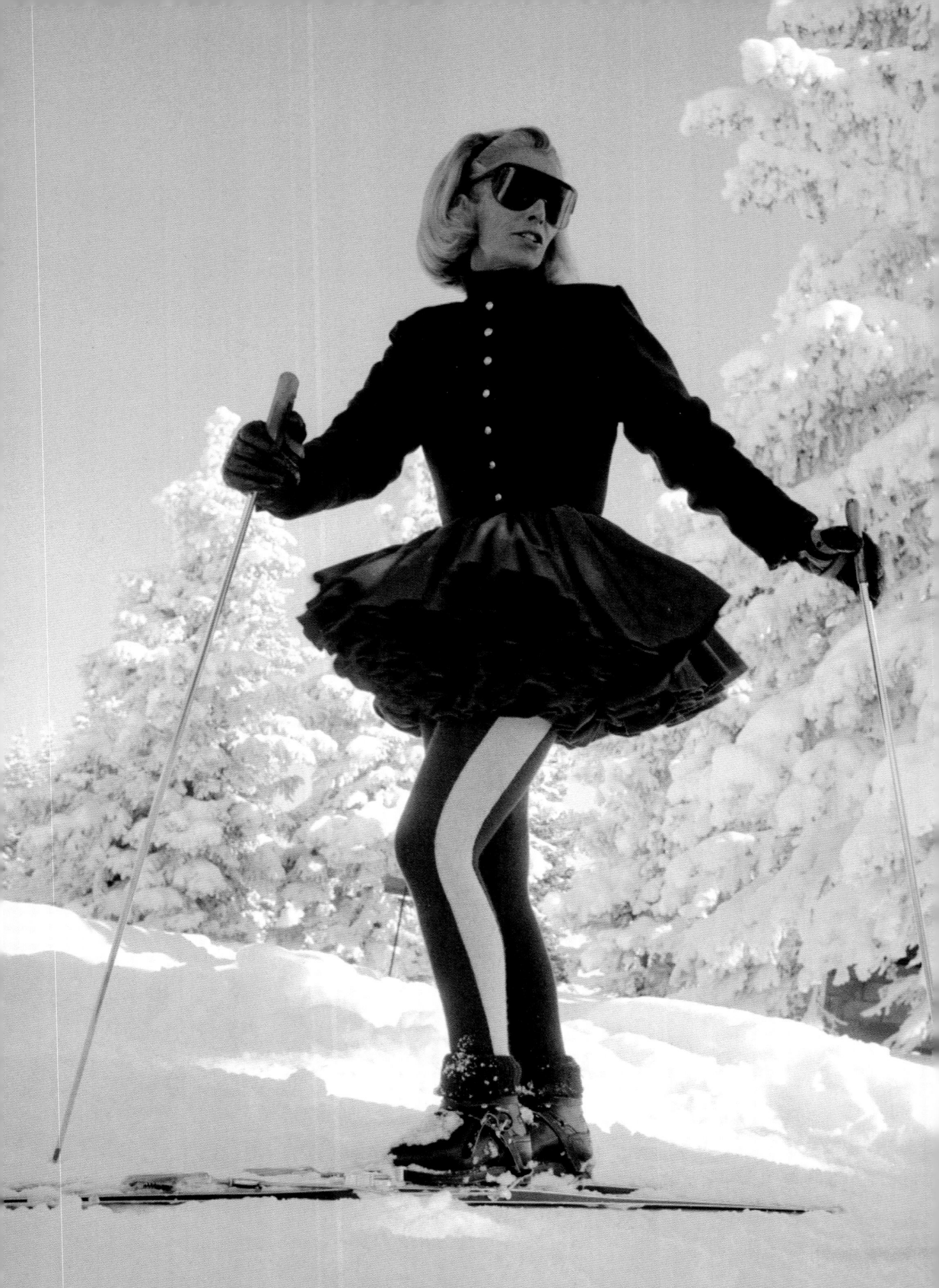

A Personal
Point of View

—

Individual style inspired by different ski regions began to emerge in the 1960s and '70s. A laid-back California look developed on the slopes of Lake Tahoe and Mammoth Mountain; Western flair mixed with gonzo oddball looks in Aspen and across the Rockies; and glamorous fashion inspired by the runway took hold in Gstaad, St. Moritz, and Cortina d'Ampezzo. People had always dressed for ski and après-ski, but in this era, personal taste and regional fashions infused ski style with a fresh perspective.

◄ Ann Bonfoey Taylor, seen here in 1964, had a fearless fashion sensibility and a major influence on the fashion scene at Vail.

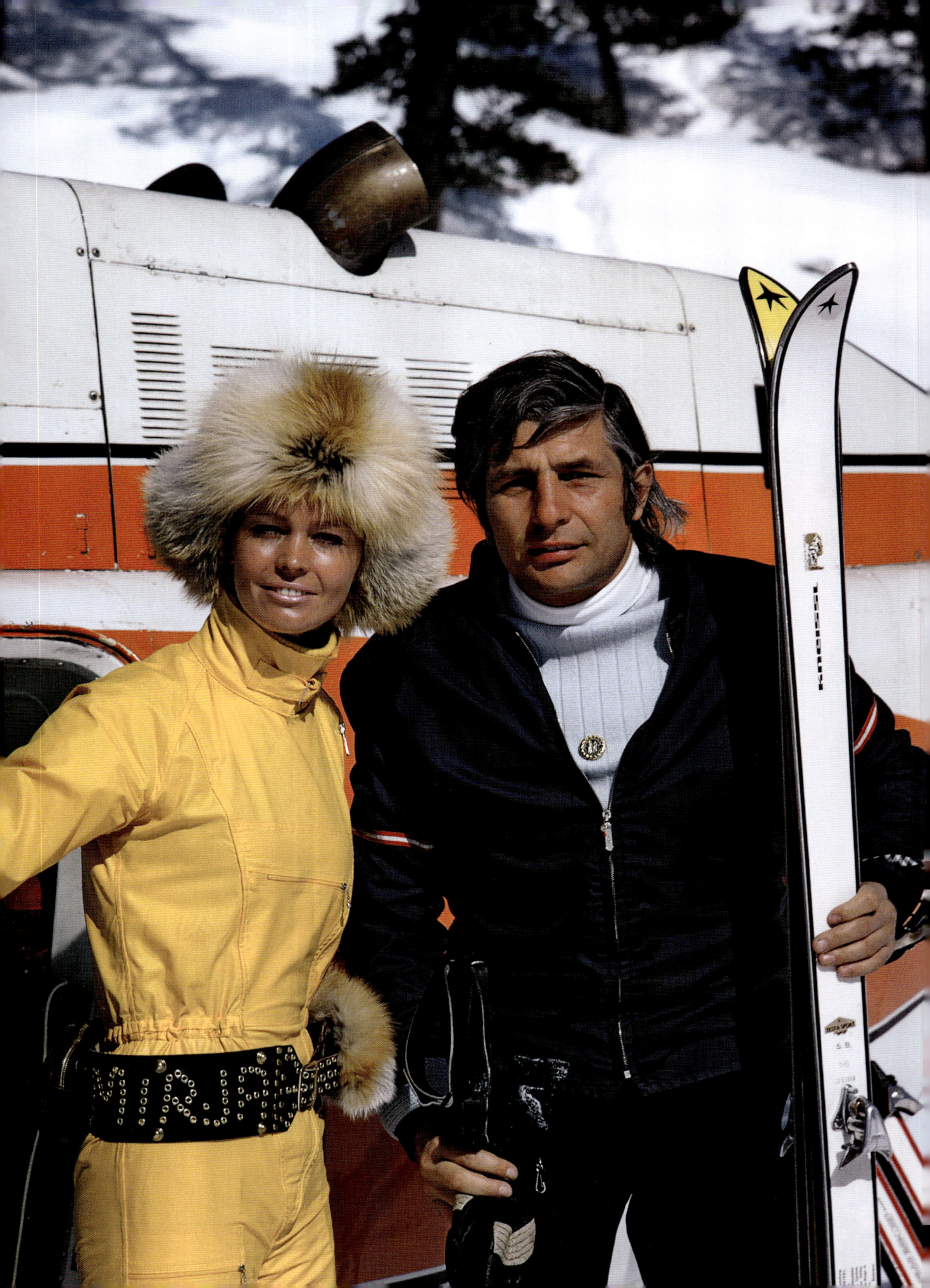

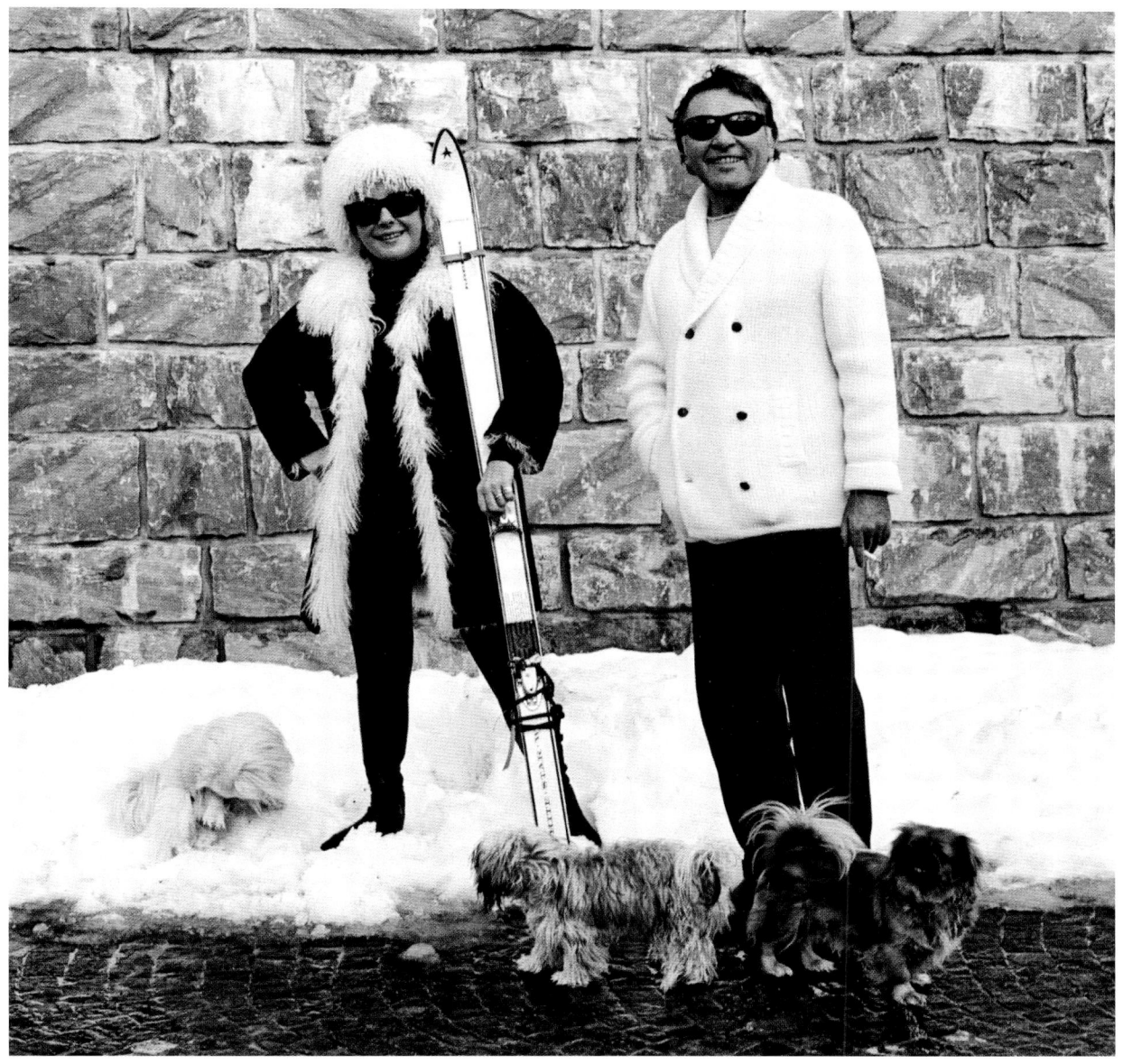

▲ Elizabeth Taylor and her husband Richard Burton on a ski vacation in 1967

◄ Model Mirja Sachs, wearing a bright monochromatic ski suit accessorized with a personalized belt, with her husband Gunter in St. Moritz in 1970

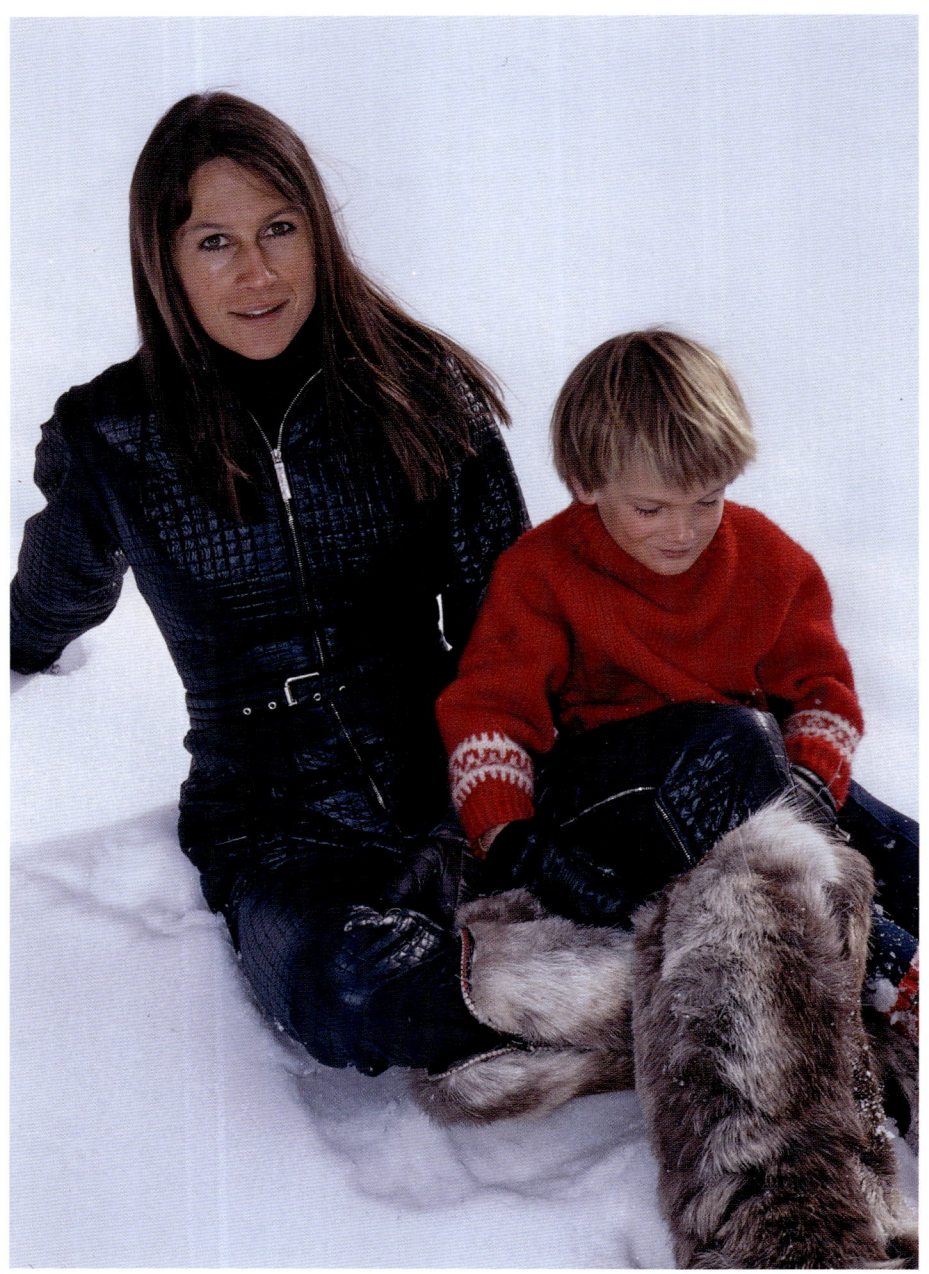

▲ Aspen local Meta Burden in a one-piece ski suit paired with oversized boots—a look that would still be perfect for après-ski today—photographed in Aspen with her son W. Douglas Burden III, 1970

▶ Casual, mountain-chic après-ski style on actress Jane Birkin and singer-songwriter Serge Gainsbourg as they go for a stroll through French resort Avoriaz, 1976

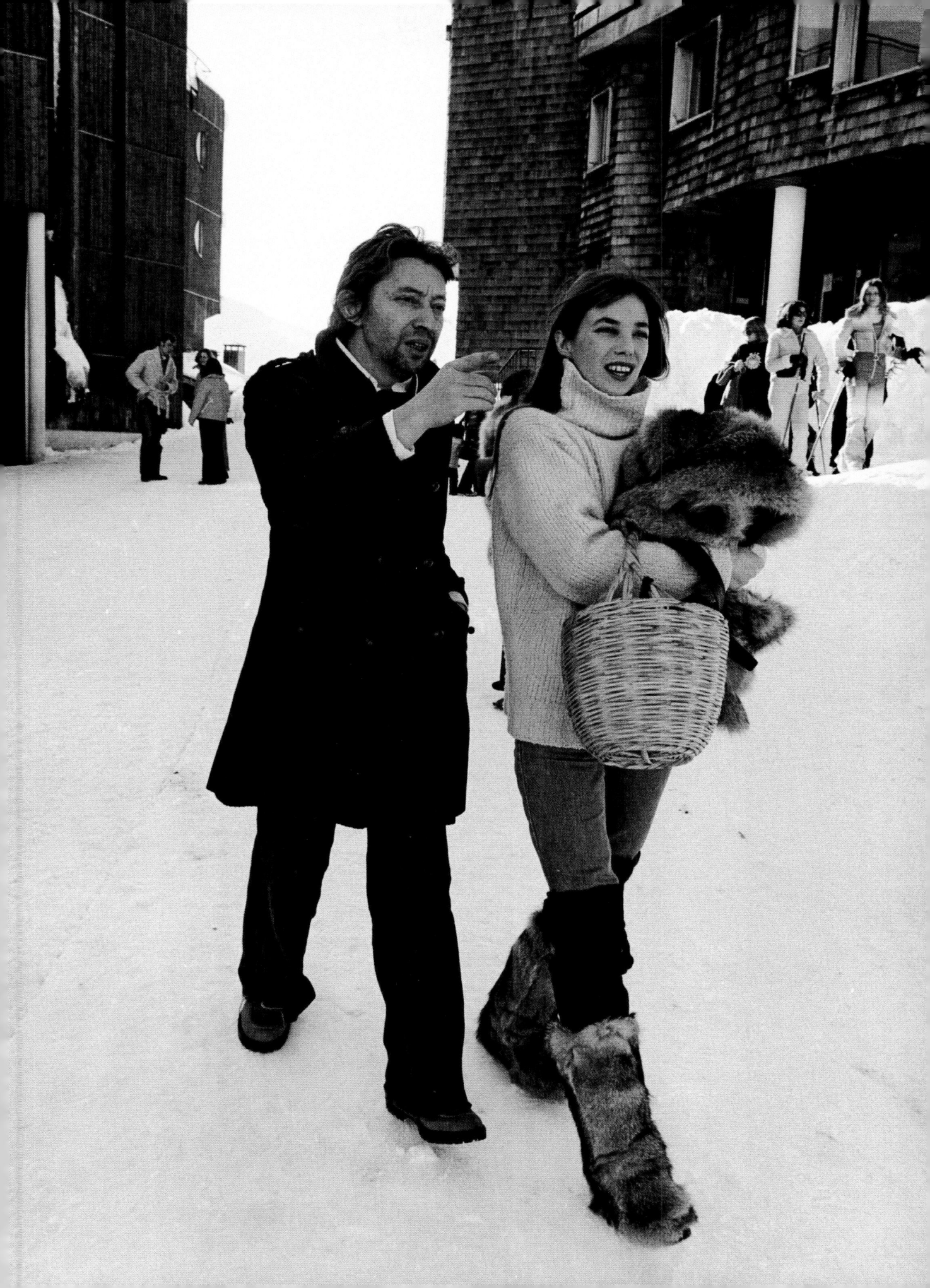

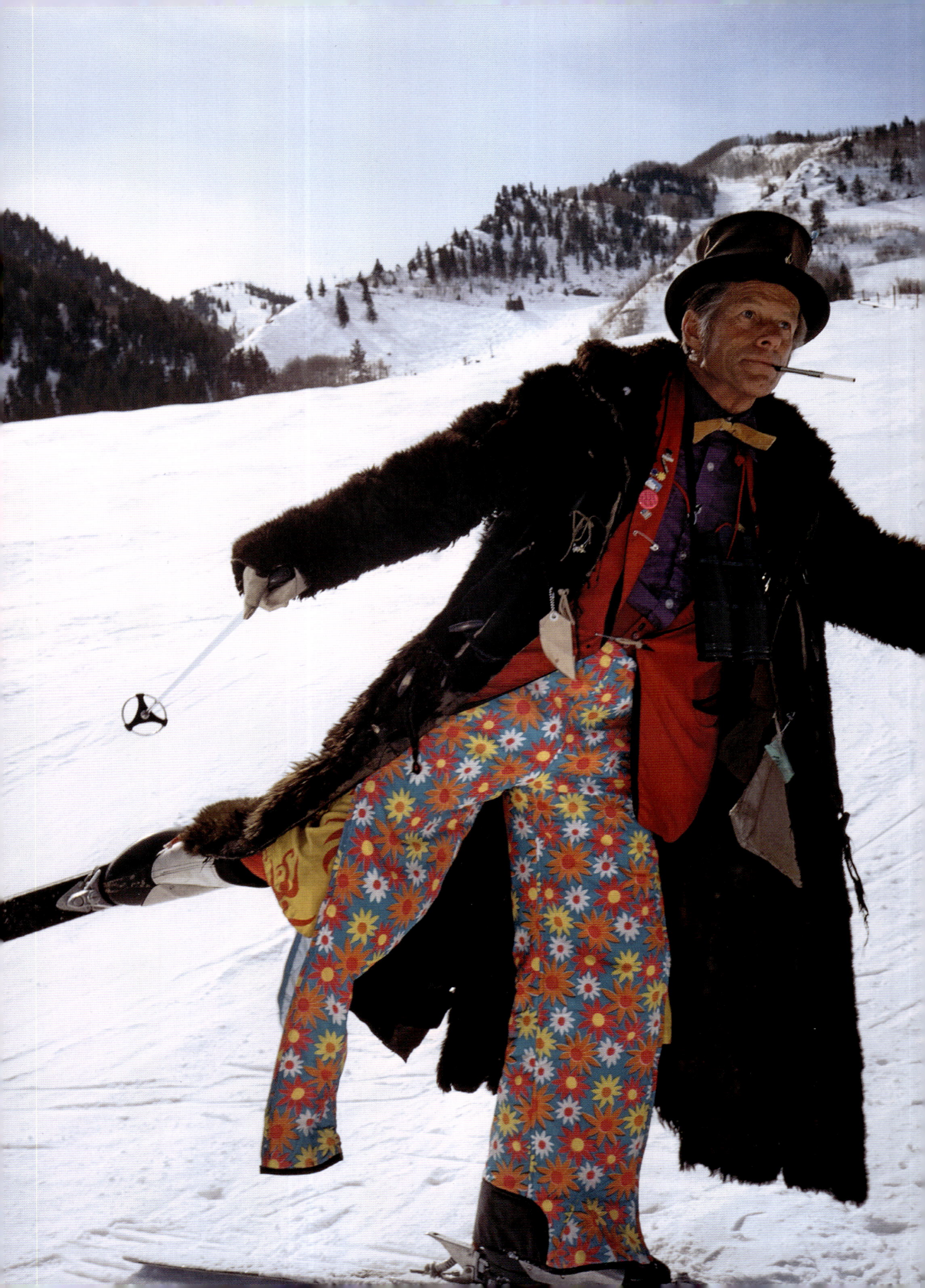

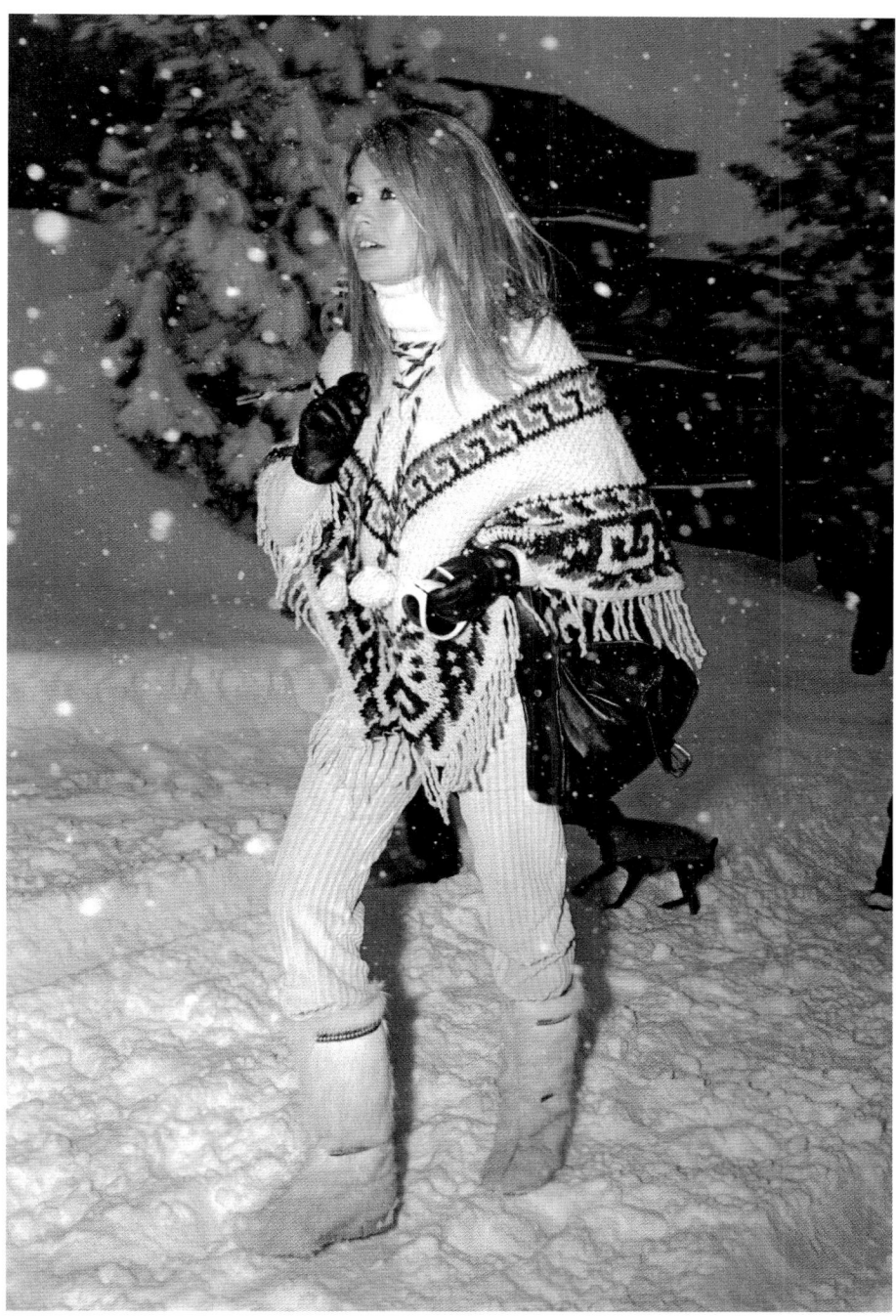

▲ Brigitte Bardot wearing a knit poncho and furry boots, circa 1960 in France

◀ Eccentricity on skis, self-proclaimed "clown prince" Ralph Jackson was a local legend in Aspen in the 1970s.

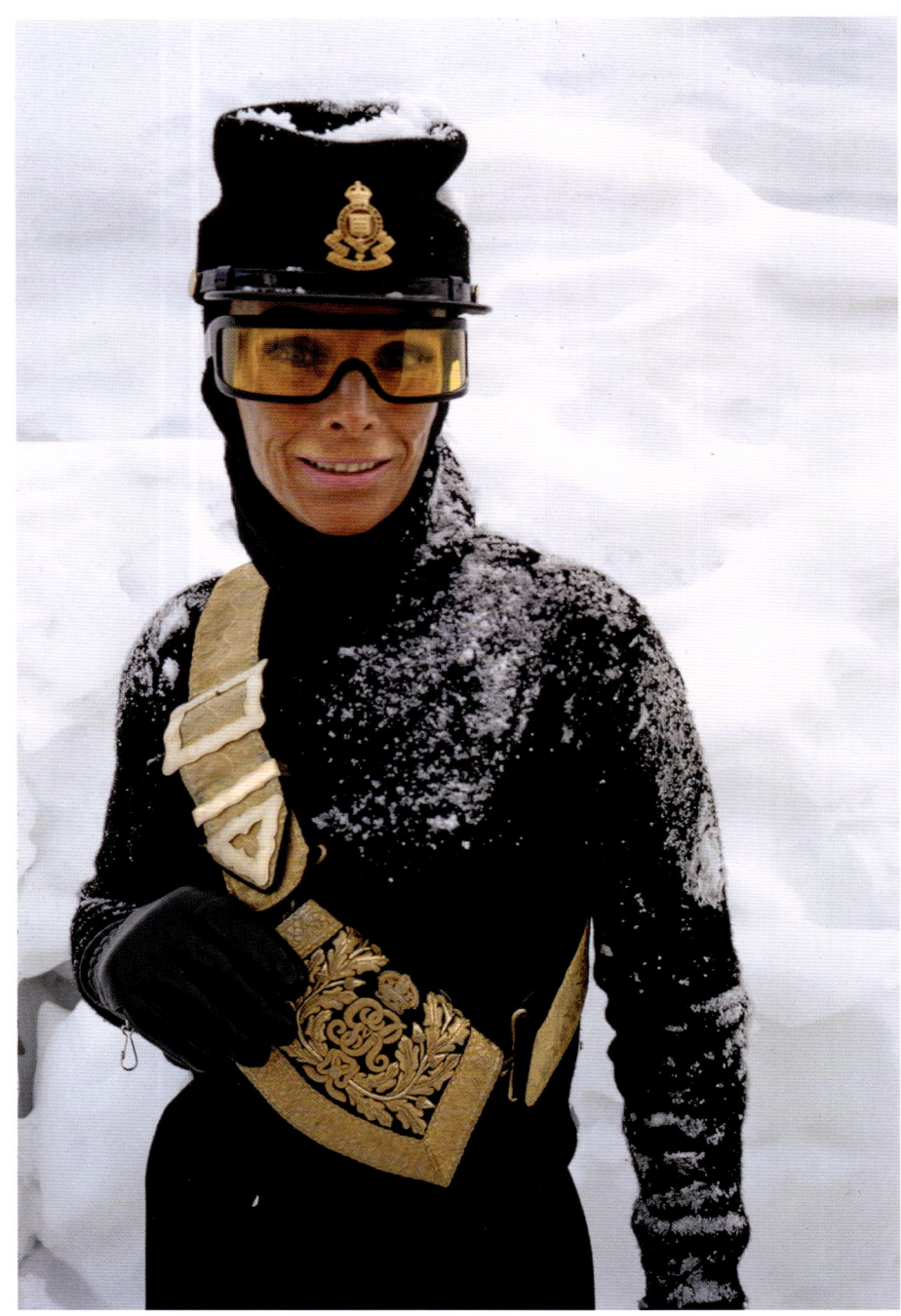

▲ Long before the term "fanny pack" was even coined, style maven Ann Bonfoey Taylor had the good fashion sense to sling a waist belt bag as a crossbody.

▶ A distinctly Californian skier at Mammoth Mountain in 1976

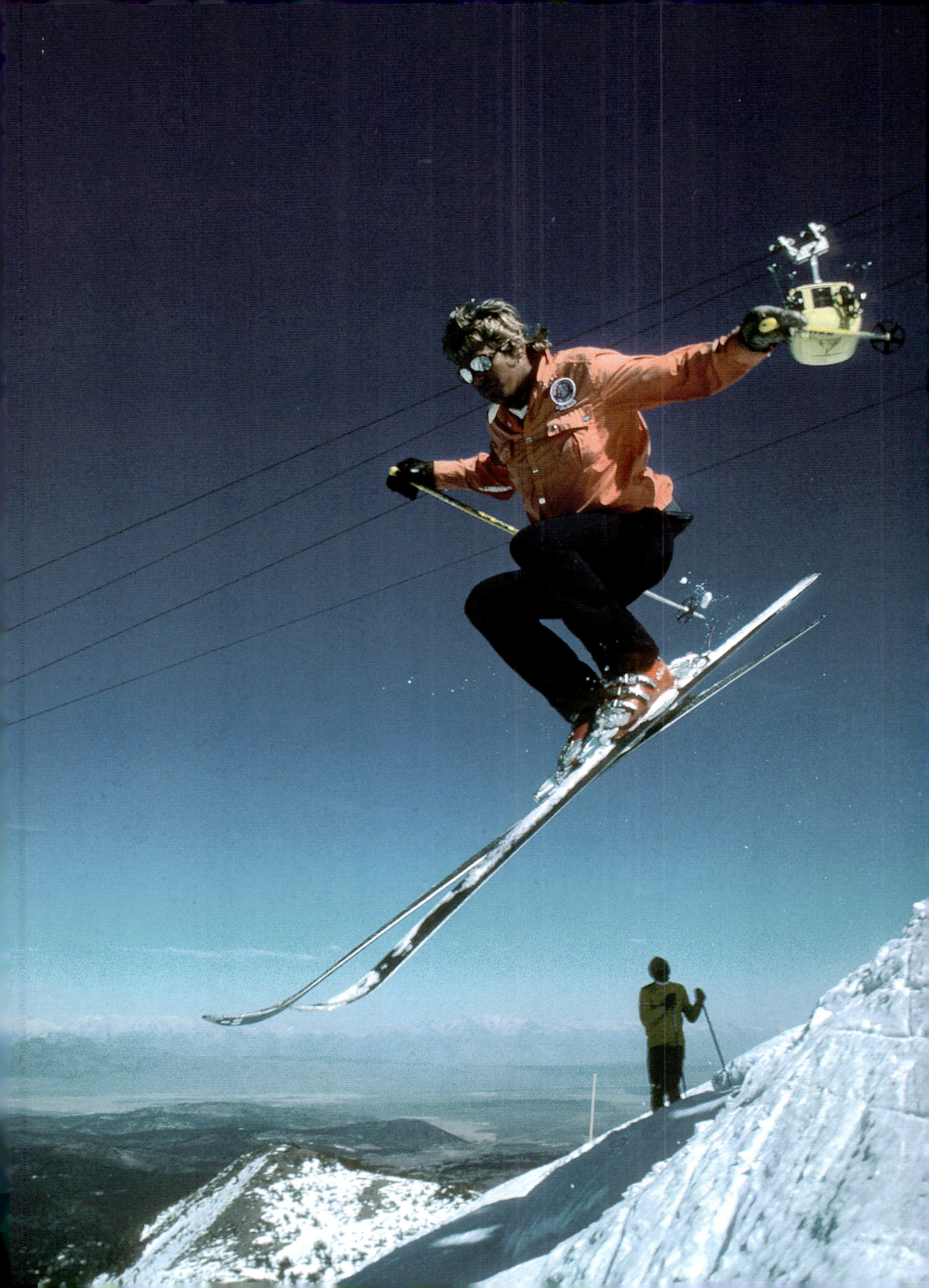

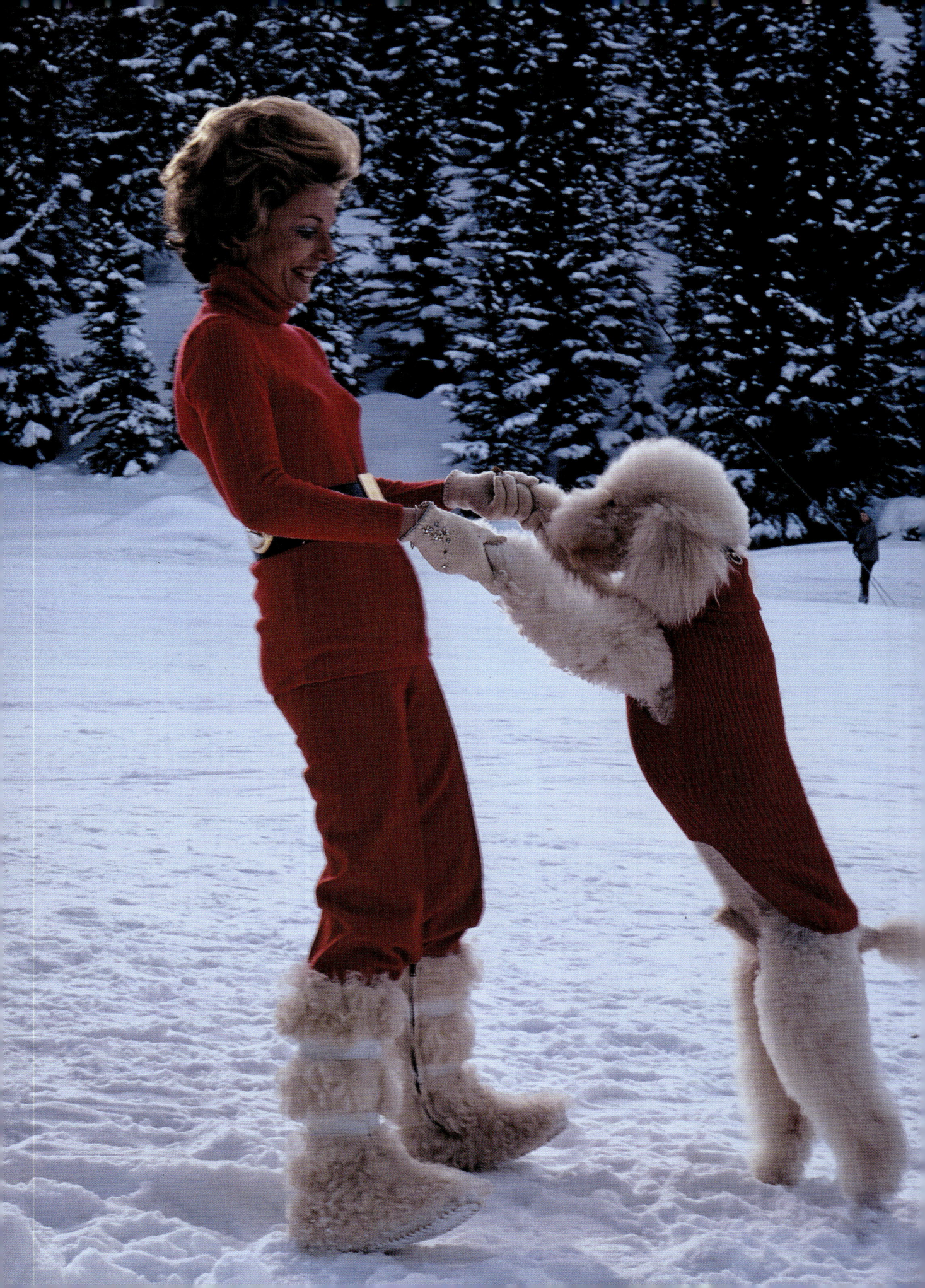

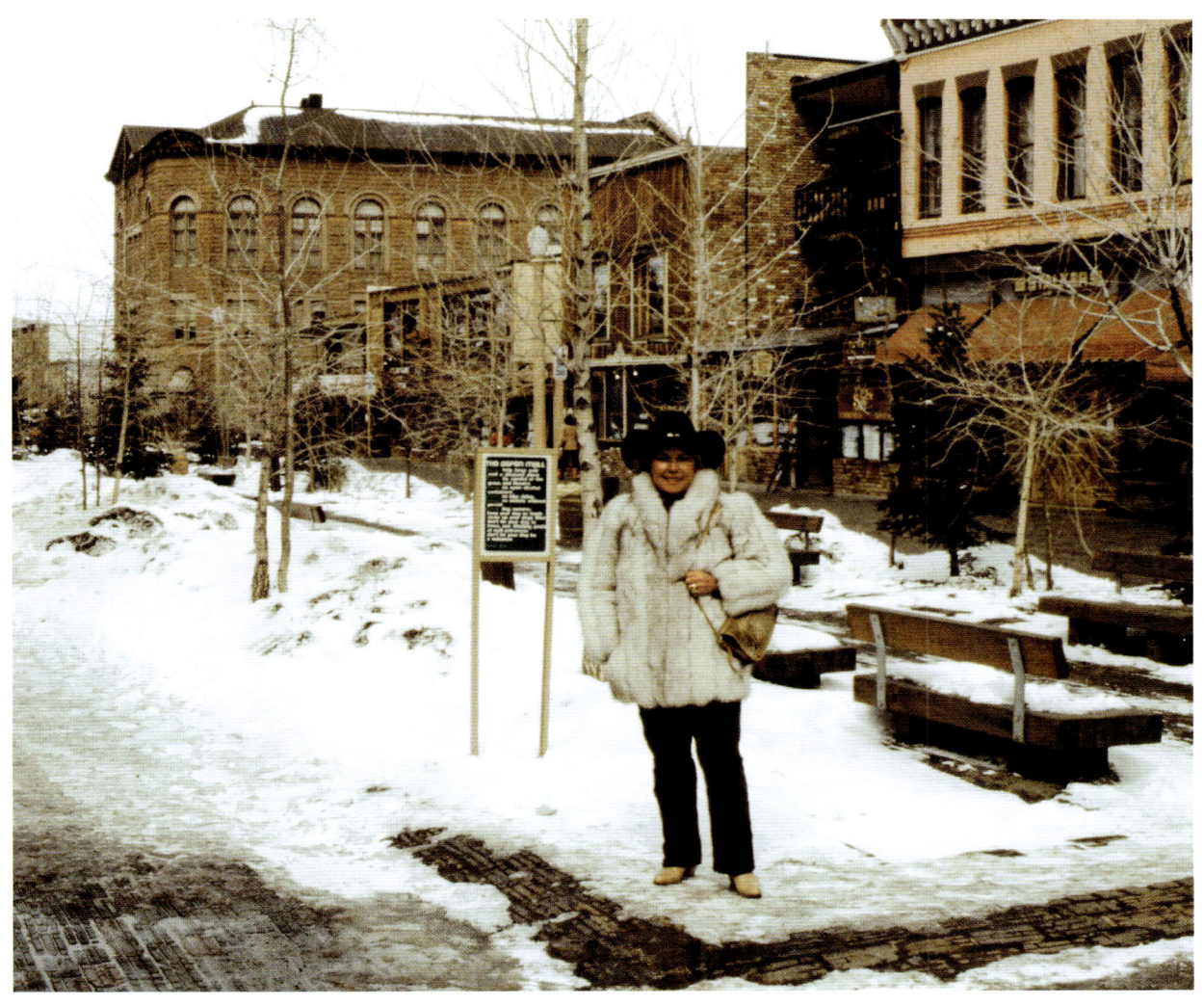

▲ Like many US ski towns out West, Aspen's modern history began with its establishment as a rugged mountain mining town. The Western aesthetic has persisted throughout the decades since, complete with cowboy boots and hats, as seen here in 1975.

◀ Socialite Annik Schäffler coordinating her après-ski look with her furry companion in Courchevel, 1970

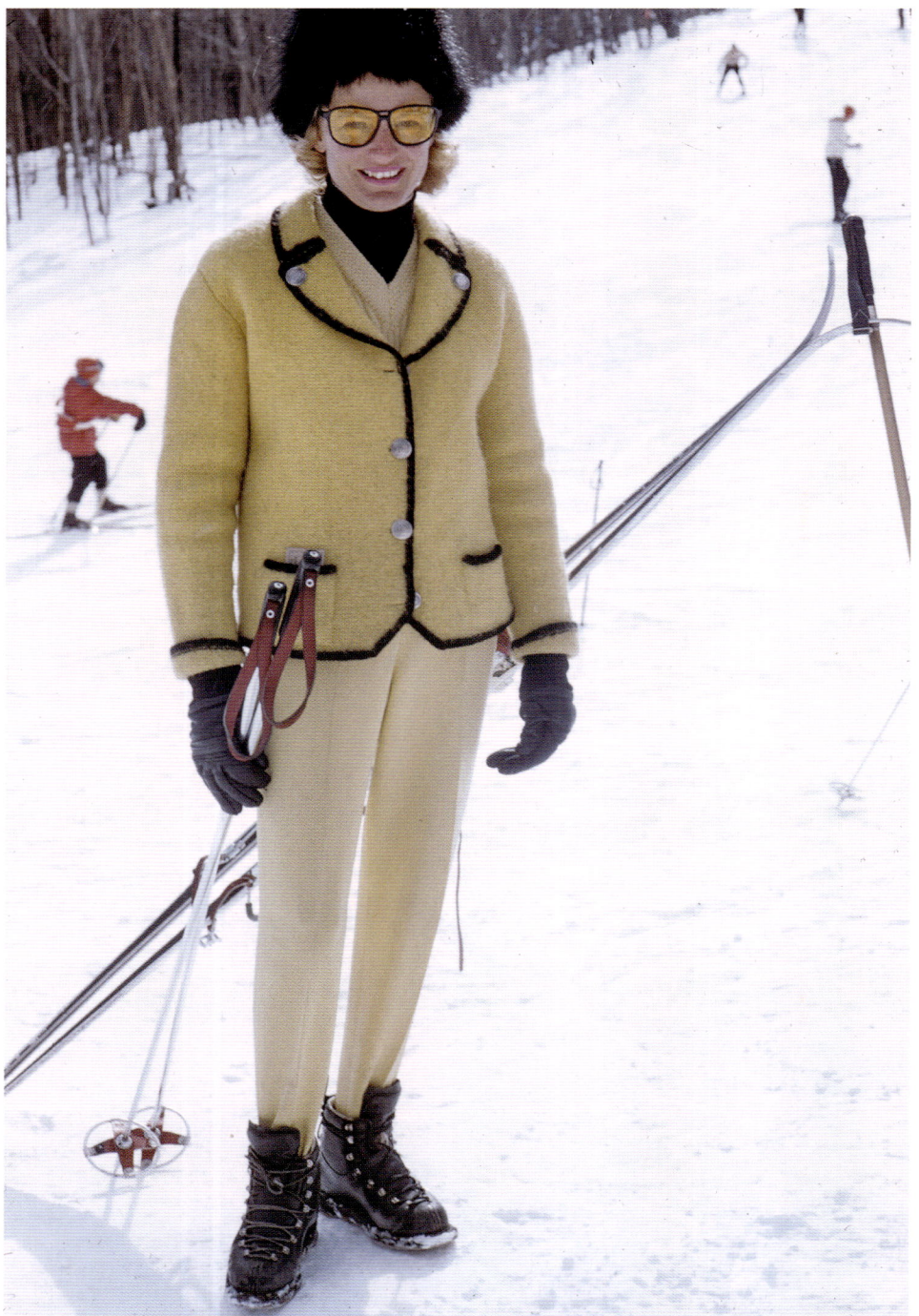

◂ Quirky northeast ski fashion at Sugarbush, 1959

▸ Former US Ski Team member and Olympian Suzy Chaffee displaying her superpowers and ski fashion influence in Vail, 1969

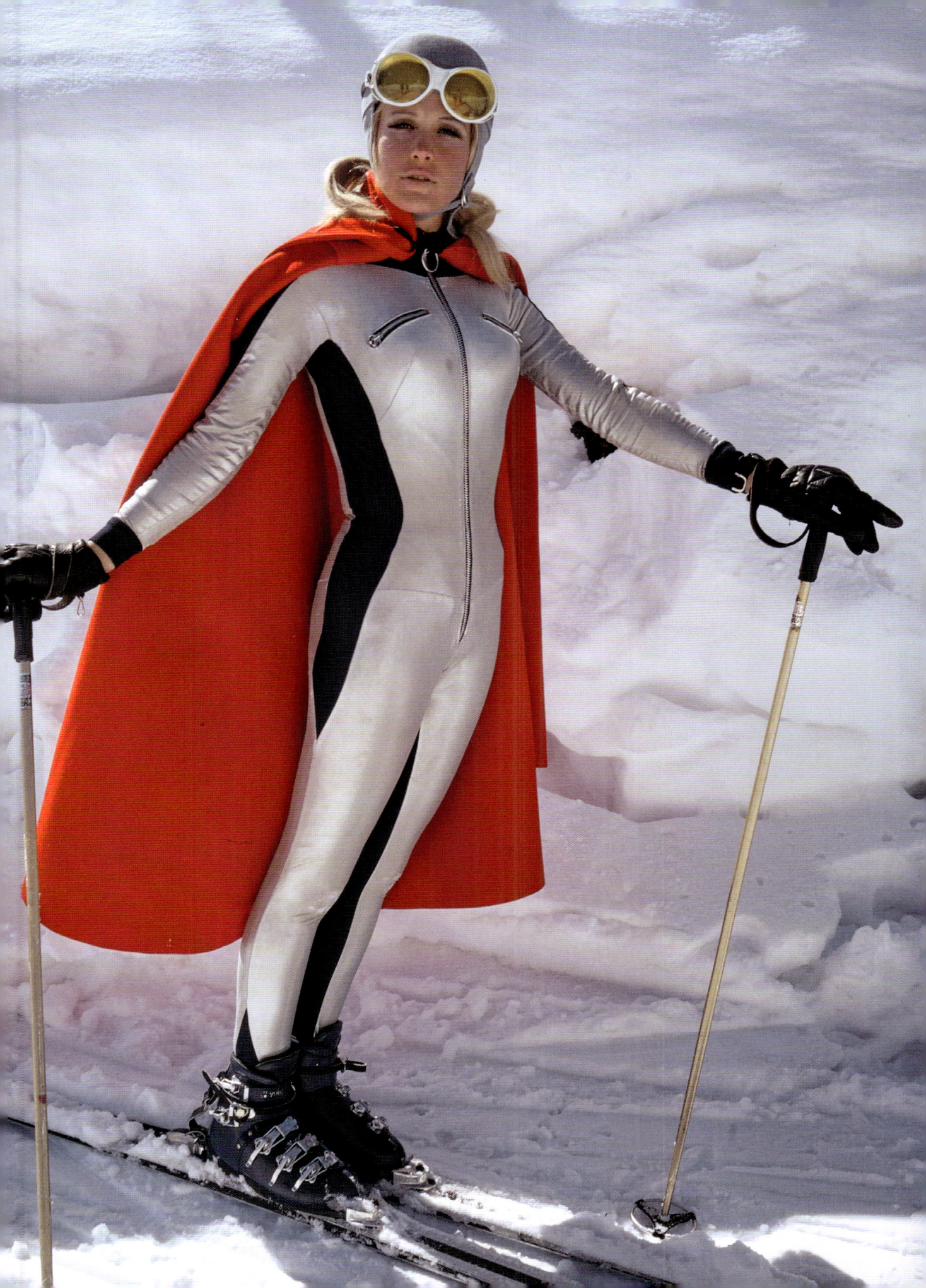

FOOTWEAR

At the end of a ski day, stiff cold boots come off and are ideally replaced with a warm, cozy après-ski option. As always, style matters and adventurous options are encouraged.

▼ Socialites Isa Genolini and Maria Antonia on the street in Cortina d'Ampezzo, 1982

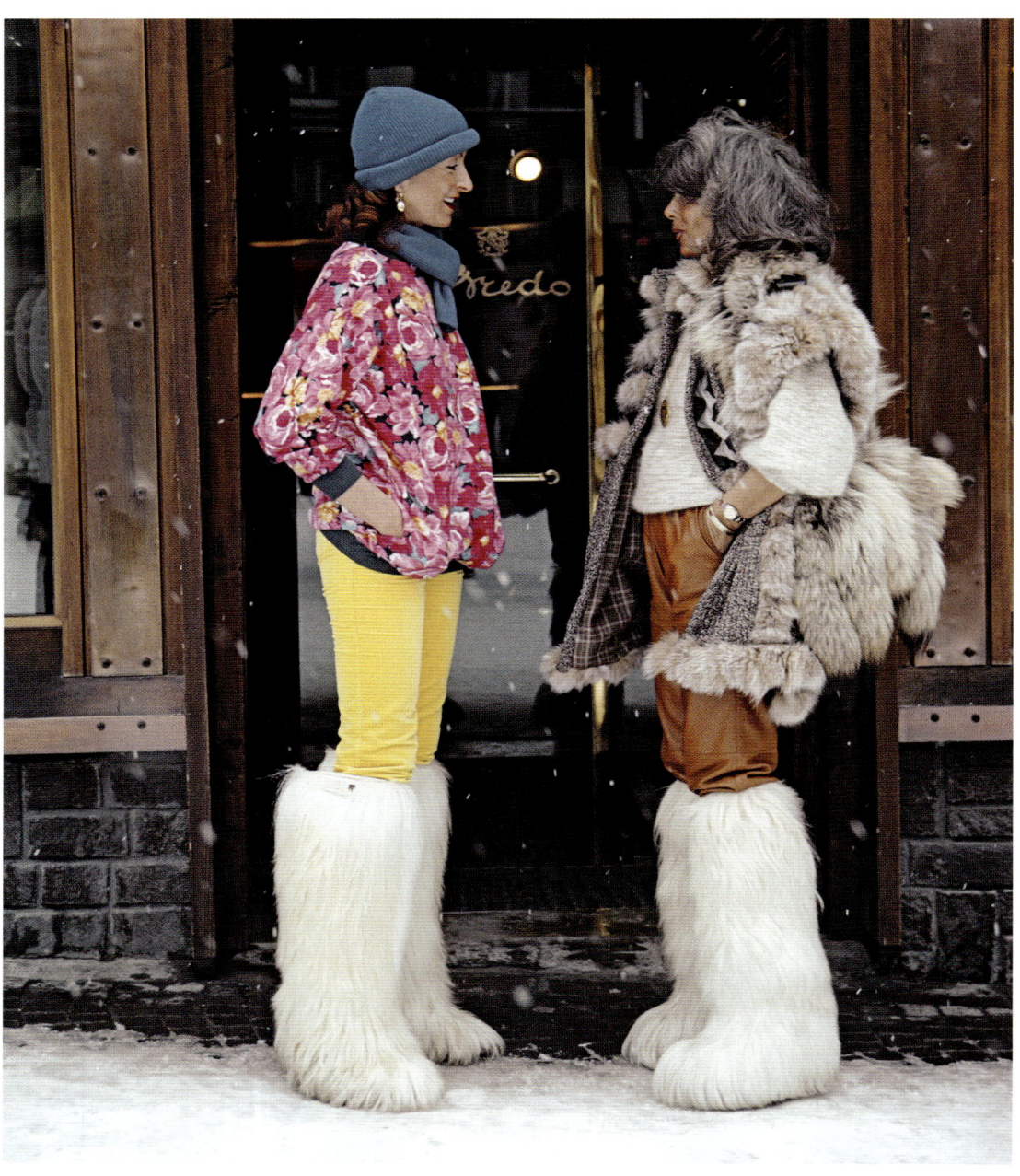

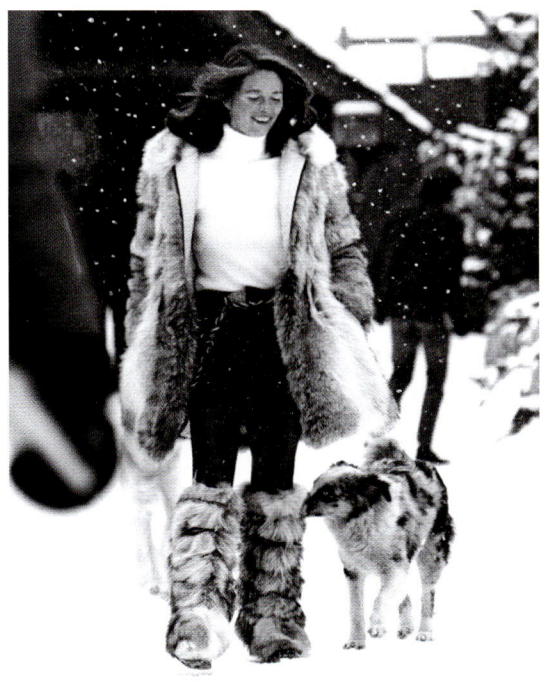

▲ Actress Charlotte Rampling wearing stretch ski pants tucked into oversized furry boots, 1970

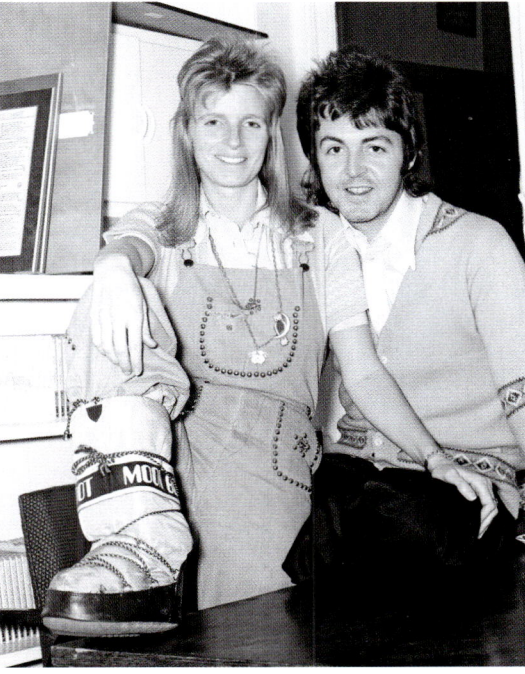

▲ Photographer Linda McCartney, shown here with her Beatles husband, Paul, brought the après-ski moon boot look to the streets of 1970s London.

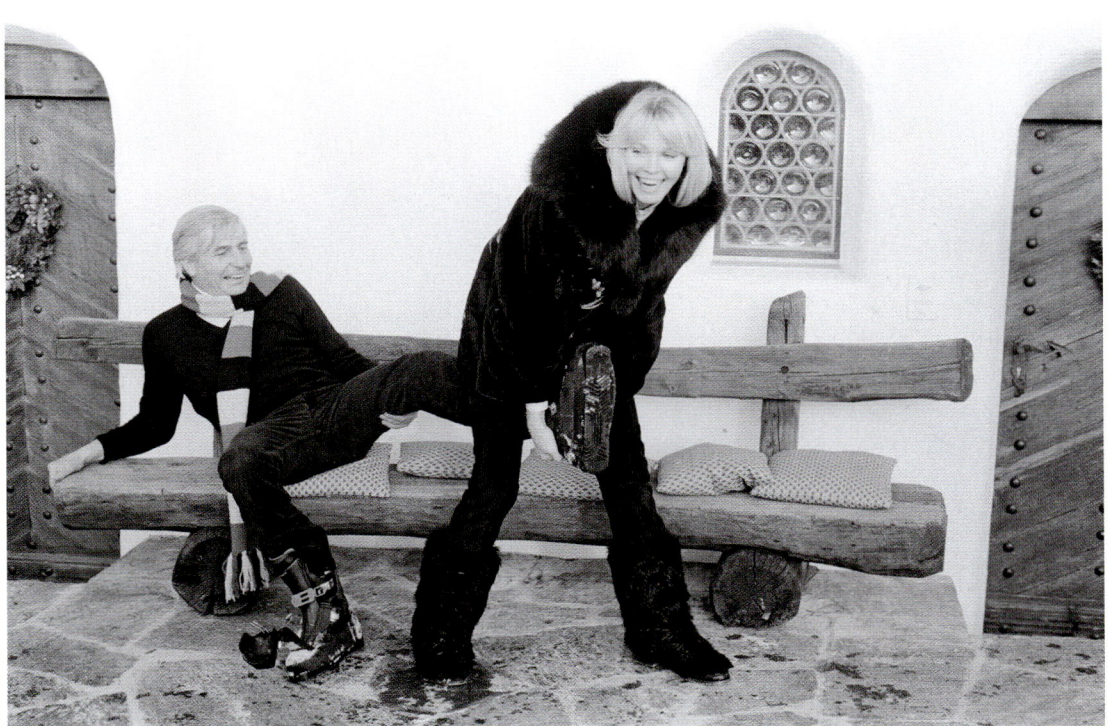

▲ Mirja Sachs helping her husband Gunter out of his ski boots after a day on the slopes of Gstaad, 1979

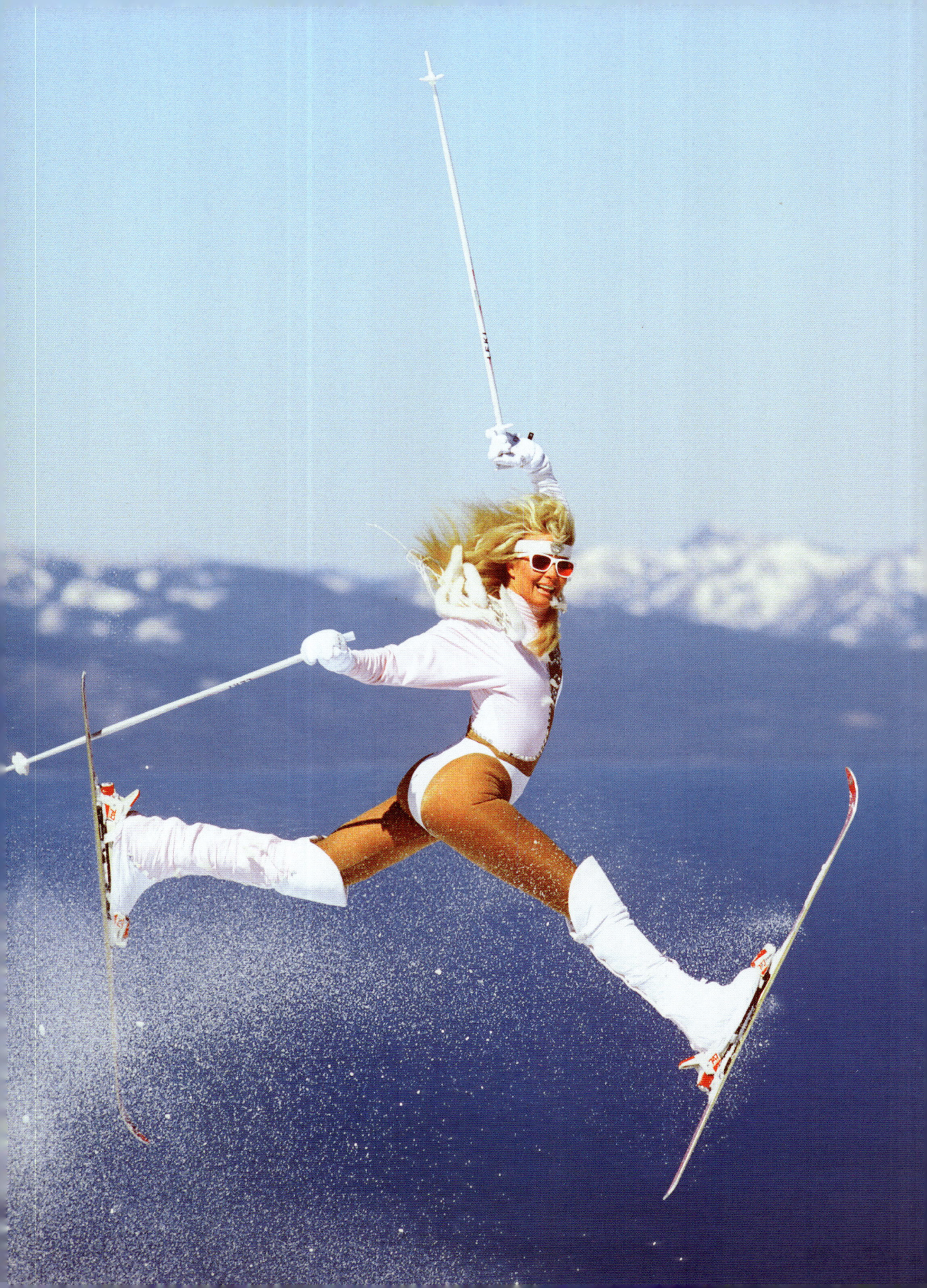

Eighties Fashion Collision

—

The confluence of pop culture and ski fashion continued into the 1980s, with a wild new look emerging on the slopes and streets of ski towns. While stretch pants remained, looser puffy pants and jackets were added into the ski fashion vernacular. *Star Wars*–inspired headwear and jacket silhouettes appeared, and neon was born. Bright colors and bright personalities were abundant in this carefree era.

◀ Suzy Chaffee embodying the spirit of 1980s ski style at the Heavenly Ski Resort in California, 1988

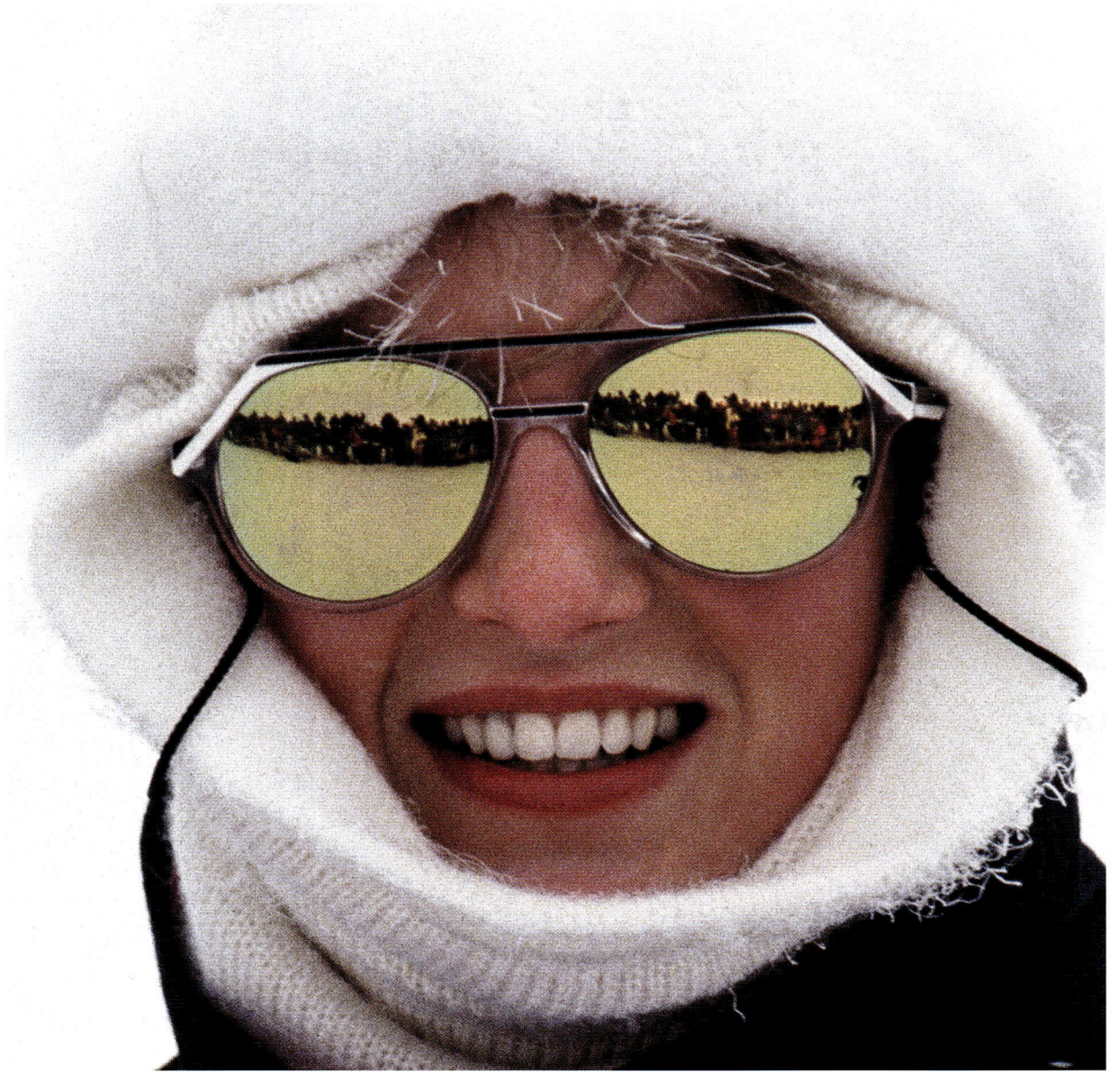

▲ Diana, Princess of Wales, channeling *Star Wars* princess Leia in 1980s knitwear
while on ski holiday in Klosters in 1987

▶ 1980s style icon Tina Turner on vacation in Gstaad in 1986

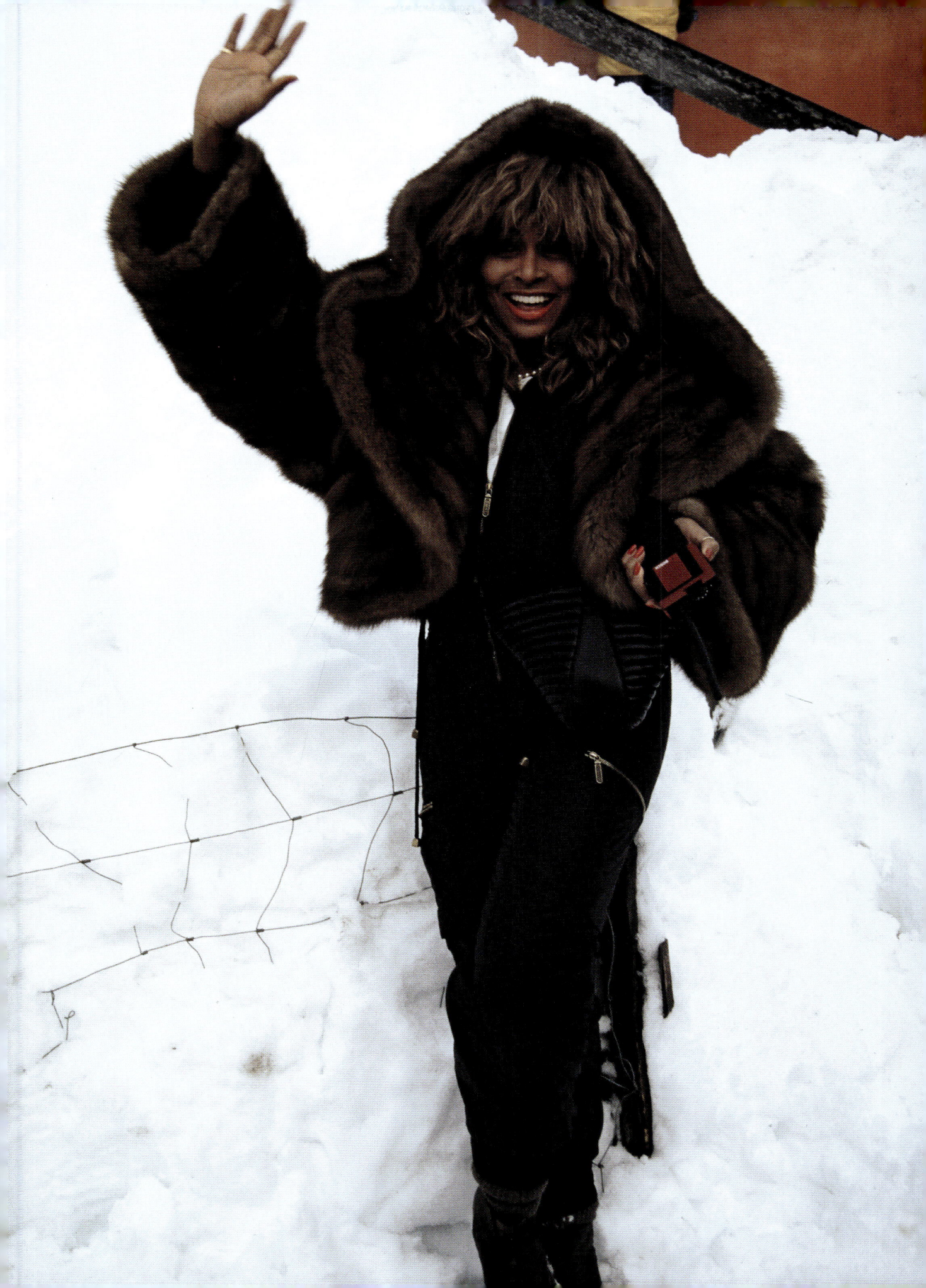

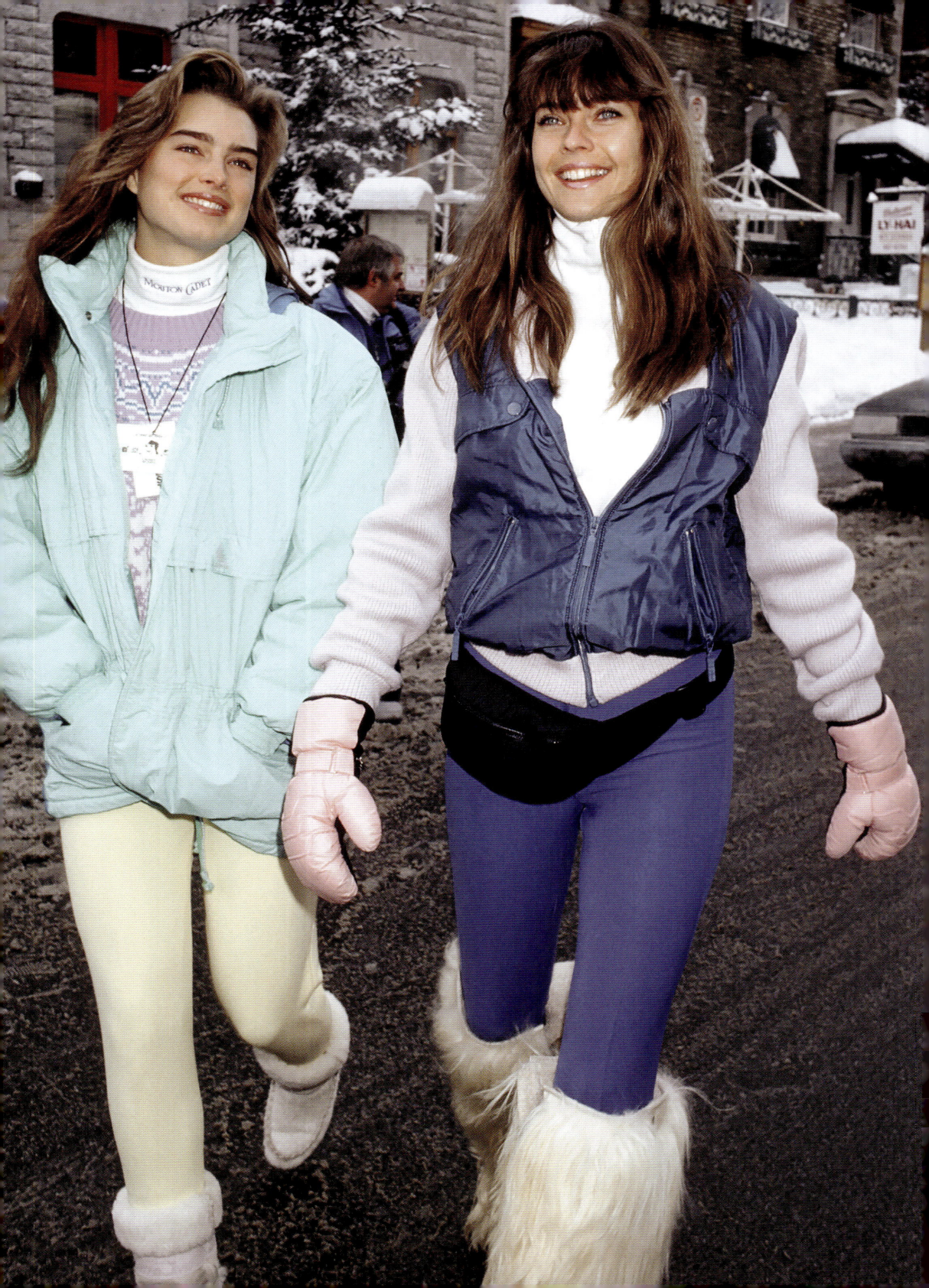

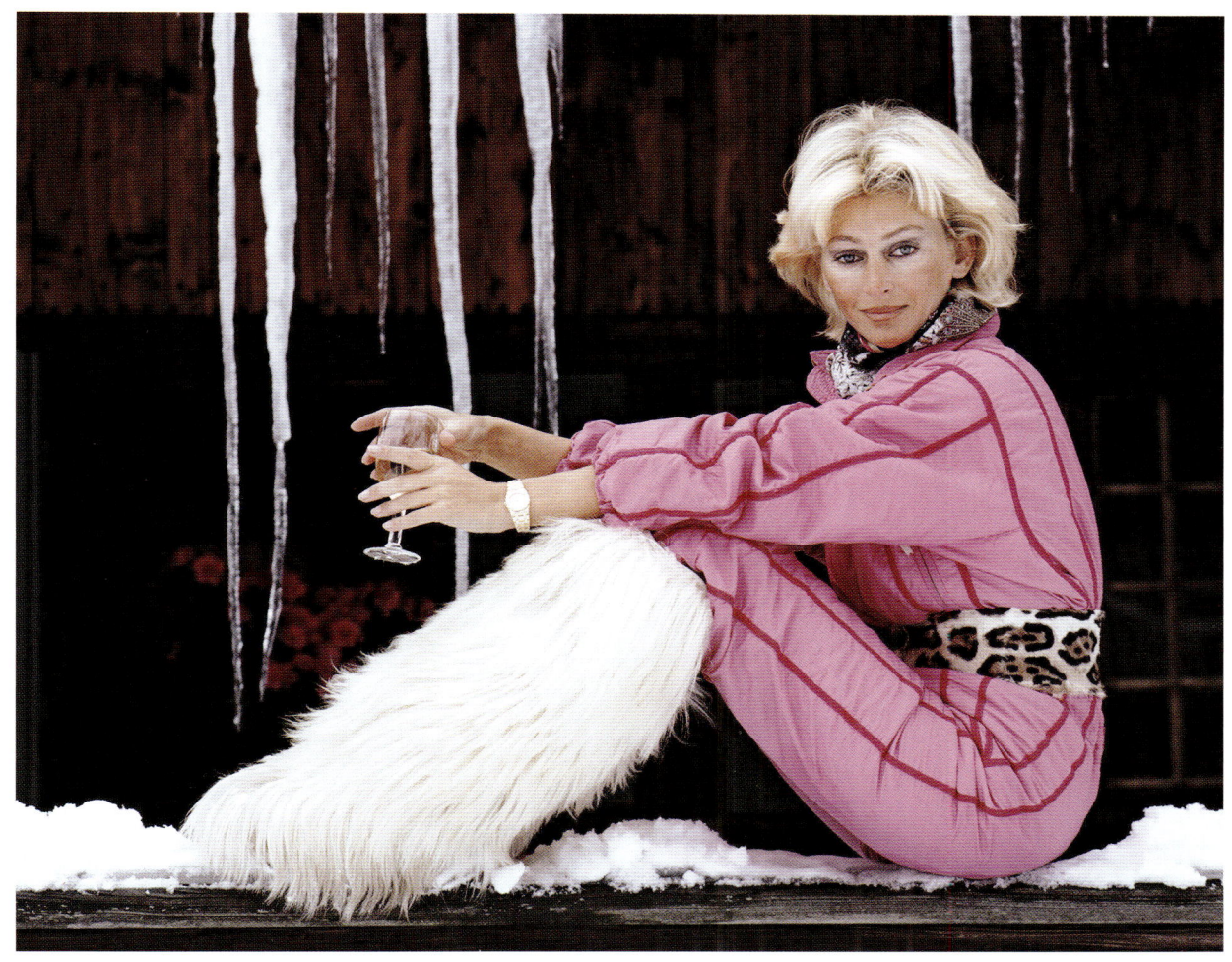

▲ Princess Bianca von Hanau, embodying decadent eighties ski fashion, at her Gstaad chalet in 1985

◀ Supermodels Brooke Shields and Carol Alt walking the streets of Mont-Sainte-Anne in Beaupré, Quebec, Canada, in 1988

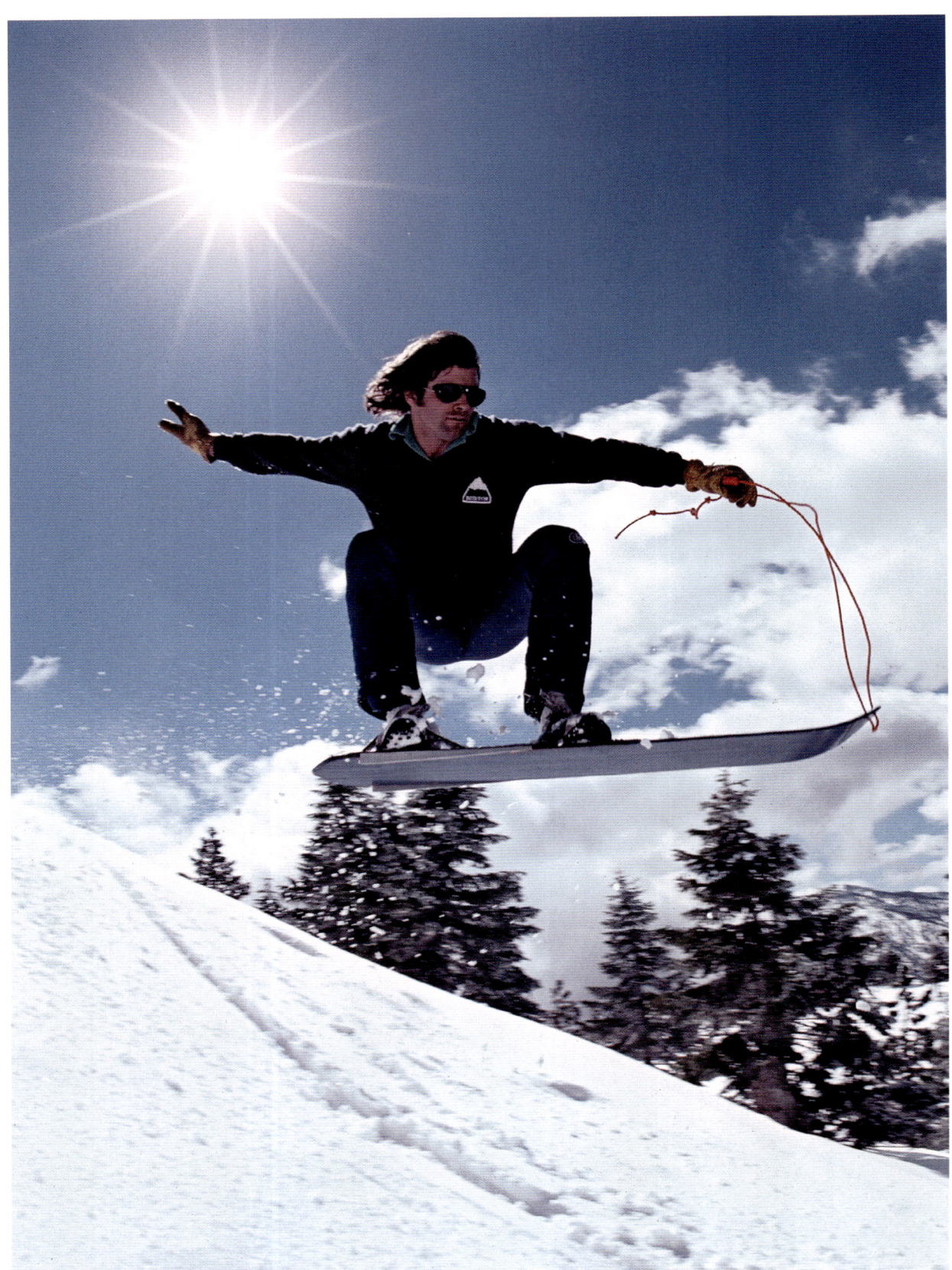

Extreme
Sports(wear)

—

The eighties also gave birth to extreme skiing and saw the emergence of snowboarding as a new sport—and along with them, a new streetwear-inspired look. Jake Burton Carpenter (in the world of snowboarding) and Glen Plake (in extreme skiing) had profound impacts on both snow sports and snow style. The mountains were forever changed by these movements.

◄ Jake Burton Carpenter, who founded Burton Snowboards in 1977, led the charge of pioneers for this new sport and helped define a new style for the mountains.

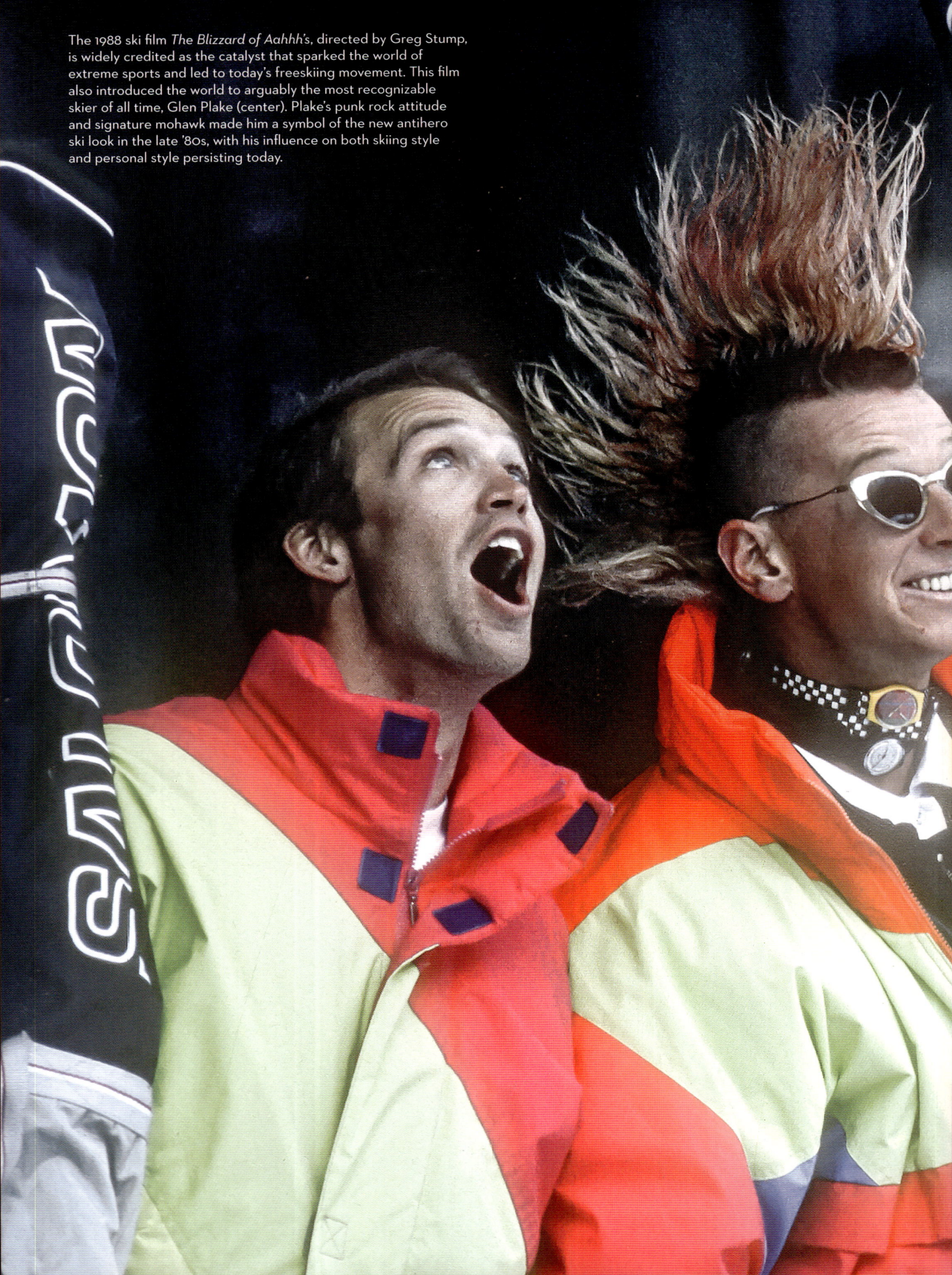

The 1988 ski film *The Blizzard of Aahhh's*, directed by Greg Stump, is widely credited as the catalyst that sparked the world of extreme sports and led to today's freeskiing movement. This film also introduced the world to arguably the most recognizable skier of all time, Glen Plake (center). Plake's punk rock attitude and signature mohawk made him a symbol of the new antihero ski look in the late '80s, with his influence on both skiing style and personal style persisting today.

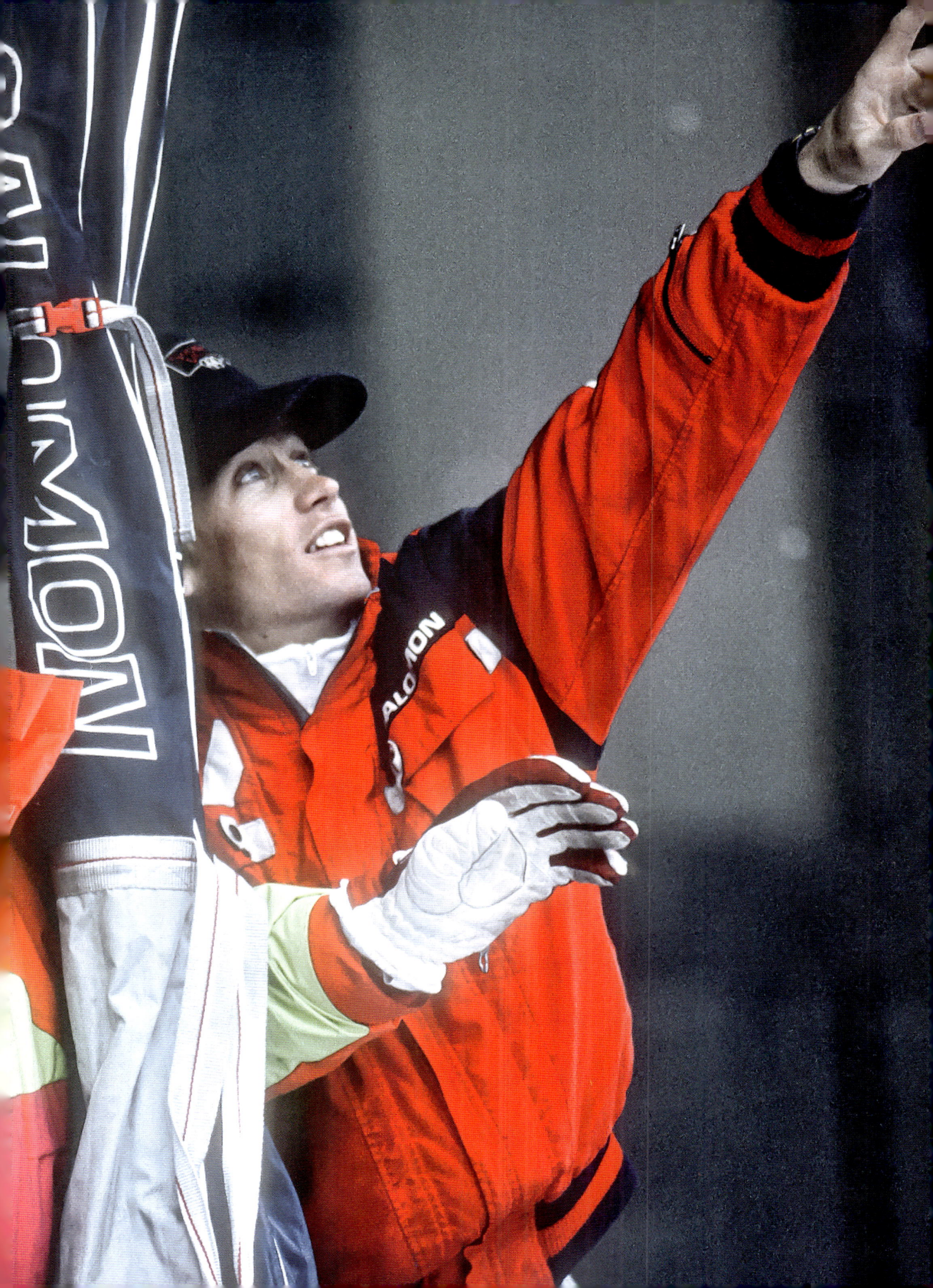

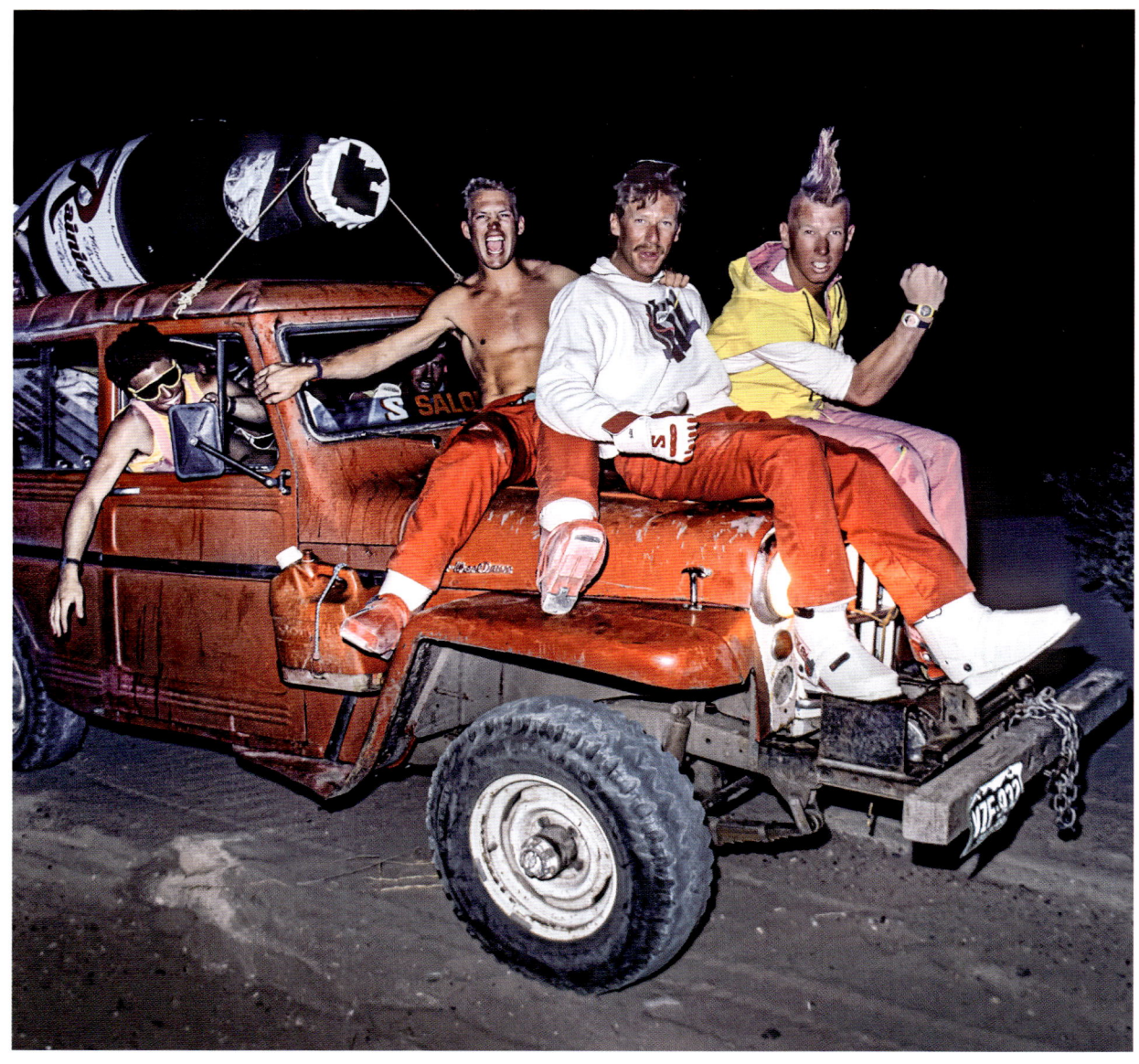

▲ During the making of Greg Stump's film *Maltese Flamingo* in 1986, this group of pro skiers took a side trip to ski the sand dunes outside Beatty, Nevada. From left: Robert Aguirre, Dan Curtis, Mike Hattrup, Scott Kennett, and Glen Plake

▶ From left: pro skiers Chris Haslock, Mike Hattrup, and Lynn Weiland, with photographer Bruce Benedict, on a break during the filming of *Maltese Flamingo* in Val d'Isère, 1986

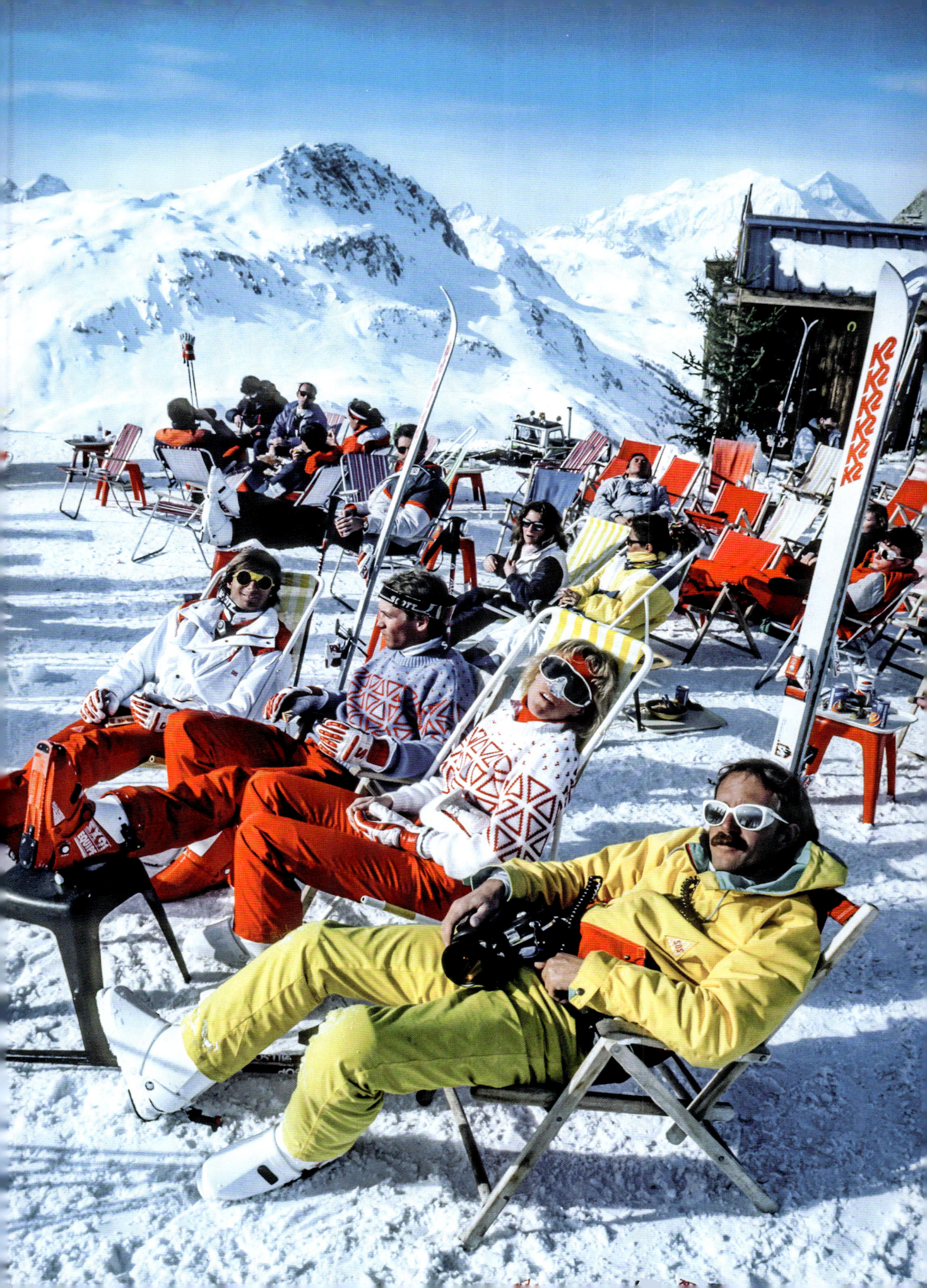

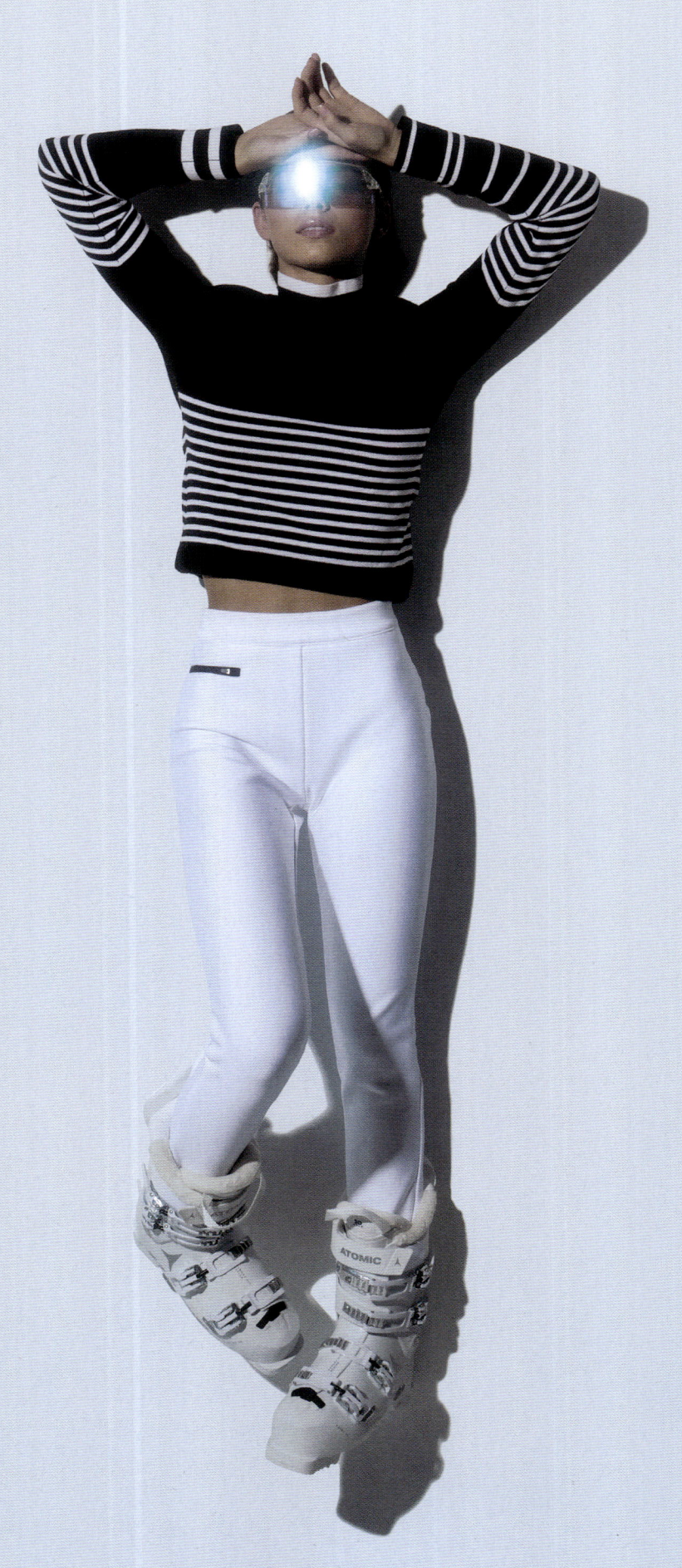

Vintage Revival

—

After two decades of wild color, followed by tired looks and a male-focused style evolution back toward baggy pants and function-over-fashion skiwear, the 2000s ushered in a vintage revival. Indie ski designers (such as myself), bored by the dearth of fashion available for young stylish skiers, took inspiration from skiing's golden era to challenge the skiwear establishment. Once again, things got slimmer, sexier, and a whole lot more fun.

Material innovations offered new possibilities for pairing vintage styles with new technology. Wool, which had disappeared almost entirely from skiwear, came back in refined, functional forms. And thanks to growing concern over the synthetics and forever chemicals used in most skiwear for several decades, development of recycled, circular, and natural fibers and finishes allowed for improvements to all elements of ski style.

Real fur went away, recycled high-performance insulations offered an alternative to goose down, and waterproof finishes that mimicked nature's ability to repel water without the use of harsh chemicals were developed.

◄ Despite pushback from the high-performance mentality among most ski retailers at the time, in-the-boot stretch pants returned and along with them nostalgia for the glamorous, fashion-driven eras of ski fashion. Here is a modern take on shimmery 1980s ski glamour from Erin Snow Winter 2023/24.

Seeing opportunity in the once-again growing ski industry, luxury fashion houses have introduced (or reintroduced) ski and après-ski collections since the early aughts. Moncler, founded in 1952 as a mountaineering gear and apparel brand, revived its technical ski and après-ski apparel collection with the introduction of its Grenoble line in 2010. And Pucci—a pivotal design house at the start of the history of ski fashion (see page 86)—recently created a new ski collection in collaboration with heritage skiwear brand Fusalp.

▶ For their Winter 2024 collection, Moncler staged a runway show on the snow in St. Moritz.

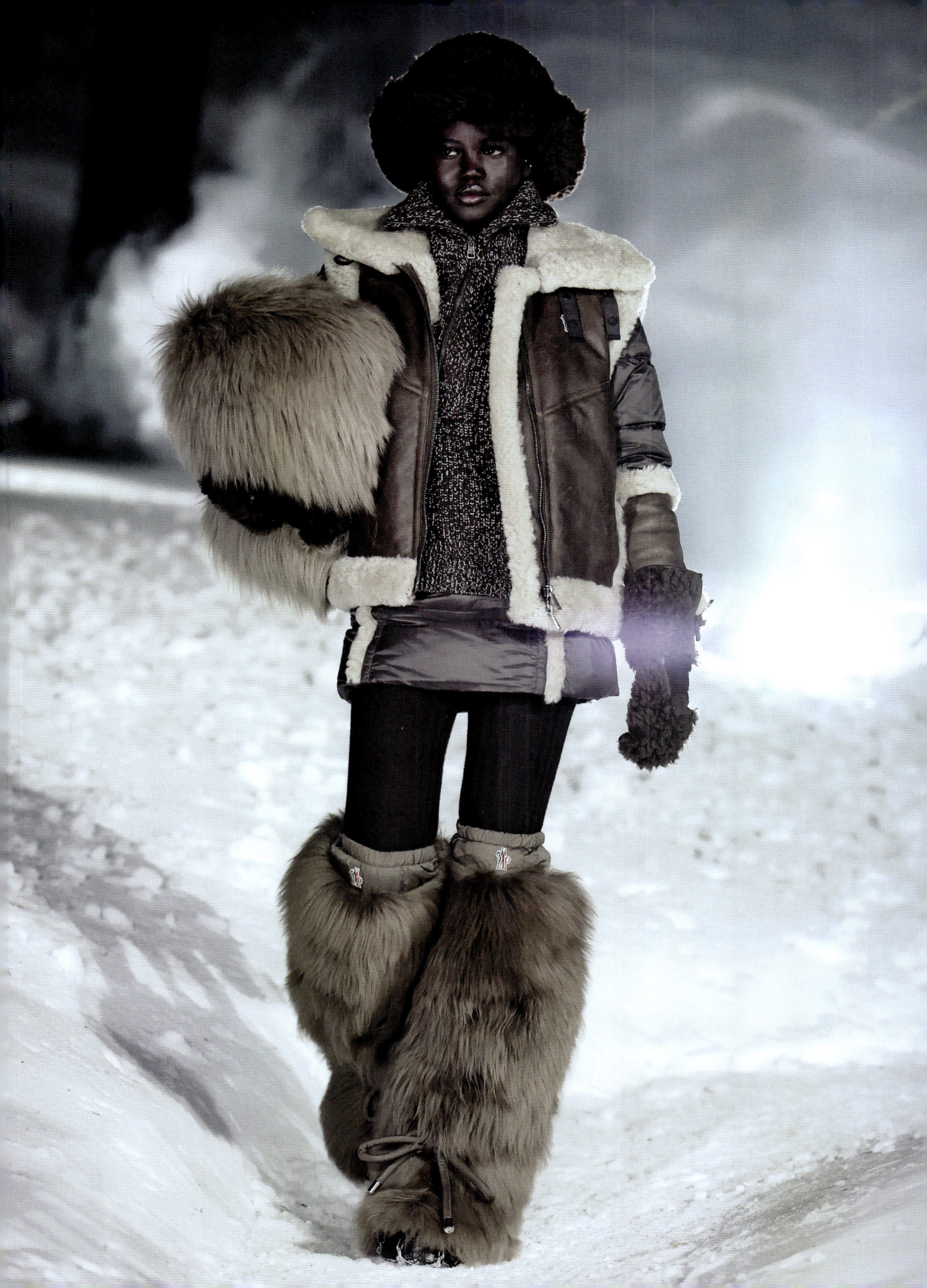

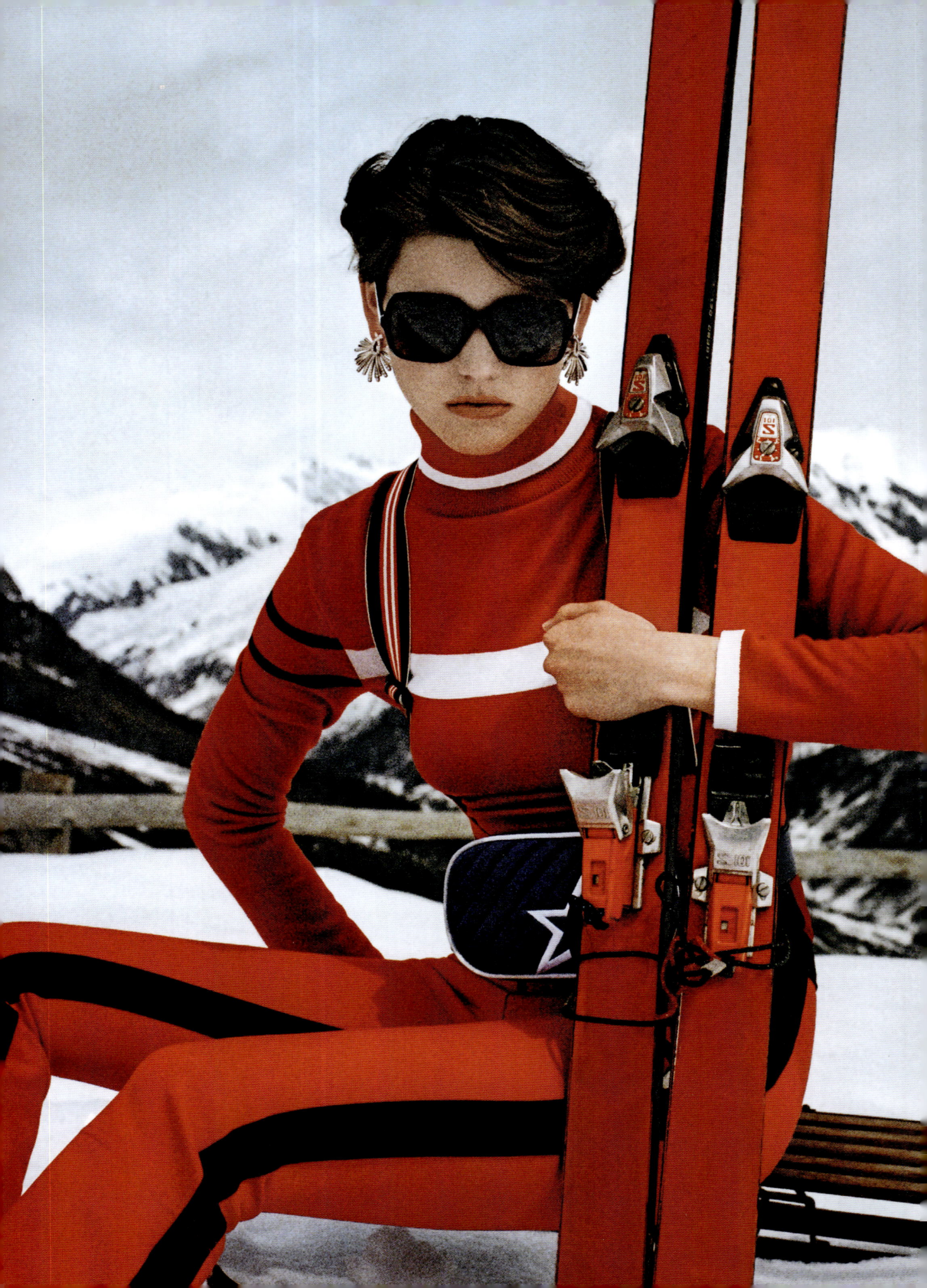

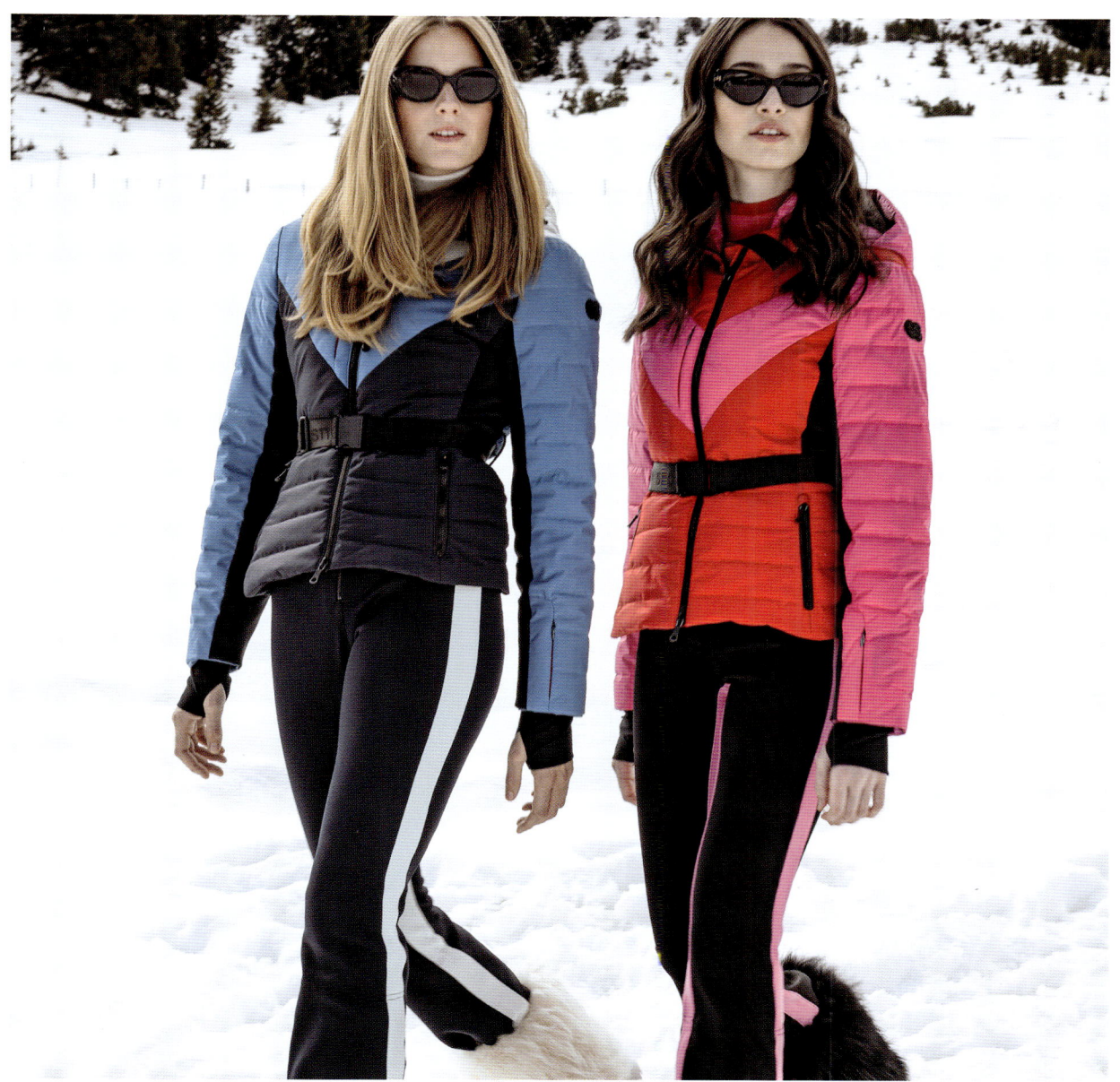

▲ Vivid colors and racing stripes reimagined for Erin Snow Winter 2023/24 and shot on the slopes of Lech, Austria

◀ Striped salopettes and fitted sweater, reminiscent of late 1960s and '70s racing-inspired skiwear, from Erin Snow Winter 2019/20

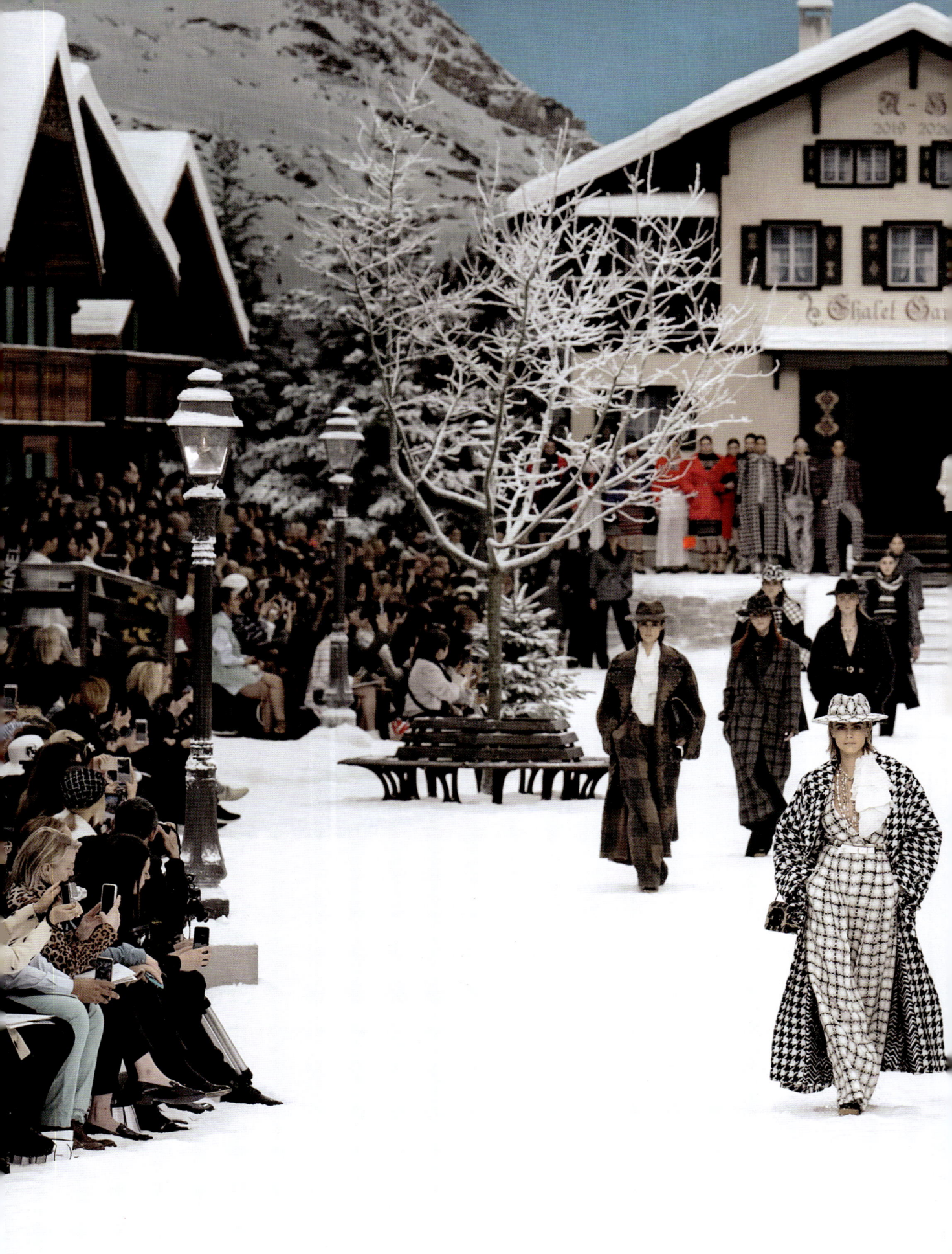

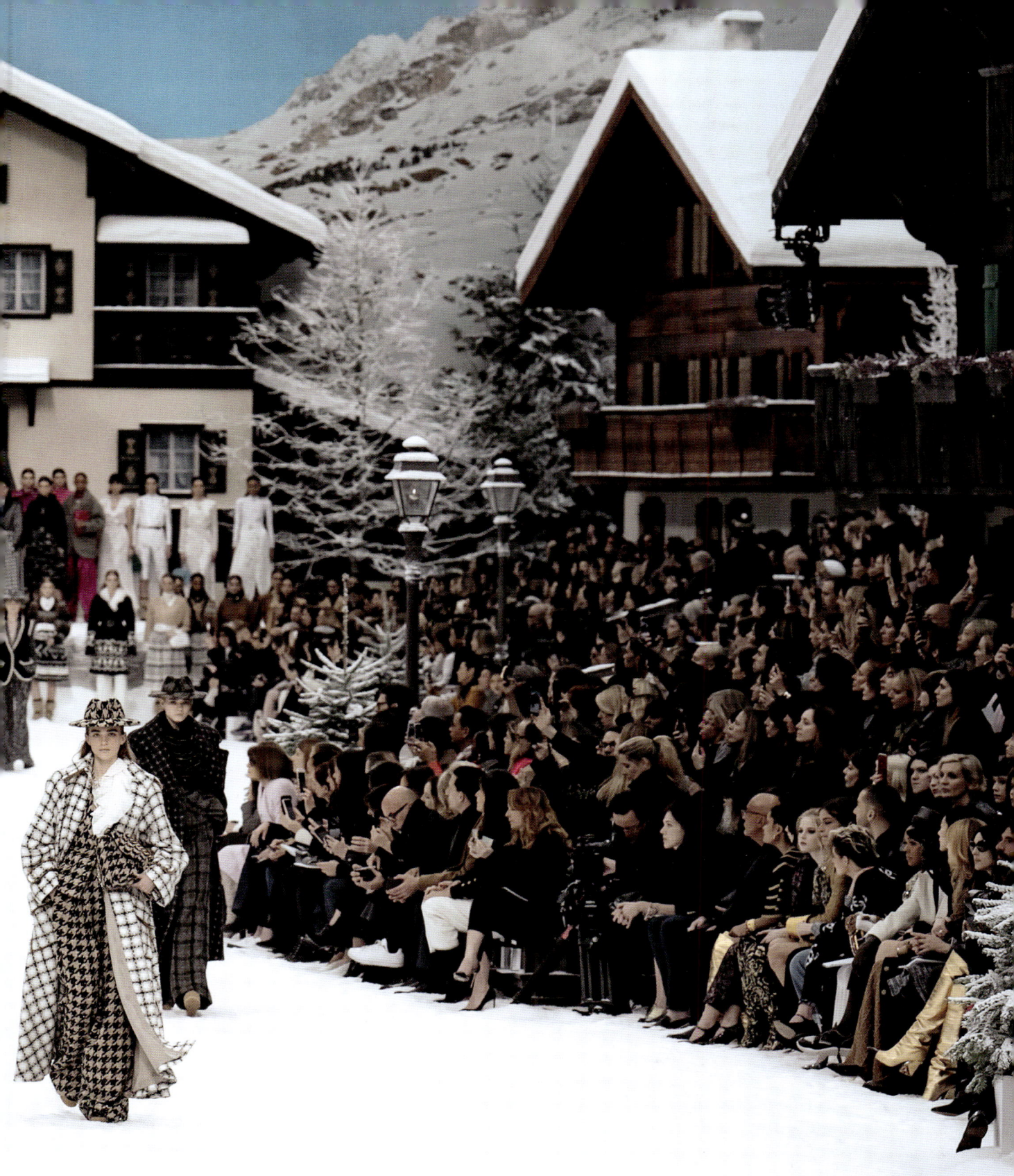

Fashion designer Karl Lagerfeld's last collection, for Chanel (Fall-Winter 2019/20), was not technically a ski collection, but the runway show was held on a set built to mimic a ski village in the Alps and featured beautiful items perfect for après-ski.

Ski Resorts for the Fashion Set

Some ski areas attract the more technical skiers, who tend to have a no-nonsense style; others are very casual, with a duct-taped-jacket type of crowd. Fashion-forward skiers who wish to dress for the occasion will feel right at home at the following resorts (and resort towns).

AUSTRIA
Lech
St. Anton

FRANCE
Courchevel
Megève
Méribel
Val d'Isère

ITALY
Cortina d'Ampezzo

JAPAN
Niseko

SWITZERLAND
Gstaad
Klosters
St. Moritz
Verbier
Zermatt

UNITED STATES
Aspen Snowmass
Deer Valley
Sun Valley

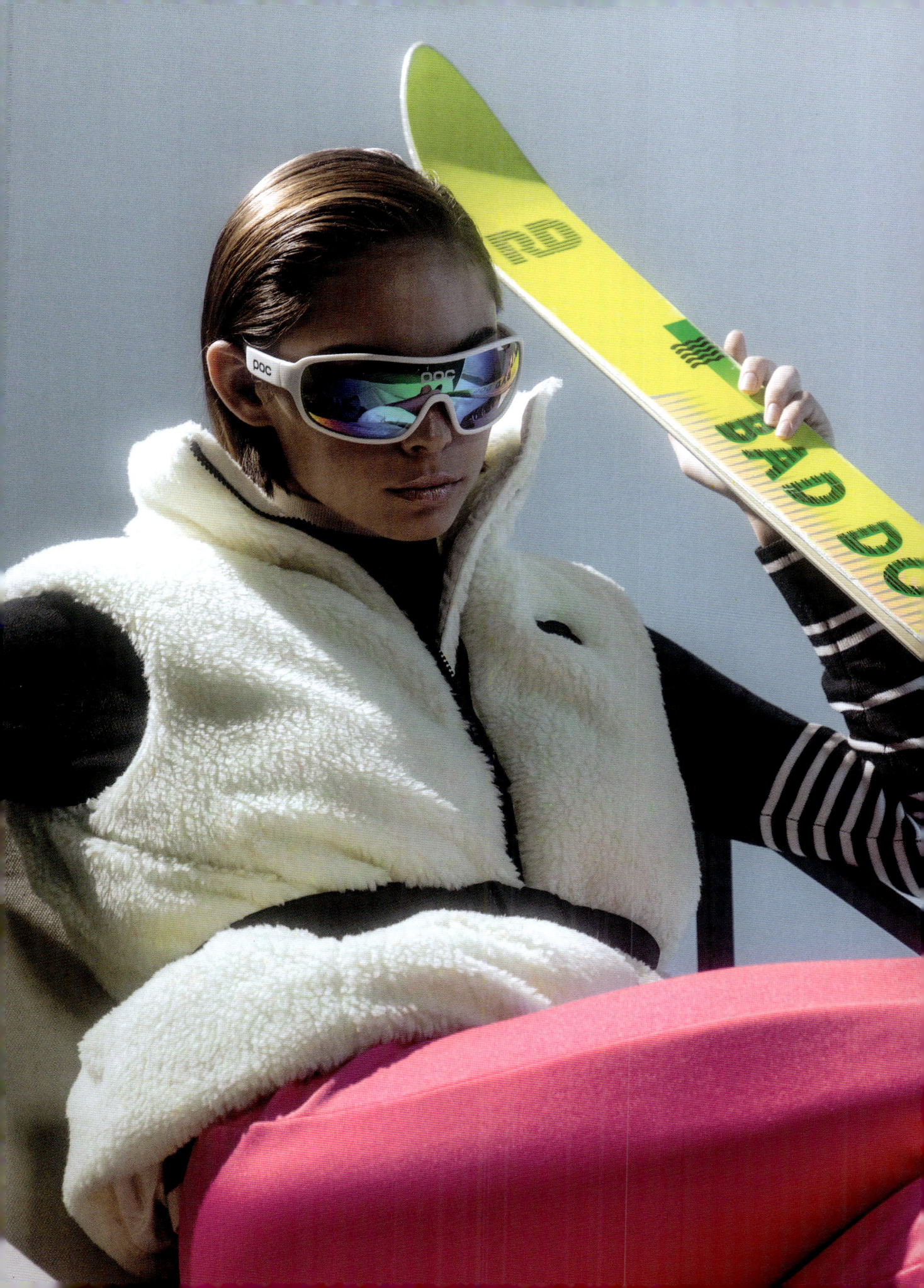

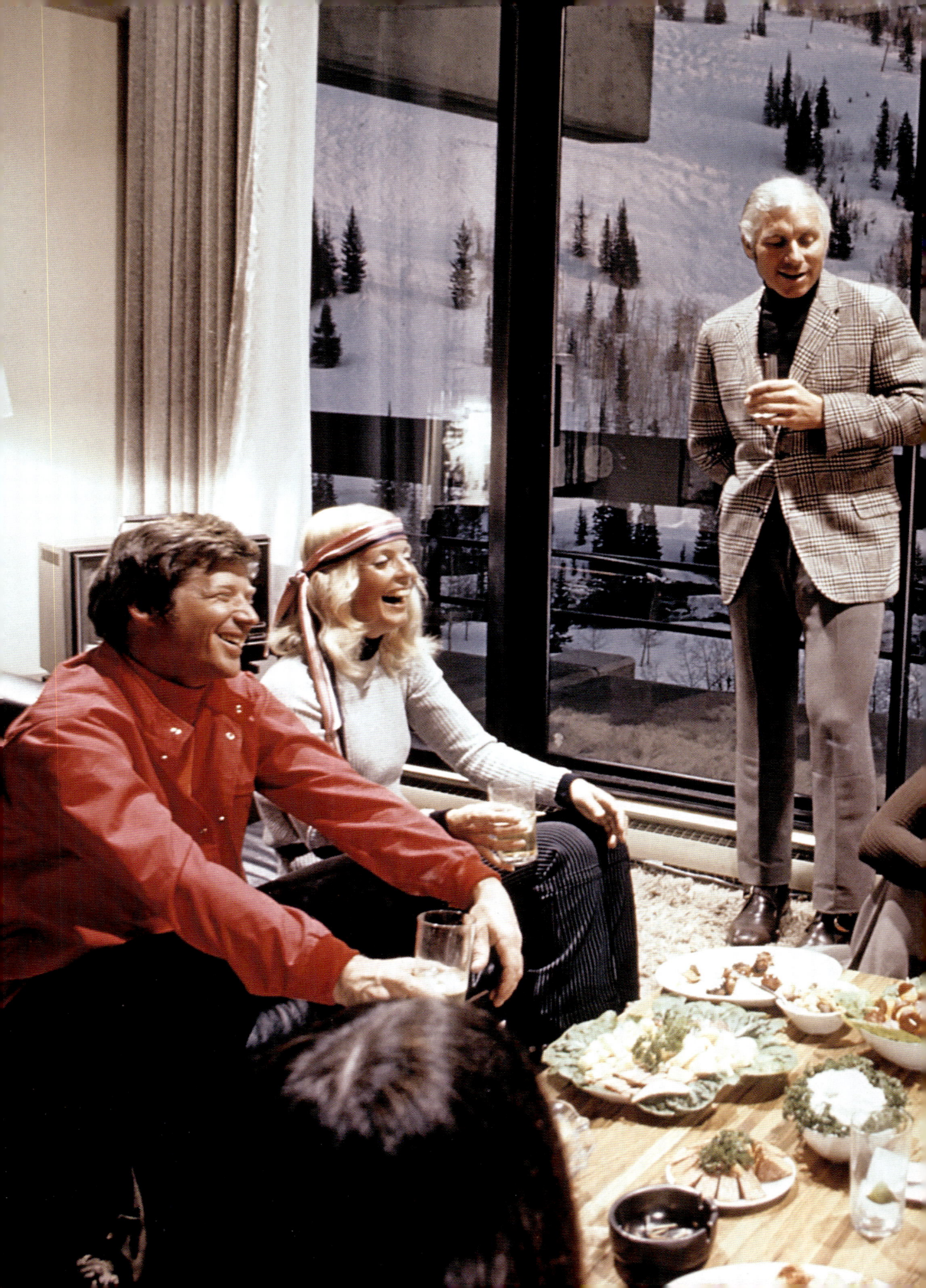

The Menu

Food and drinks enjoyed after skiing are meant to warm you up and replenish your reserves. For some revelers, après-ski indulgence cannot begin soon enough, with ski lunches turning into decadent affairs. Others may wait until the lifts shut down to make an après-ski pit stop for nachos and beer. No matter how long or hard you ski, after burning calories on the slopes, the urge to splurge is justified. The pages that follow will take you on a culinary and libation tour of various ski regions across the globe, with recipes for some iconic menu items from the mountains of the United States, Canada, and Europe.

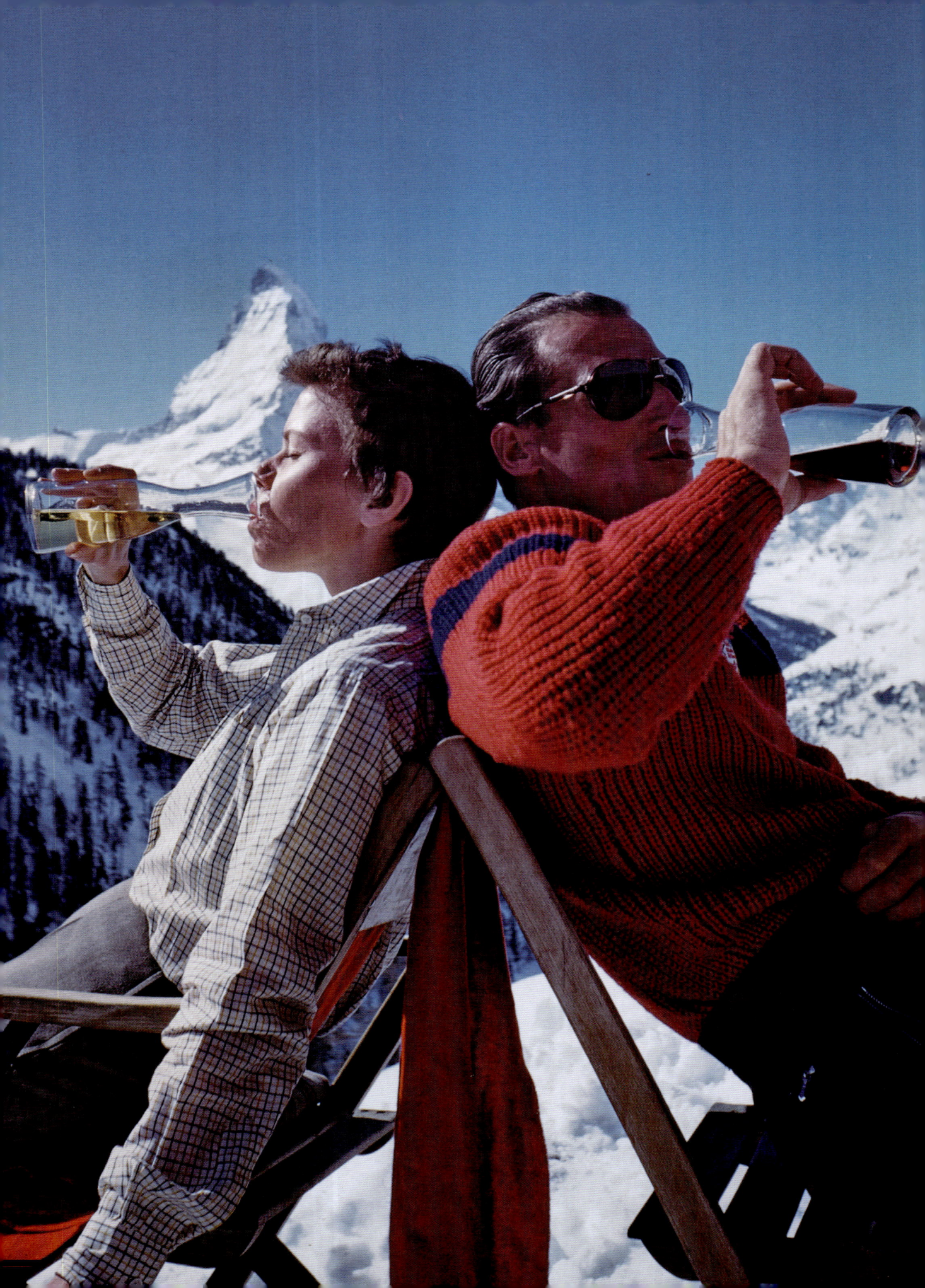

Drinks

—

The tradition of having a drink after skiing is believed to have originated in Norway during the mid-1800s, when aquavit was passed around after a day on the snow to warm Scandinavian skiers. After even a few hours on the slopes, nothing is better than a special beverage to toast the day and swap stories. And when you're traveling with kids, the promise of a warm, sugary après-ski treat goes a long way toward coaxing little ones into their ski gear on a cold winter morning.

◂ Enjoying a drink under the blue skies of Switzerland in Zermatt, 1955

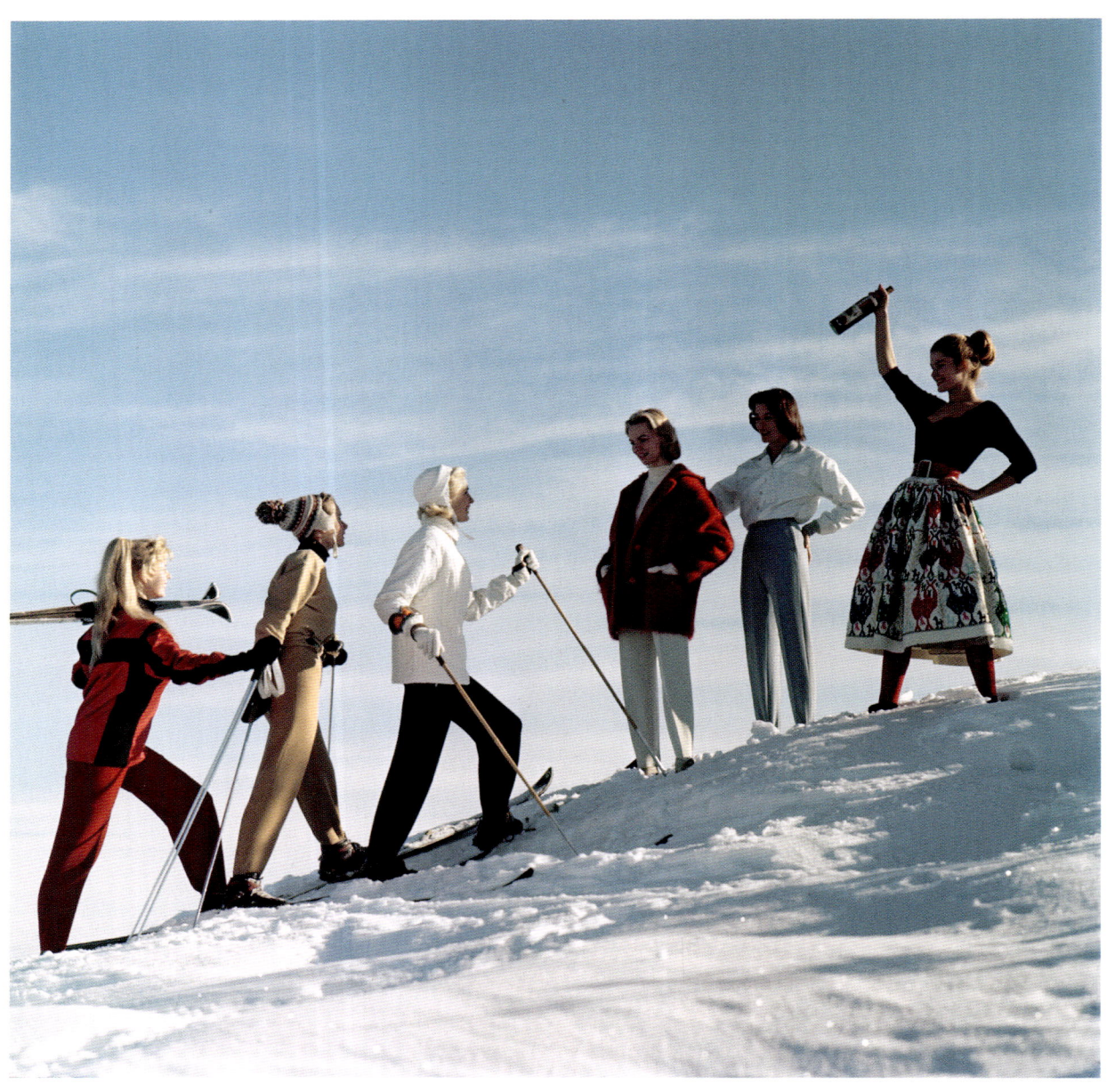

▲ Friends at the ready with an après-ski cocktail for returning skiers, 1955

▶ A waiter delivering drinks on ice skates in St. Moritz, 1932

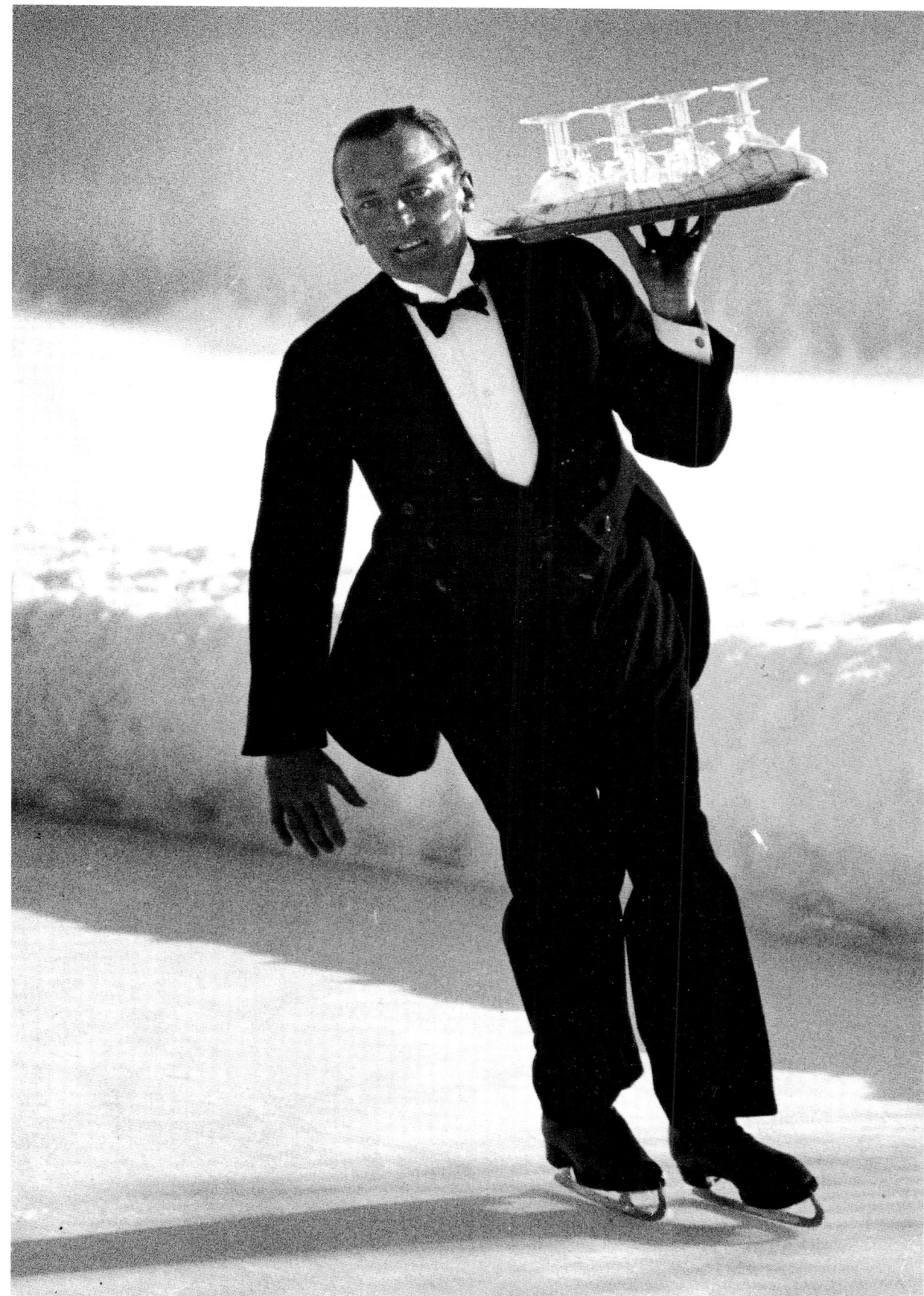

APEROL SPRITZ

Serves 1

1½ ounces (45 ml) Aperol
3 ounces (90 ml) Prosecco
¾ ounce (20 ml) club soda
Slice of orange, for garnish

The spritz is said to have originated in the Veneto region of Northern Italy in the 1800s. Visitors and soldiers from other parts of what was then the Austro-Hungarian Empire apparently found Italian wines too strong, so they added a splash of water to their glass to lighten it up. Still water was later updated to soda water, and many fabulous spritz drinks were born, among them the Aperol Spritz. Incredibly refreshing and light, this drink is traditionally made with equal parts Aperol and Prosecco. My recipe ups the amount of Prosecco to cut the bitterness of the Aperol.

◇◇◇◇◇◇◇

Fill a wineglass halfway with ice. Add the Aperol, Prosecco, and club soda and give a gentle stir. Garnish with an orange slice.

KIR ROYALE

Serves 1

1 ounce (30 ml) crème de cassis
Champagne (or sparkling wine)
A few fresh blackberries

Champagne is a fine choice for a celebratory occasion, and any number of cocktails can be made with this sparkling wine. A popular and refreshing aperitif served in many ski resorts in the Alps is the Kir Royale. Adding a few fresh blackberries (or another berry of your choice) to the traditional recipe gives it a nice garnish and something to nibble at the bottom of your drink.

◇◇◇◇◇◇

Pour the crème de cassis into a champagne flute. Fill the remainder of glass with champagne, then drop in a few blackberries.

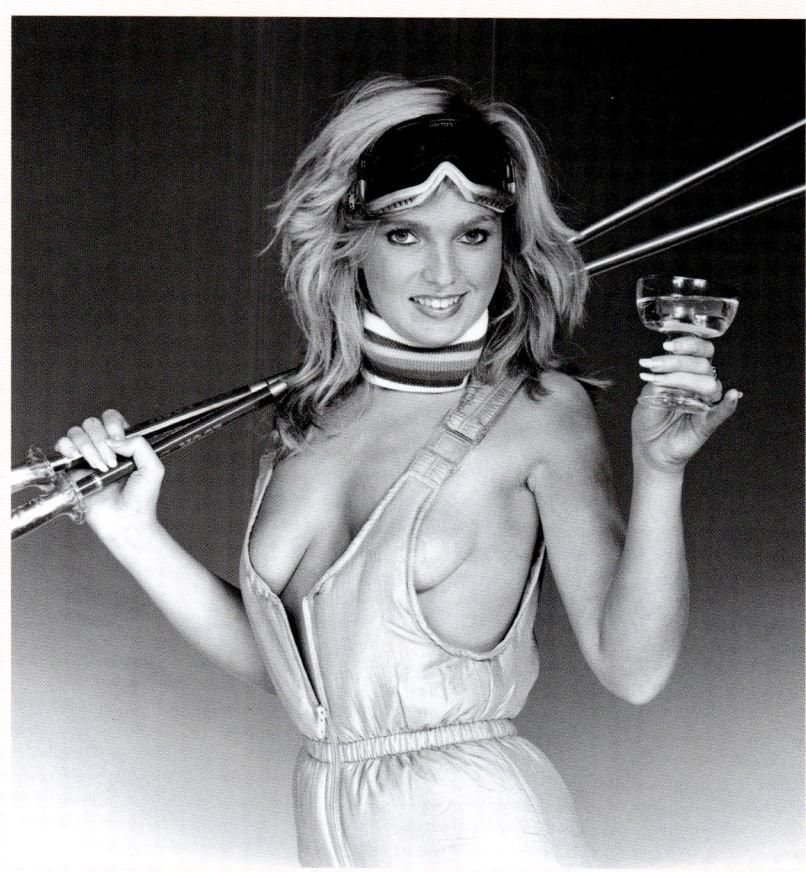

▶ Showcasing the naughty side of après-ski with a cocktail in hand, 1983

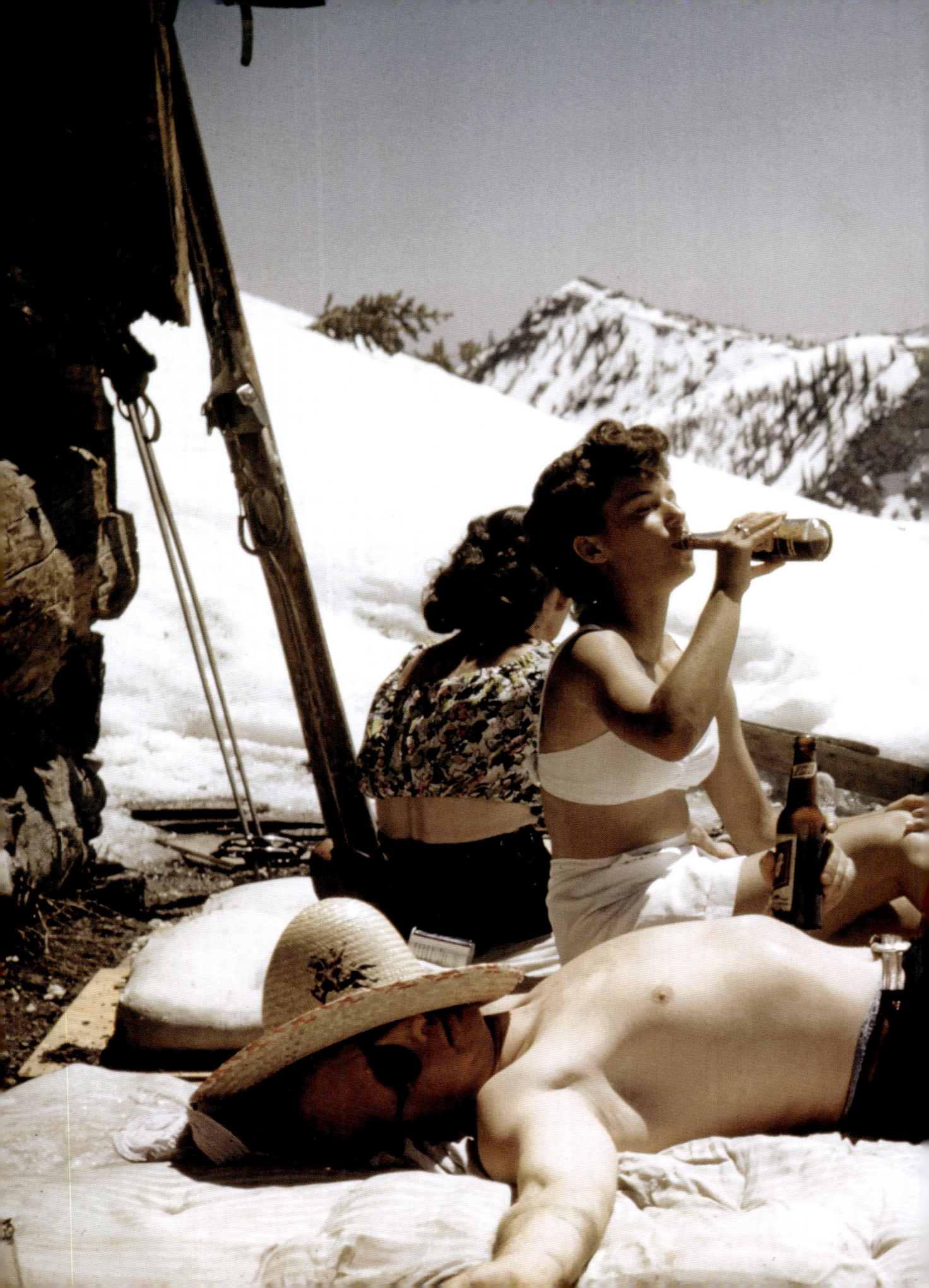

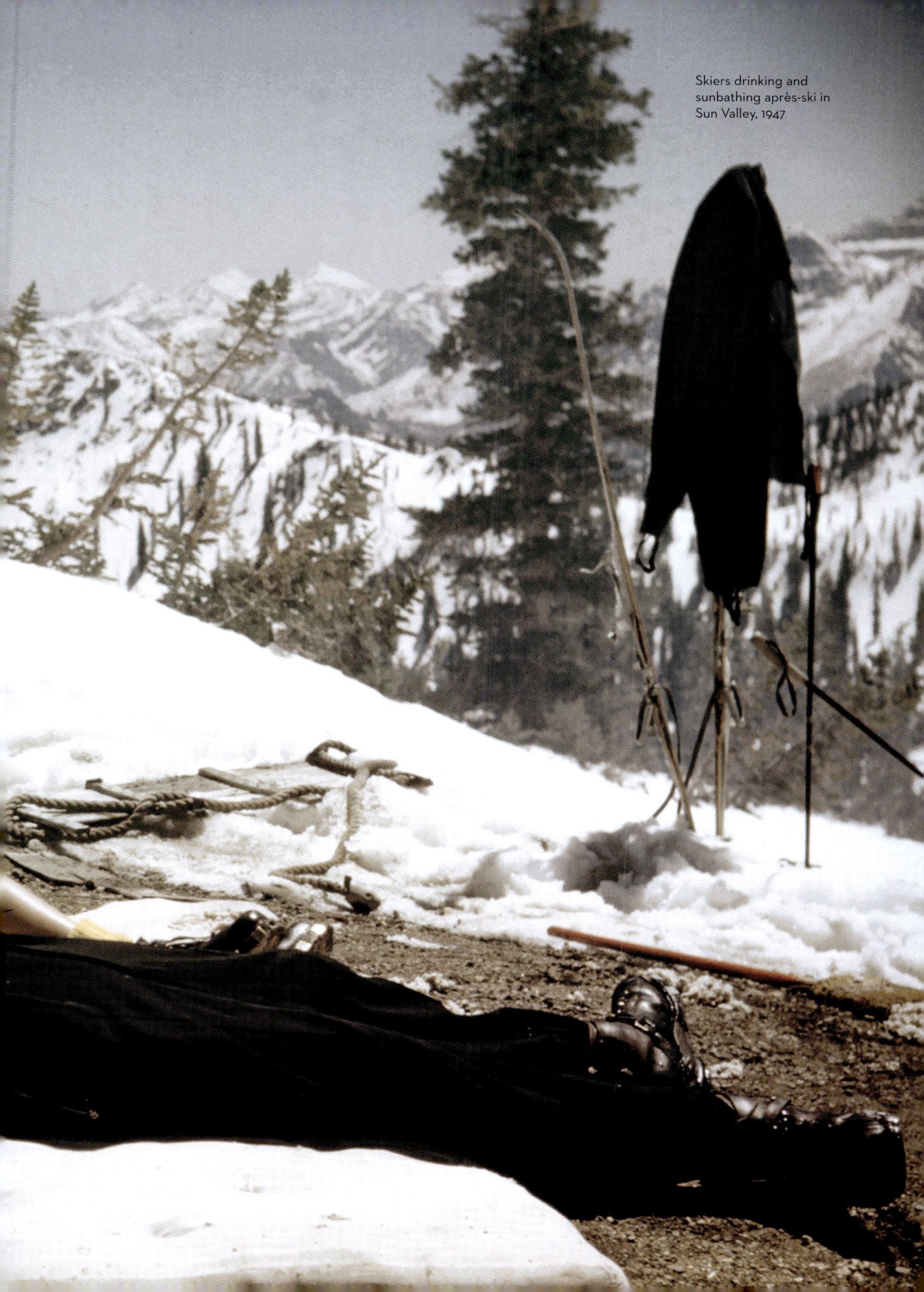

Skiers drinking and
sunbathing après-ski in
Sun Valley, 1947

BEER CULTURE

Beer is popular at ski resorts all over the world, with a long history steeped in local tradition. In America, many craft breweries have opened in ski country throughout Colorado, Utah, California, Wyoming, and Vermont, inspired by and paying tribute to their surrounding mountains and ski culture. No après-ski fête would be complete without a bucket of ice filled with ski-themed craft beers. For a more elevated experience, keep a variety of beer glassware (pint glasses, mugs, and pilsner glasses) at the ready in the freezer.

▼ Self-service ice-cold bucket of beer in Sun Valley, 1950

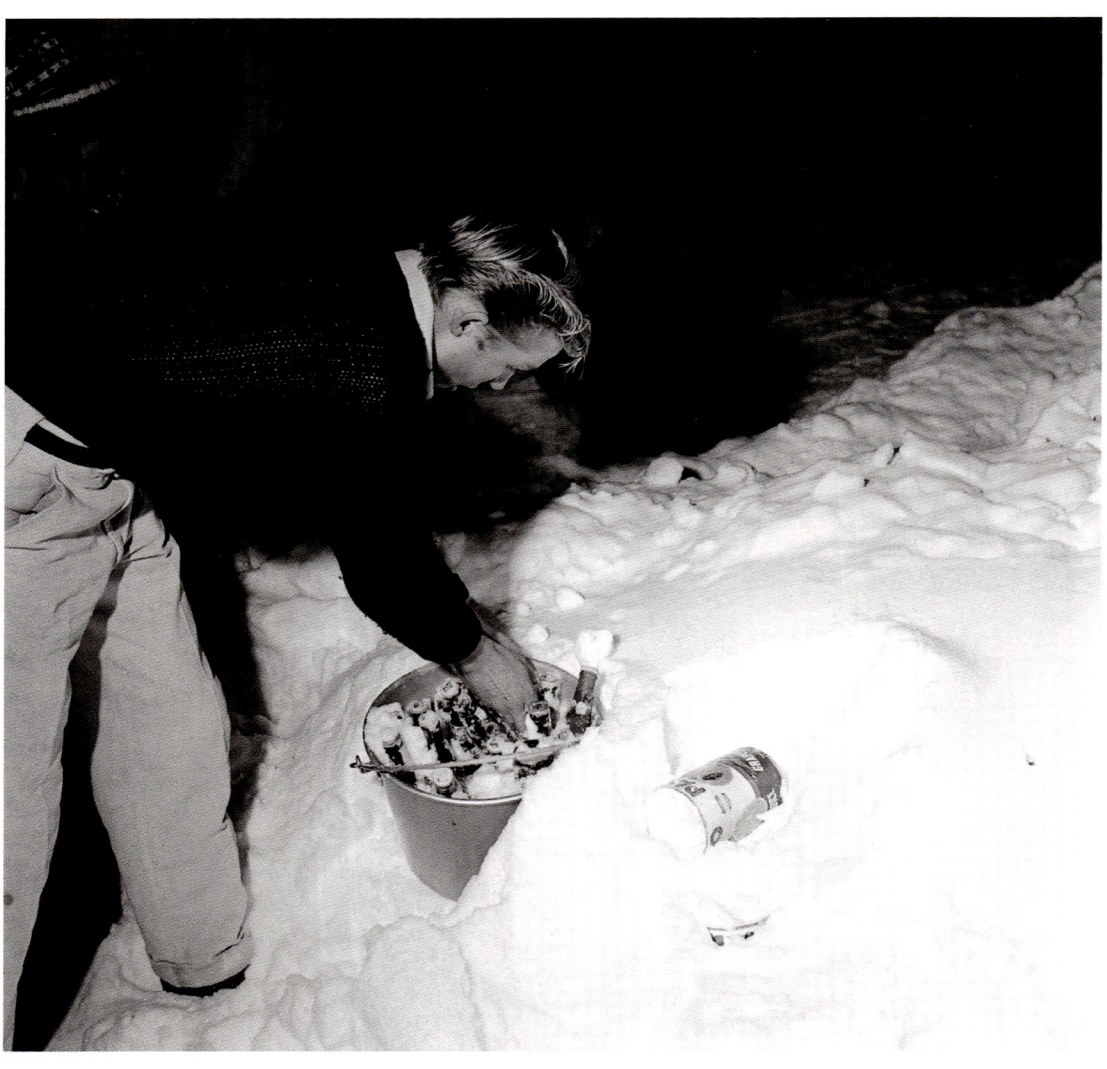

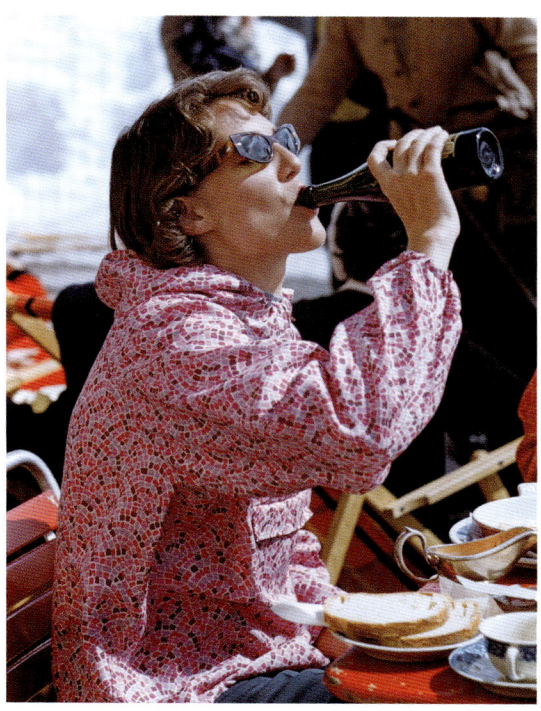

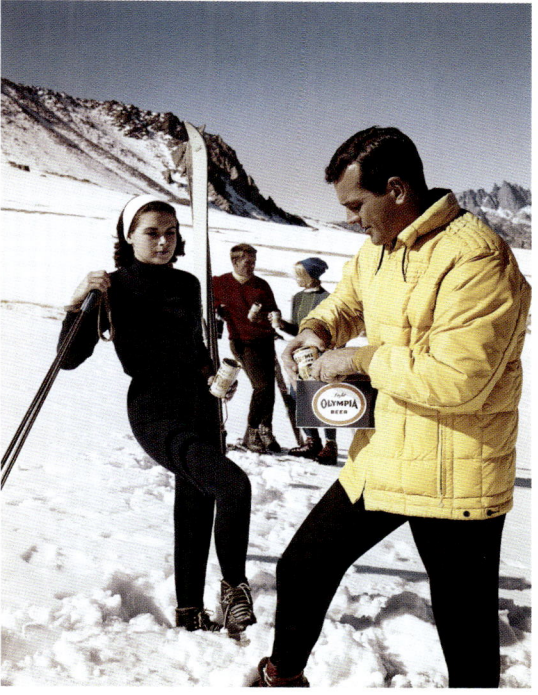

▲ A Pucci-clad skier enjoying beer from the bottle in Zermatt, 1956

▲ Beers shared slope-side, circa 1962

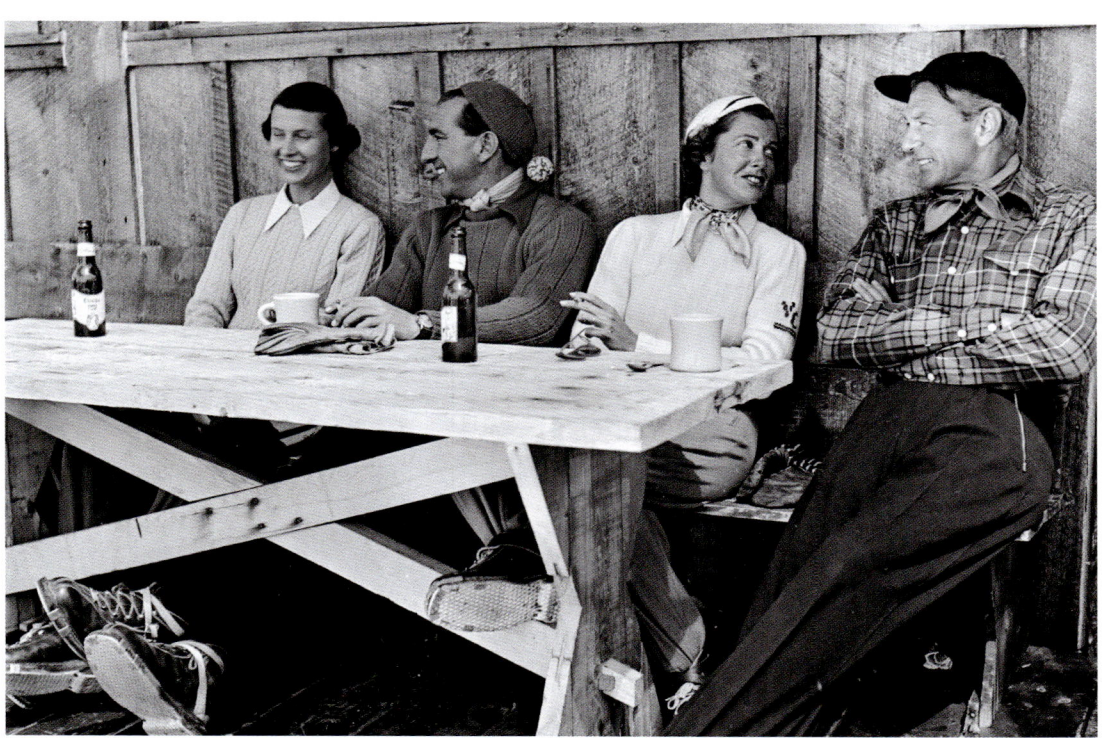

▲ Actor Gary Cooper (far right) and his wife, Veronica (second from right), enjoying après-ski beers with friends near their Aspen home in 1952

BOMBARDINO

Serves 1

3 ounces (90 ml) zabaglione
1½ ounces (45 ml) brandy
Whipped cream, store-bought or
    homemade (see page 198)
Ground cinnamon

The Bombardino is a quintessential après-ski concoction found across the Dolomites. The aptly named drink ("little bomb" in Italian) delivers a tiny but mighty punch of tasty alcoholic warmth in the form of Italian eggnog. While zabaglione is traditionally homemade, you can also use Advocaat or Zabov egg liqueurs.

◇◇◇◇◇◇◇◇

Warm the zabaglione in a saucepan over medium heat, stirring occasionally. Meanwhile, pour the brandy into a glass mug. When the zabaglione is hot (but not boiling), slowly pour it into the mug and stir well to combine. Top your Bombardino with a generous dollop of whipped cream and finish with a sprinkle of cinnamon.

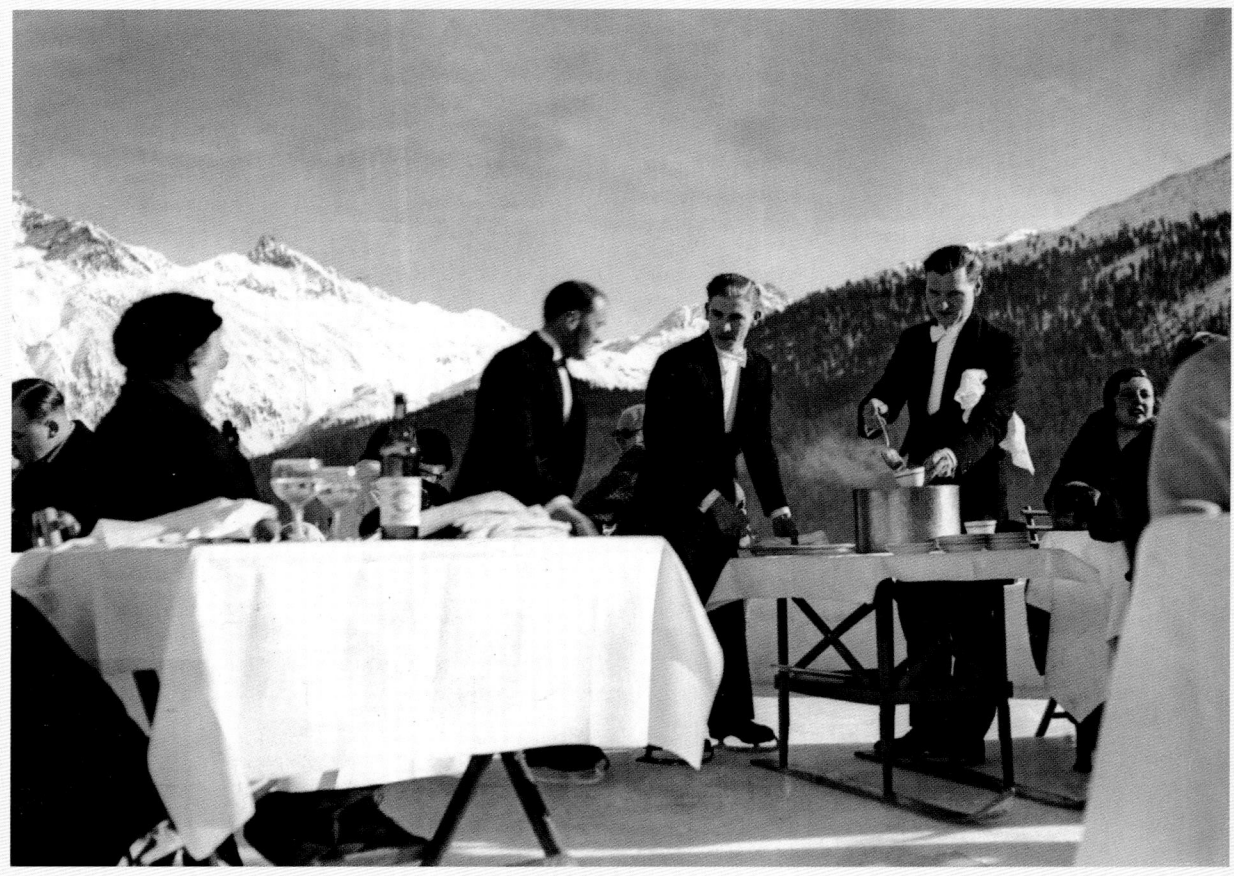

VIN CHAUD

Serves 2

1 cup (240 ml) dry red wine (Cabernet
    Sauvignon or Merlot work well)
½ ounce (15 ml) Armagnac or other
    brandy
2 tablespoons dark brown sugar
Juice of 1 large orange
3 cardamom pods, plus more for
    serving
2 cinnamon sticks, plus more for
    serving
2 cloves, plus more for serving
1 whole star anise, plus more for
    serving

While it is said that the Vin Chaud dates back to Roman times, this warm spiced wine is now a popular winter holiday and après-ski drink across France and worldwide. You can whip it up in the morning before heading out for a day of skiing, let the wine infuse with the spices all day, then reheat gently when you're ready to serve.

◇◇◇◇◇◇◇◇

Combine all the ingredients in a small saucepan and slowly bring to a very gentle simmer, stirring occasionally. Never allow the drink to reach a boil or else the alcohol will begin to evaporate, with a negative impact on the flavor. Let simmer very gently for 2 minutes, then remove the pan from the heat and let stand at room temperature for at least an hour. When you're ready to serve, rewarm and pour into two glass mugs, with an extra cinnamon stick and some spices in each cup.

HOT TODDY

Serves 1

Boiling water
1½ ounces (45 ml) bourbon
1 tablespoon light honey
2 teaspoons fresh lemon juice
Cinnamon stick, for garnish (optional)
Lemon peel, for garnish (optional)
Whole star anise, for garnish (optional)

The hot toddy has a long history and infinite variations. Essentially a spiked lemon tea, it's like a therapeutic bath in a cup. The classic base is a combination of hot water, lemon, honey, and whiskey. To mix it up, throw in some spices like cinnamon and star anise, infuse your hot water with black or chamomile tea, or substitute maple syrup or sugar for the honey. The spirits can also be swapped, depending on your preference; give rum, bourbon, or brandy a try.

◇◇◇◇◇◇◇◇

Fill a mug with boiling water and set aside for 1 minute to warm the mug. Pour out the water, then add the bourbon, honey, and lemon juice. Top with additional hot water and stir until the honey is dissolved. Garnish with the cinnamon stick, lemon peel, and star anise, if desired.

◄ Hot beverage delivery on ice
in St. Moritz, 1933

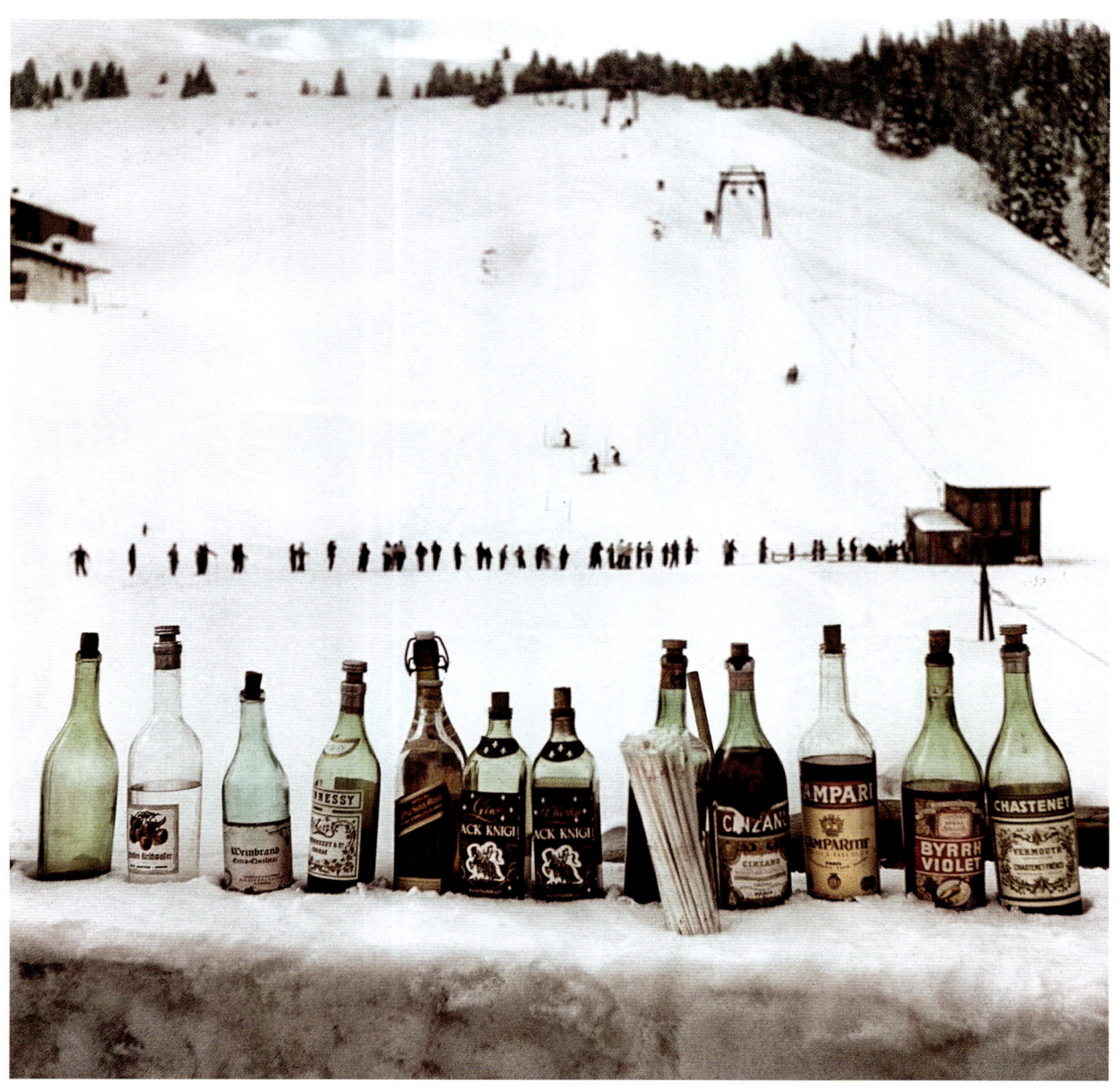

A fully stocked ice bar in Zürs, 1950

An ideal après-ski cocktail in hand from the Zürs ice bar

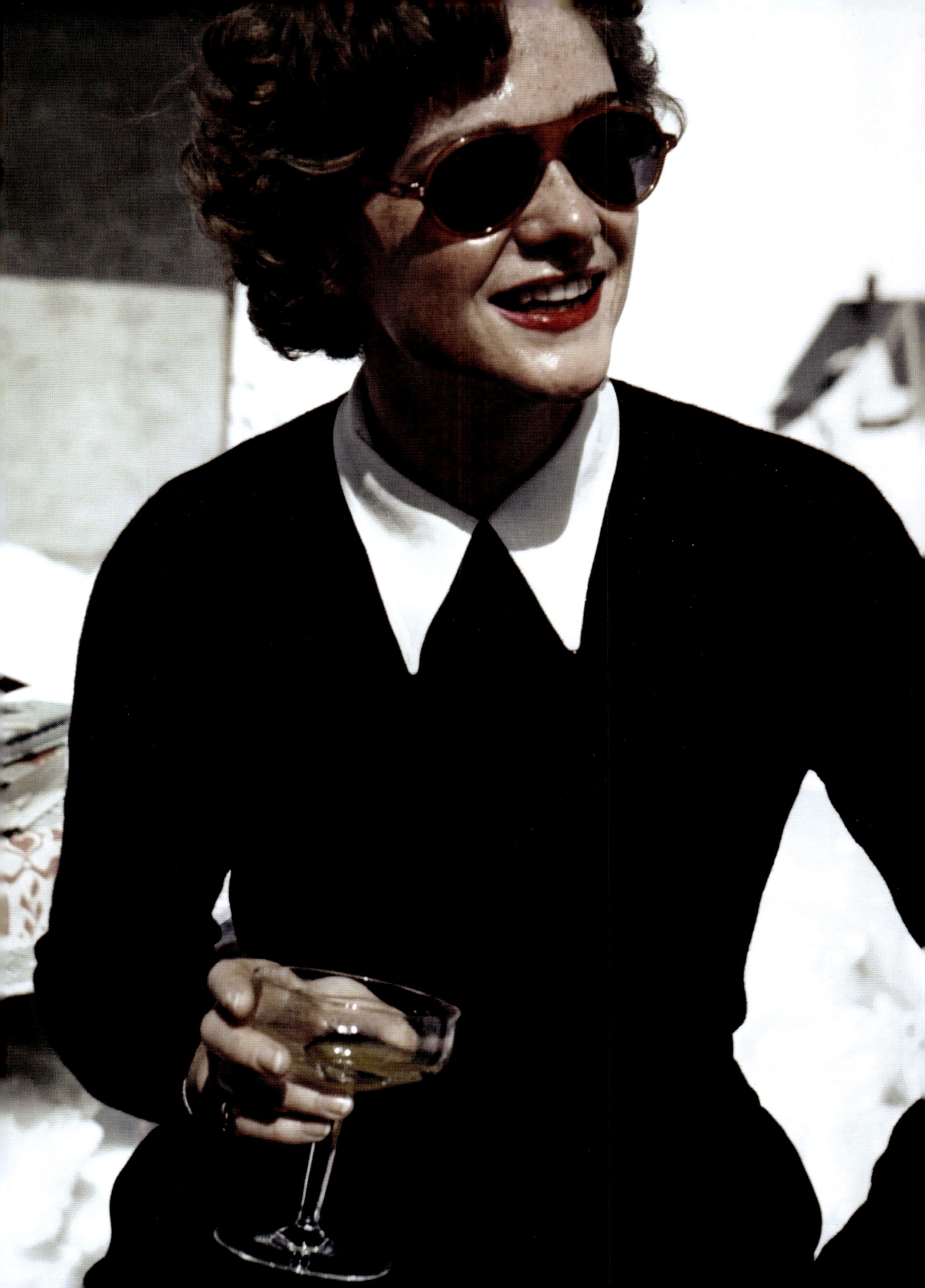

HOT
CHOCOLATE

Serves 4

6 ounces (170 g) semisweet chocolate,
   finely chopped
1 quart (1 L) whole milk
Liquor of choice (optional)
Marshmallows (to learn how to make your
   own, see page 203)

Families that play together stay together. Hence, we can't forget the little ones when planning post-ski-day fun. Hot chocolate needs no introduction; however, this next-level hot chocolate is another matter completely. Always look for the absolute best-quality bar of chocolate you can find. This recipe calls for semisweet (60 to 65% cocoa) chocolate, but bittersweet also works. Add a spiked floater for the adults (aged or dark rum, peppermint schnapps, Baileys, and Kahlúa are personal favorites) and revelers of all ages will be giddy.

◇◇◇◇◇◇◇

Combine the chocolate and milk in a heavy saucepan over medium heat and cook, whisking constantly. When tiny bubbles begin to form, after about 5 minutes, reduce the heat slightly and continue to whisk until the chocolate completely melts, about 1 minute more. Pour into mugs. Adults can spike their hot chocolate with the liquor of their choice, if desired. Top with a marshmallow and enjoy!

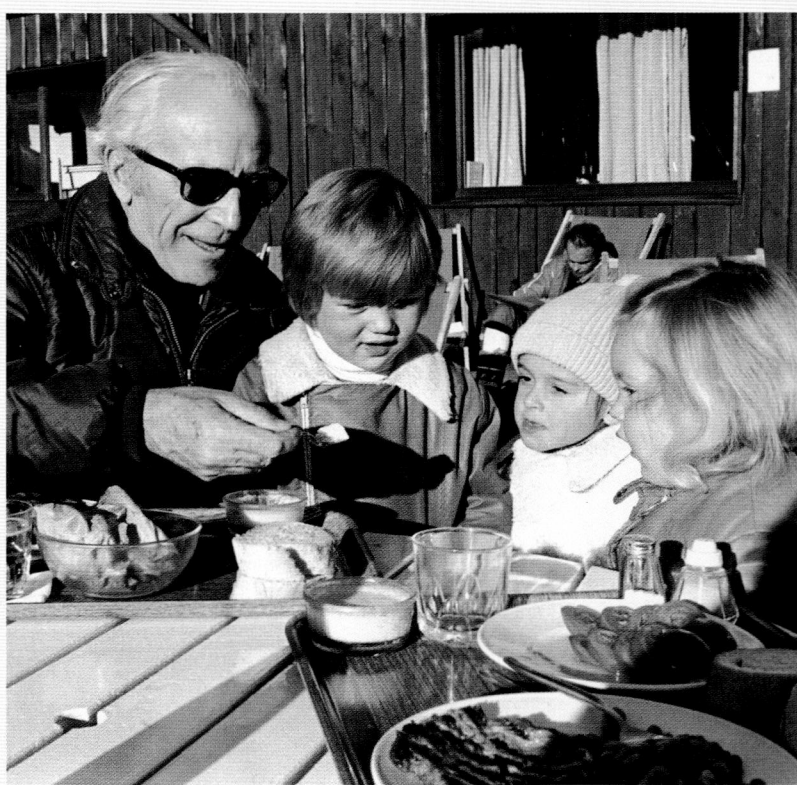

▸ Henri Ziegler, father of the
Concorde airplane, sharing treats
with his family in Courchevel in 1976

ESPRESSO MARTINI

Serves 1

1 ounce (30 ml) Licor 43 (or your
    preferred vanilla-infused liqueur)
1 ounce (30 ml) vodka
½ ounce (15 ml) Kahlúa
1 ounce (30 ml) chilled espresso
Ground cinnamon or whole espresso
    beans, for garnish

While the classic Espresso Martini is a simple combination of vodka, Kahlúa, espresso, and simple syrup, this recipe is inspired by the one served at the Goldener Hirsch in Deer Valley, Utah. Of course, most people do not typically stock the variety of extracts used in the Goldener Hirsch's excellent cocktail, but this version is an homage to its greatness. Consider swapping out the vodka for tequila to add a bit more flavor.

◇◇◇◇◇◇◇

Combine the Licor 43, vodka, Kahlúa, and espresso in a cocktail shaker with ice. Shake vigorously for about 30 seconds, until foam forms, then strain into a chilled martini or coupe glass. Top with a sprinkle of cinnamon or the classic garnish of three espresso beans, signifying health, wealth, and happiness.

JÄGERMEISTER

Serves 1

1½ ounces (45 ml) Jägermeister

No après-ski book would be complete without a nod to this iconic German herbal liqueur commonly enjoyed in Austrian and Swiss resorts. It will warm you up from the inside out.

◇◇◇◇◇◇◇

You can serve Jägermeister at room temperature or pour it over ice in a glass, but chilling the bottle in a freezer (or snow bank) and serving in a chilled shot glass is the preferred and iconic après-ski method of consumption.

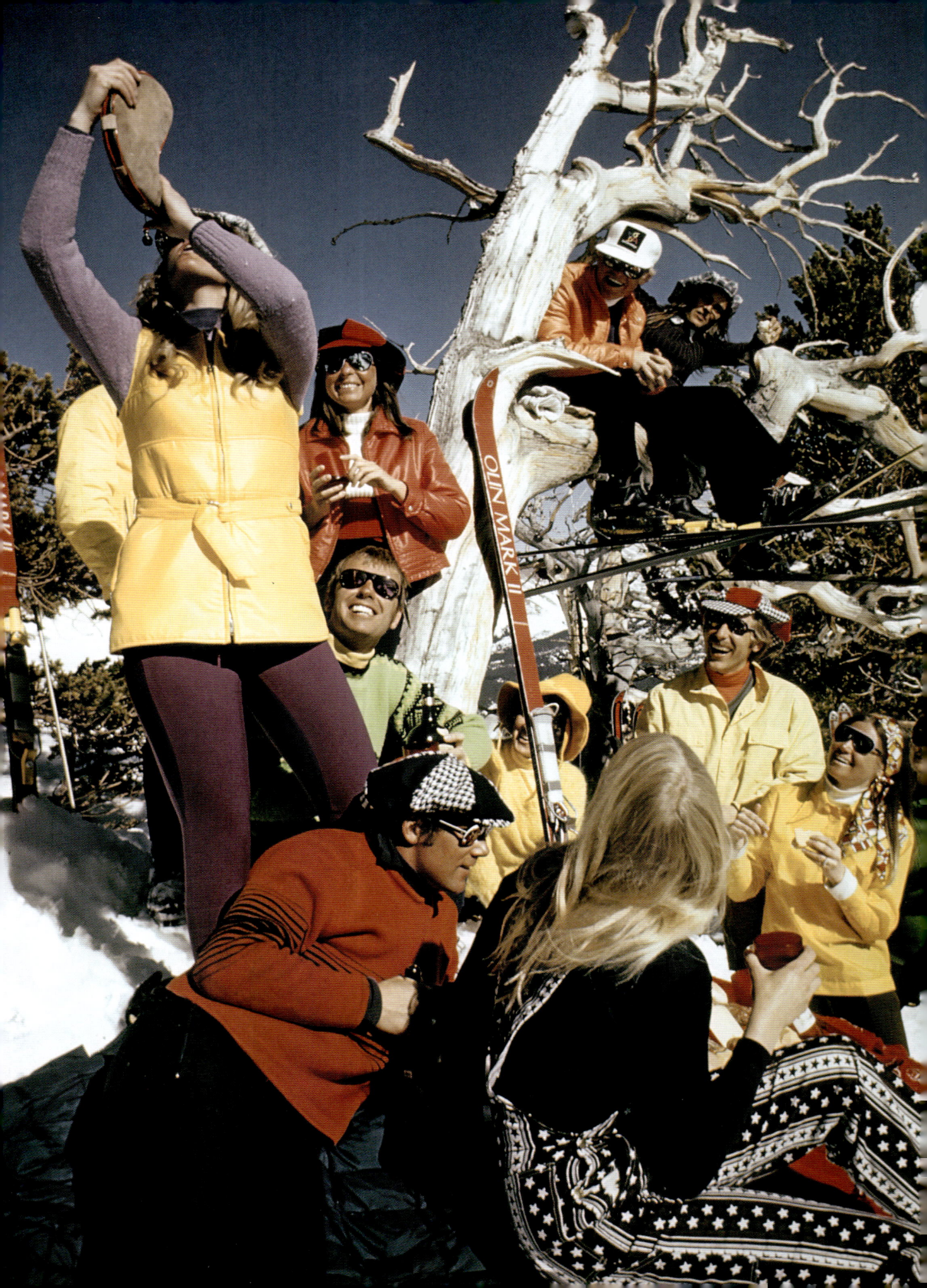

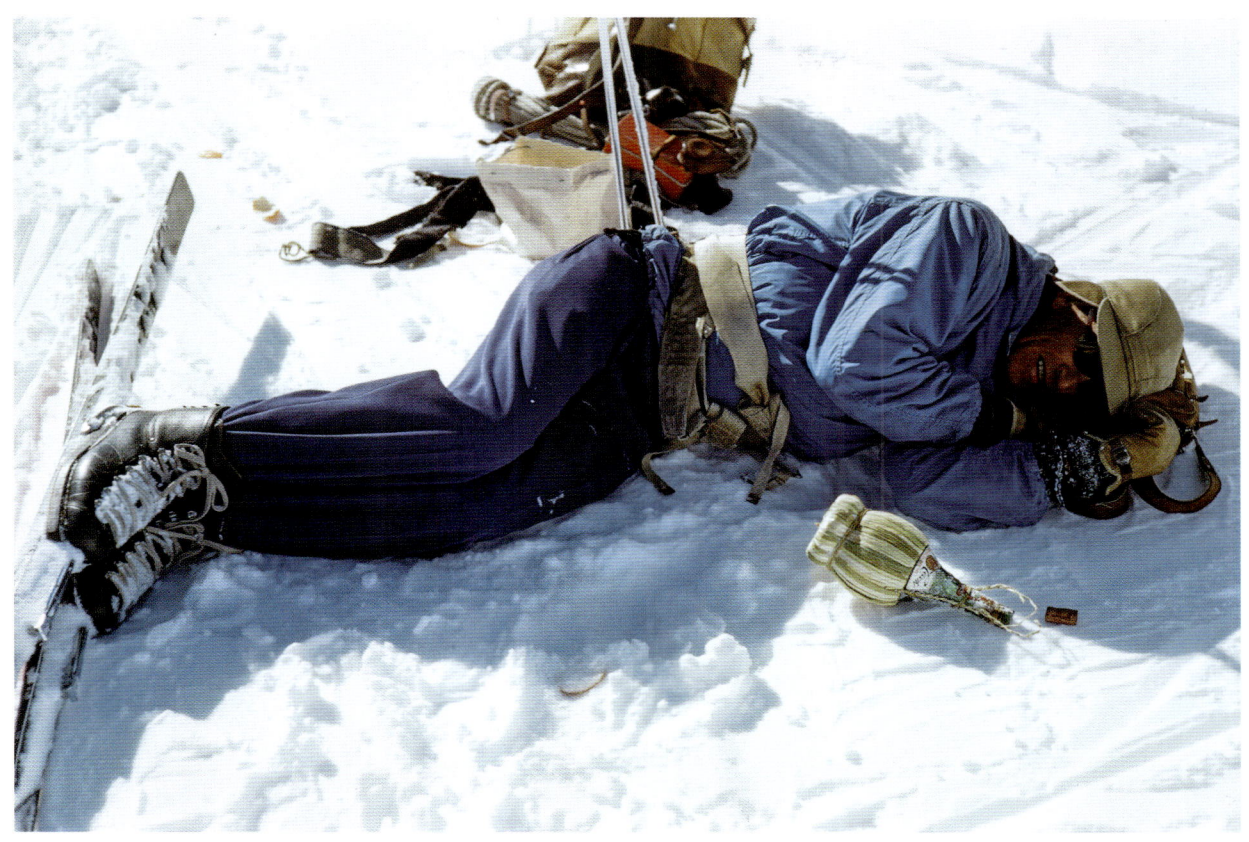

▲ After hours on the slopes and perhaps too much to drink, it's time for food in Zermatt, 1955.

◀ Après-ski in Breckenridge, Colorado, 1972

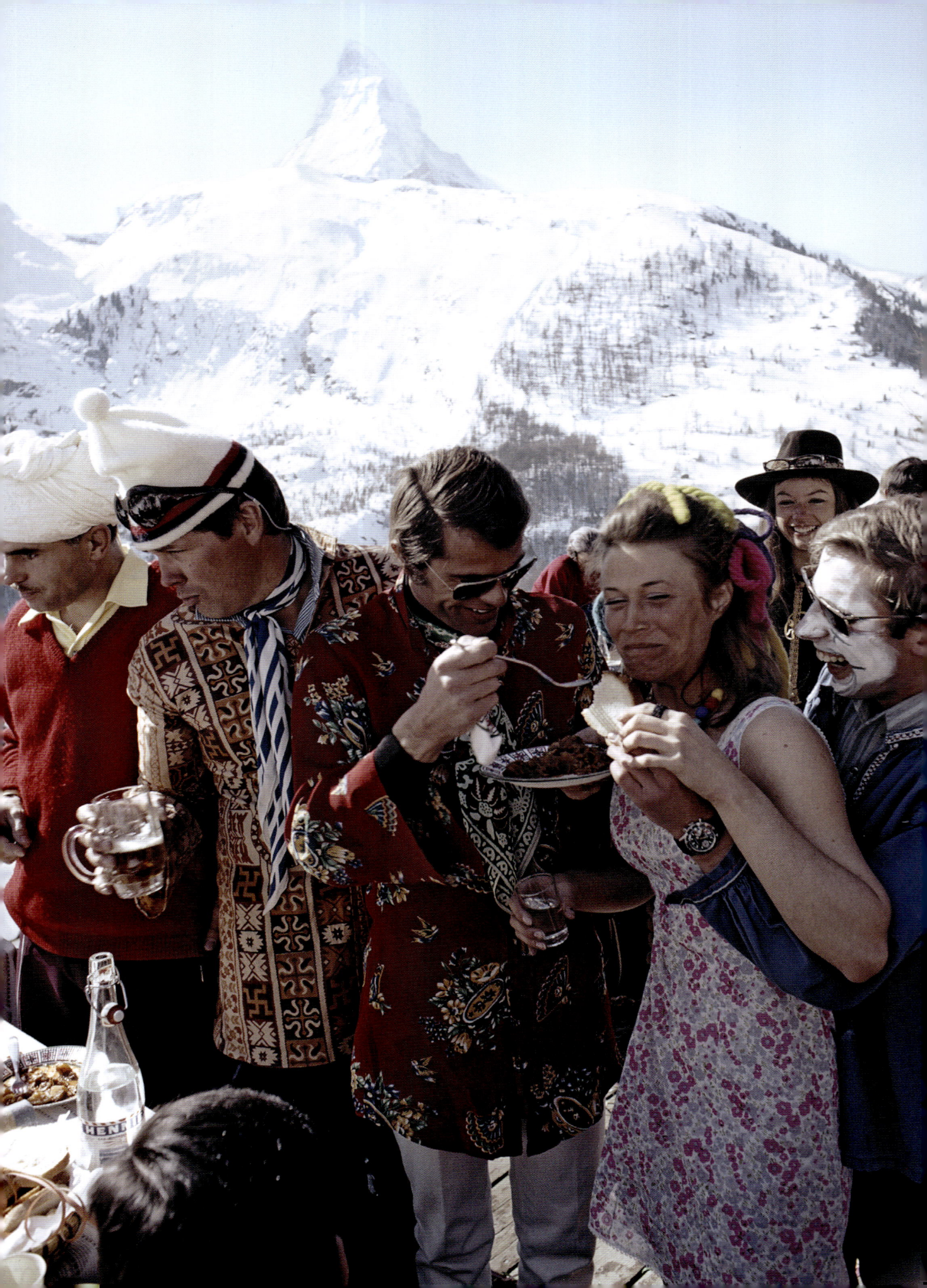

Food

—

Every ski region around the world boasts its own iconic dishes, from the cheese fondue of the Swiss Alps to the poutine of Quebec's Laurentian Mountains. As such, ski trips offer not only incredible scenery but also the discovery of beloved regional culinary traditions, shared with a sense of camaraderie. Whether a slope-side nibble or a complete meal, an après-ski menu is essential to a complete ski experience. These recipes are an indulgence, but after a day on the slopes, a bit of decadence has been earned.

A note about cooking at high altitudes: Due to lower air pressure, liquids evaporate more quickly and boil at a lower temperature the higher you are above sea level. I have included some helpful tips for those recipes that might require modification if being prepared at a high altitude.

◄ Après-ski with a side of food, liquor, and frivolity in Zermatt, 1968

BRAISED SHORT RIB AND BLACK BEAN NACHOS

Serves 8

FOR THE SHORT RIBS

4 pounds (1.8 kg) bone-in beef short ribs, patted dry
4 teaspoons coarse kosher salt
1½ teaspoons freshly ground black pepper
5 garlic cloves, smashed and peeled
2 jalapeño or serrano peppers, halved lengthwise, seeded if desired
1 onion, peeled and quartered lengthwise
1 (28-ounce/794 g) can chopped tomatoes
½ cup (20 g) coarsely chopped cilantro stems (reserve the leaves for topping)
2 teaspoons dried oregano
2 tablespoons extra-virgin olive oil
1 to 2 tablespoons chili powder
2 teaspoons ground coriander
2 teaspoons ground cumin
1 tablespoon tomato paste
1 (12-ounce/355 ml) bottle Mexican lager (Modelo Negra works well)

FOR THE BLACK BEANS

1 (15-ounce/425 g) can black beans
½ teaspoon chili powder
½ teaspoon ground coriander
½ teaspoon ground cumin
Kosher salt

No ski day is complete without nachos, at least in the US. The classic foundation of chips and cheese can be built upon with any number of toppings and proteins. Nachos can, of course, be made vegetarian, but my recipe takes them up a notch with the addition of braised short ribs and seasoned black beans.

NOTE: Ideally, cook the short ribs the day before, let them cool, and refrigerate the whole pot overnight. This will allow the flavors to come together and facilitate easier shredding before the nacho prep.

◇◇◇◇◇◇

Braise the short ribs: Season the short ribs with 3 teaspoons salt and the black pepper. Let rest while you prepare the sauce.

Place a large Dutch oven over high heat on the stovetop. Combine the garlic, peppers, and onion in the dry pot and cook, turning occasionally, until lightly charred all over, about 10 minutes.

Turn off the heat and transfer the garlic, peppers, and onion to a blender. Add the chopped tomatoes with their juices, cilantro stems, oregano, and remaining 1 teaspoon salt. Puree until smooth.

Preheat the oven to 350°F (175°C).

Return the Dutch oven to the stovetop over medium-high heat and add the olive oil. Sear the short ribs in batches until well browned all over, about 20 minutes. Transfer the browned ribs to a bowl.

Reduce the heat to medium, add the chili powder, coriander, and cumin to the pot, and cook, stirring, until fragrant, about 30 seconds. Stir in the tomato paste and cook until it begins to caramelize, 1 to 2 minutes. Stir in the tomato-pepper puree and beer and bring to a simmer. Return the short ribs to the pot, cover, and transfer to the oven. Bake for 1 hour 45 minutes, then uncover the pot, give the meat a stir, and continue baking until the ribs are fork-tender and falling off the bone, 45 to 60 minutes more. (Note: A longer cooking time may be needed at high altitude.)

FOR THE NACHOS

1 (16-ounce/455 g) bag restaurant-style tortilla chips (look for a sturdy chip)

1 to 2 jalapeños (depending on their heat), halved lengthwise and thinly sliced

8 ounces (225 g) sharp cheddar cheese, grated (about 2 cups)

8 ounces (225 g) Monterey Jack cheese, grated (about 2 cups)

4 avocados, peeled, pitted, and diced

Juice of 1 lime

Flaky sea salt (ideally Maldon)

½ small red onion, very thinly sliced

1½ cups (355 g) fresh salsa (preferably salsa verde)

1 cup (240 g) Mexican crema or sour cream (optional)

Hot sauce (optional)

Chopped fresh cilantro leaves (optional)

On the day of serving, remove the short ribs from the pot, reserving the sauce. Remove and discard the fat, bones, and gristle and shred the meat. Place the pot on the stove and reheat the sauce over medium heat. If it seems thin, simmer until it thickens. Return the meat to the pot and heat until warmed through.

Prepare the beans: Drain but do not rinse the beans. In a bowl, combine the beans with the chili powder, coriander, cumin, and salt to taste.

Assemble the nachos: Preheat the oven to 400°F (200°C). Line 2 rimmed baking sheets with parchment paper and divide the chips between them. Top the chips with small scoops of the bean mixture. Sprinkle evenly with the jalapeño slices and both cheeses, but don't go too heavy—the key to crispy nachos is to keep the toppings light when the chips go in the oven. Bake for 8 to 10 minutes, until the cheese is melted and bubbling and the edges of the chips are just beginning to brown.

Meanwhile, in a small bowl, mash together the avocados, lime juice, and salt to taste. Remove the nachos from the oven and top with the short ribs, dollops of the prepared avocado, red onion, and salsa. If desired, add crema, drizzle with hot sauce, and sprinkle with cilantro, or prepare small serving bowls with these toppings on the side. Serve immediately and dig in.

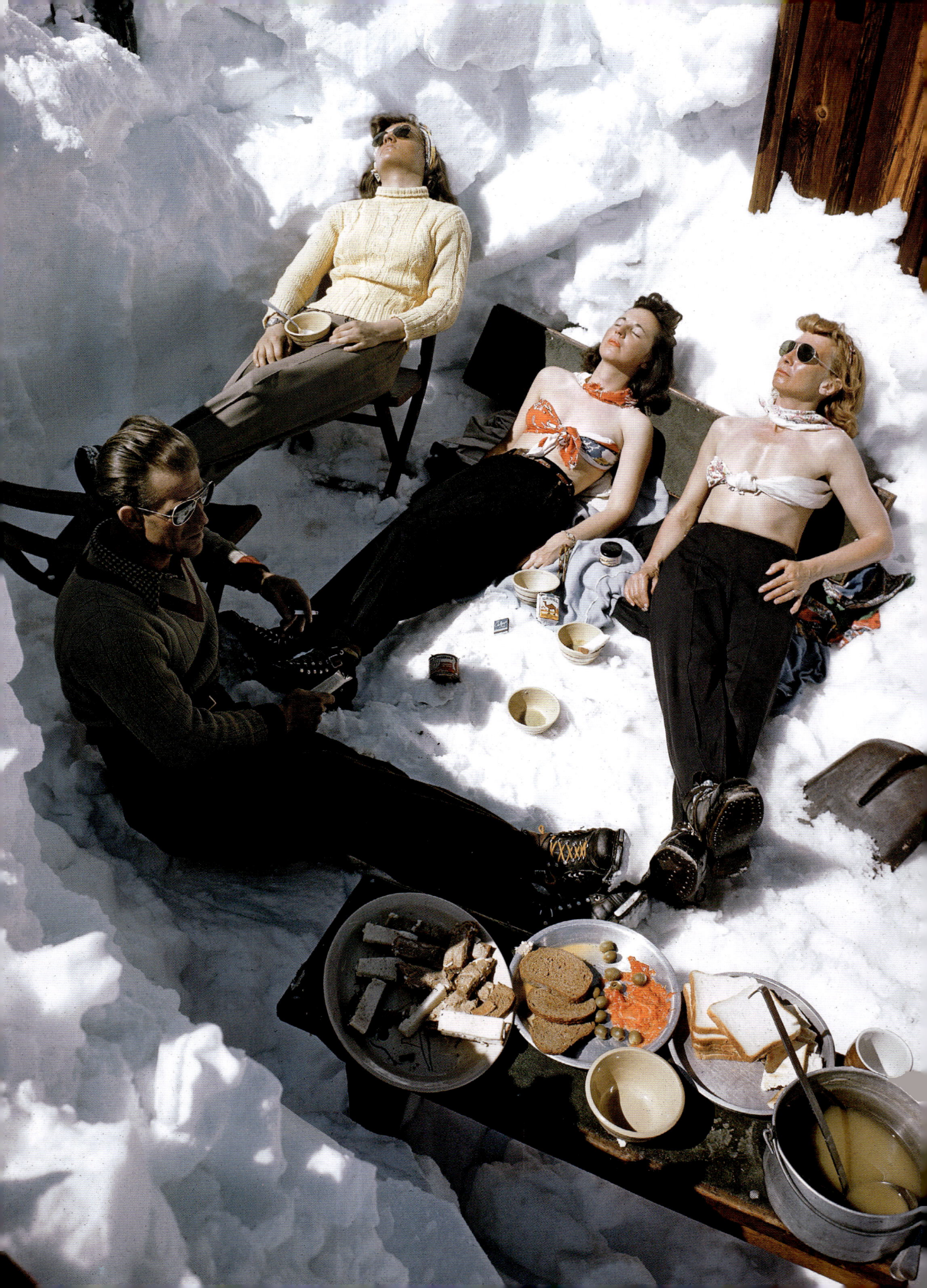

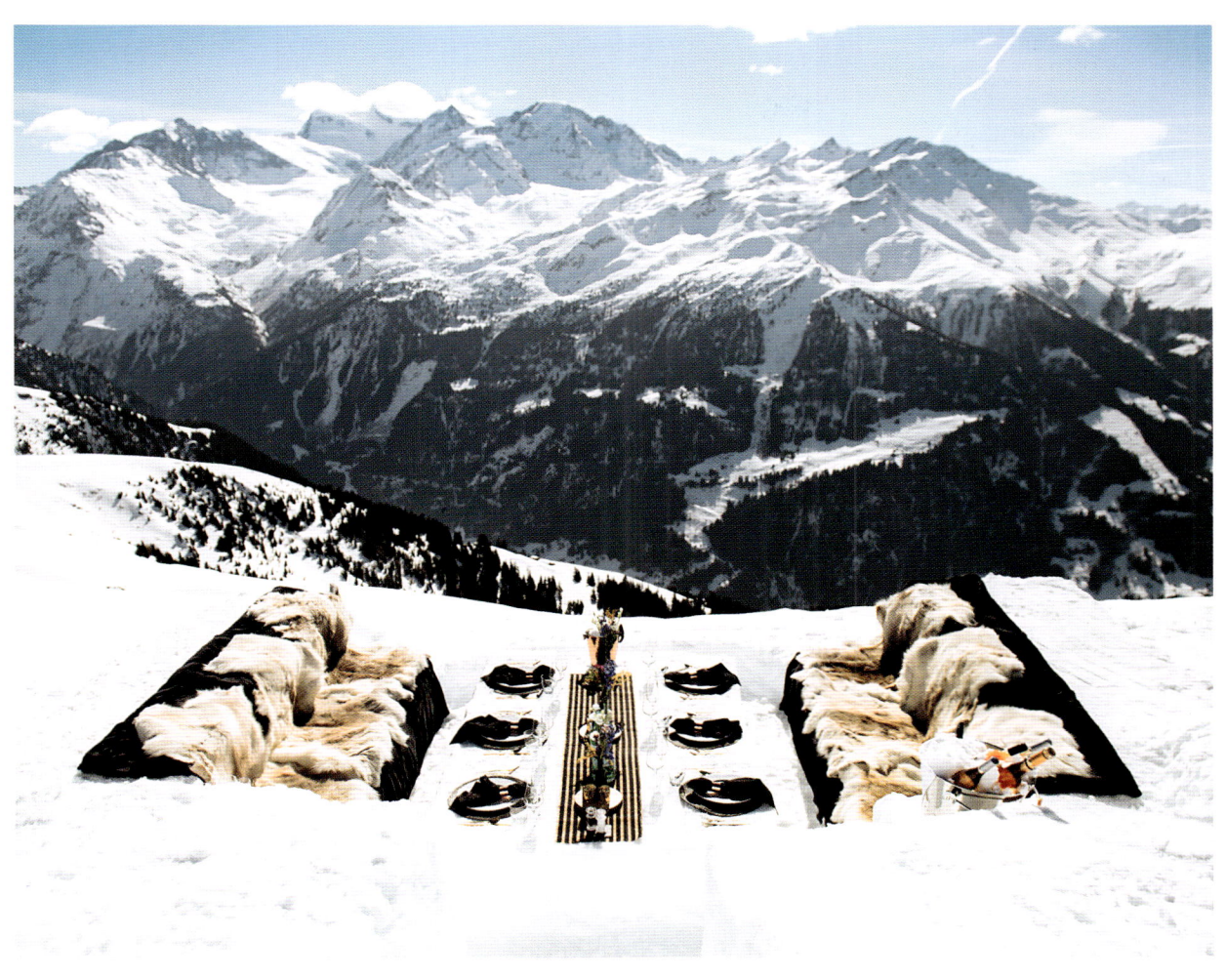

A superb tablescape for après-ski food and drinks on the slopes of the Alps, 2019

Dining and sunbathing in Sun Valley, 1946

APRÈS-SKI BOARD

Serves 6 to 8

FOR THE BOARD

10 ounces (285 g) soft cheese (such as Murray's Cave Aged Reserve Greensward)

1 pound (455 g) semi-hard cheese (such as Comté or Gruyère), sliced

1 pound (455 g) hard cheese (such as aged Manchego or Gouda), sliced

Fig jam

Honeycomb

1 Granny Smith apple, cored and thinly sliced, with skin on

1 Bartlett pear, cored and thinly sliced, with skin on

Selection of pickled vegetables (I like Pacific Pickle Works Carriots of Fire and Rick's Picks Mean Beans)

Green and red seedless grapes

Crisps (I recommend Raincoast Crisps Fig and Olive Crackers)

French baguette or sourdough loaf, cubed

6 ounces (170 g) beef salami, sliced (a favorite is Red Bear Tipsy Cow Beef & Brandy Salami)

3 ounces (85 g) bresaola, sliced

Cornichons

Castelvetrano olives (preferably unpitted)

Kalamata olives (preferably unpitted)

Unsalted roasted almonds or Marcona almonds

Pistachios

Dried apricots

Dried or fresh figs (if fresh, sliced in half)

Rosemary or thyme sprigs, for garnish

Dehydrated citrus slices, for garnish

Boards are great for any occasion. For après-ski, they provide a canvas for all types of nibbling food and make a great sidekick for Cheese Fondue (page 191) or Raclette (page 192). Alternatively, you can include wedges of cheese on the board itself and call it good. The quality of your ingredients here is essential: Look for artisanal specialty products for the best spread. Any type of board will work, but the idea is for the board to fill the center of your table, so plan appropriately, depending on your setting and the size of your crowd. The suggestions below are for 6 to 8 people and would fill a 14-by-20-inch (35 by 50 cm) board, but you can scale up or down as needed. More is more when it comes to a board. Load it up and forget about it while you enjoy your evening.

◇◇◇◇◇◇◇

Arrange your cheeses at intervals on your board to create a foundation. Remove the top layer of rind on your soft cheese. Place a small bowl filled with fig jam and the honeycomb (either right on the board or in a bowl) near the cheeses.

Arrange rows of sliced apple and pear and neat piles of pickled vegetables on the board. Cut small clusters of grapes and add them throughout.

Arrange rows of crisps and mounds of bread cubes at the ends of your board. If desired, serve additional bread cubes in a bowl or basket alongside the board.

Insert the meats between the other groupings.

Wedge in a pile of cornichons. Scatter clusters of olives, nuts, and dried fruit between the other groupings.

Finally, insert sprigs of rosemary and/or thyme and scatter dehydrated citrus slices throughout. Place serving tools, such as a small spoon for the jam and spreading knives for the soft cheese and honeycomb, where needed and have small plates ready nearby.

SWEET & SPICY CHICKEN WINGS

Serves 6

1 cup (320 g) gochujang
½ cup (120 ml) fresh orange juice
¼ cup (60 ml) honey
¼ cup (60 ml) light soy sauce
2 tablespoons toasted sesame oil
5 pounds (2.2 kg) chicken wings, split
Kosher salt
Freshly ground black pepper
2 scallions, green parts only, thinly sliced
Toasted sesame seeds (optional)

You will find chicken wings on nearly every bar menu in American ski towns. This recipe calls for gochujang, a fermented Korean red pepper paste, in a nod to our ski friends from Seoul. Serve these wings with ice-cold beer and a giant pile of napkins, or even better, wet wipes.

◇◇◇◇◇◇◇

In a medium bowl, whisk together the gochujang, orange juice, honey, soy sauce, and sesame oil.

Pat the chicken wings dry with paper towels and place in a large bowl. Add half of the marinade to the bowl with chicken and toss, making sure that each piece is coated. Cover and refrigerate for at least 2 hours and up to 8 hours. Reserve the remaining marinade.

Remove the chicken from the refrigerator 30 minutes before you plan to cook. Line 2 rimmed baking sheets with aluminum foil and place a few paper towels on each sheet. Divide the wings equally between the prepared baking sheets, setting them in a single layer on the paper towels, and pat dry.

Preheat the oven to 325°F (165°C). Remove the paper towels, wiping up any marinade from the foil as you go and making sure that the wings remain in a single layer. Season very lightly with salt and pepper (the marinade already contains salt from the soy sauce, so be sparing). Bake for about 30 minutes, until the fat begins to render and the skin gets lightly browned. Remove the pans from the oven. Increase the oven temperature to 450°F (230°C).

Using tongs, remove the wings to a large bowl and discard any juices from the baking sheets. Toss the wings with enough of the remaining marinade to fully coat, reserving some to serve for dipping. Using tongs, return the wings in a single layer to the baking sheets. Bake until a glaze develops and they are slightly charred, 10 to 15 minutes. Use an instant-read thermometer to confirm that the chicken has reached an internal temperature of 175°F (79°C). (Note: This may take longer at high altitude.) Transfer the wings to a serving platter and garnish with scallions and sesame seeds, if desired. Serve while hot!

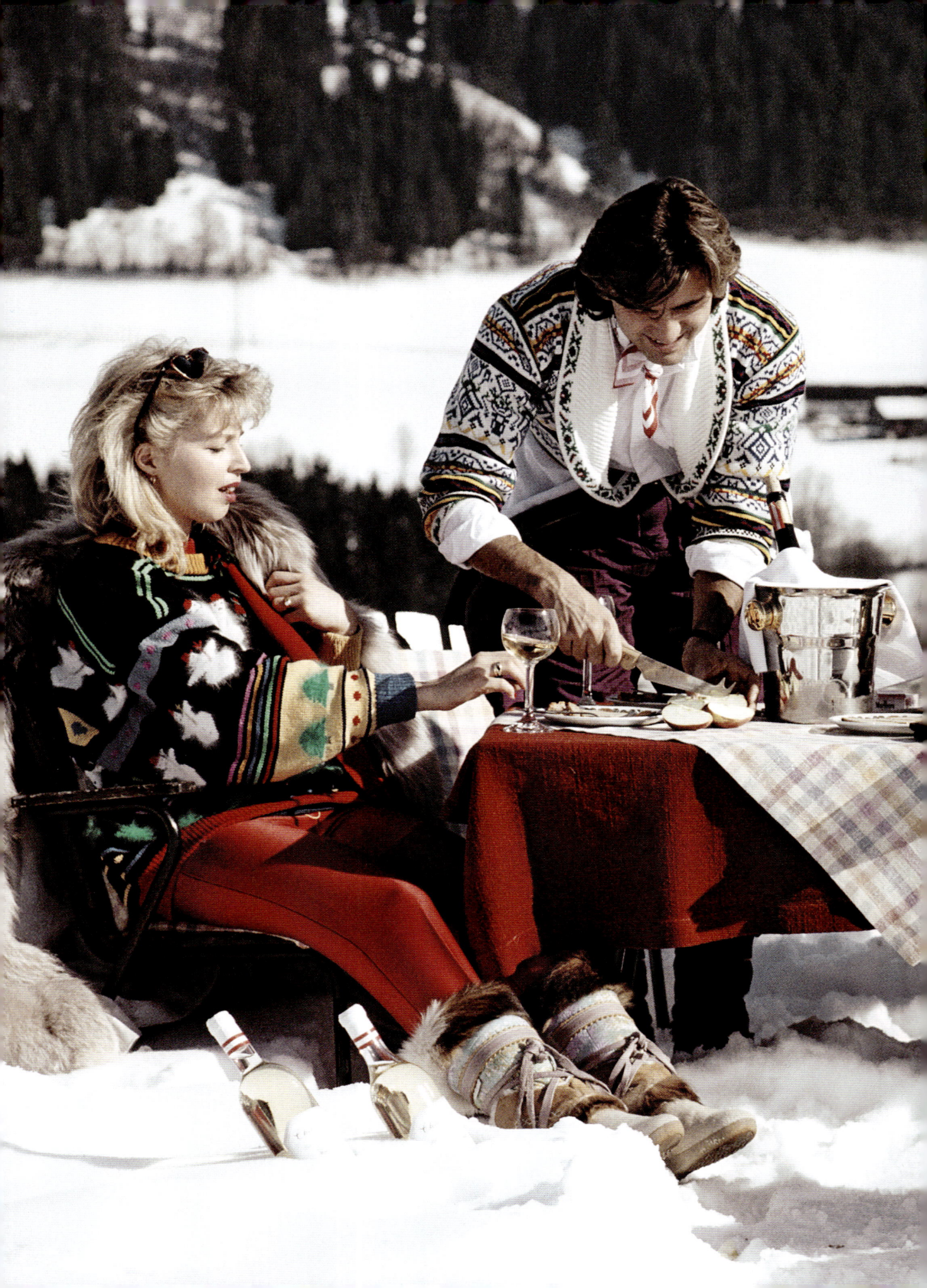

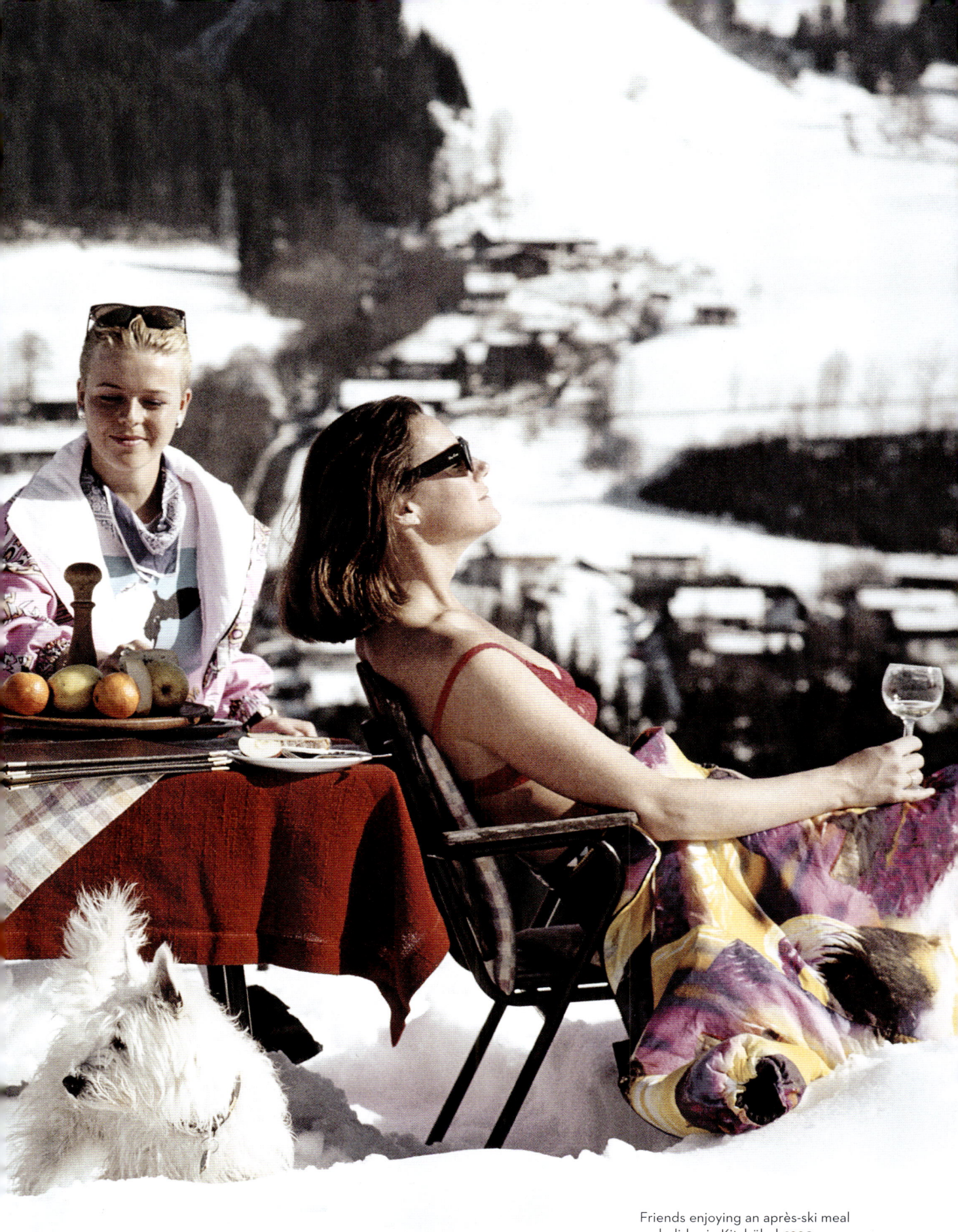

Friends enjoying an après-ski meal
on holiday in Kitzbühel, 1990

POUTINE

Serves 6 to 8

1 tablespoon vegetable oil
1 pound (455 g) boneless beef chuck,
    chopped into small pieces
4 tablespoons (55 g) unsalted butter
1 cup (150 g) diced white onion
Kosher salt
Freshly ground black pepper
Cayenne pepper (optional)
⅓ cup (40 g) all-purpose flour
1 quart (1 L) beef stock (see Note),
    homemade or store-bought (look
    for the best-quality low-sodium
    option you can find)
1 pound (455 g) crinkle-cut frozen
    french fries
1 cup (140 g) cheese curds (try
    Ellsworth Cooperative Creamery
    Cheddar Cheese Curds)
1 scallion, green parts only, thinly sliced

For the brave skiers of Quebec, who often face frigid temperatures, poutine is a beloved après-ski indulgence. This dish can be found all over the province and has made its way south to many US ski resorts as well. In fact, poutine has become as ubiquitous as nachos in some ski towns. For this recipe, you can save yourself some trouble and use high-quality store-bought french fries. The real star of the dish is the gravy, and for a twist on the traditional preparation, I've added beef chuck.

◇◇◇◇◇◇◇

Preheat the oven according to the french fry package instructions.

Set a large sauté pan over high heat and drizzle in the oil. When it's hot, add the beef and stir. Continue to cook until the released juices have evaporated, the beef has browned nicely, and some caramelization has formed on the bottom of the pan, 5 to 7 minutes.

Add the butter and reduce the heat to medium, stirring until the butter fully melts. Add the onions and a pinch each of salt, black pepper, and cayenne (if using), and stir, scraping the fond from the bottom of the pan. Sauté until the onions soften and turn golden brown, 2 to 3 minutes, then add the flour and cook, stirring constantly, for 3 to 4 minutes to create a roux. It will be ready when the raw flour smell is gone.

Stir in the beef stock and increase the heat to high. Let the mixture come to a simmer, then reduce the heat to medium and continue simmering, uncovered, until it reduces to a gravy consistency (but one that's thin enough to nicely coat your french fries), stirring occasionally and deglazing the sides of the pan along the way, 15 to 20 minutes.

While your gravy simmers, bake your french fries following the package instructions. Once you've removed the fries from the oven, switch on the broiler.

When the gravy reaches the desired consistency, check your meat for tenderness and add a pinch more salt if needed.

Divide the fries evenly between individual au gratin dishes or arrange them on one large ovenproof serving dish. Sprinkle the cheese curds evenly over the fries. Place under the broiler for just a few moments, until the cheese curds begin to melt, then remove from the oven, ladle the gravy over the fries, sprinkle with scallions, and serve.

NOTE: If preparing this recipe at a high altitude, the stock in the gravy may evaporate more quickly; you may wish to add ½ cup (120 ml) more beef stock.

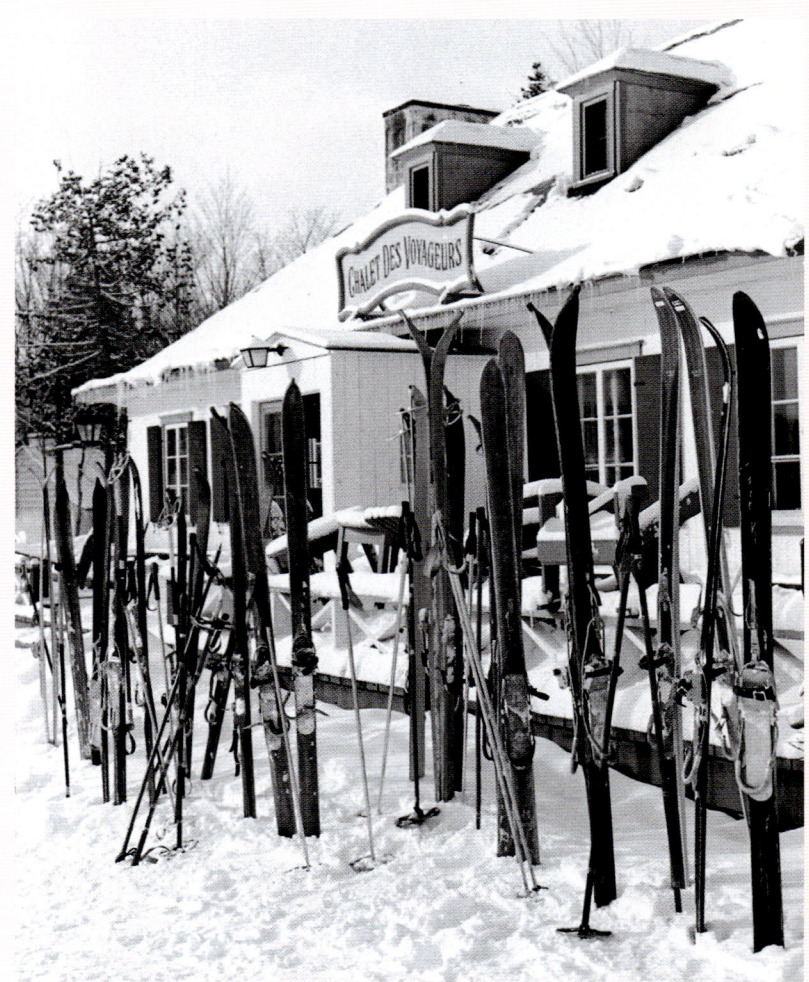

▶ With freezing temperatures, hearty food such as poutine is best enjoyed indoors (as in Mont Tremblant, captured here in 1945).

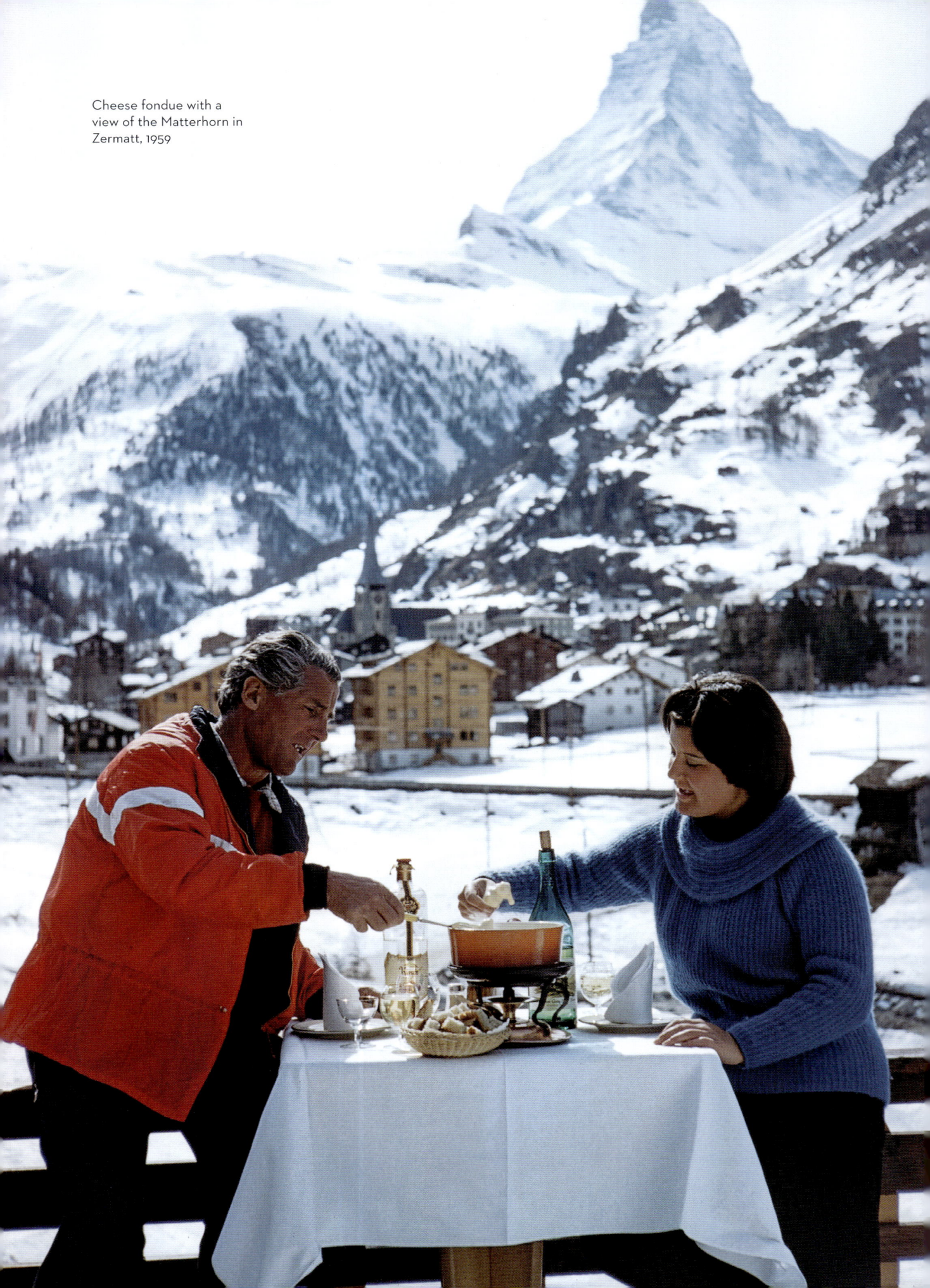

Cheese fondue with a
view of the Matterhorn in
Zermatt, 1959

CHEESE FONDUE

Serves 4 to 6

FOR THE FONDUE

1 garlic clove, lightly crushed
2 cups (480 ml) dry white wine
2 tablespoons cornstarch
2 tablespoons warm water
8 ounces (225 g) Gruyère cheese,
    coarsely grated
8 ounces (225 g) Emmental cheese,
    coarsely grated
1 tablespoon kirsch (optional)

SUGGESTIONS FOR DIPPING

1 Fuji apple, cored and sliced (or
    cubed), with skin on
1 Granny Smith apple, cored and sliced
    (or cubed), with skin on
2 Bartlett pears, cored and sliced (or
    cubed), with skin on
1 large artisan French boule, cubed
Blanched broccoli florets
Roasted mini potatoes

SPECIAL EQUIPMENT

Fondue pot
Fondue forks

Fondue has been bringing Alpine families together since the eighteenth century. This Swiss winter tradition took America by storm after appearing at the New York World's Fair in the Swiss Pavilion's Alpine restaurant in 1964. There is no standard recipe, and cheese type preferences can vary by region—I'm partial to Emmental and Gruyère. You can serve this fondue alongside the Après-Ski Board (page 184) and use some of the board ingredients for dipping, or offer it with a side plate piled with sliced fruit, cubed bread, and vegetables. Just don't lose your food in the pot, or you will be sentenced to dish duty!

◇◇◇◇◇◇◇

Rub the inside of a heavy saucepan with the garlic clove, then discard. Add the wine to the pot and bring to a simmer over medium heat.

In a cup, stir together the cornstarch and warm water.

Gradually add both cheeses to the pot of simmering wine, using a wooden spoon to stir constantly in a zigzag pattern. Do not stir in a circular motion or the cheese might form into a ball. Continue to stir until the cheese has just melted and is creamy, being careful not to allow the mixture to boil.

Give a quick stir to your cornstarch mixture and slowly stir it into the fondue. Let simmer, continuing to stir, until the fondue has thickened, 5 to 8 minutes. Stir in the kirsch, if using. When it's ready, carefully transfer to a fondue pot and place the pot over a tea candle or canned heat burner, with fondue forks at the ready and your dipping ingredients alongside.

RACLETTE

Serves 4

1½ pounds (680 g) baby potatoes
Extra-virgin olive oil
½ teaspoon coarse kosher salt or flaky
   sea salt (such as Maldon)
1 medium yellow onion, thinly sliced
14 ounces (400 g) raclette cheese,
   ideally a wheel segment with a
   curved edge of rind, but a wedge or
   slices will also work
1 cup (150 g) cornichons, sliced into
   rounds

Another favorite Alpine cheese experience involves melted semi-soft raclette. I first encountered this cheese on a trip to Chamonix, France, but it is produced on both the French and Swiss sides of the Alps and is very popular throughout the region. Typically, a half wheel or wedge of raclette is placed onto a fascinating contraption with a hot iron used to melt the surface on demand. A plate of small potatoes, cornichons, and pickled onions is prepared, and when enough cheese is melted it is simply scraped and drizzled directly over the plate. This quintessential après-ski culinary experience can be easily re-created at home without any special tools. Instead of using boiled potatoes and pickled onions, my recipe calls for pan-frying the vegetables before slathering them with cheese. The method of quartering the potatoes results in a contrast of crunchy and creamy textures and dark and light surfaces. You can serve individual portions, but to get the party started faster, I recommend preparing one large cast-iron skillet with enough ingredients and cheese to share.

◇◇◇◇◇◇◇

Cut the potatoes in half and place them on your cutting board cut side down; then halve them again but keep these halves together. Add enough olive oil to a large (at least 12 inches/30 cm) cast-iron skillet to coat the bottom with about ⅛ inch (3 mm) of oil. Heat over medium heat until the oil begins to shimmer. Sprinkle salt evenly over the oil. Place the cut potatoes on the salt in the pan without separating the quarters (so each still appears as one half). Cook without disturbing the potatoes for about 10 minutes. Then gently turn over one potato half to see if the bottom has browned nicely. If it hasn't, continue to cook for a few more minutes and check again.

When the browning looks good, remove the pan from the heat for a few seconds to let it cool down, turn the heat down to the lowest setting, cover the pan, and return it to the burner. This will allow the potatoes to steam and continue to brown. Cook for another 20 minutes, or until a sharp knife slips easily into a potato.

Use a spatula to transfer the potatoes to a plate. Drain off all but about 2 tablespoons of the olive oil.

Return the pan to medium heat. Add the onions and sauté for about 8 minutes, until they are soft and lightly browned; reduce the heat if you see that they are browning too quickly. Remove from the heat and return the potatoes to the pan in a single layer, cut side up, allowing the halves to separate and reveal the unbrowned surfaces. Set the pan aside.

Fire up the broiler. Line a small rimmed baking sheet with aluminum foil and brush lightly with olive oil. Place the cheese on the baking sheet, rind side down (if using a wheel segment), and set it directly under the broiler. Watch closely; as soon as the cheese begins to melt and bubble, after about 2 minutes, remove the baking sheet from the oven, tip the cheese over the pan with the potatoes and onions, and scrape the melted cheese evenly over the top. You might need to repeat this step a time or two to melt enough cheese to cover the pan. Try to work fast because the cheese will cool quickly. Sprinkle evenly with cornichon rounds and serve immediately.

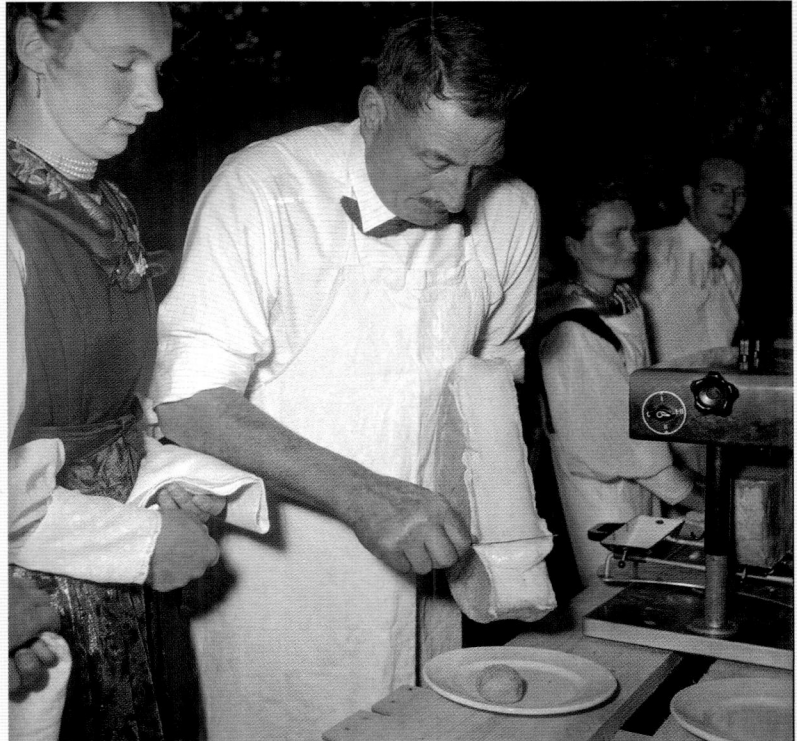

▶ Raclette served in Sion, Switzerland, 1959

SOUPE A L'OIGNON (FRENCH ONION SOUP)

Serves 6

FOR THE SOUP

3 tablespoons unsalted butter

1 tablespoon vegetable oil

2 pounds (910 g) yellow onions, thinly sliced

1 teaspoon kosher salt, plus more as needed

½ teaspoon freshly ground black pepper, plus more as needed

2 quarts (2 L) beef stock (see Note), homemade or store-bought (look for the best-quality low-sodium option you can find)

3 tablespoons flour

½ cup (120 ml) dry white wine or vermouth

FOR THE CROÛTES

1 good crusty French baguette, cut into at least twelve ¾- to 1-inch-thick (2 to 3 cm) slices

Extra-virgin olive oil

1 or 2 garlic cloves, halved lengthwise

FOR SERVING

3 teaspoons (15 ml) sherry, or cognac

8 ounces (225 g) Gruyère cheese, grated (or a combination of Gruyère and Parmesan)

Extra-virgin olive oil

SPECIAL EQUIPMENT

6 oven-safe soup bowls

Though it did not originate on the slopes of the Alps, this dish, which was created in the center of Paris, has worked its way onto many great après-ski menus. It is hard to imagine a more ideal way to savor the end of a day of skiing than with a bowl of French onion soup. For this recipe, the onions need a long, slow cook. Pour yourself a glass of wine and be patient while they fully caramelize.

◇◇◇◇◇◇◇

Prepare the soup: Combine the butter and oil in a 4- to 5-quart (4 to 5 L) heavy-bottomed saucepan or Dutch oven over medium-low heat. When the mixture begins to bubble, add the onions, cover, and cook for 15 minutes, stirring often. Remove the lid, increase the heat to medium, add the salt and pepper, and cook, uncovered, stirring occasionally, until the onions are caramelized (look for a rich golden brown color and a very soft but not mushy texture), 35 to 40 minutes. If the onions are browning too quickly, reduce the heat.

Meanwhile, bring the beef stock to a boil in a medium saucepan.

Sprinkle the caramelized onions with the flour and cook, stirring, for 3 minutes, until a slightly toasted, nutty aroma develops. Move the pan off the heat and gently add the boiling stock, stirring. Add the wine and taste; adjust the seasoning if needed. Return the pan to low heat and simmer, partially covered, for 30 to 40 minutes, skimming the fat occasionally, until the soup develops a rich color and flavor. Taste once again for seasoning, adding salt and pepper if needed.

If desired, the soup can be made ahead to this point and refrigerated for up to 3 days.

Prepare the croûtes: Preheat the oven to 325°F (165°C). Arrange the bread slices in a single layer on a rimmed baking sheet. Bake for 15 minutes, then remove from the oven. Using a pastry brush, brush both sides of each slice with olive oil. Arrange the slices with their other sides face up (so both sides have a turn face up on the sheet), return to the oven, and bake for 15 minutes, until the bread is lightly browned and thoroughly dried. Remove from the oven and rub each slice with the cut side of the garlic.

If you're making these ahead of time, store the croûtes in an airtight container at room temperature for up to 3 days.

Assemble for serving: When you're ready to serve, position a rack in the top third of your oven and preheat the oven to 375°F (190°C). Bring the soup to a boil on the stovetop.

Place the oven-safe bowls on a rimmed baking sheet, add ½ teaspoon sherry to each bowl, and ladle in the soup, leaving at least 1 inch (3 cm) of space at the top of the bowl. Float at least 2 croûtes on top of each bowl of soup and divide the cheese evenly among the bowls, sprinkling to completely cover the croûtes as well as the soup. The more cheese, the better. Drizzle the cheese with a little olive oil. Bake for 10 to 20 minutes, until the cheese is melted and bubbling, then switch on your broiler and broil for 1½ to 2 minutes, until the tops have browned lightly. Serve immediately.

NOTE: If preparing this recipe at a high altitude, the stock in the soup may evaporate more quickly; you may wish to add 1 cup (240 ml) more beef stock.

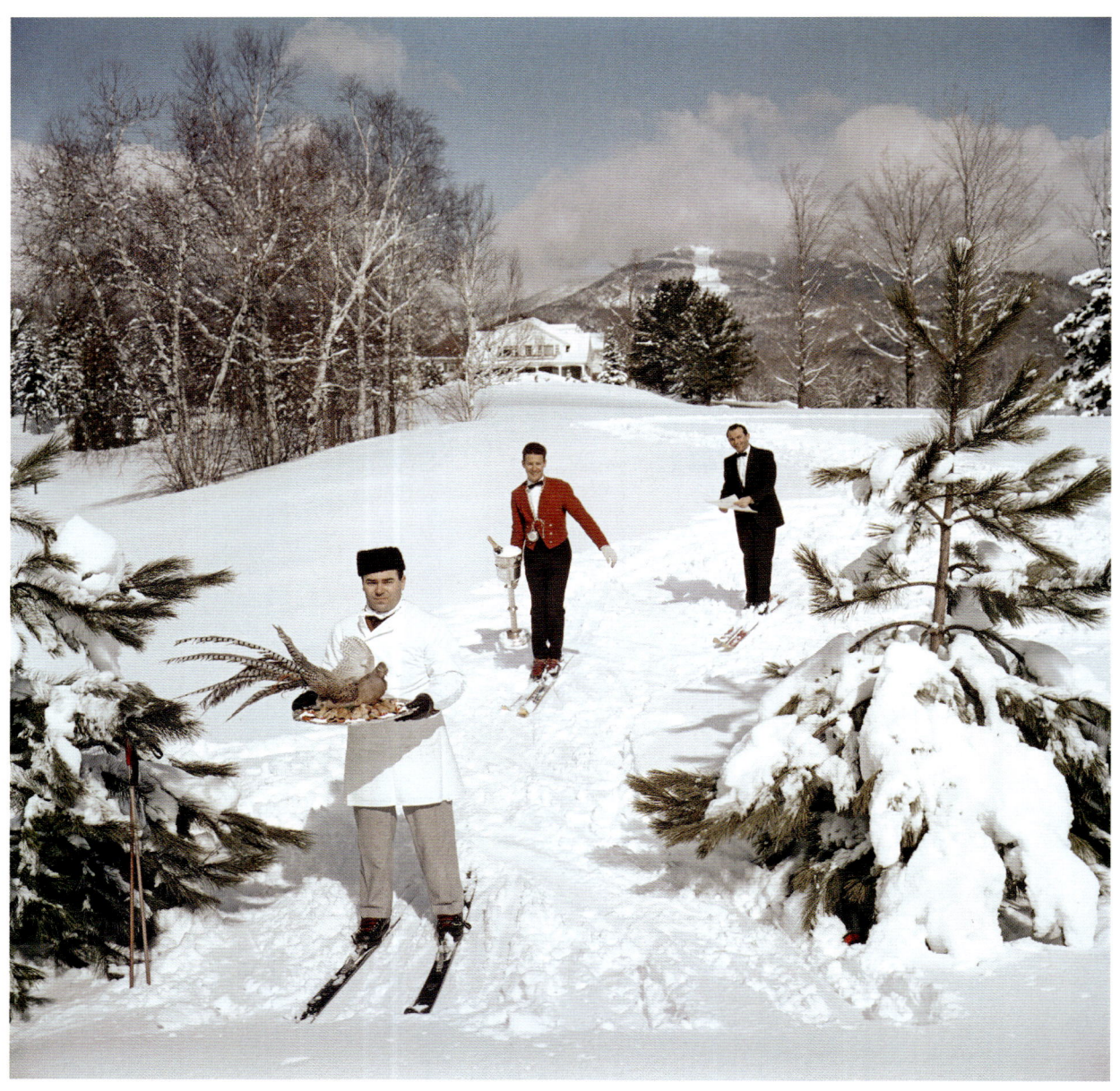

▲ Skiing waiters in Stowe, 1962

▶ Après-ski meal on ice in St. Moritz, 1931

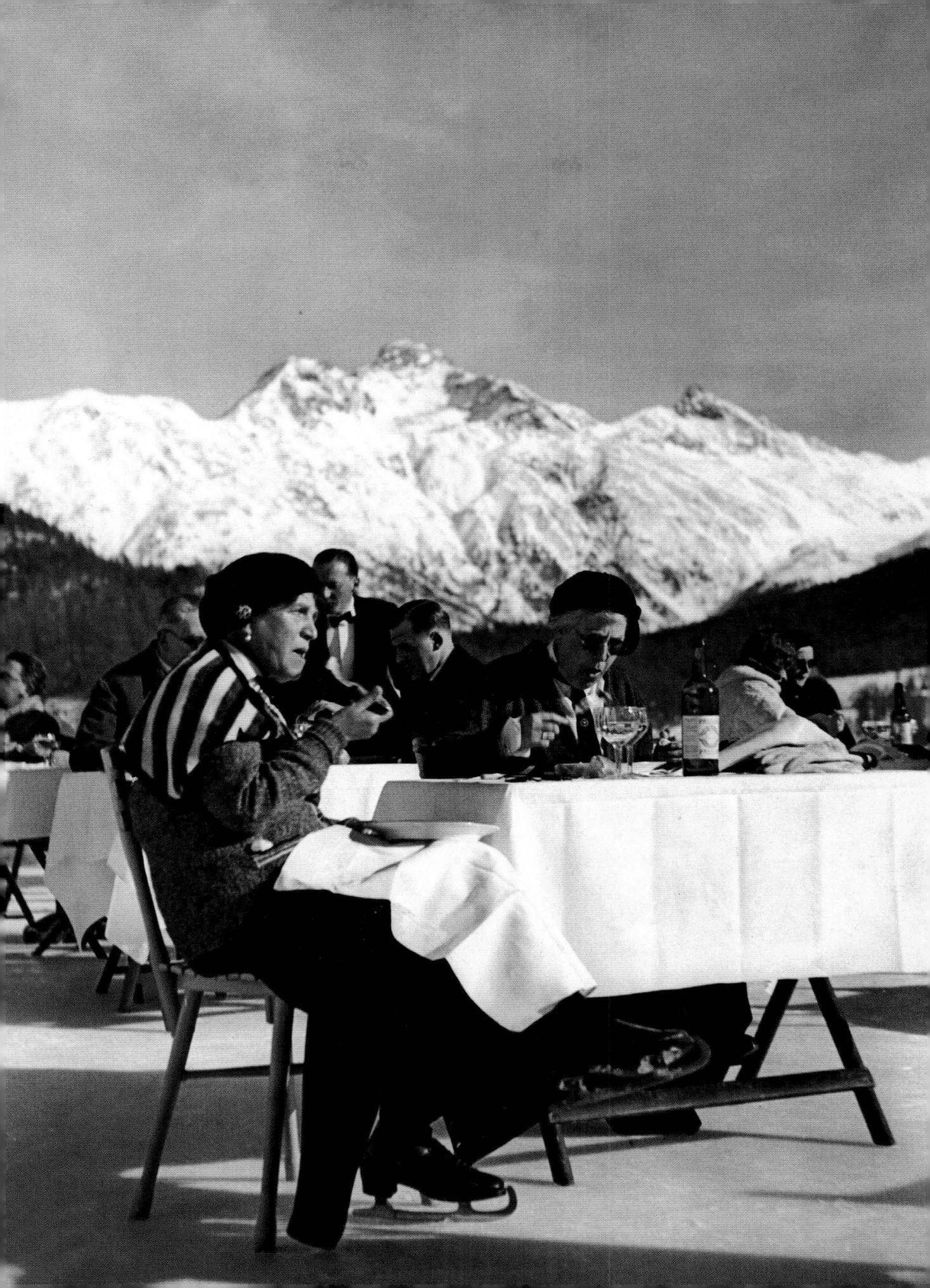

APPLE STRUDEL

Serves 8 to 10

FOR THE STRUDEL
¼ cup (50 g) raisins
3 tablespoons rum or lukewarm water
8 tablespoons (115 g) unsalted butter
½ cup (60 g) fine dried breadcrumbs
⅓ cup (65 g) granulated sugar
½ teaspoon ground cinnamon
1½ pounds (680 g) tart apples (such
    as Granny Smith or Pink Lady),
    peeled, quartered, and thinly sliced
    crosswise (see Notes)
12 (13-by-17-inch/33 by 43 cm) phyllo
    sheets
Powdered sugar, for dusting

FOR THE WHIPPED CREAM
1 cup (240 ml) chilled heavy cream or
    heavy whipping cream
¼ cup (30 g) powdered sugar
1 teaspoon pure vanilla extract

NOTES: After slicing your apples, you can squeeze some fresh lemon juice over them to keep them from browning.

Soaking the raisins will plump them up, rehydrate them, and, if rum is used, give them a nice boozy flavor.

Flaky pastry with warm, spiced apple chunks enjoyed next to the fire with your favorite cocktail makes for an idyllic end to the ski day and start of the evening. Strudel is often served with a vanilla sauce or vanilla ice cream, but this recipe calls for a simple homemade vanilla whipped cream that's also a perfect topping for Hot Chocolate (page 174). You can absolutely make homemade strudel dough, but to save time and achieve a flaky, thin dough very similar to traditional German apfelstrudel, this recipe uses store-bought phyllo sheets.

◇◇◇◇◇◇

Prepare the strudel: Combine the raisins and rum or water in a small bowl. Let soak for 10 minutes.

Meanwhile, melt 2 tablespoons butter in a small skillet over medium heat. Add the breadcrumbs and toast, stirring constantly, until they are golden brown, about 4 minutes. Transfer the breadcrumbs to a large bowl and let them cool. Set aside the skillet.

In a small bowl, combine the granulated sugar and cinnamon. Add the mixture to the buttered breadcrumbs, stirring to combine.

Drain the raisins and combine them with the apples in a large bowl.

Melt the remaining 6 tablespoons (85 g) butter in the reserved skillet and transfer to a small bowl.

Preheat the oven to 375°F (190°C) and set a rack in the center of the oven.

Lay a strip of parchment or waxed paper longer than your phyllo sheets on a work surface, with a long side closest to you. Place a sheet of phyllo in the center of the paper (again, with a long side closest to you) and use a pastry brush to lightly brush its surface with the melted butter. Lay the next sheet of phyllo directly on top of the first and repeat the process until you have a stack of 6 buttered sheets.

Leaving a 2-inch (5 cm) border, spread half of the prepared breadcrumbs over the lower half of the top phyllo sheet (the side closest to you). Then spread half of the apple mixture over the breadcrumbs. Fold the short ends of the phyllo stack over the filling to keep it from spilling out during rolling. Starting at the long end closest to you, use the paper to help you pick up the bottom edge, roll the phyllo over the filling, and continue rolling away from you to create a tight strudel with its seam side down. Then trim the paper so it is just wide enough to hold the strudel, and use the paper to transfer the strudel (still seam-side down) to a rimmed baking sheet.

Repeat the process with the remaining 6 phyllo sheets and the remaining breadcrumbs and apple mixture to create another strudel and place it seam-side down on its paper next to the first strudel on the baking sheet. Brush both with the remaining melted butter.

Bake on the middle rack until the strudels are golden brown, 35 to 45 minutes. (Note: The baking time may be slightly longer at high altitude.) Remove from the oven and let cool slightly.

Prepare the whipped cream: Place a medium mixing bowl in the refrigerator to chill for at least 15 minutes before getting started, and keep your heavy cream refrigerated and cold until you are ready to use it.

Put the cream, powdered sugar, and vanilla extract in your chilled bowl and use a hand-held electric mixer to beat the ingredients together, starting on a low speed and gradually increasing to high as the mixture begins to firm.

Beat until stiff peaks form, 60 to 90 seconds, stopping halfway to scrape down the sides of the bowl with a spatula. Whipped cream can be stored in the refrigerator in an airtight container for up to 2 days.

To serve: The strudel should be served warm. If made ahead, reheat it in a 400°F (200°C) oven for 15 minutes. Use a slotted spatula to carefully transfer the strudels to a serving platter, slice them diagonally, and dust with powdered sugar. Load whipped cream into a serving bowl and serve alongside the strudel slices.

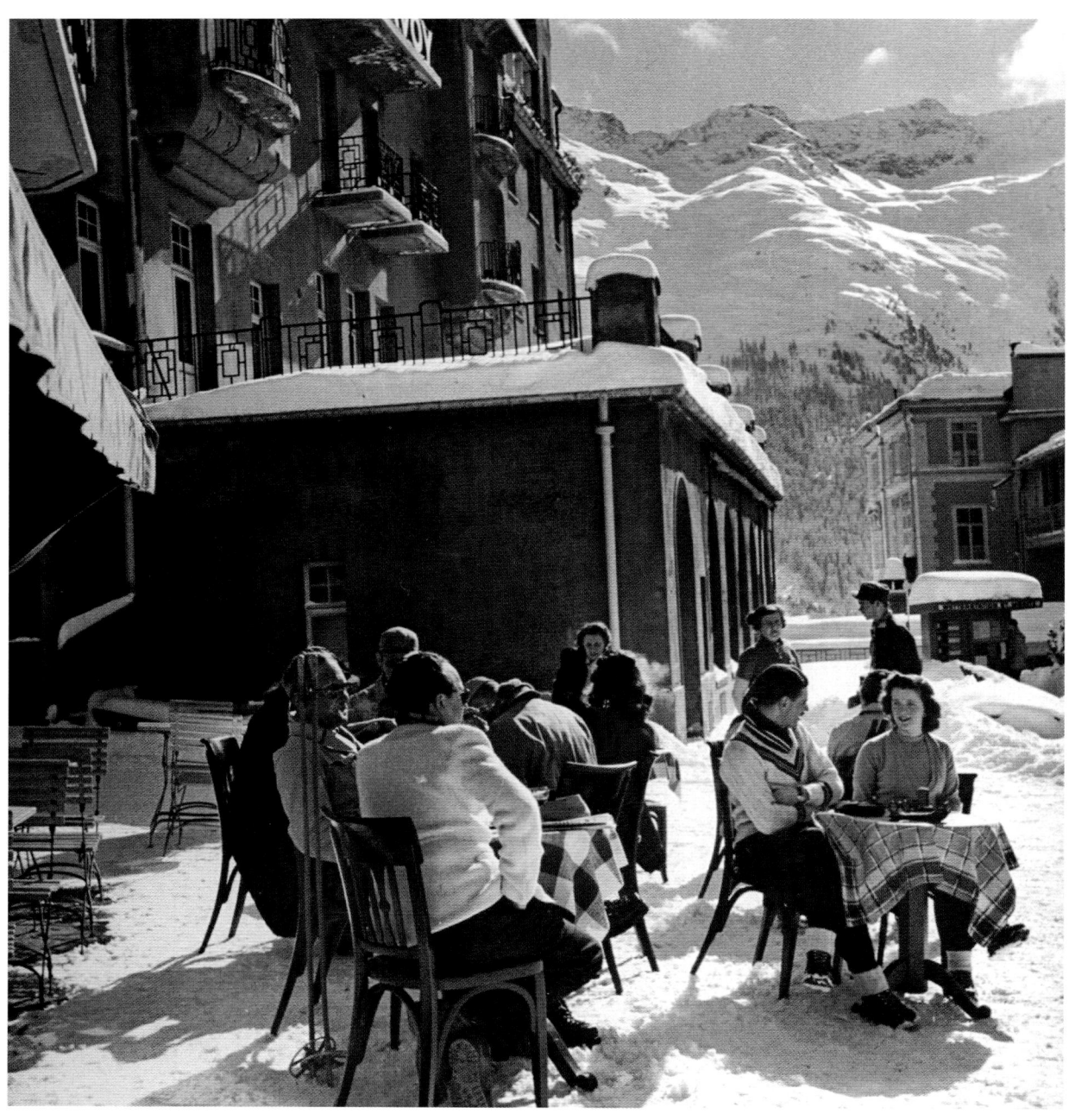

▲ Après-ski dining at an outdoor café in St. Moritz, 1947

▶ American film actor Tyrone Power and actress Linda Christian on
their honeymoon in Kitzbühel, 1949

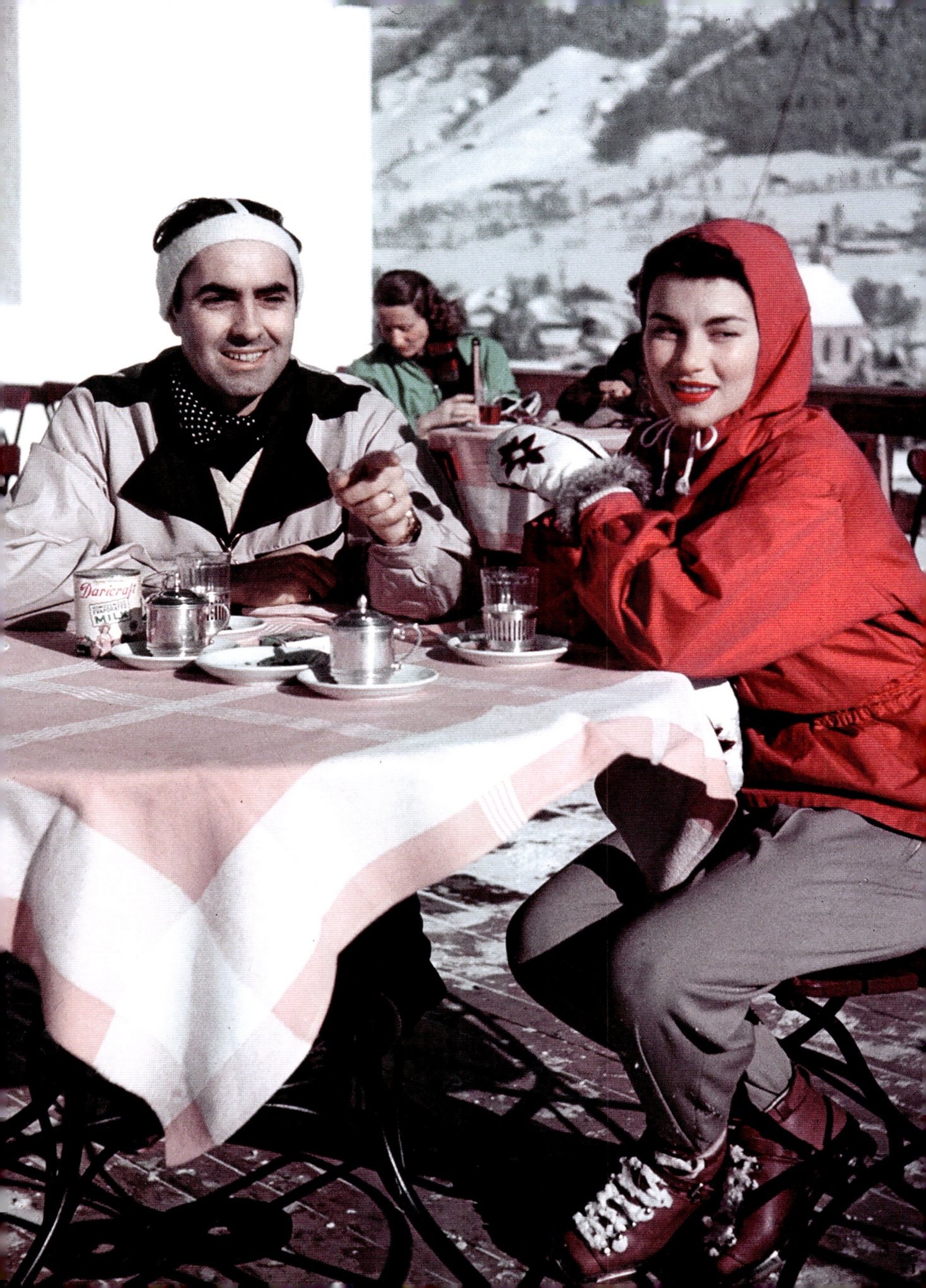

CHOCOLATE FONDUE

Serves 4 to 6

FOR THE FONDUE
¾ cup (180 ml) heavy cream
1 tablespoon (14 g) unsalted butter
1 to 2 tablespoons (15 to 30 ml) liquor
    of choice (optional)
8 ounces (225 g) high-quality
    bittersweet baking chocolate (avoid
    chocolate chips), finely chopped

SUGGESTIONS FOR DIPPING
Bananas, cut into 1-inch (3 cm) rounds
Strawberries, washed and dried with
    green tops still attached
Granny Smith apple, cored and sliced
    (or cubed), with skin on
Fresh pineapple, cubed
Raspberries, washed and dried
Dried apricots
Pound cake or angel food cake, cut
    into cubes
Pretzel sticks
Marshmallows, store-bought or
    homemade (see page 203)
Maldon sea salt

SPECIAL EQUIPMENT
Fondue pot
Fondue forks

This dessert is always a crowd-pleaser. It is incredibly easy to prepare and adds an element of entertainment to your après-ski festivities. The quality of the ingredients is crucial: Look for a premium chocolate for the best flavor. As with Cheese Fondue (page 191), you can select from any number of dipping ingredients, from cubed cake to sliced or dried fruit. Artfully arrange them on a serving platter, alongside a finger bowl of Maldon sea salt flakes for garnish. Feel free to spike your fondue with your liquor of choice (brandy and bourbon work well, or you can add Frangelico for a spiked hazelnut fondue).

◇◇◇◇◇◇◇

Combine the cream, butter, and liquor (if using) in a heavy saucepan over medium heat and bring to a simmer, stirring occasionally. Remove from the heat, add the chocolate, and stir until the chocolate has melted and the mixture is smooth. Carefully transfer the chocolate mixture to the fondue pot and set over a tea candle or canned heat burner. Have your fondue forks ready and serve alongside your dipping ingredients.

S'MORES BAR

Serves 18 to 20

FOR THE VANILLA MARSHMALLOWS
Vegetable oil
Powdered sugar, for dusting (you'll
   need at least 1 cup/120 g)
3 (¼-ounce/7 g) envelopes powdered
   unflavored gelatin
1 cup (240 ml) cold water
1½ cups (300 g) granulated sugar
1 cup (240 ml) light corn syrup
¼ teaspoon salt
2 teaspoons vanilla extract (or 1
   teaspoon vanilla extract plus 1
   teaspoon extract of your choice)

FOR THE S'MORES
Store-bought honey graham crackers,
   split into squares
Fine-quality milk chocolate bars
   (s'mores purists can opt for classic
   milk chocolate Hershey's bars)
Fine-quality dark chocolate bars
Store-bought large marshmallows

SPECIAL EQUIPMENT
Fine-mesh sieve
Candy thermometer
Long wooden s'mores sticks (left
   soaking until use in a water-
   filled container) or extendable
   marshmallow roasting sticks

There is nothing wrong with eating s'mores before dinner. Consider it a well-deserved amuse-bouche. This classic American treat was dreamed up by the Girl Scouts back in the 1920s and is often associated with summertime campfires. However, roaring fires and après-ski were made for each other, and s'mores have worked their way onto the agenda of nearly every ski lodge in America. Take your s'mores to another level by creating a s'mores bar with an array of high-quality chocolate squares (look for a variety of options, like chocolates with sea salt, caramel, cayenne, and hazelnut or other nut flavors) alongside both homemade and store-bought marshmallows.

The marshmallow recipe here yields a vanilla-flavored confection, but you can easily make marshmallows in other flavors by swapping out 1 teaspoon of the vanilla extract for any flavor extract you desire (peppermint, maple syrup, almond, and strawberry are great options). Let the creativity flow and allow your guests to combine these ingredient choices into an endless s'more tasting experience.

◇◇◇◇◇◇◇

Prepare the vanilla marshmallows: With a pastry brush or paper towel, lightly grease the inside of a 9-by-13-inch (23 by 33 cm) pan or ceramic baking dish with vegetable oil. Use a fine-mesh sieve to dust the surface with powdered sugar. Set aside.

In the bowl of a stand mixer fitted with the whisk attachment, dissolve the gelatin in ½ cup (120 ml) cold water and allow it to soften.

Combine the remaining ½ cup (120 ml) water with the granulated sugar, corn syrup, and salt in a medium heavy-bottomed saucepan over medium-high heat and gently stir until the sugar is dissolved and the mixture reaches a boil. Attach a candy thermometer to the pan and continue to boil without stirring (but watching carefully) until the sugar syrup reaches 240°F (116°C). (Note: If you're preparing this at a high altitude, for every increase of 1,000 feet/300 m in elevation above sea level, decrease the target sugar temperature by 2°F/1°C.)

Remove the pan from the heat and wait a few seconds for the bubbles to reduce. Then set the mixer to low speed and slowly pour the sugar syrup into the gelatin mixture. Gradually increase the mixer speed to medium-high and continue whisking until the mixture turns white and fluffy and thickens to form a ribbon when the whisk is lifted, 10 to 12 minutes. Add the vanilla (and any other) extract and increase the mixer speed to the highest setting for 1 minute to blend.

Scrape the mixture into the prepared pan and use either wet fingers or a spatula brushed with oil to spread it evenly. Tap the pan gently on the counter a few times to remove any air bubbles, and allow the marshmallow to stand at room temperature until it has firmed, is no longer sticky, and can be gently pulled away from the edge of the pan,

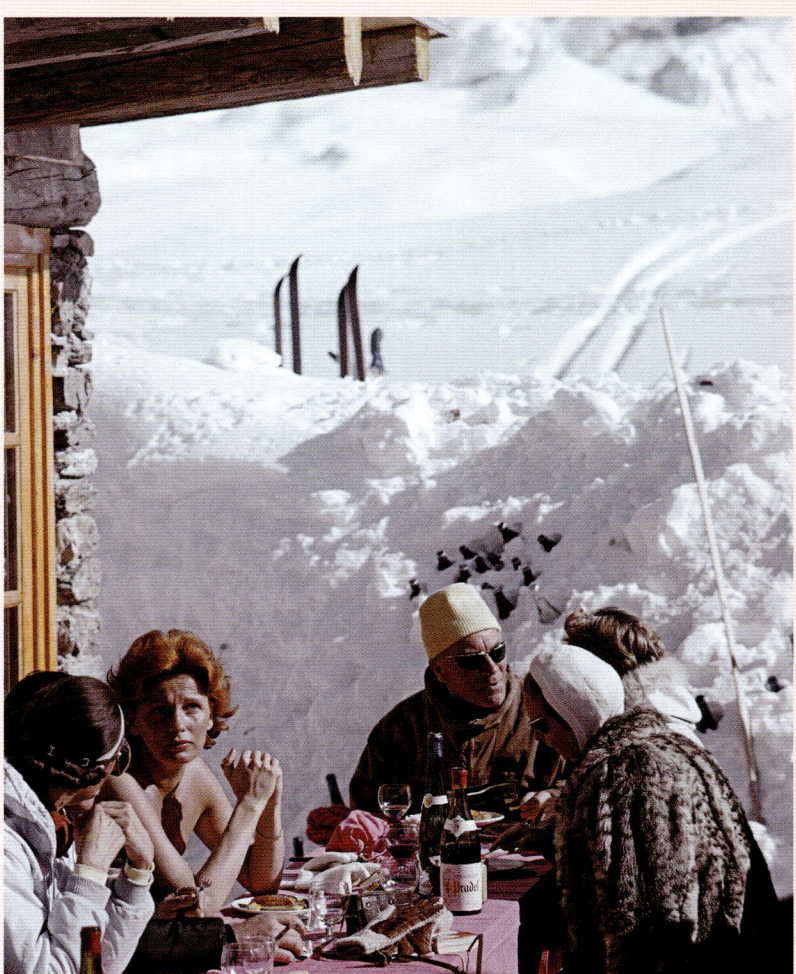

▶ A sunny après-ski meal in Courchevel, 1970

at least 4 hours. The mixture does not need to be covered, but if you prefer, cover it with aluminum foil (plastic wrap can sink and stick to the top of the marshmallow).

When the marshmallow is ready, dust a cutting board with powdered sugar, use a flexible spatula to pull the marshmallow away from the edges of the pan, and invert it onto the prepared board. Dust the top with powdered sugar. Brush a long thin knife with vegetable oil and dust it with powdered sugar to prevent sticking. Use the knife to cut the marshmallow lengthwise and crosswise into 6 even rows, yielding 36 large, rectangular marshmallows, then dust all the edges with more powdered sugar and shake off any excess.

You can store the marshmallows layered between sheets of waxed or parchment paper in an airtight container in a dry location at cool room temperature for a week or more.

Prepare the s'mores: Arrange squares of graham crackers neatly on a serving platter. Split your chocolate options into individual serving sizes (if the bars are made with a small rectangle design, split them into 2-rectangle sections; if they're made with a large square design, split them into single squares) and set them next to the graham crackers. Have your sticks at the ready.

Prepare your fire source. Outdoor firepits are great, but a small tabletop version can be fun as well.

When you're ready to make s'mores magic, place a square of chocolate on a square of graham cracker; have another graham cracker square waiting. Place 1 homemade vanilla or store-bought marshmallow on a stick and hold it above the flame, rotating slowly until it begins to puff; with homemade marshmallows, this could be as quick as 20 to 30 seconds. Ideally have a friend help with the next step of assembly: Catch the toasted marshmallow between the bottom graham cracker loaded with chocolate and the plain top graham cracker while you slowly pull out the stick. Squeeze the crackers together gently to spread your marshmallow and allow it to melt your chocolate slightly before indulging in your creation. Feel free to repeat as many times as you like.

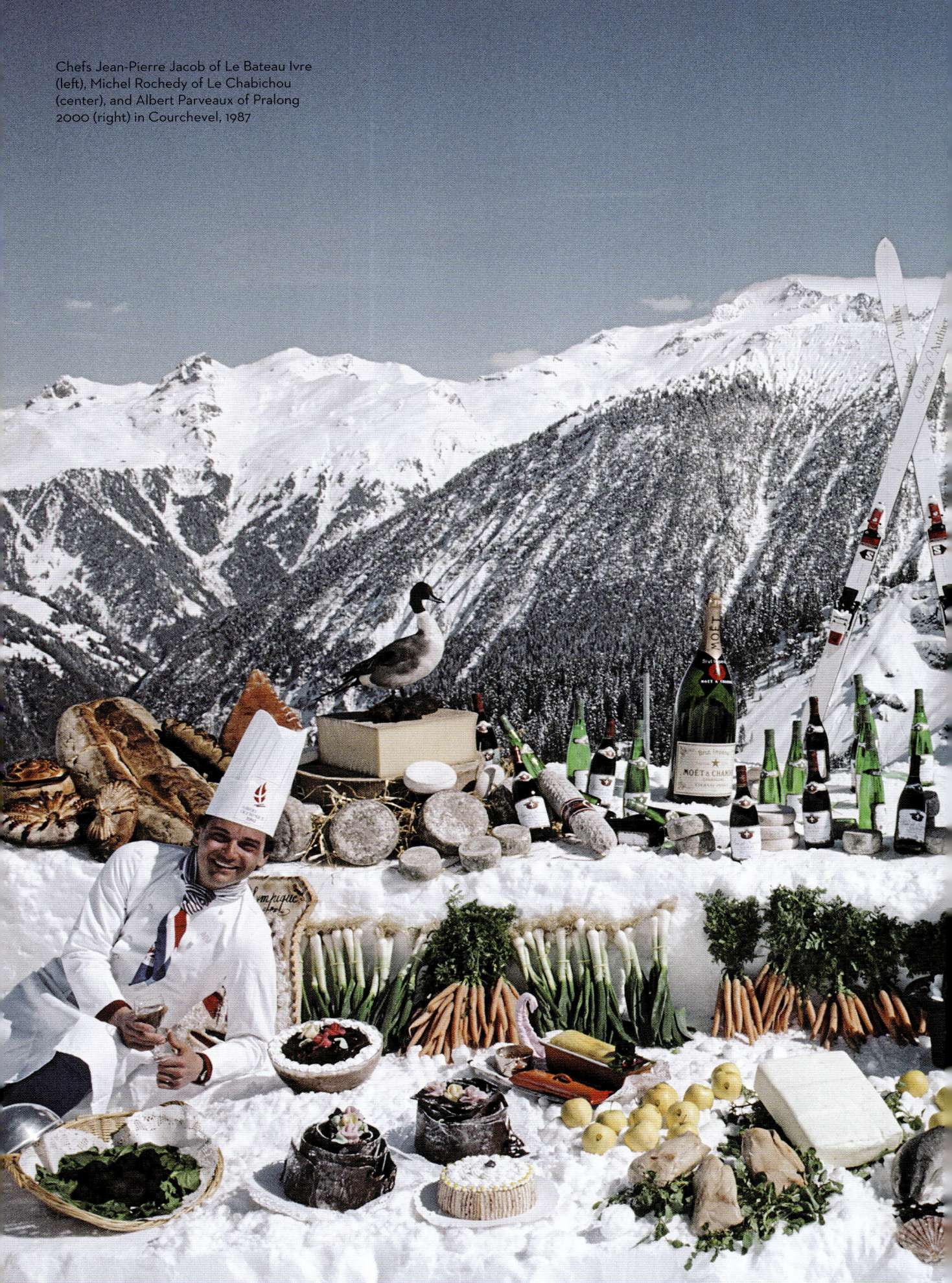

Chefs Jean-Pierre Jacob of Le Bateau Ivre
(left), Michel Rochedy of Le Chabichou
(center), and Albert Parveaux of Pralong
2000 (right) in Courchevel, 1987

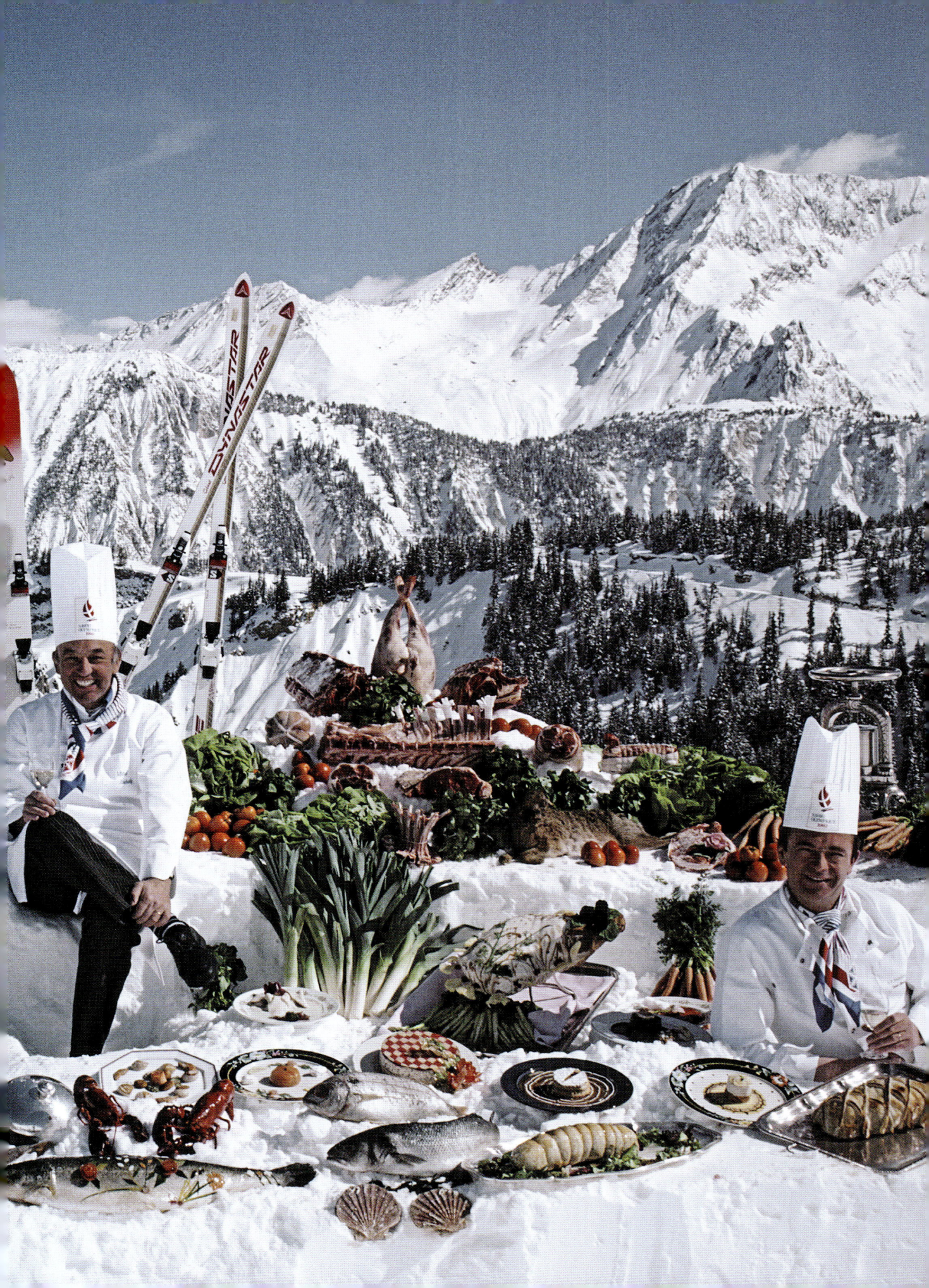

Ski Resorts for the Gourmand

While the list is not definitive, these resorts (and resort towns) have some of the best food; some are home to Michelin-starred restaurants that offer a truly exceptional culinary experience après-ski.

AUSTRIA

Ischgl

Kitzbühel

Lech

St. Anton

St. Christoph

CANADA

Whistler Blackcomb

FRANCE

Chamonix

Courchevel

Megève

Tignes & Méribel

Val d'Isère

Val Thorens

ITALY

Alta Badia

Cortina d'Ampezzo

Corvara

Courmayeur

San Cassiano

Val Gardena

JAPAN

Niseko

SWITZERLAND

St. Moritz

Verbier

Zermatt

UNITED STATES

Aspen Snowmass

Park City

Stowe

Vail

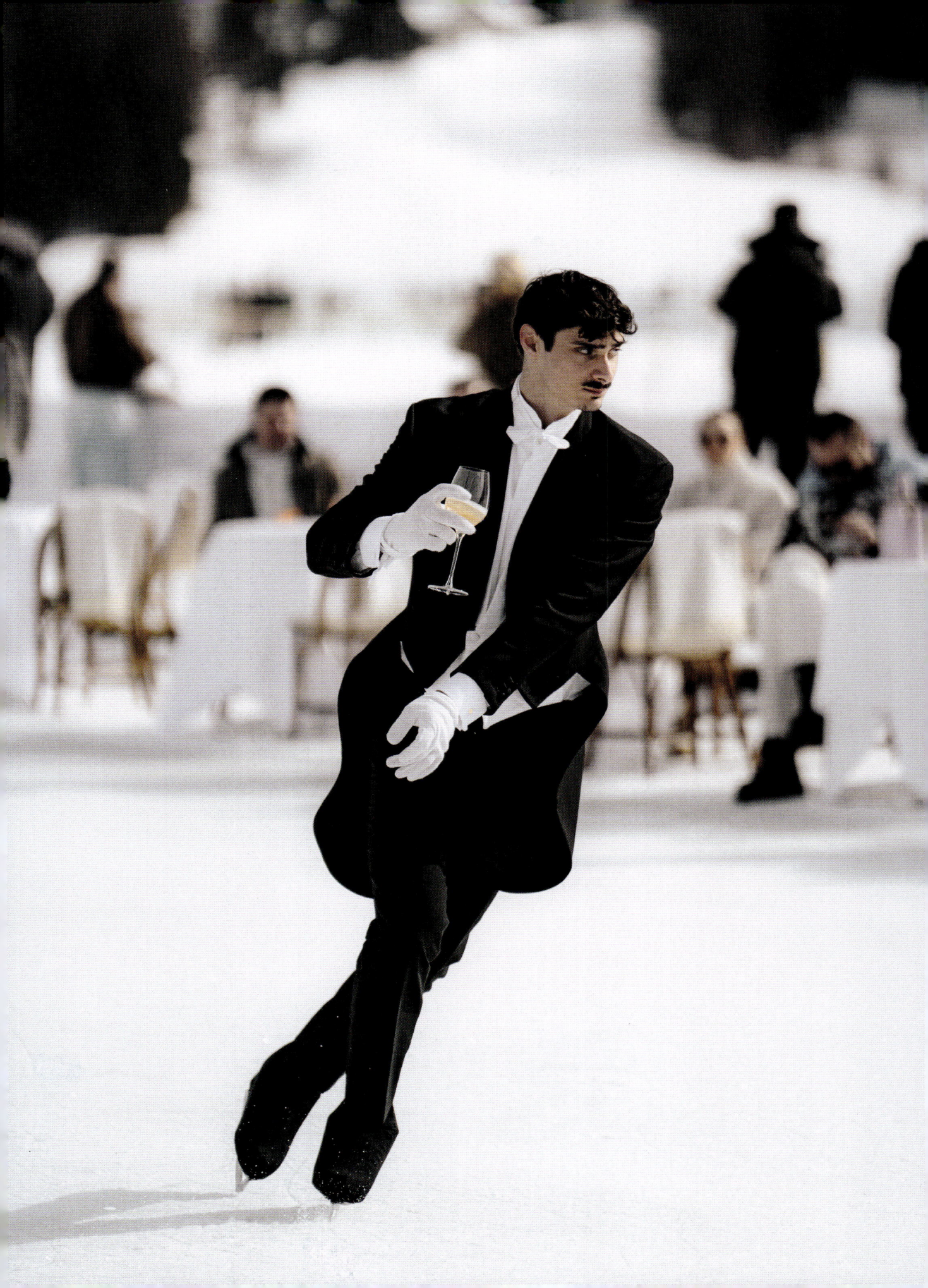

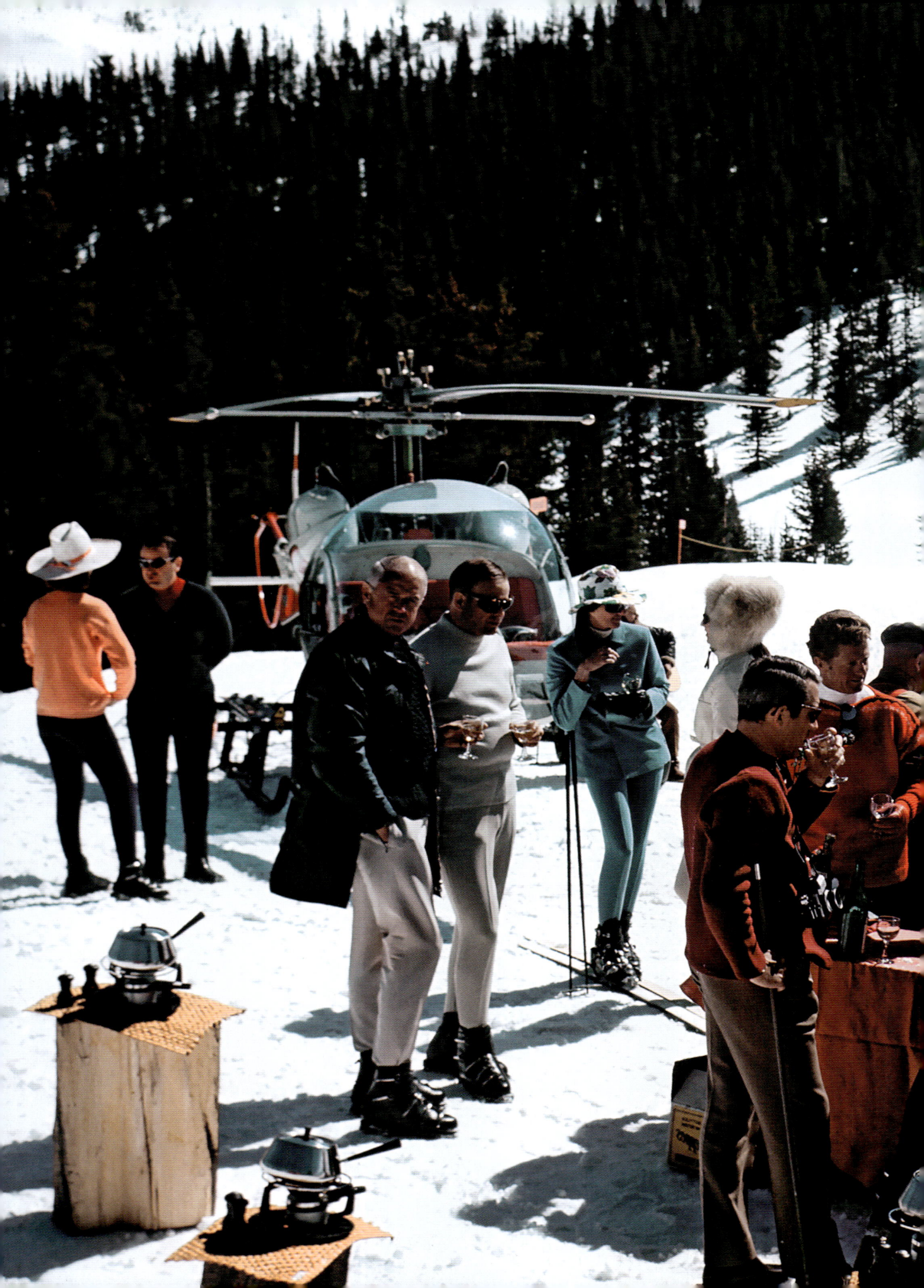

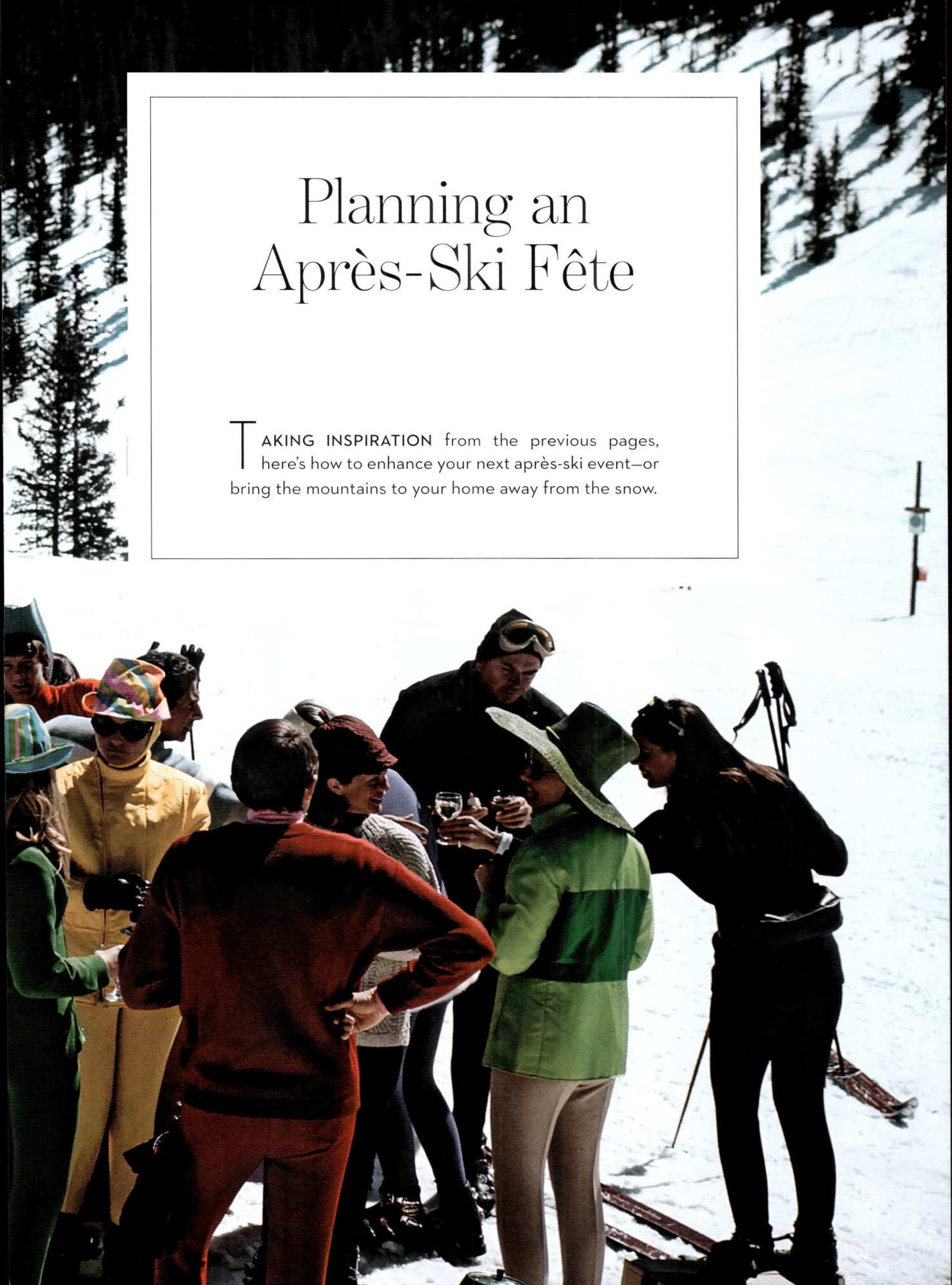

Planning an Après-Ski Fête

TAKING INSPIRATION from the previous pages, here's how to enhance your next après-ski event—or bring the mountains to your home away from the snow.

Setting the Scene

Infuse your environment with the following six elements of a ski holiday, anywhere and anytime of year.

1. **The bar.** While it does not need to be made of ice, it should ideally evoke the mountains, with natural elements such as wood, and it should be well-stocked.

2. **Seating.** A mix of chairs and stools at different heights allow for conversation and gathering. Cushions for the floor in front of a fire are also appreciated.

3. **Tables.** A coffee table or side tables provide a surface for food and games (or dancing).

4. **A fire element.** For indoor gatherings, utilize your fireplace if you have one. Outdoors, a fire pit is ideal both for warming hands and toes and for making s'mores (see page 203). Tabletop fire pits for indoor or outdoor use are also an option.

5. **Games.** Prepare a variety of games, preferably ones that work for multiple people. For an indoor gathering, you might turn to board games, cards, and maybe a game of Twister. Outdoor settings with snow could include sleds and tools for building a snowman.

6. **Décor.** This might include sherpa throws, blankets, natural elements such as wood and naturally shed antlers, a vintage sled, and ideally a pair or two of vintage skis.

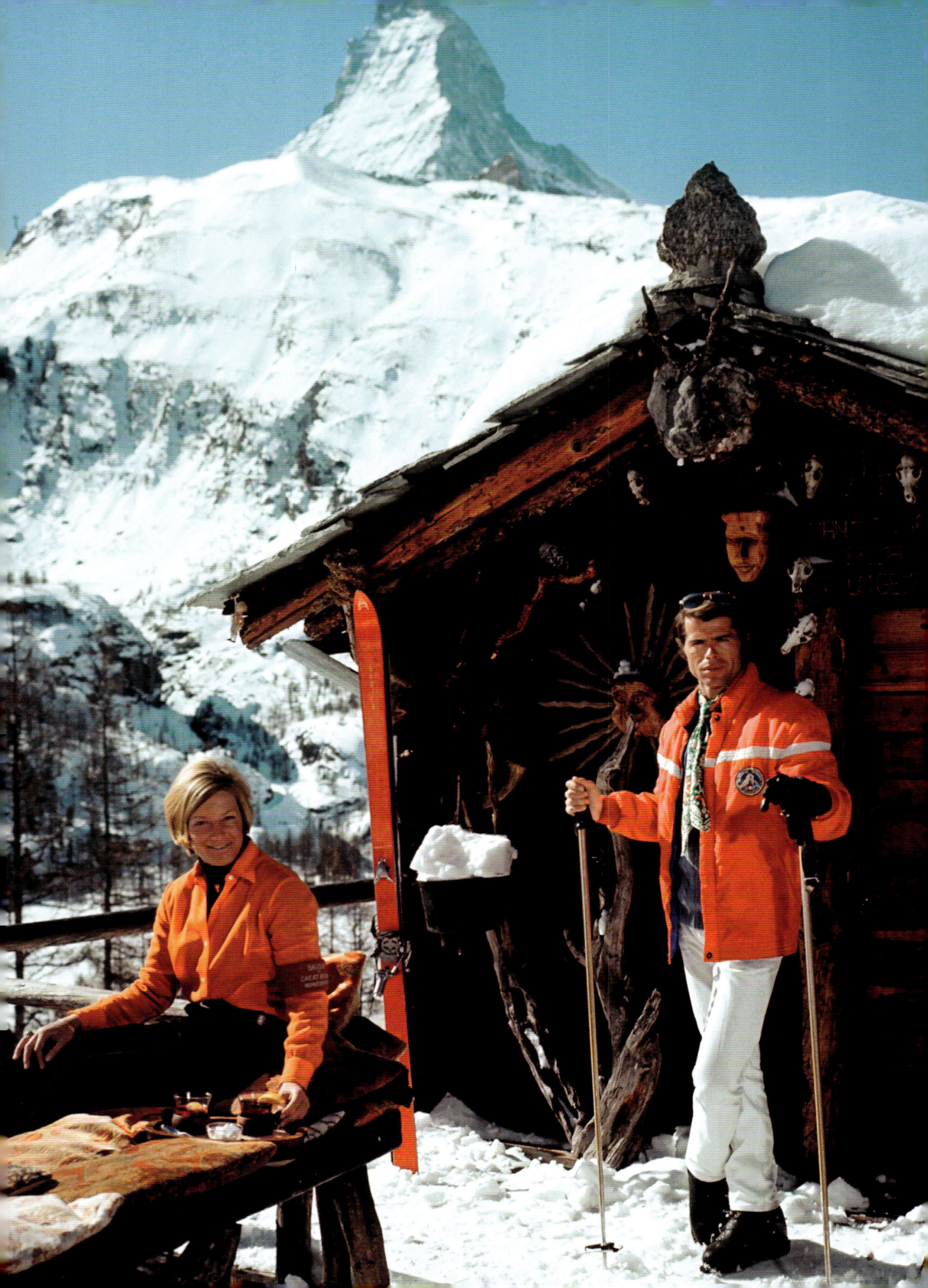

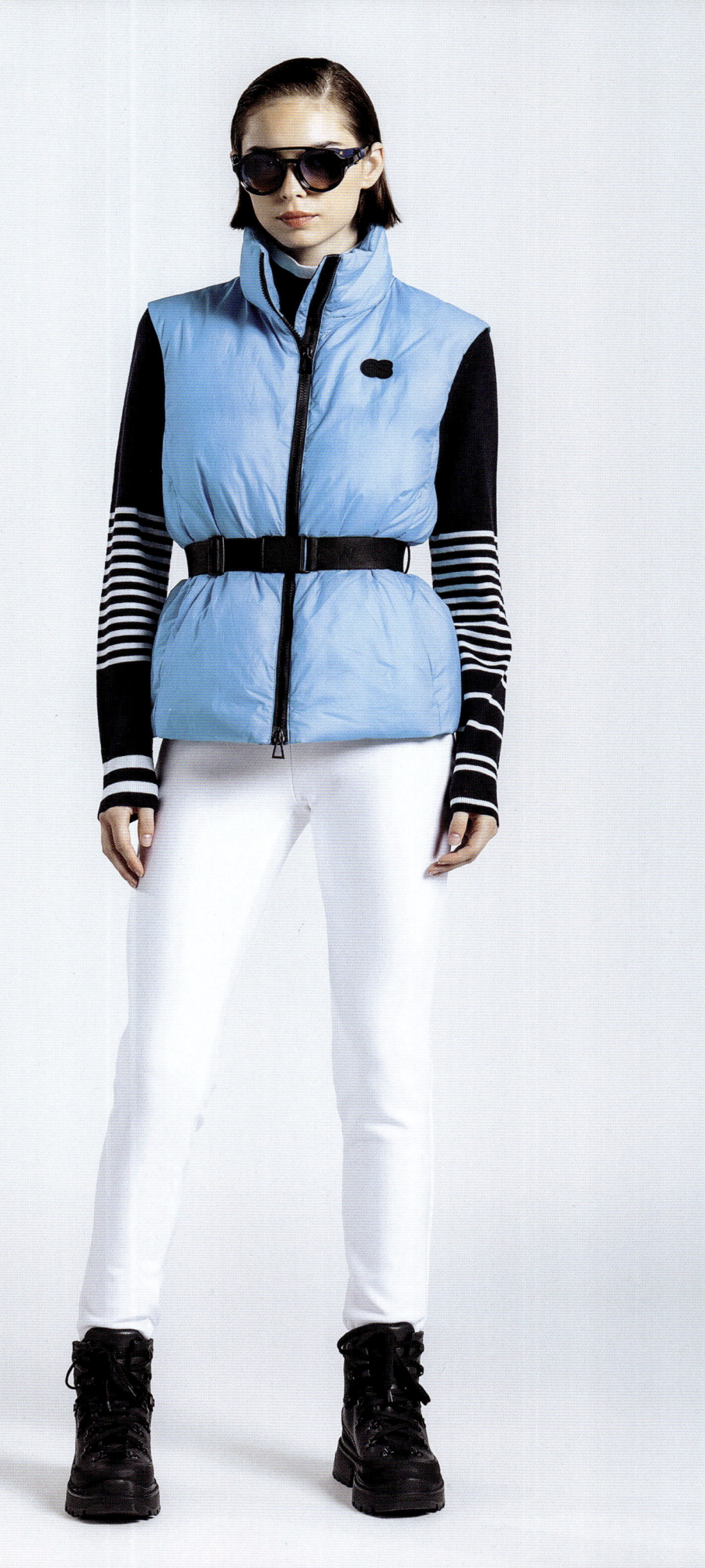

Dressing the Part

Whether you are inspired by the sophistication of the 1940s and '50s, the sex appeal of the '60s and '70s, or the individualism and streetwear influence of the '80s and '90s, your look can be broken down into four key elements:

1. **Sweater or top.** The revival of the classic ski sweater—whether in the form of a Norwegian design, a sporty striped number, or chunky cable knit—can be found on many patrons of the sun deck après-ski. Form-fitting turtlenecks and half-zip tops are also great options, especially because they can be worn from the mountain straight to après. Throw on a vest for extra warmth.

2. **Double-duty pants.** Fitted, in-the-boot pants can be worn on the slopes but also provide a chic look with enough warmth and protection for a stroll through a ski town or village on a cold, snowy evening. Salopettes (suspender pants) typically go over the boot and work equally well. Anyone uncomfortable with the sleek fit of a stretch pant may want to at least exchange any baggy ski pants for a more tailored option.

3. **Footwear.** Whether you are looking for a lug-soled leather lace-up boot, an oversized moon boot, or rugged Sorels, the originals are thankfully still available today, as are a new crop of vintage-inspired options.

4. **Accessories.** A baseball hat or knit option for après-ski will rescue you from the inevitable helmet hair. Similarly, swapping out ski goggles for a chic pair of sunglasses makes for a seamless transition to après-ski. Holding on to your hot chocolate or Vin Chaud with bulky ski gloves can be a challenge, so glove liners or knit mittens can come in handy for outdoor après-ski activities. If you can fit all of this into your jacket pockets, do so. Otherwise, a hip pouch or fanny pack is once again fashionable and comes in handy for carrying your après-ski accessories.

Crafting the Menu

An après-ski menu should evoke a feeling of nostalgia for a snowy landscape or a ski region of the world. Whether you're planning a party for two or twenty, keep these four elements in mind.

1. **Consider your audience.** What is the size of your gathering? Are children involved? Based on this information you can formulate a theme or direction for your menu—for example, a fondue party with both cheese (page 191) and chocolate (page 202) options; an American Rockies theme with beer, nachos (page 180), and wings (page 185); an Italian Dolomites theme with Bombardinos (page 170); a board (page 184) featuring bresaola and Italian olives; and apple strudel (page 198). Options span the globe and a variety of tastes.

2. **Inventory your supplies.** As soon as you have your menu in mind, pull out all necessary cookware, servingware, and glassware, make sure they are smudge-free, and use sticky notes to organize and label each for their intended use. If you are on a ski trip and working with what you have available in a rented cabin, taking stock of your available resources before finalizing your menu will be crucial.

3. **Select a signature drink or two.** Vin Chaud (page 171) is a great option to prepare ahead and have on hand, ready to reheat. Craft beer can be selected and chilled ahead of time. Finally, depending on the mood, select a composed cocktail (see pages 161–177 for ideas) and either prepare a round before guests arrive or have the ingredients prepped and ready. Don't forget garnishes!

4. **Prep the meal.** Always have a shareable spread ready to serve when guests arrive. For your other menu items, either have them ready for reheating and assembly or work backward to create a timeline and ensure that cooking will be complete at the optimal time for serving. Using a phone alarm set to remind you of tasks at the appropriate times comes in very handy and keeps you on schedule, especially if you've poured yourself a glass of wine while cooking!

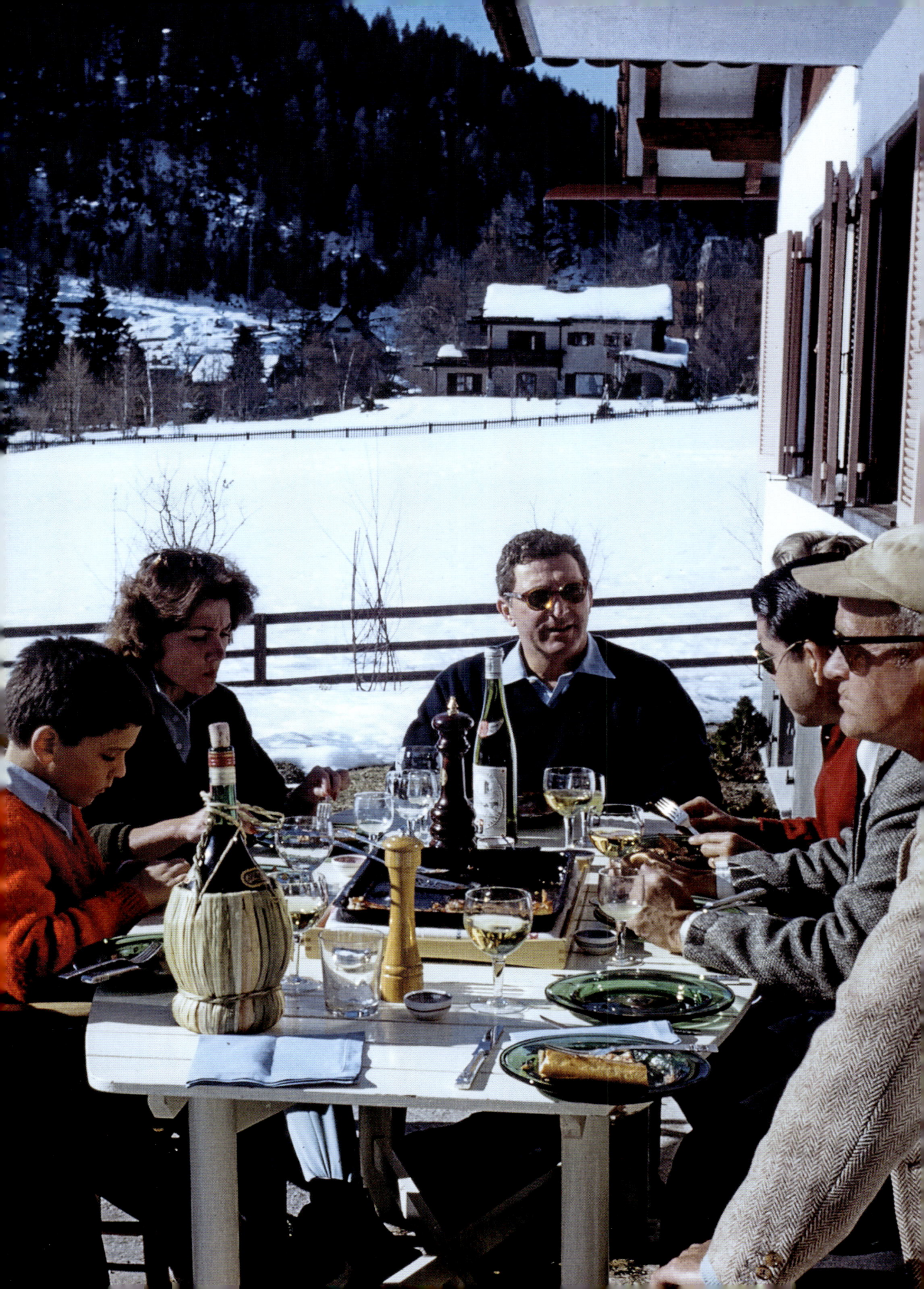

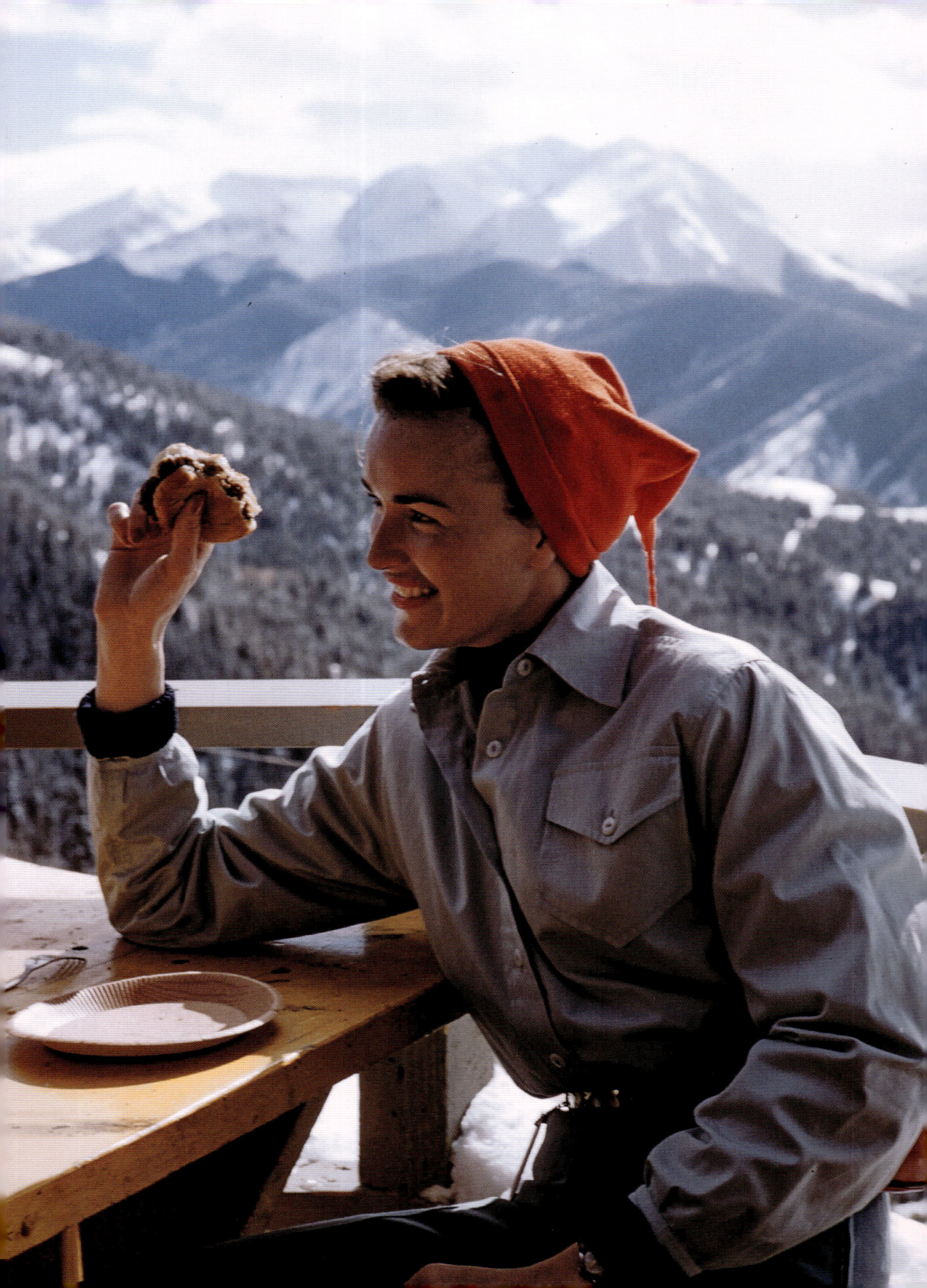

Afterword

WHILE DOING RESEARCH for this book, I was struck by the sense of escapism and joy that the world of ski culture has brought to humans around the world. Skiing took hold as a popular sport in post–World War I Europe and grew in popularity in the Americas after World War II. The same photographer (Robert Capa) who was present on Omaha Beach on D-Day to capture the American troop landing also took sojourns to Austria and Switzerland in the aftermath of the war to capture moments of pleasure and holiday. Looking through photo archives of the era, it is evident that skiing played a role in returning a sense of relief and humanity to a war-torn world for some very lucky individuals.

As a lifelong skier who has built my career around the sport, the thing I love most about skiing and being in the mountains is the sense of peace it brings me. When I race down a steep slope making deep edge turns, I focus on nothing beyond what's in front of me. The rest of the world and all its worries fade away. The day, especially when I share it with my family and close friends, is usually followed by an après-ski celebration of food, drinks, relaxation, games, or whatever feels interesting.

As you have seen in the pages of this book, people from all different walks of life share in the joy of skiing. Swapping stories about an epic powder day transforms strangers into simpaticos. Whether you are a serious skier or simply in it for the cocktails and nachos, the mountains bring us all together.

Acknowledgments

To my family: Thank you for introducing me to the mountains and for infusing me with an appreciation for adventure, Stein style, travel, and hard work. I am so honored to carry on our family tradition with the next generation. I treasure our tree-run laps, swimming in heated outdoor mountain pools, mint chocolate s'mores, spicy wings, and tubing après-ski. And thank you for being my sounding board, cocktail drinking partners and taste-testers while writing this book.

To my dear friends: Thank you for encouraging me to take on this project and for offering opinions and feedback along the way.

To my Erin Snow family: Thank you for over twenty years of partnership, support and friendship. I am incredibly proud of the work we have done and the mountains we have climbed together.

To Kitty Cowles: Thank you for thinking of me. I am truly grateful.

To Bridget Monroe Itkin: Thank you for your partnership while writing this book. I have cherished our talks and your witty, smart insights.

To Nina Simoneaux: Thank you for your creative partnership and design eye. This book came to life thanks to you.

To the rest of the Artisan team: Thank you to Lia Ronnen, Ken Yu, Julia Perry, Laura Cherkas, Nancy Ringer, Hillary Leary, Suet Chong, Kim Ehart, Elissa Santos, Zach Townsend, Donna Brown, Zach Greenwald, Moira Kerrigan, MacKenzie Collier, and Alana Bonfiglio for your keen eyes, expertise, editing, and direction. Working with this talented team, both while writing and editing this book and onward into the future, has been a tremendous honor.

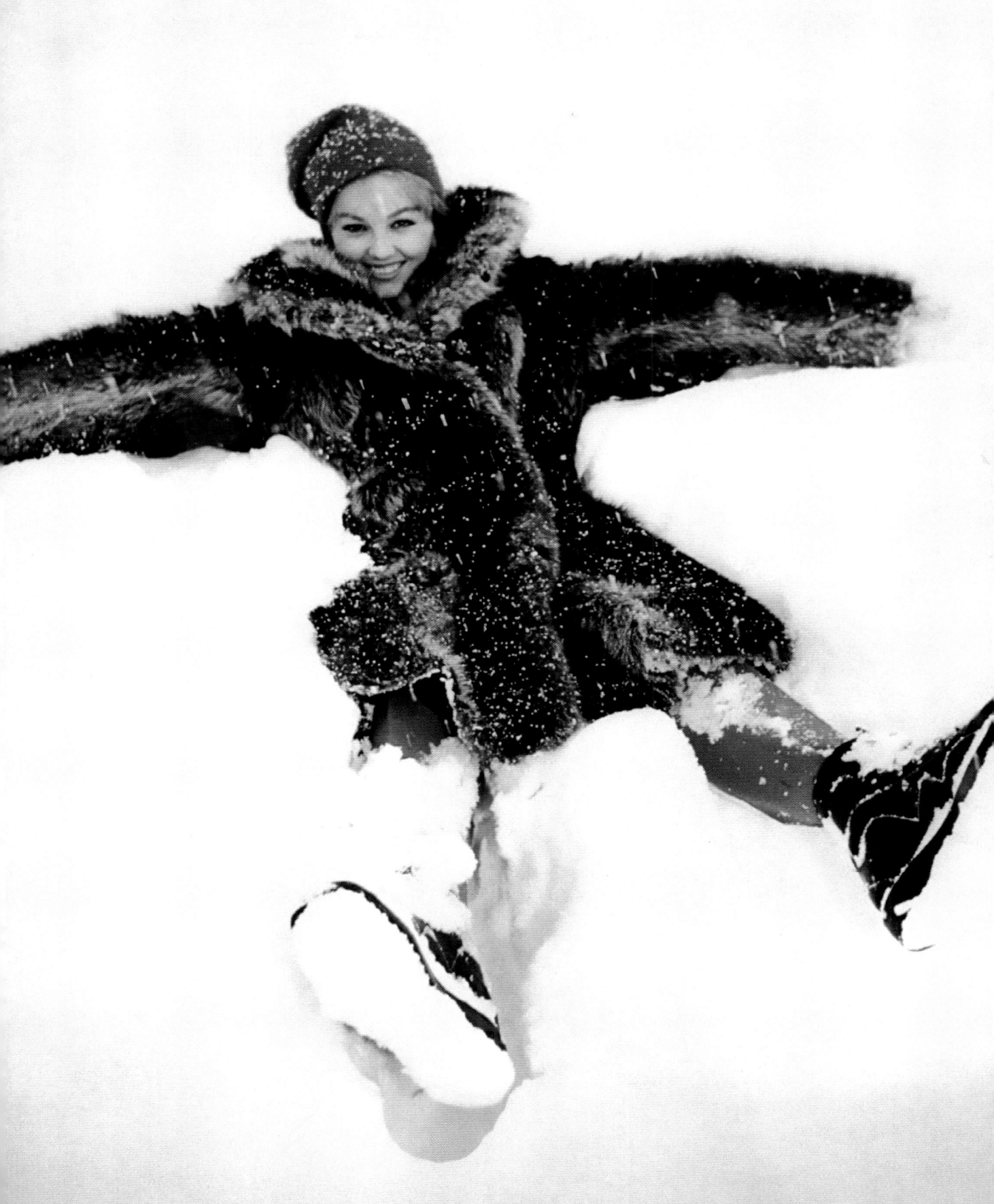

Photography Credits

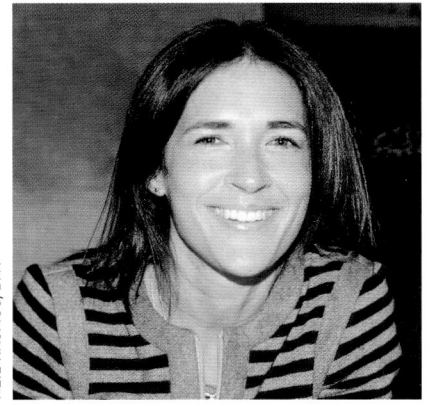

ERIN ISAKOV is the cofounder of global ski and outdoor apparel brand Erin Snow, which she began with her husband in 2003. Erin grew up an avid skier and snowboarder (her father was a ski patroller at Mammoth Mountain, California) and travels the world to hit the slopes with her family and friends.

More than twenty years since its founding, Erin Snow has been sold through fashion retailers, luxury ski resorts, and specialty ski stores throughout the Americas, Europe, and Asia. The brand has been regularly featured in national publications, including *Vogue, WWD, W, Glamour, Condé Nast Traveler, The New York Times*, and *SNOW*, and in 2017 won the inaugural CFDA + Lexus Fashion* Initiative for its commitment to sustainable fashion design.